Ichigo Takano presents

Dreamin'
Sun

5

volume
five

Dreamin'
Sun

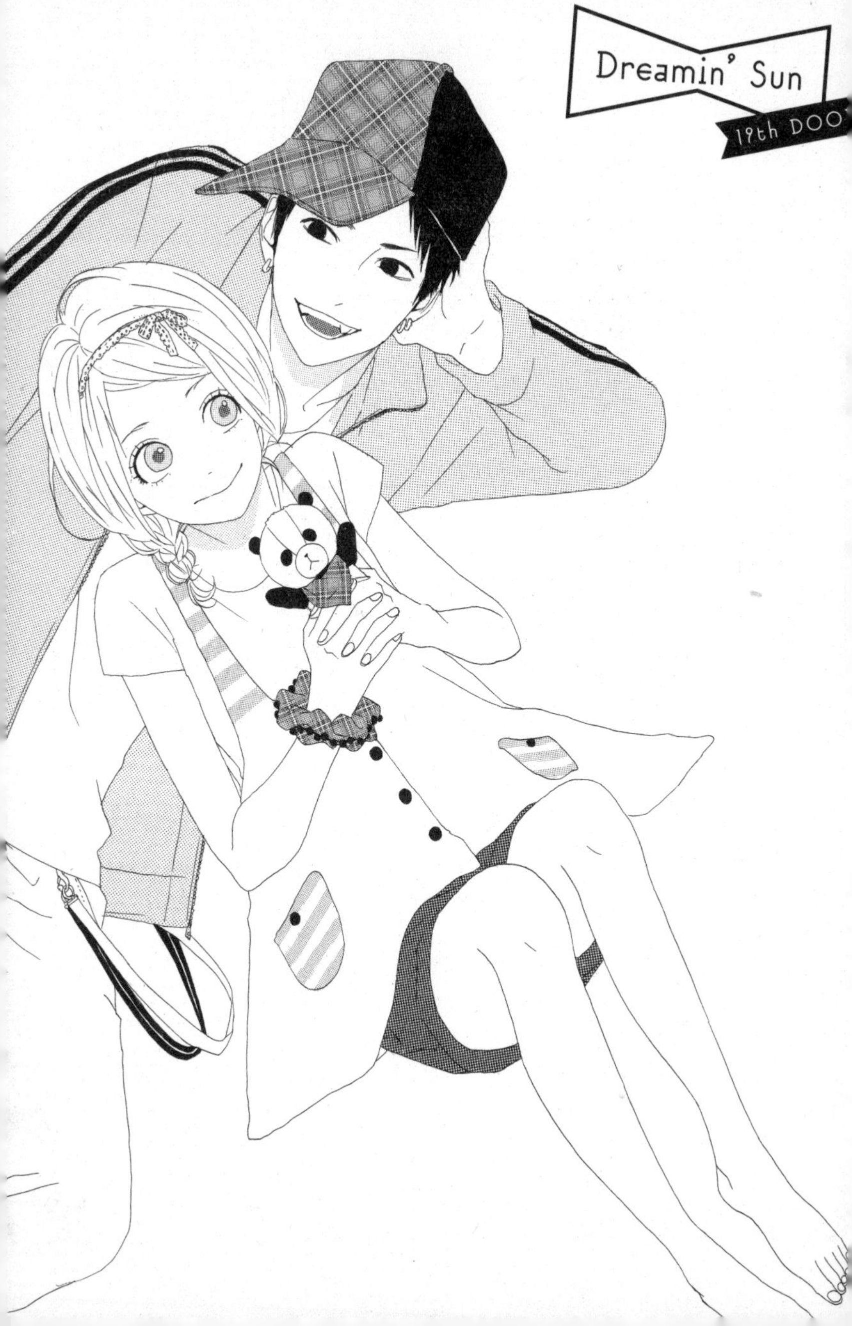
Dreamin' Sun
19th DOO

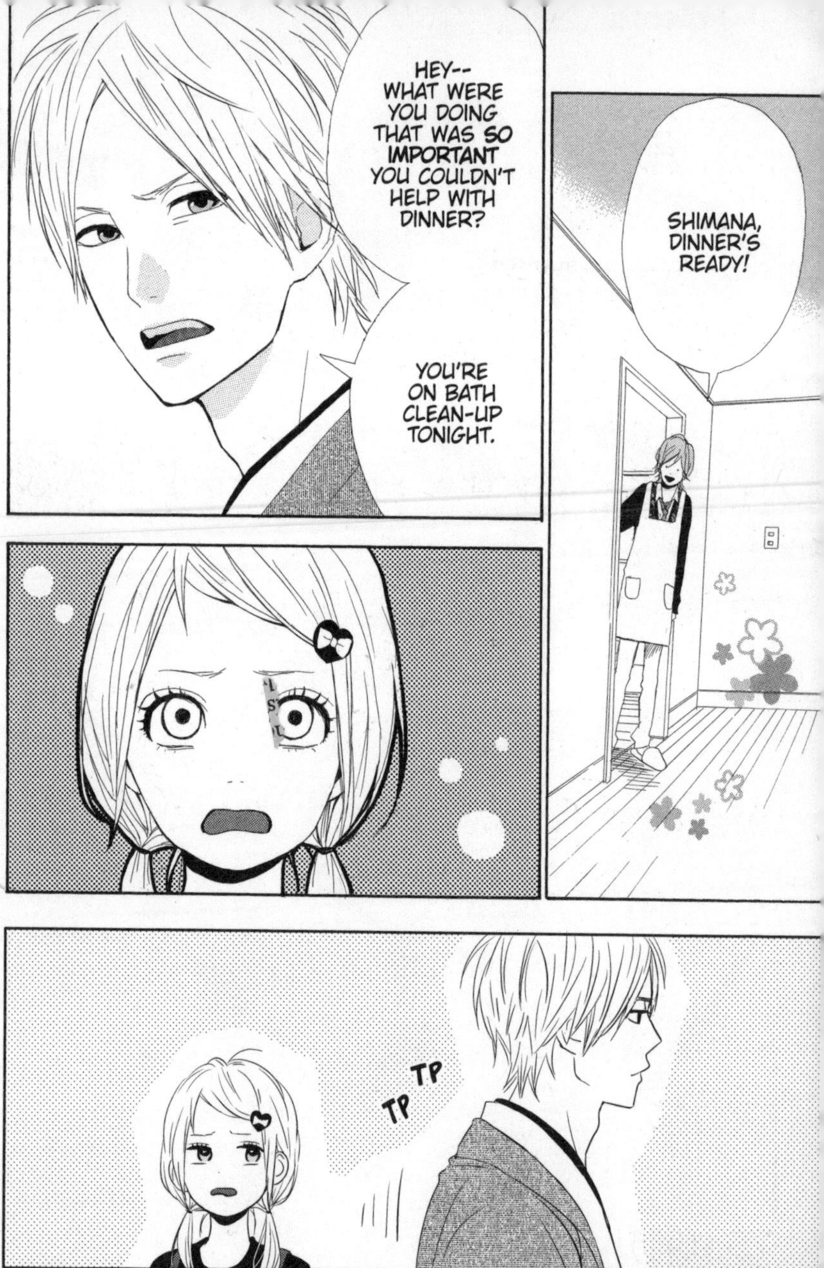
SHIMANA, DINNER'S READY!
HEY-- WHAT WERE YOU DOING THAT WAS SO IMPORTANT YOU COULDN'T HELP WITH DINNER?
YOU'RE ON BATH CLEAN-UP TONIGHT.
TP TP

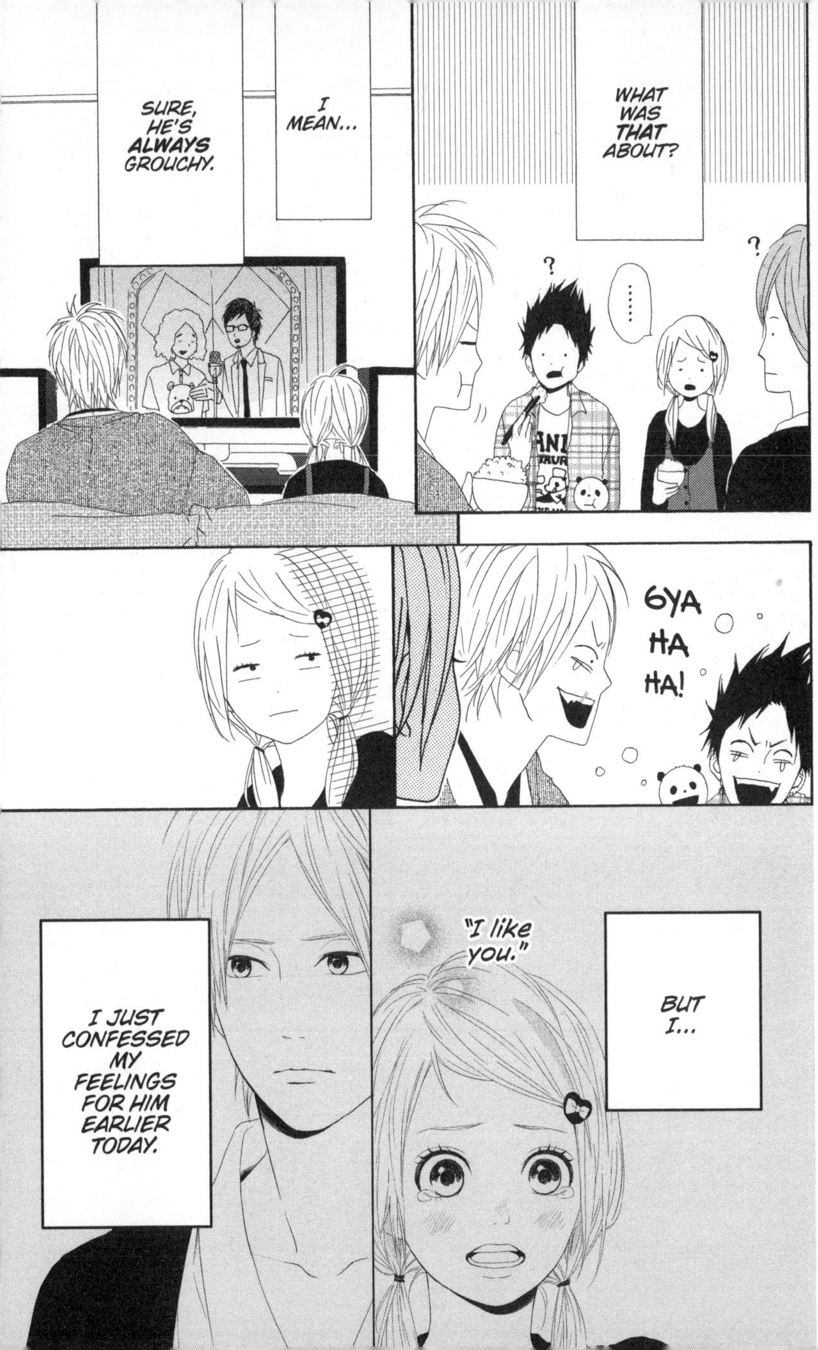
WHAT WAS THAT ABOUT?
?
......
?
I MEAN...
SURE, HE'S **ALWAYS** GROUCHY.
GYA HA HA!
BUT I...
"I like you."
I JUST CONFESSED MY FEELINGS FOR HIM EARLIER TODAY.

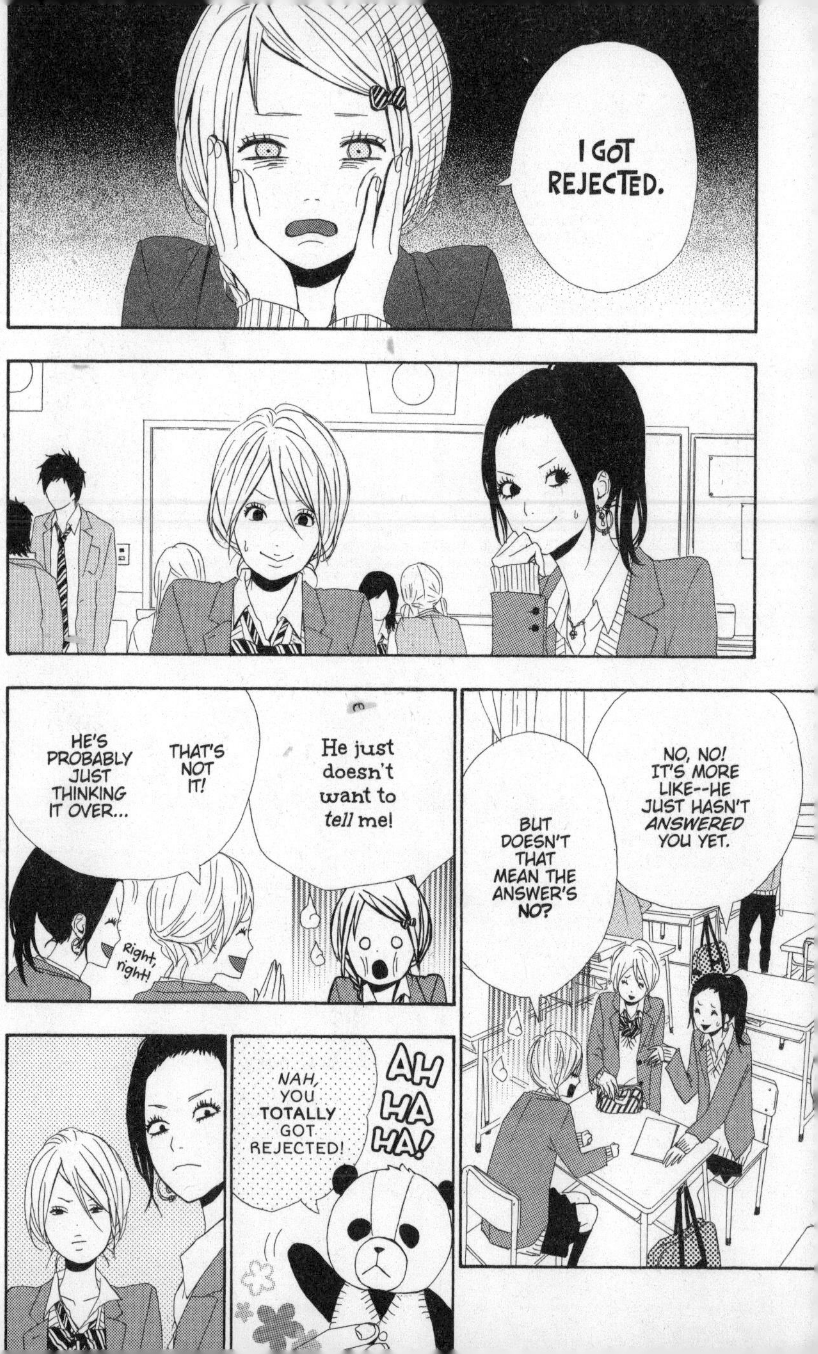
I GOT REJECTED.
NO, NO! IT'S MORE LIKE--HE JUST HASN'T *ANSWERED* YOU YET.
BUT DOESN'T THAT MEAN THE ANSWER'S NO?
He just doesn't want to *tell* me!
THAT'S NOT IT!
HE'S PROBABLY JUST THINKING IT OVER...
Right, right!
AH HA HA!
NAH, YOU TOTALLY GOT REJECTED!

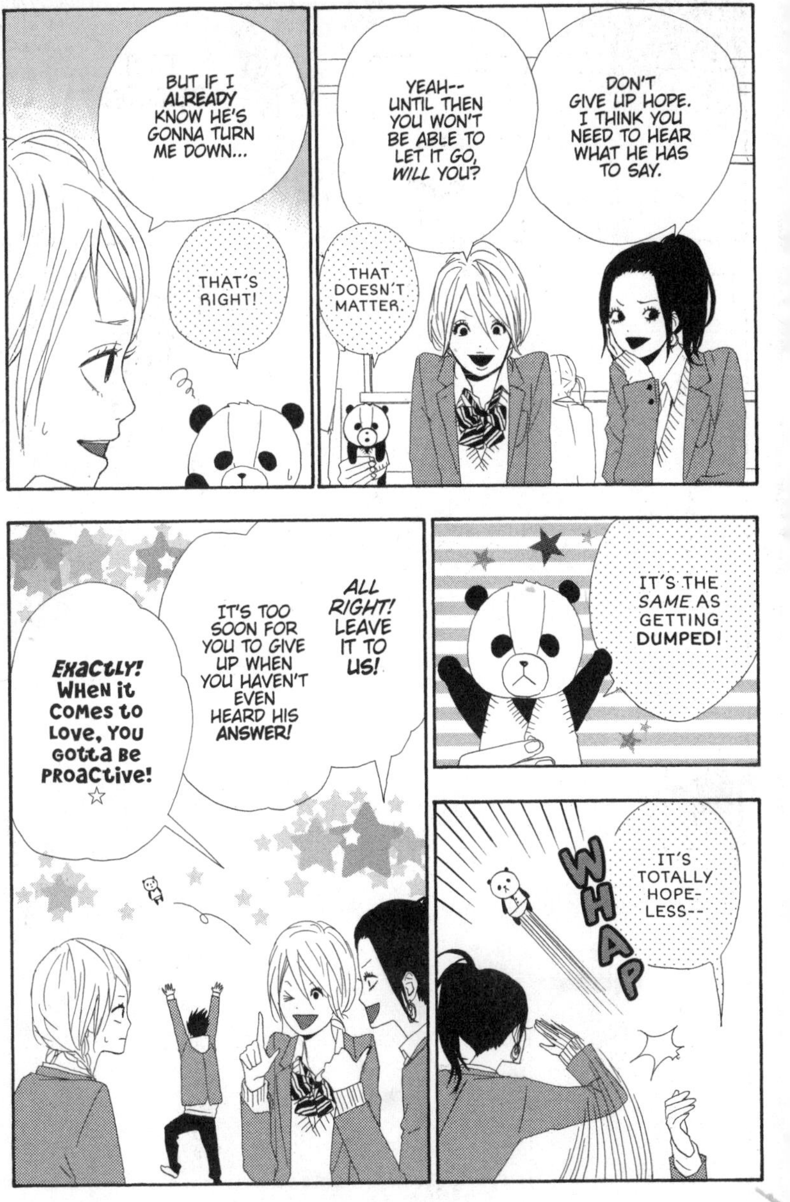
DON'T GIVE UP HOPE. I THINK YOU NEED TO HEAR WHAT HE HAS TO SAY.
YEAH-- UNTIL THEN YOU WON'T BE ABLE TO LET IT GO, WILL YOU?
THAT DOESN'T MATTER.
BUT IF I ALREADY KNOW HE'S GONNA TURN ME DOWN...
THAT'S RIGHT!
IT'S THE SAME AS GETTING DUMPED!
IT'S TOTALLY HOPE-LESS--
WHAP
ALL RIGHT! LEAVE IT TO US!
IT'S TOO SOON FOR YOU TO GIVE UP WHEN YOU HAVEN'T EVEN HEARD HIS ANSWER!
EXACTLY! WHEN IT COMES TO LOVE, YOU GOTTA BE PROACTIVE! ☆

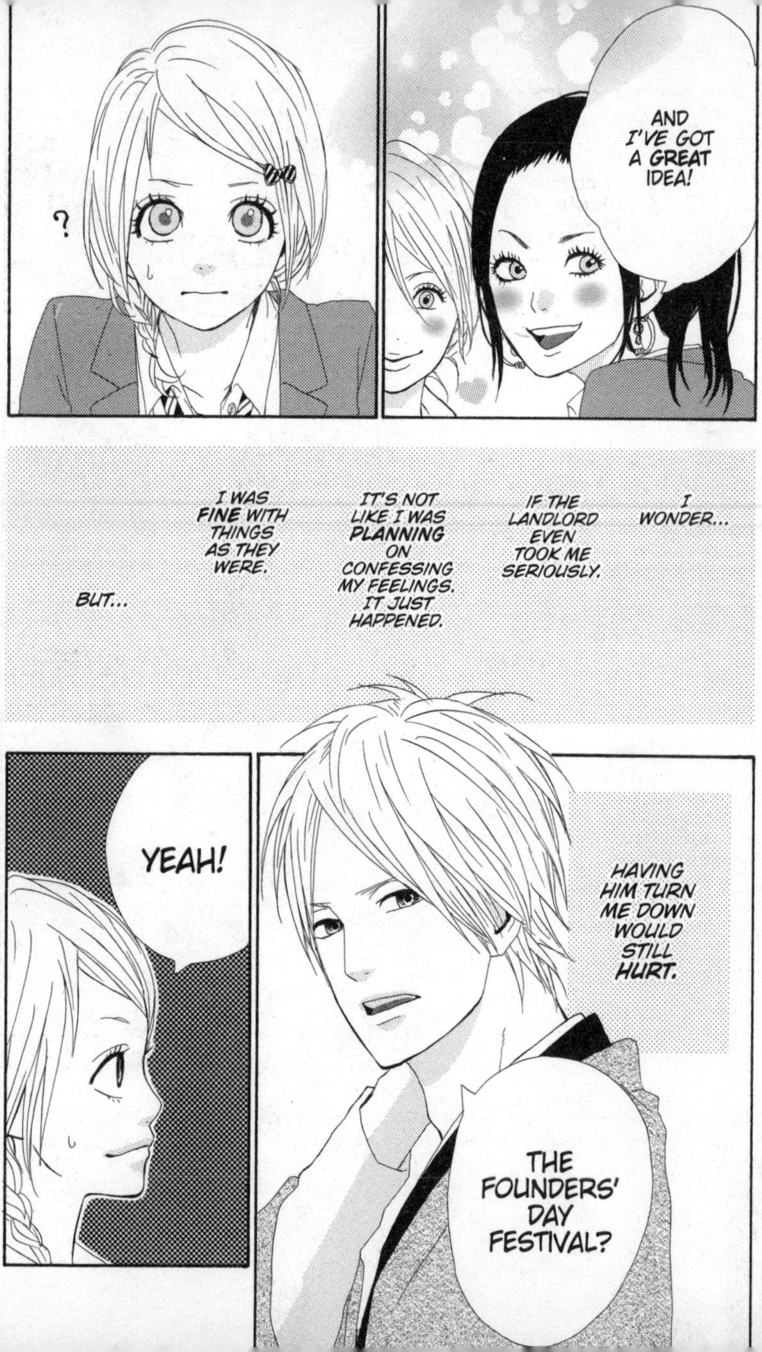
AND I'VE GOT A GREAT IDEA!
?
I WONDER...
IF THE LANDLORD EVEN TOOK ME SERIOUSLY.
IT'S NOT LIKE I WAS PLANNING ON CONFESSING MY FEELINGS. IT JUST HAPPENED.
I WAS FINE WITH THINGS AS THEY WERE.
BUT...
HAVING HIM TURN ME DOWN WOULD STILL HURT.
THE FOUNDERS' DAY FESTIVAL?
YEAH!

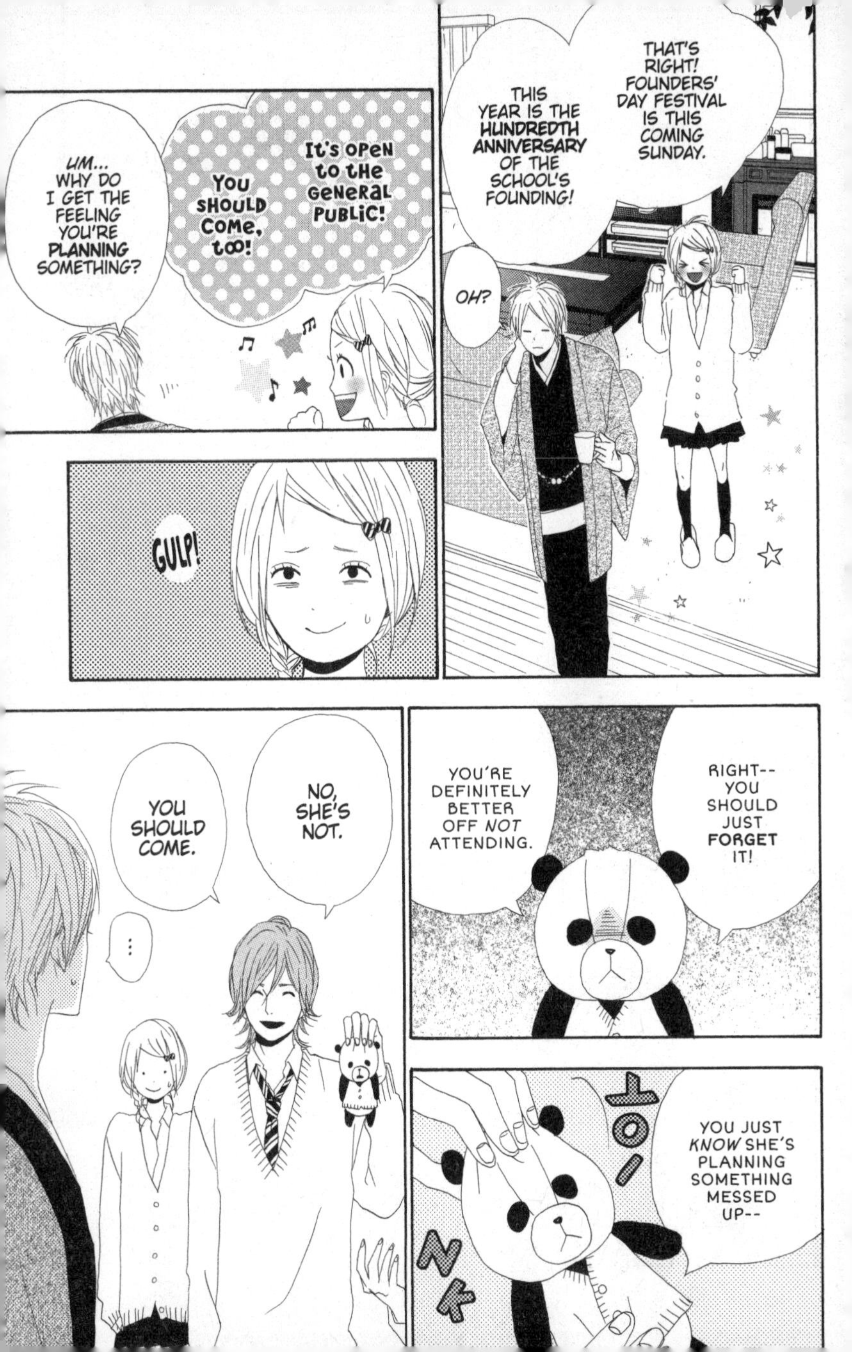
THAT'S RIGHT! FOUNDERS' DAY FESTIVAL IS THIS COMING SUNDAY.
THIS YEAR IS THE HUNDREDTH ANNIVERSARY OF THE SCHOOL'S FOUNDING!
OH?
It's open to the general public!
You should come, too!
UM... WHY DO I GET THE FEELING YOU'RE PLANNING SOMETHING?
GULP!
RIGHT-- YOU SHOULD JUST FORGET IT!
YOU'RE DEFINITELY BETTER OFF *NOT* ATTENDING.
TOINK
YOU JUST *KNOW* SHE'S PLANNING SOMETHING MESSED UP--
NO, SHE'S NOT.
YOU SHOULD COME.
...

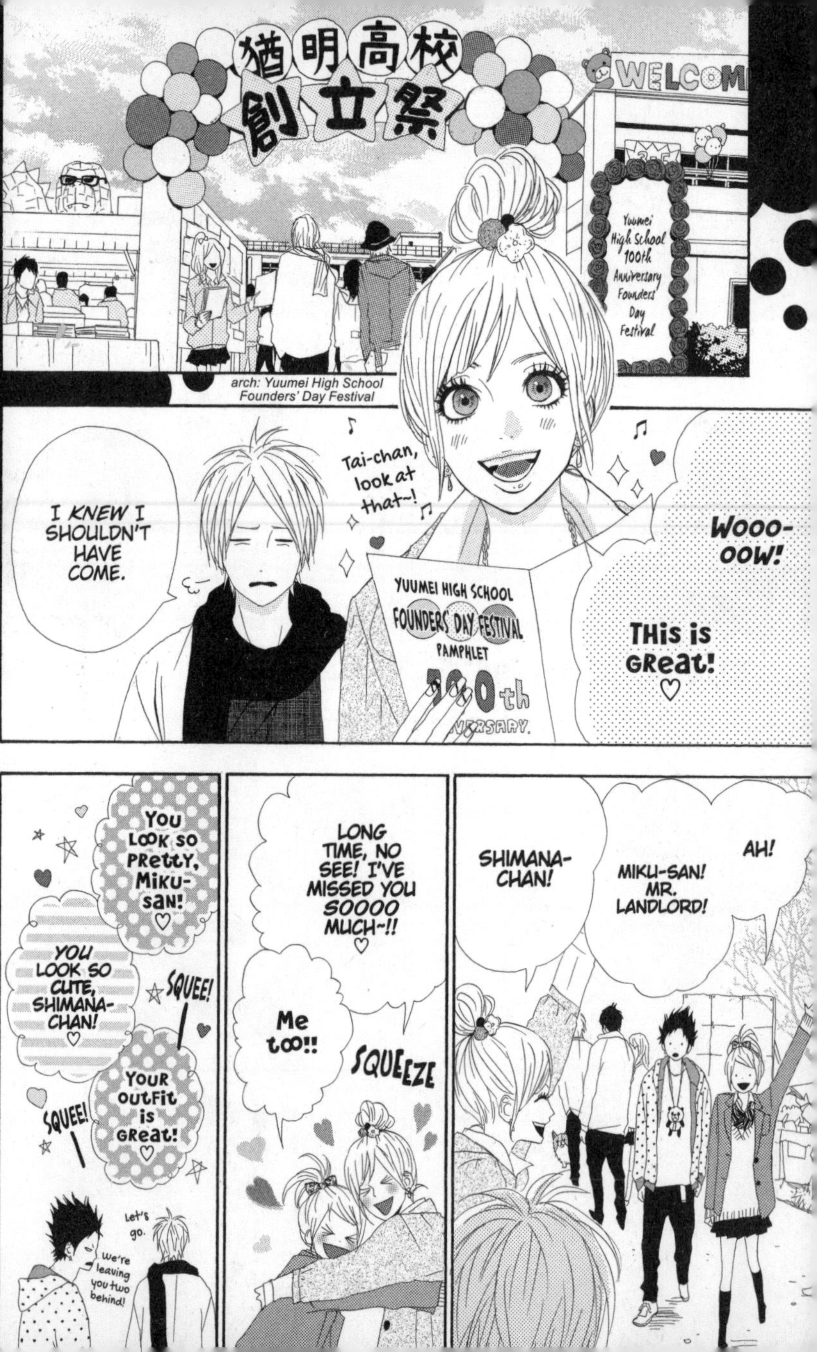
猶明高校
創立祭
WELCOM
Yuumei High School 100th Anniversary Founders Day Festival
arch: Yuumei High School Founders' Day Festival
Wooo-oow!
This is great! ♡
Tai-chan, look at that~!
YUUMEI HIGH SCHOOL FOUNDERS' DAY FESTIVAL PAMPHLET
I KNEW I SHOULDN'T HAVE COME.
AH!
MIKU-SAN! MR. LANDLORD!
SHIMANA-CHAN!
LONG TIME, NO SEE! I'VE MISSED YOU SOOOO MUCH~!! ♡
Me too!!
SQUEEZE
You look so pretty, Miku-san! ♡
YOU LOOK SO CUTE, SHIMANA-CHAN! ♡
SQUEE!
Your outfit is great! ♡
SQUEE!
Let's go.
We're leaving you two behind!

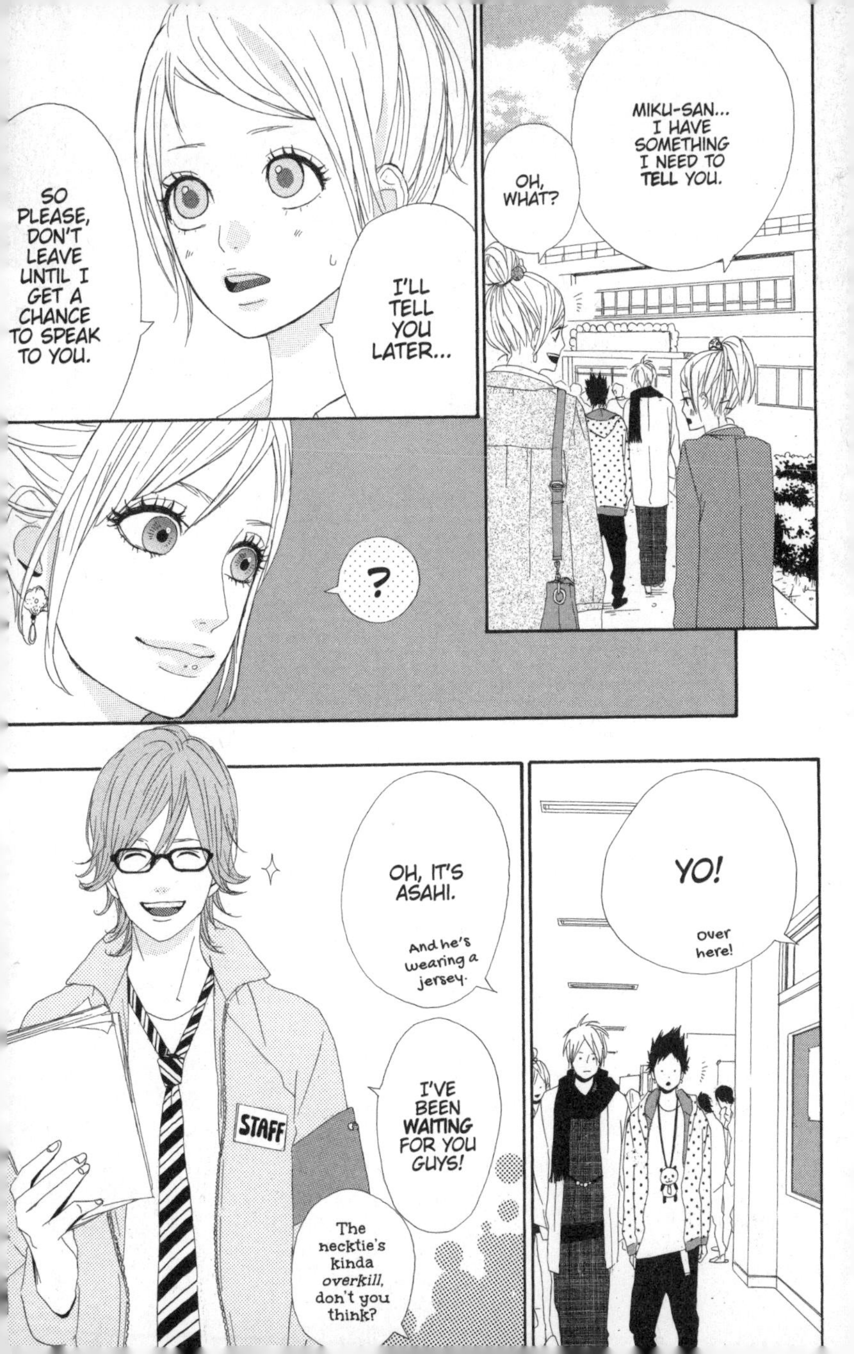
MIKU-SAN... I HAVE SOMETHING I NEED TO TELL YOU.
OH, WHAT?
I'LL TELL YOU LATER...
SO PLEASE, DON'T LEAVE UNTIL I GET A CHANCE TO SPEAK TO YOU.
?
YO!
Over here!
OH, IT'S ASAHI.
And he's wearing a jersey.
STAFF
I'VE BEEN WAITING FOR YOU GUYS!
The necktie's kinda overkill, don't you think?

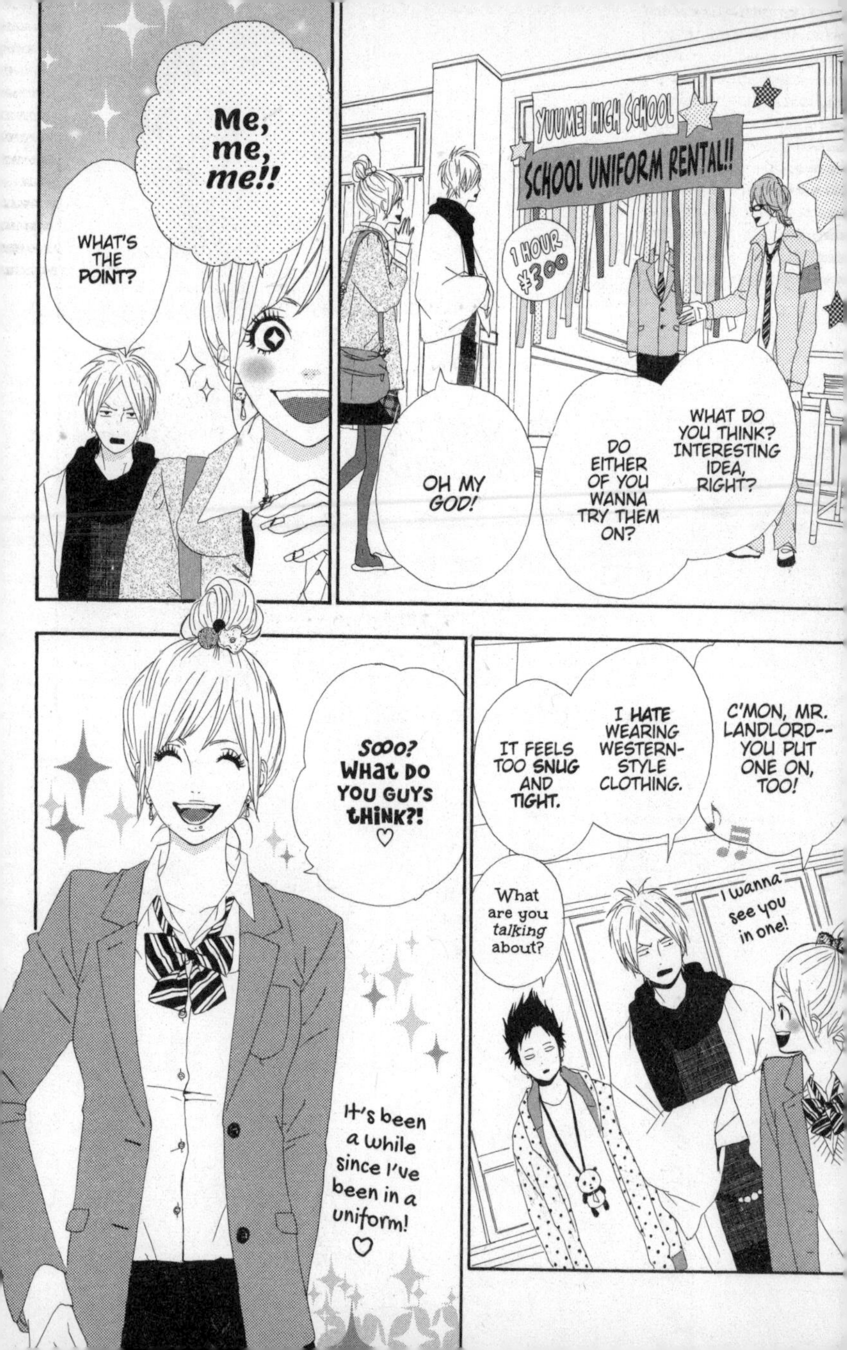
YUUMEI HIGH SCHOOL
SCHOOL UNIFORM RENTAL!!
1 HOUR ¥300
WHAT DO YOU THINK? INTERESTING IDEA, RIGHT?
DO EITHER OF YOU WANNA TRY THEM ON?
OH MY GOD!
Me, me, me!!
WHAT'S THE POINT?
C'MON, MR. LANDLORD-- YOU PUT ONE ON, TOO!
I HATE WEARING WESTERN-STYLE CLOTHING.
IT FEELS TOO SNUG AND TIGHT.
I wanna see you in one!
What are you talking about?
Sooo? What do you guys think?! ♡
It's been a while since I've been in a uniform! ♡

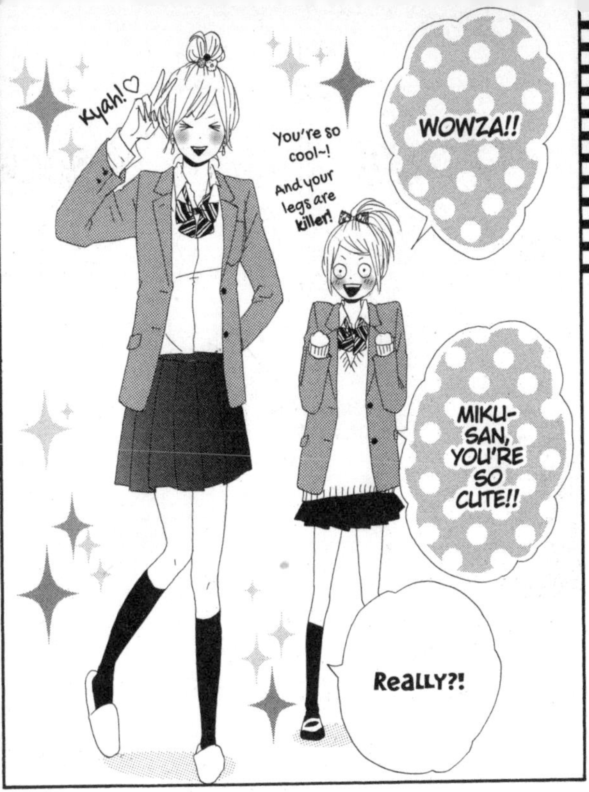
WOWZA!!
You're so cool~! And your legs are killer!
Kyah!♡
MIKU-SAN, YOU'RE SO CUTE!!
Really?!

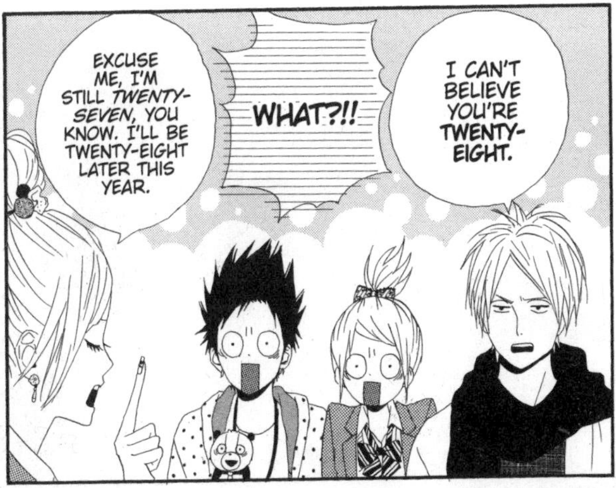
I CAN'T BELIEVE YOU'RE TWENTY-EIGHT.
WHAT?!!
EXCUSE ME, I'M STILL *TWENTY-SEVEN*, YOU KNOW. I'LL BE TWENTY-EIGHT LATER THIS YEAR.

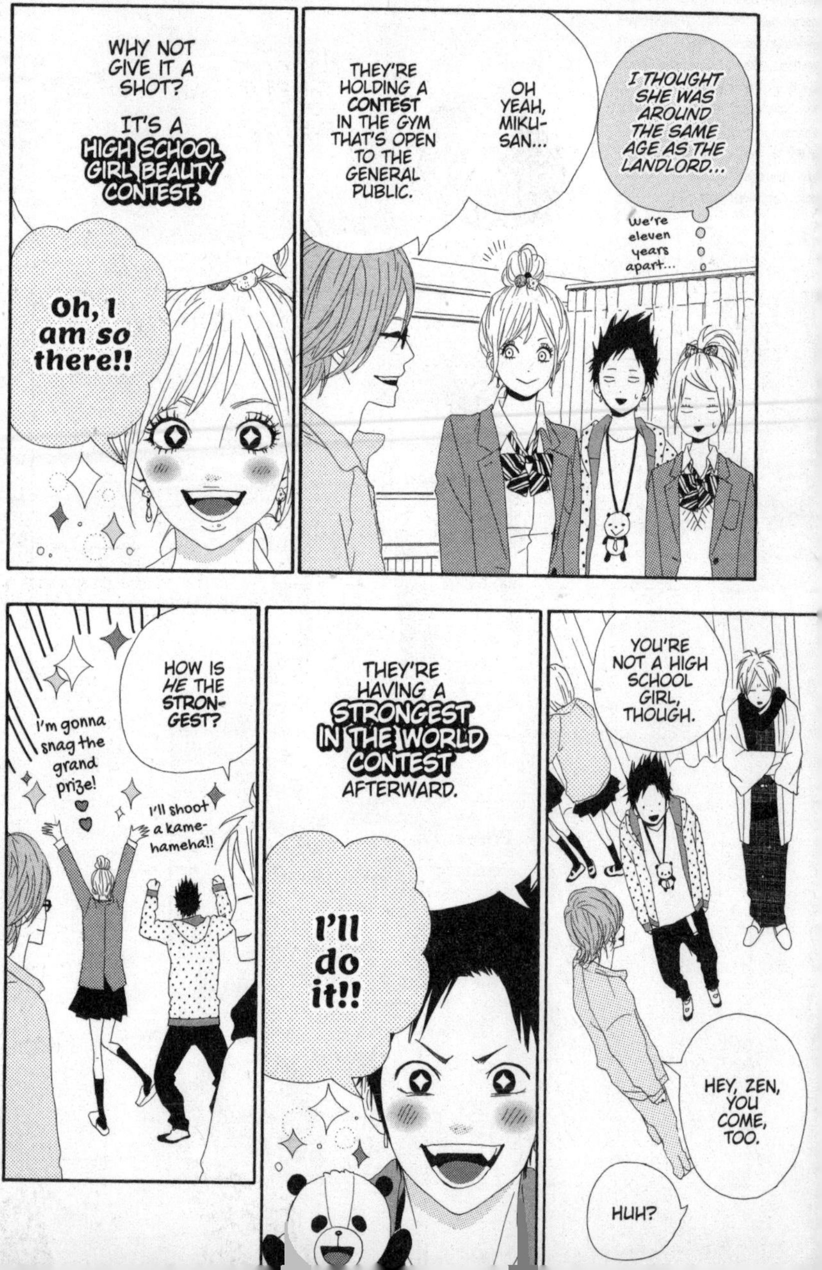
I THOUGHT SHE WAS AROUND THE SAME AGE AS THE LANDLORD...
We're eleven years apart...
OH YEAH, MIKU-SAN...
THEY'RE HOLDING A CONTEST IN THE GYM THAT'S OPEN TO THE GENERAL PUBLIC.
WHY NOT GIVE IT A SHOT?
IT'S A HIGH SCHOOL GIRL BEAUTY CONTEST.
Oh, I am so there!!
YOU'RE NOT A HIGH SCHOOL GIRL, THOUGH.
HEY, ZEN, YOU COME, TOO.
HUH?
THEY'RE HAVING A STRONGEST IN THE WORLD CONTEST AFTERWARD.
I'll do it!!
HOW IS HE THE STRONGEST?
I'm gonna snag the grand prize!
I'll shoot a kame-hameha!!

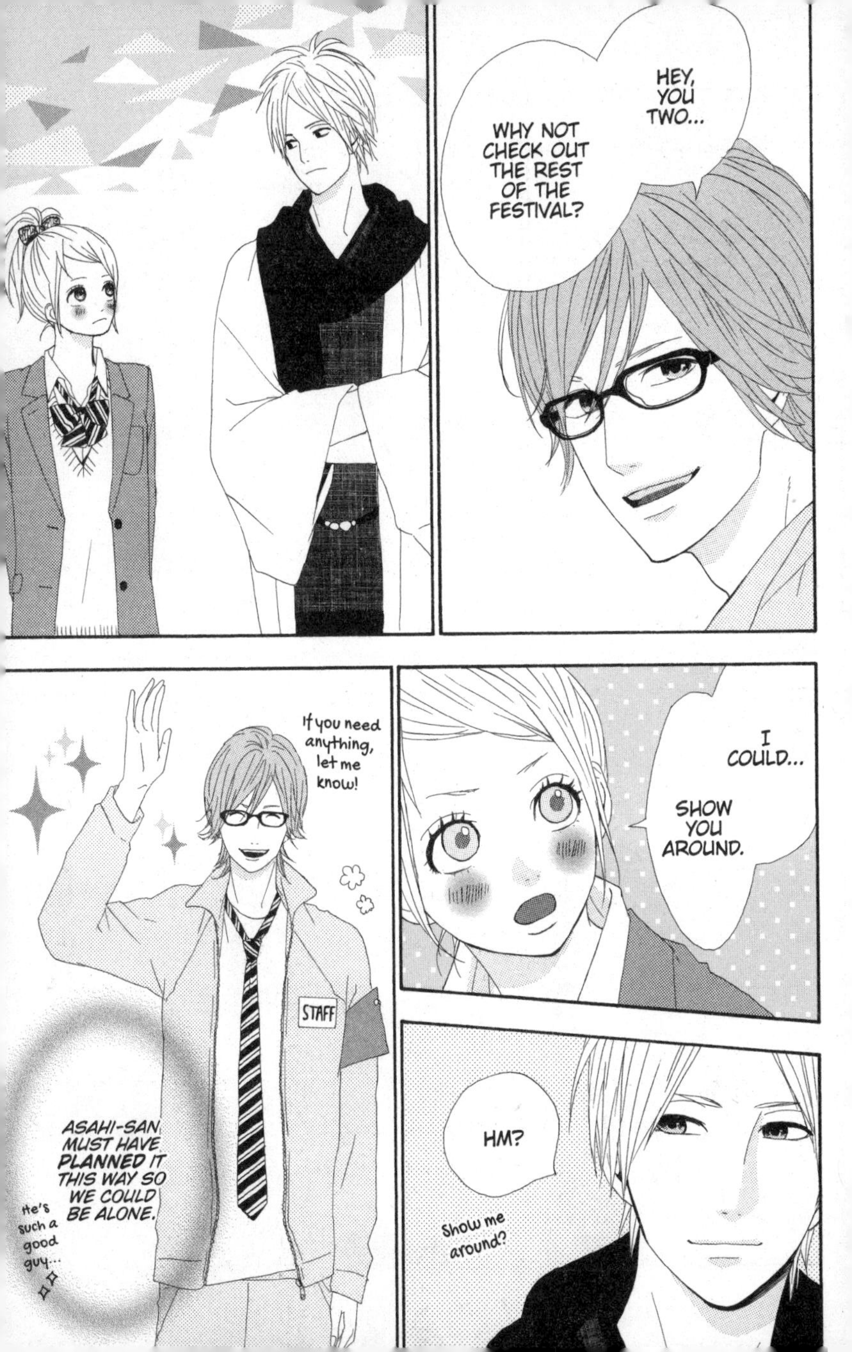
HEY, YOU TWO...
WHY NOT CHECK OUT THE REST OF THE FESTIVAL?
I COULD...
SHOW YOU AROUND.
HM?
Show me around?
If you need anything, let me know!
STAFF
ASAHI-SAN MUST HAVE PLANNED IT THIS WAY SO WE COULD BE ALONE.
He's such a good guy...

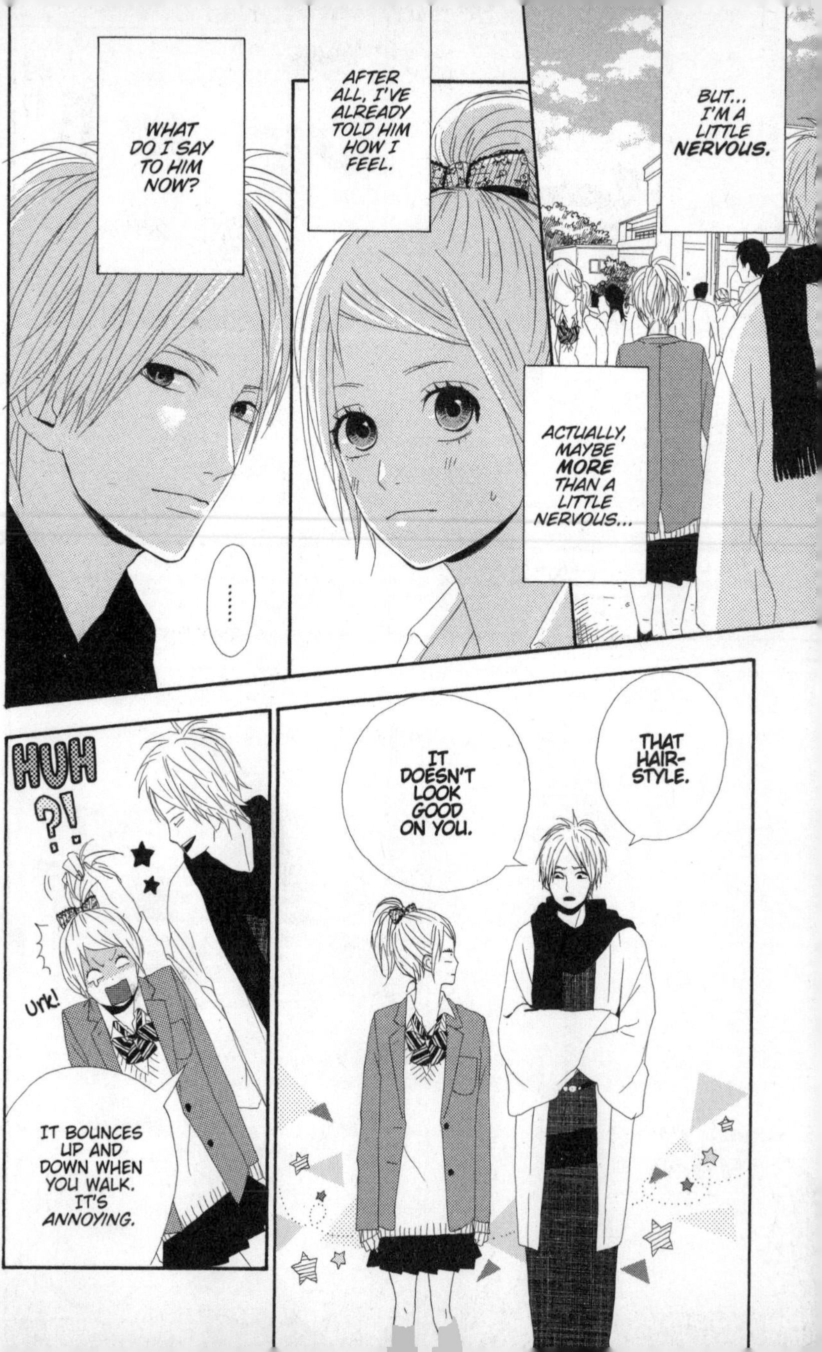
BUT... I'M A LITTLE NERVOUS.
ACTUALLY, MAYBE MORE THAN A LITTLE NERVOUS...
AFTER ALL, I'VE ALREADY TOLD HIM HOW I FEEL.
WHAT DO I SAY TO HIM NOW?
......
THAT HAIR-STYLE.
IT DOESN'T LOOK GOOD ON YOU.
HUH ?!
URK!
IT BOUNCES UP AND DOWN WHEN YOU WALK. IT'S ANNOYING.

sign: Cotton Candy, Free

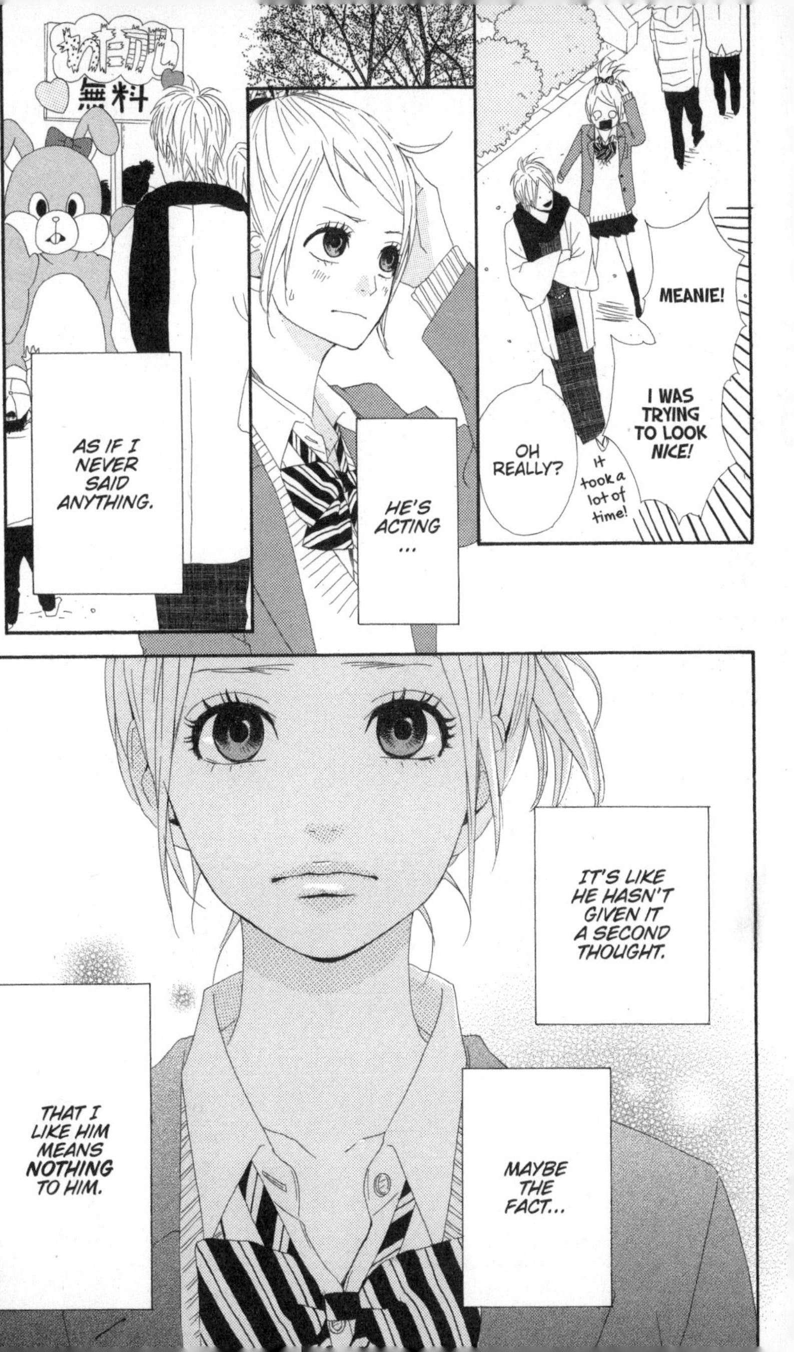
MEANIE!
I WAS TRYING TO LOOK NICE!
It took a lot of time!
OH REALLY?
HE'S ACTING...
AS IF I NEVER SAID ANYTHING.
IT'S LIKE HE HASN'T GIVEN IT A SECOND THOUGHT.
MAYBE THE FACT...
THAT I LIKE HIM MEANS NOTHING TO HIM.

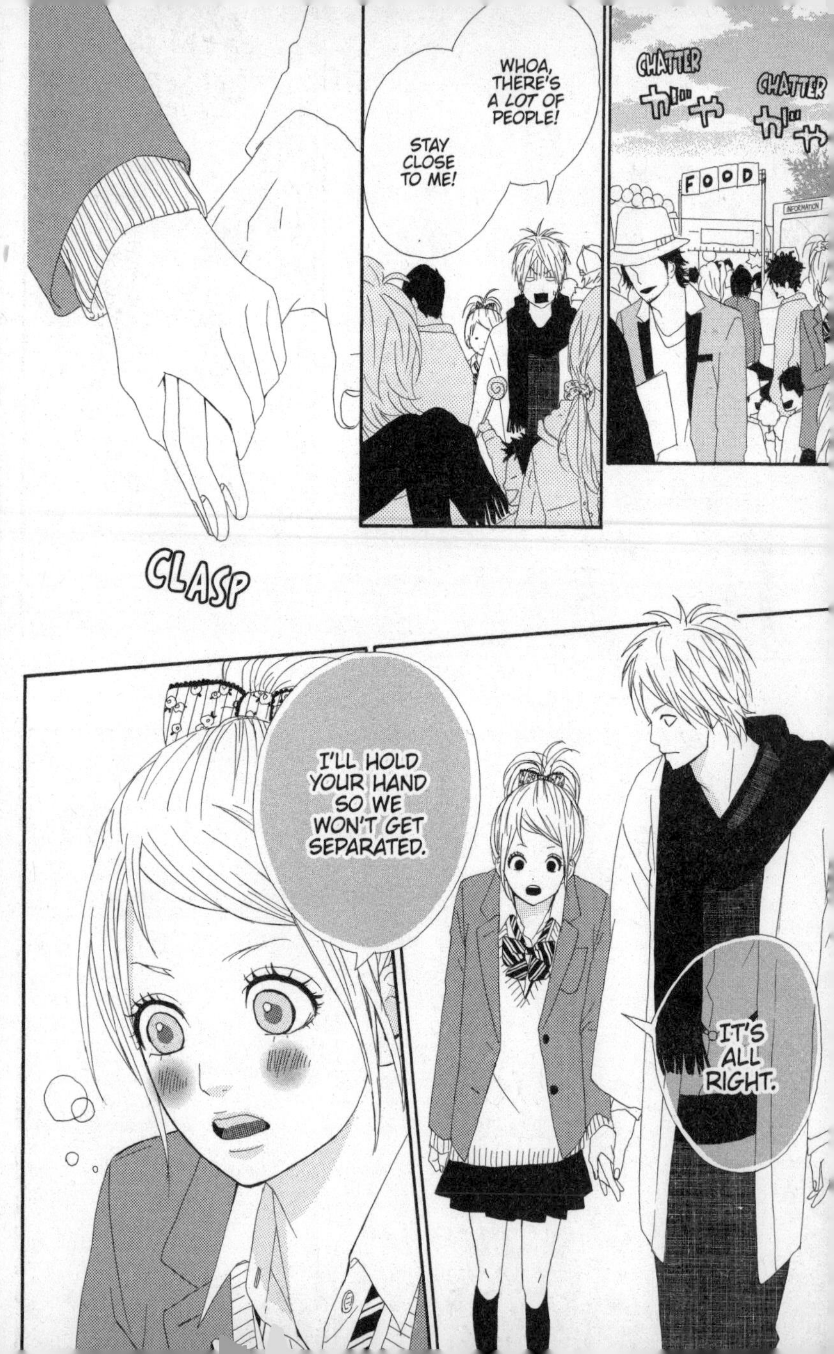
CHATTER
ガヤ
CHATTER
ガヤ
FOOD
INFORMATION
WHOA, THERE'S A LOT OF PEOPLE!
STAY CLOSE TO ME!
CLASP
IT'S ALL RIGHT.
I'LL HOLD YOUR HAND SO WE WON'T GET SEPARATED.

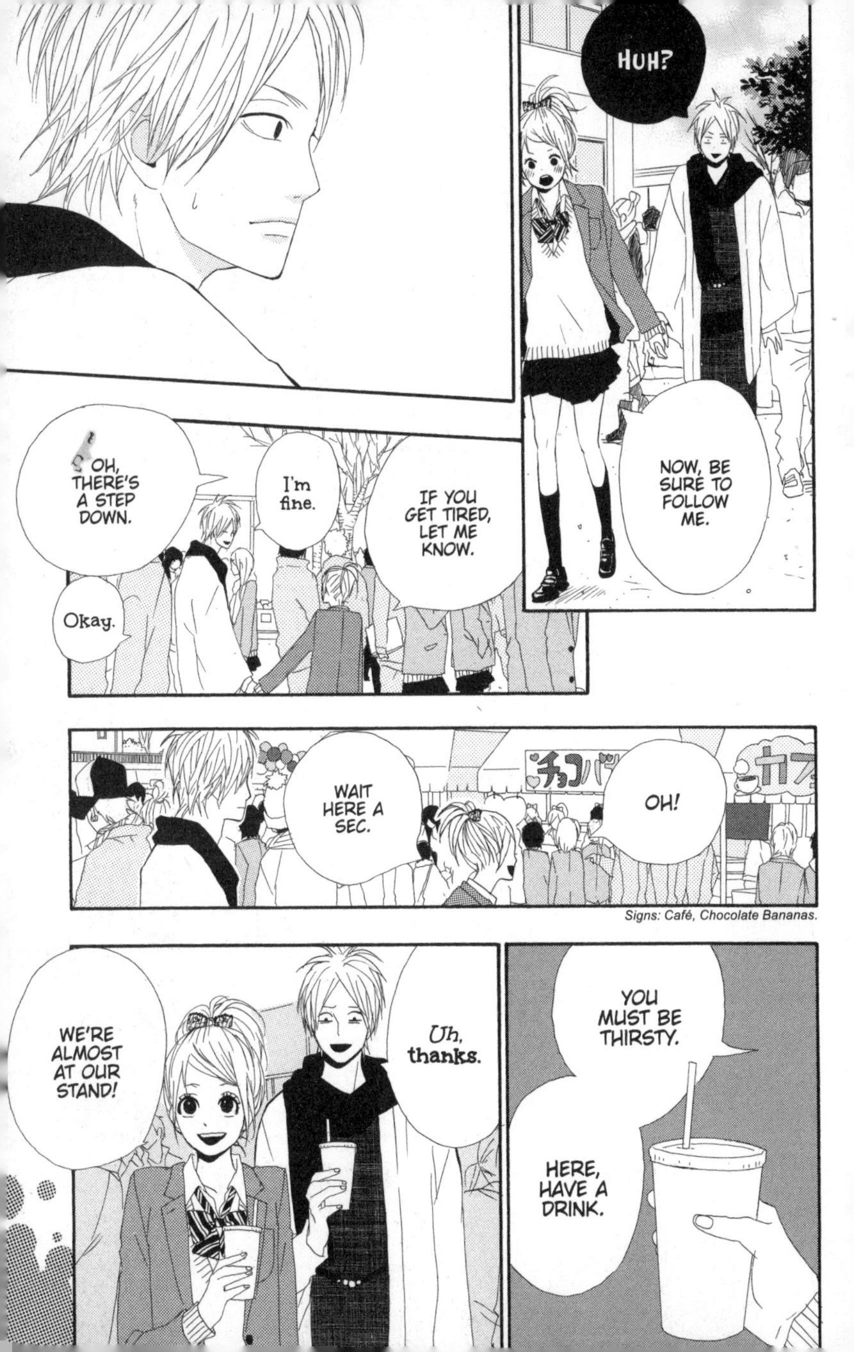
HUH?
NOW, BE SURE TO FOLLOW ME.
IF YOU GET TIRED, LET ME KNOW.
I'm fine.
OH, THERE'S A STEP DOWN.
Okay.
OH!
WAIT HERE A SEC.
YOU MUST BE THIRSTY.
HERE, HAVE A DRINK.
Uh, thanks.
WE'RE ALMOST AT OUR STAND!

Signs: Café, Chocolate Bananas.

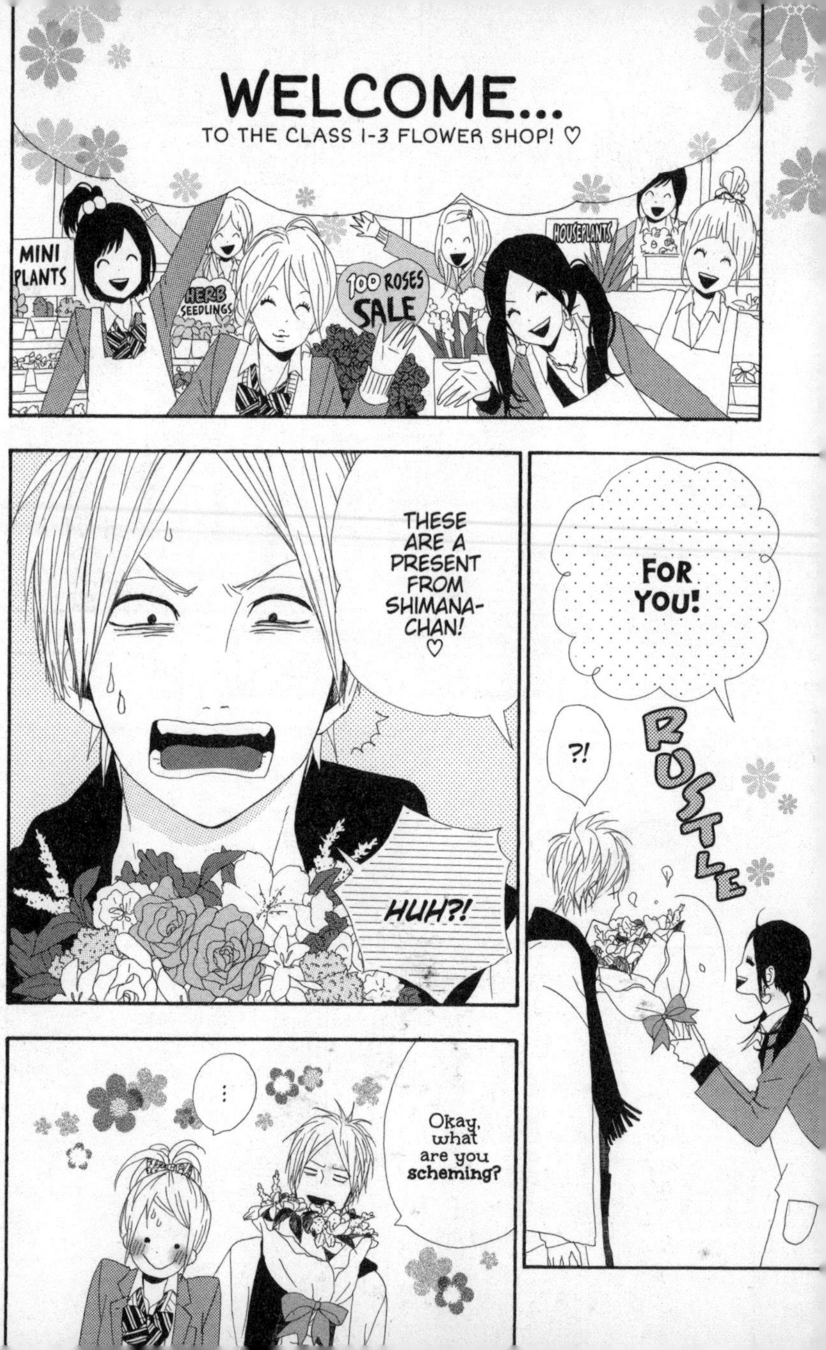
WELCOME...
TO THE CLASS 1-3 FLOWER SHOP! ♡
HOUSEPLANTS
100 ROSES SALE
HERB SEEDLINGS
MINI PLANTS
FOR YOU!
ROSTVE
?!
THESE ARE A PRESENT FROM SHIMANA-CHAN! ♡
HUH?!
Okay, what are you scheming?
...

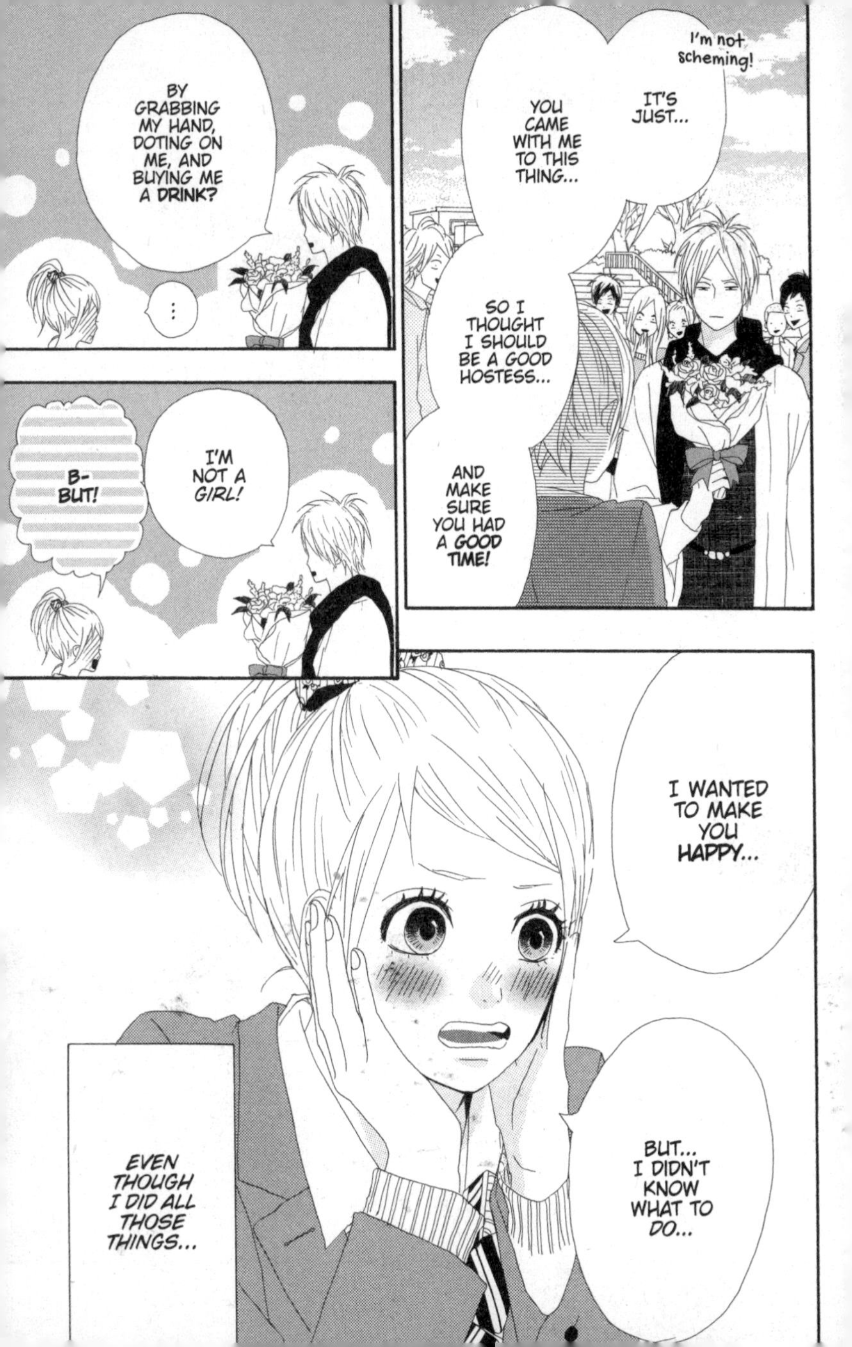

I'm not scheming!
IT'S JUST...
YOU CAME WITH ME TO THIS THING...
SO I THOUGHT I SHOULD BE A GOOD HOSTESS...
AND MAKE SURE YOU HAD A GOOD TIME!
BY GRABBING MY HAND, DOTING ON ME, AND BUYING ME A DRINK?
...
I'M NOT A GIRL!
B-BUT!
I WANTED TO MAKE YOU HAPPY...
BUT... I DIDN'T KNOW WHAT TO DO...
EVEN THOUGH I DID ALL THOSE THINGS...

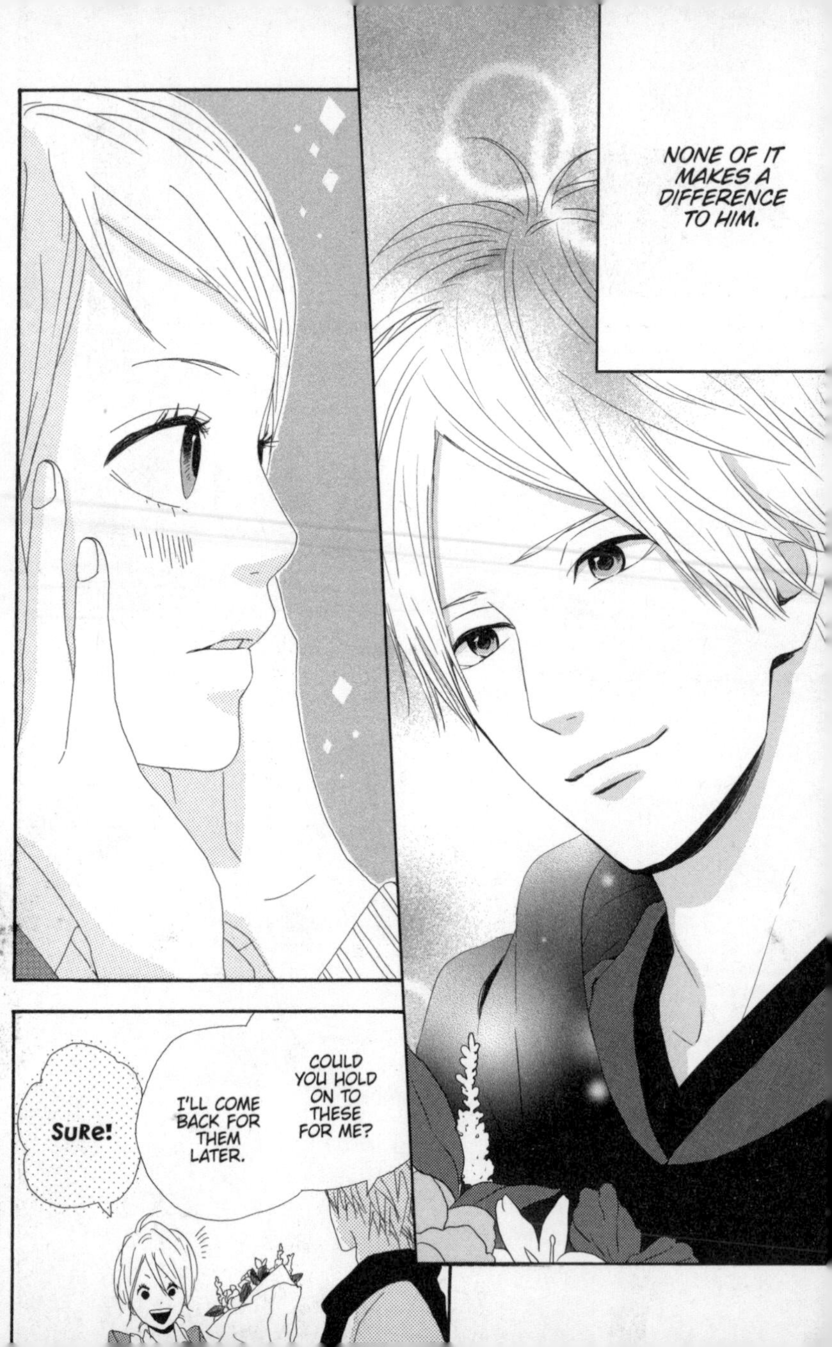
NONE OF IT MAKES A DIFFERENCE TO HIM.
COULD YOU HOLD ON TO THESE FOR ME?
I'LL COME BACK FOR THEM LATER.
Sure!

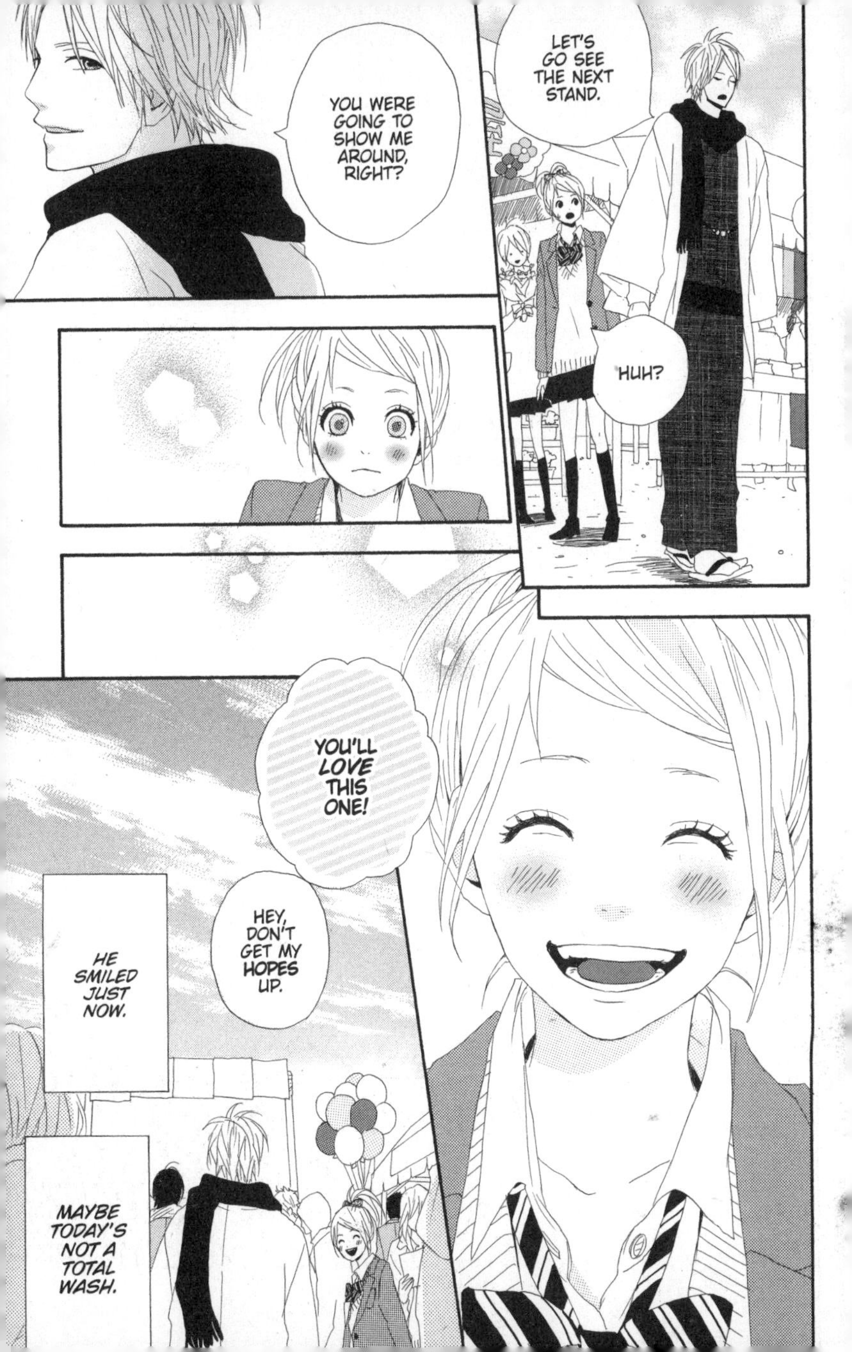
LET'S GO SEE THE NEXT STAND.
HUH?
YOU WERE GOING TO SHOW ME AROUND, RIGHT?
YOU'LL *LOVE* THIS ONE!
HEY, DON'T GET MY HOPES UP.
HE SMILED JUST NOW.
MAYBE TODAY'S NOT A TOTAL WASH.

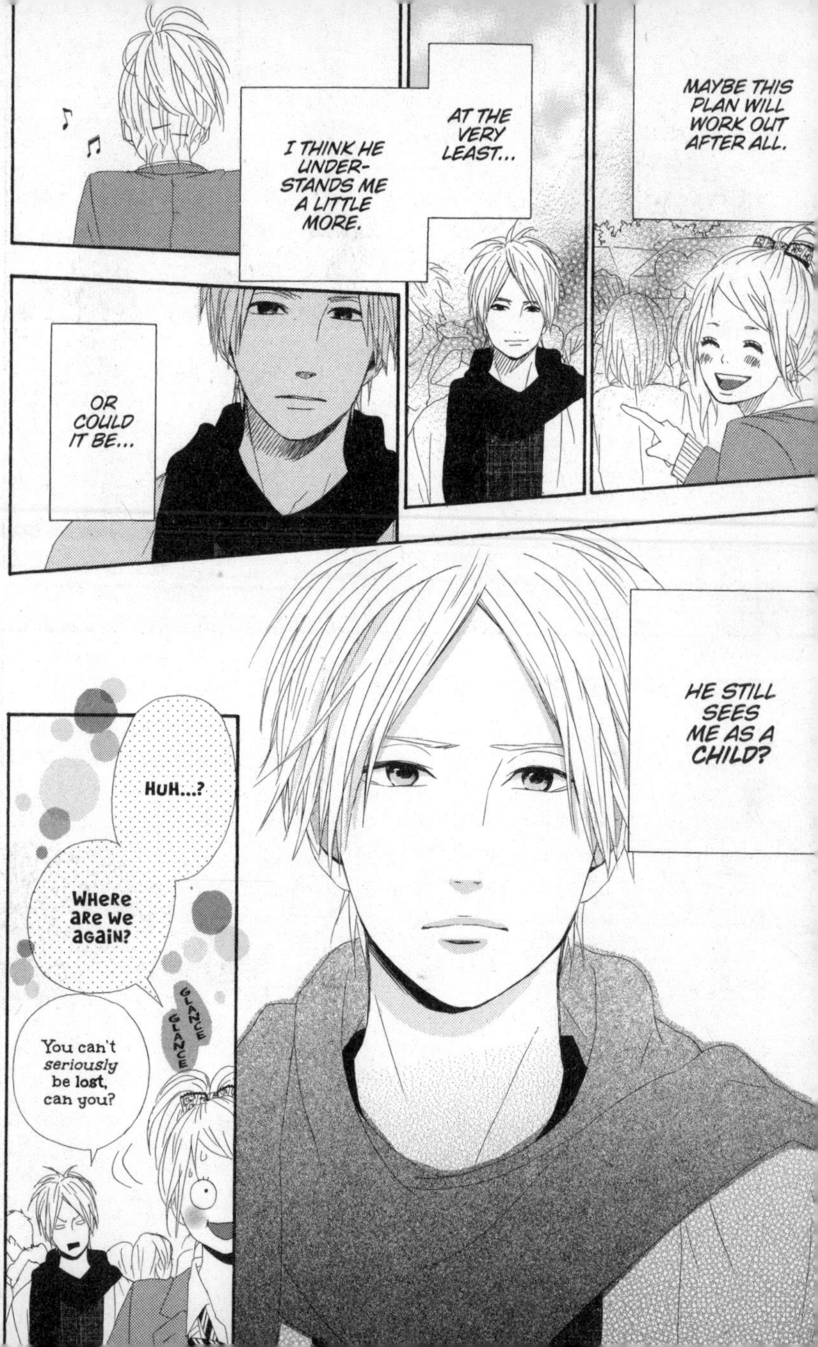

MAYBE THIS PLAN WILL WORK OUT AFTER ALL.
AT THE VERY LEAST...
I THINK HE UNDER-STANDS ME A LITTLE MORE.
OR COULD IT BE...
HE STILL SEES ME AS A CHILD?
HUH...?
Where are we again?
GLANCE GLANCE
You can't *seriously* be lost, can you?

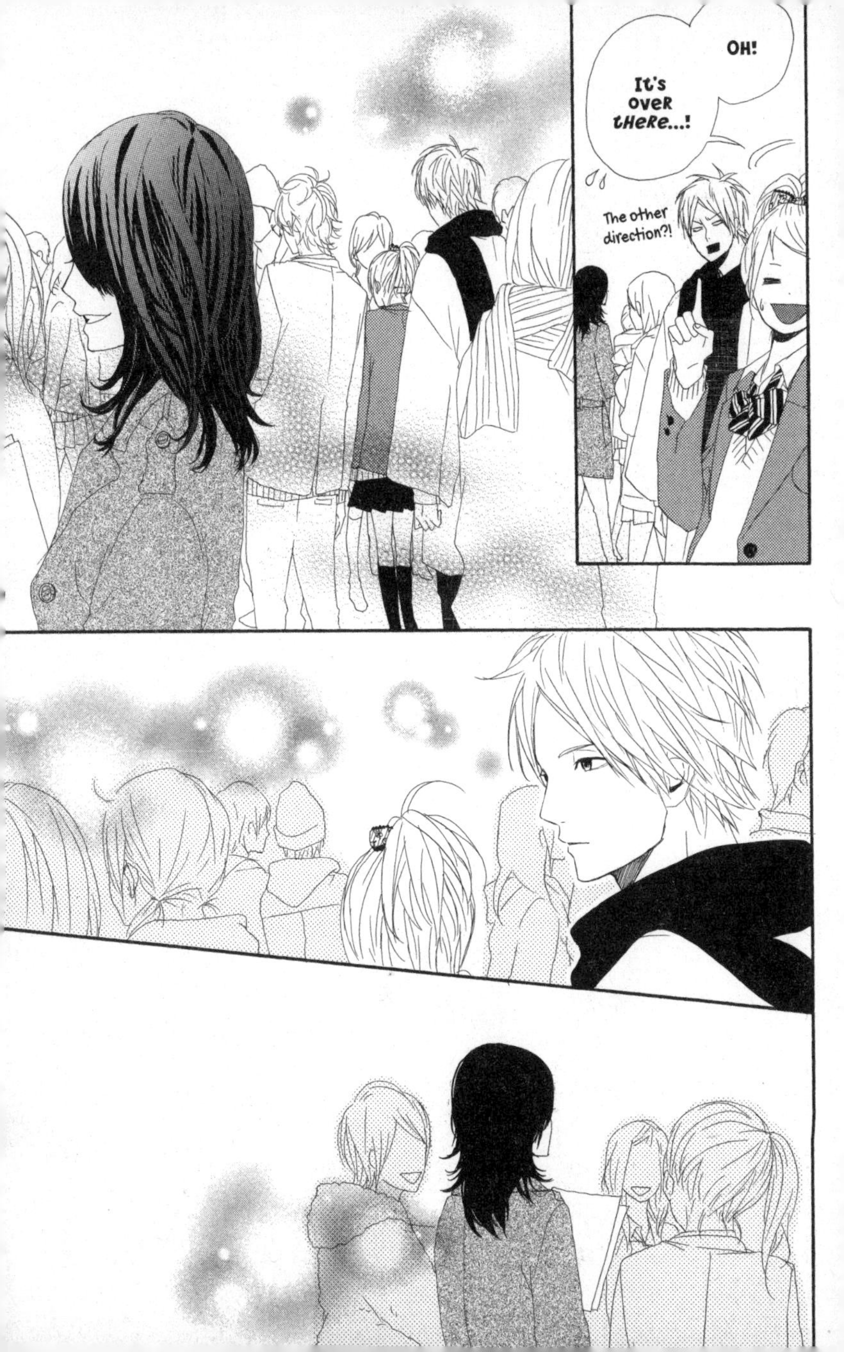
OH!
It's over there...!
The other direction?!

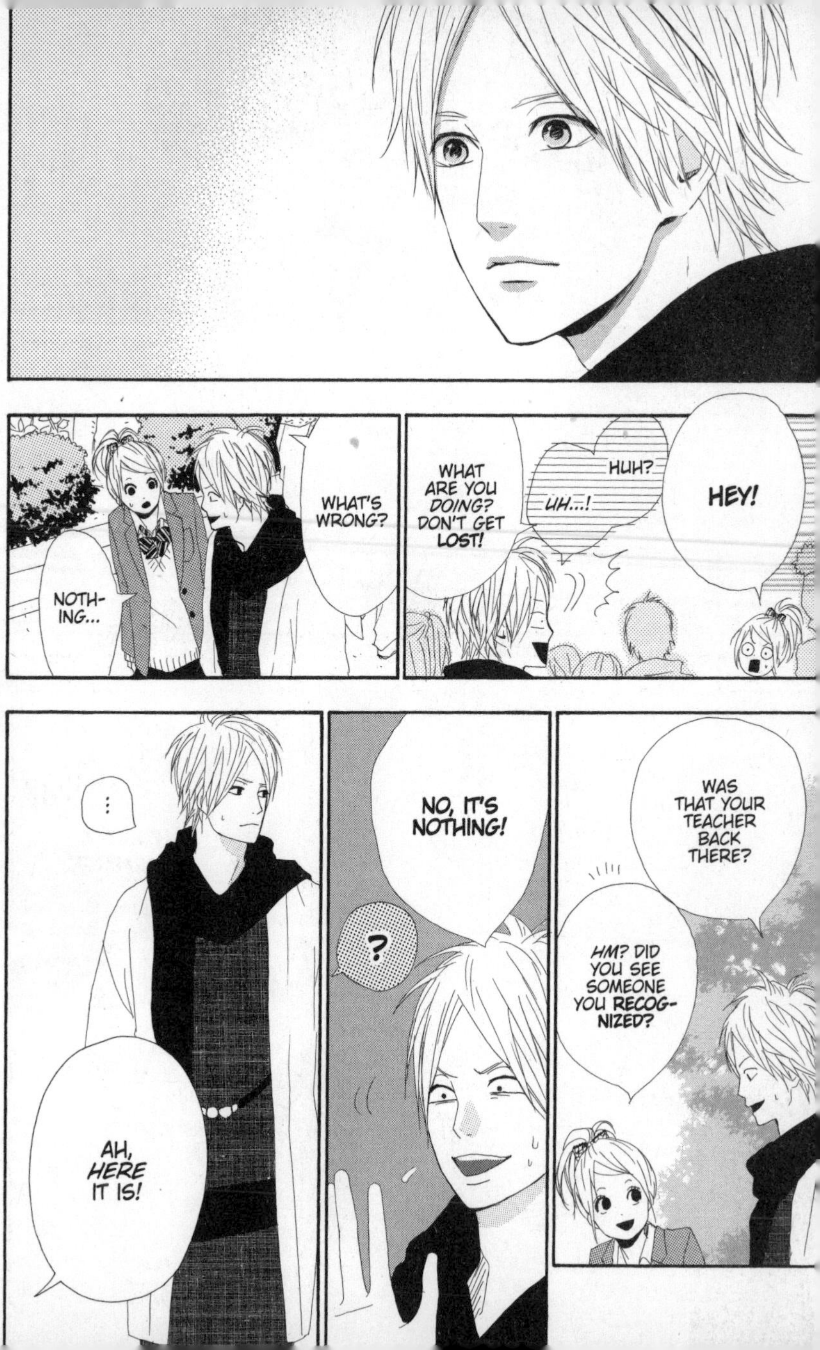
HEY!
HUH?
UH...!
WHAT ARE YOU DOING? DON'T GET LOST!
WHAT'S WRONG?
NOTHING...
WAS THAT YOUR TEACHER BACK THERE?
HM? DID YOU SEE SOMEONE YOU RECOGNIZED?
NO, IT'S NOTHING!
?
...
AH, HERE IT IS!

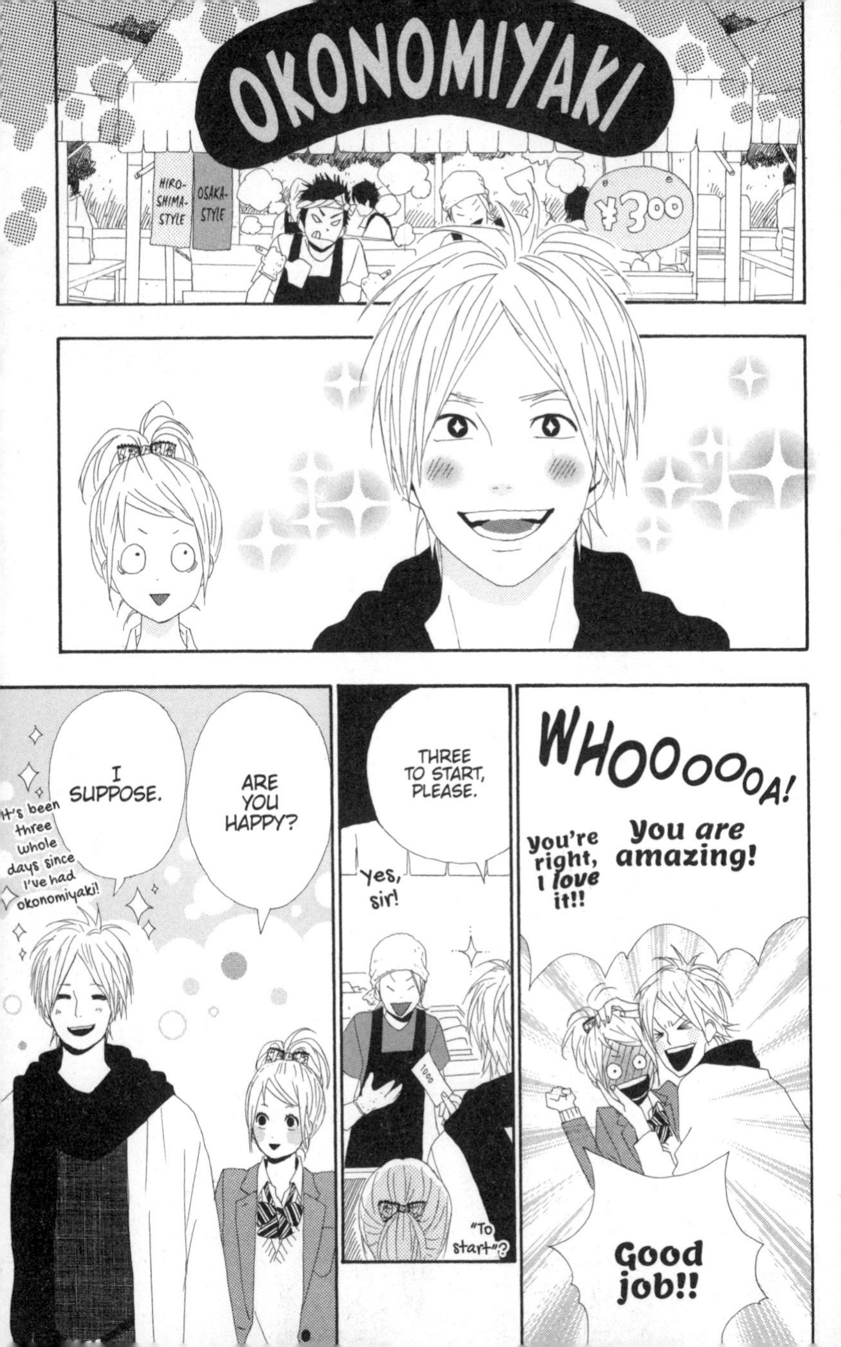

OKONOMIYAKI
HIRO-SHIMA-STYLE
OSAKA-STYLE
¥300
WHOOOOOOA!
You are amazing!
You're right, I love it!!
Good job!!
THREE TO START, PLEASE.
Yes, sir!
1000
"To start"?
ARE YOU HAPPY?
I SUPPOSE.
It's been three whole days since I've had okonomiyaki!

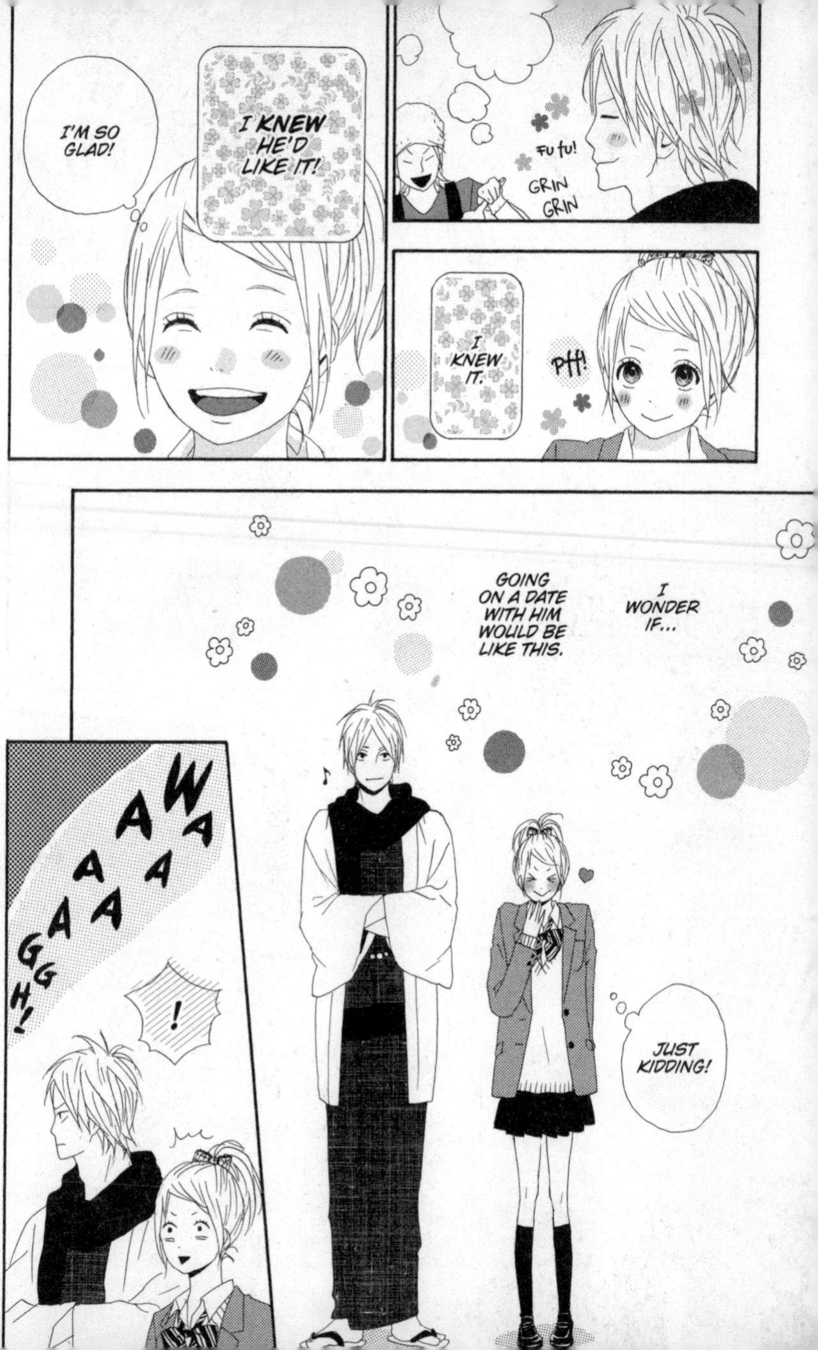
Fu fu!
GRIN GRIN
I KNEW IT.
Pff!
I KNEW HE'D LIKE IT!
I'M SO GLAD!
I WONDER IF...
GOING ON A DATE WITH HIM WOULD BE LIKE THIS.
JUST KIDDING!
WAAAAAAGGH!
!

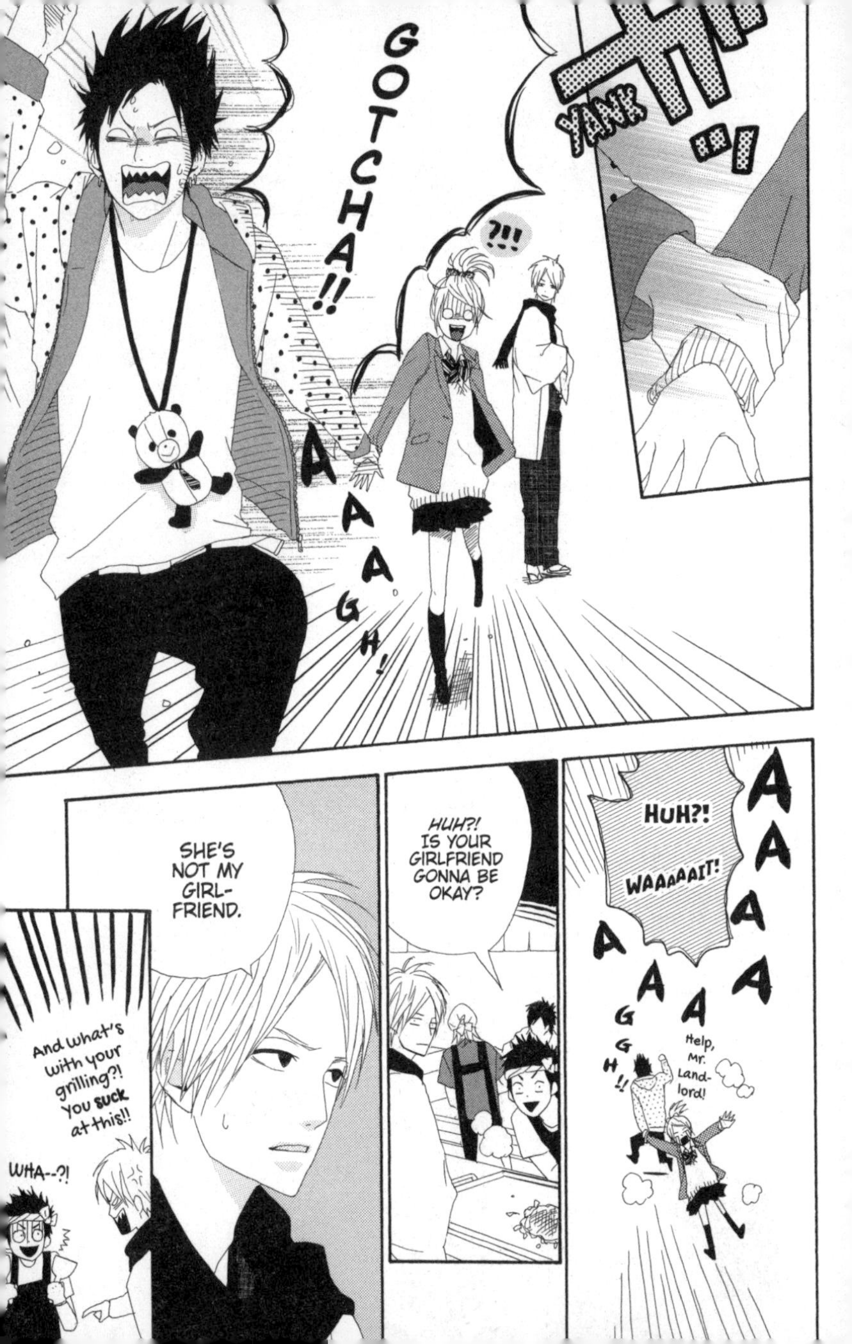
YANK
!!
GOTCHA!!
?!!
AAAGH!
HUH?!
WAAAAAIT!
AAAAAAAAAGGH!!
Help, Mr. Landlord!
HUH?! IS YOUR GIRLFRIEND GONNA BE OKAY?
SHE'S NOT MY GIRL-FRIEND.
And what's with your grilling?! You suck at this!!
WHA--?!

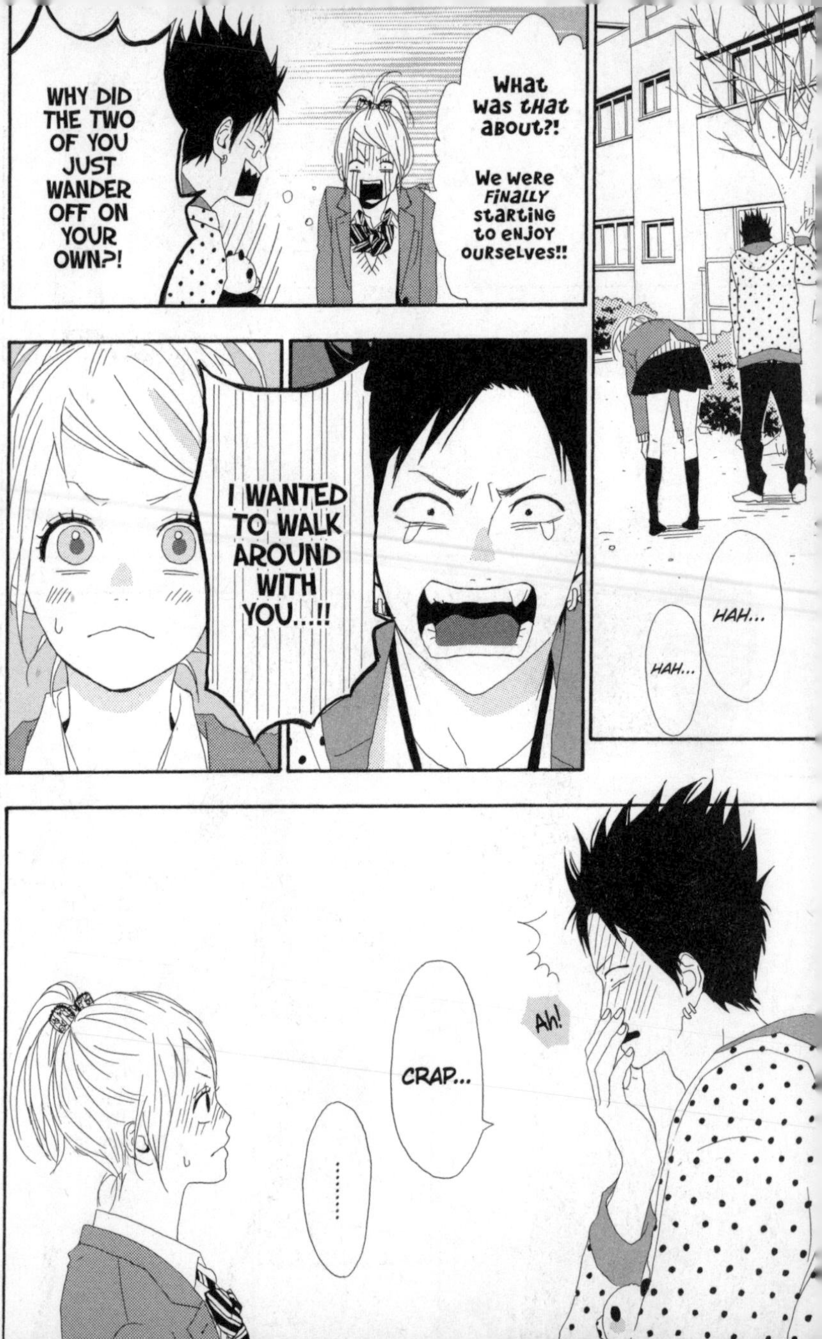
HAH...
HAH...
What was that about?!
We were finally starting to enjoy ourselves!!
WHY DID THE TWO OF YOU JUST WANDER OFF ON YOUR OWN?!
I WANTED TO WALK AROUND WITH YOU...!!
Ah!
CRAP...
......

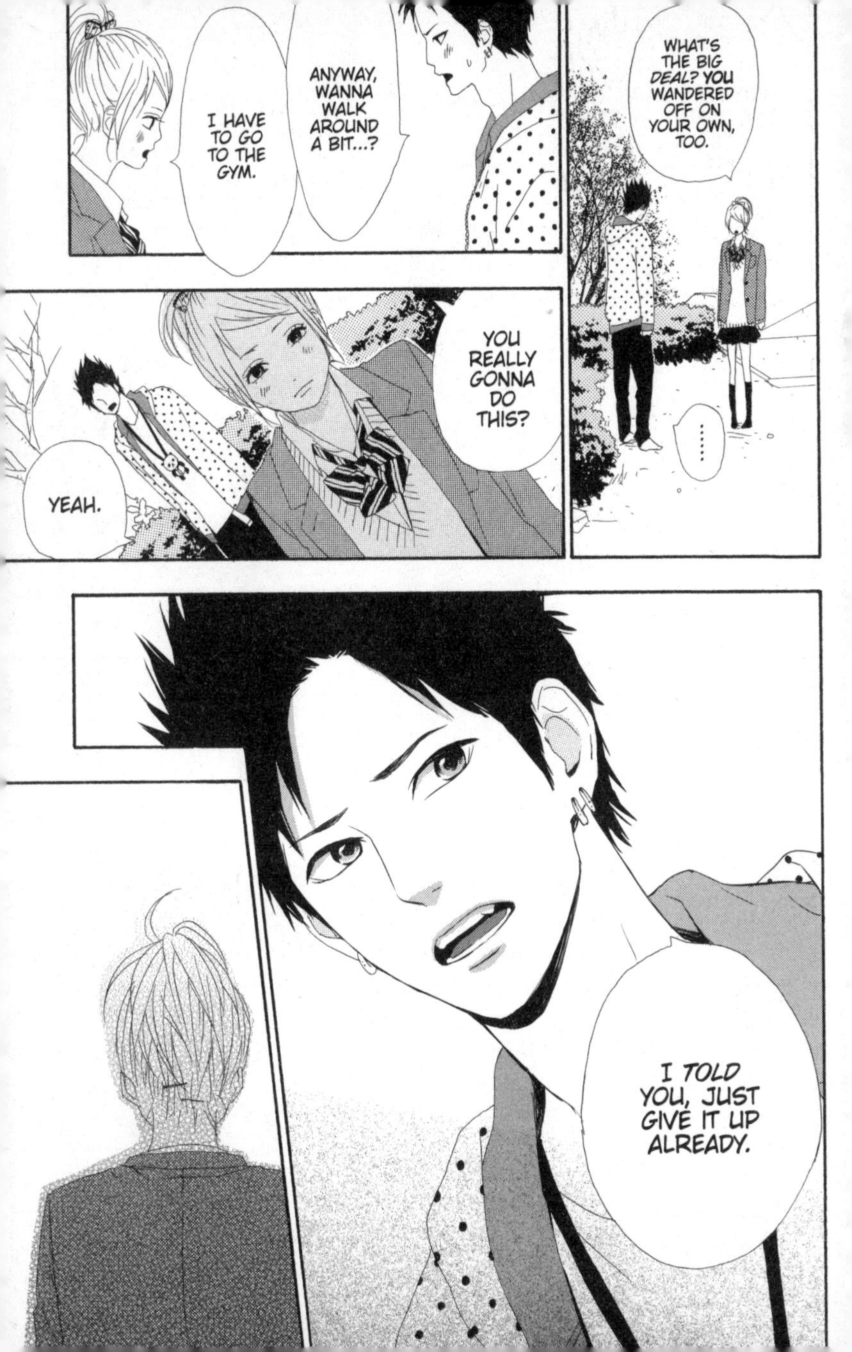
WHAT'S THE BIG *DEAL?* YOU WANDERED OFF ON YOUR OWN, TOO.
......
ANYWAY, WANNA WALK AROUND A BIT...?
I HAVE TO GO TO THE GYM.
YOU REALLY GONNA DO THIS?
YEAH.
I *TOLD* YOU, JUST GIVE IT UP ALREADY.

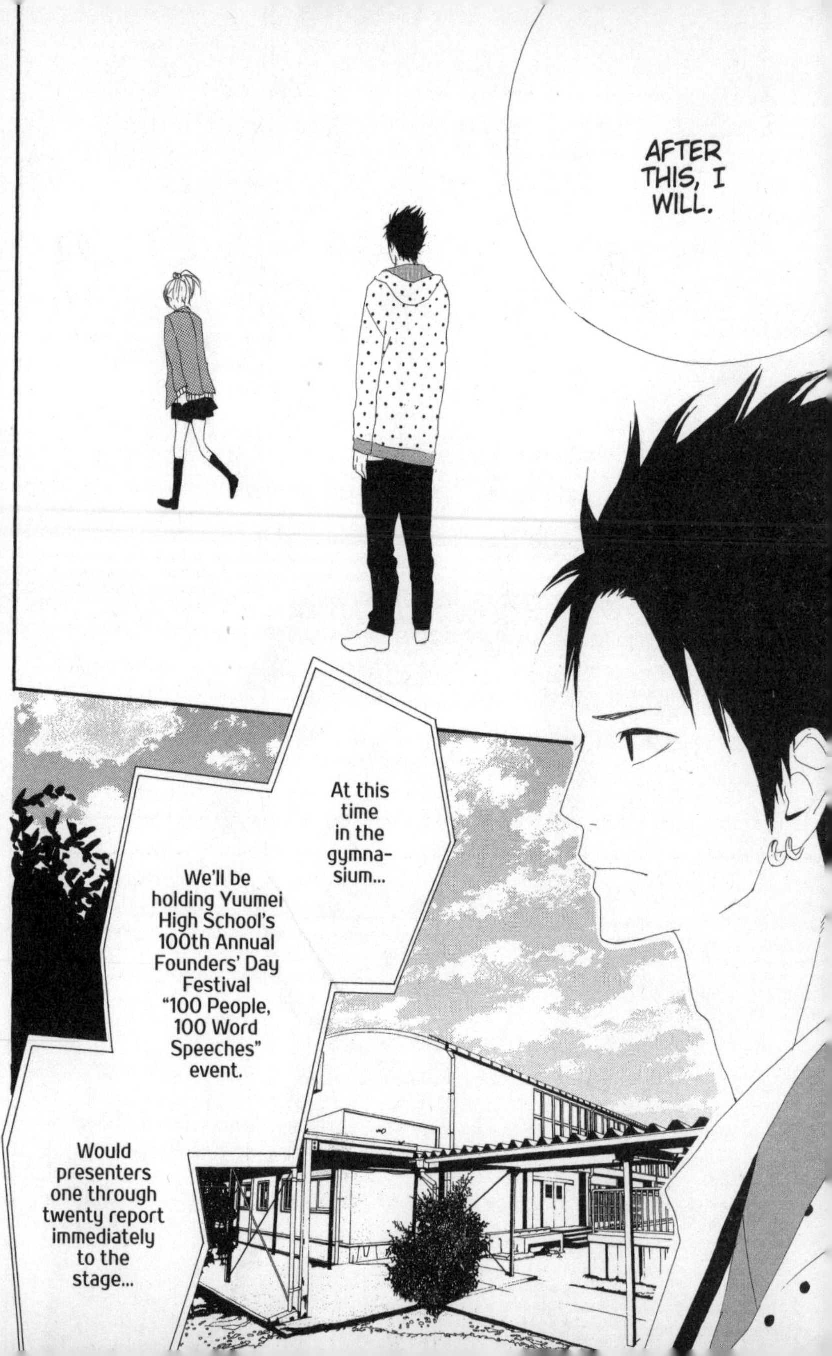
AFTER THIS, I WILL.
At this time in the gymnasium...
We'll be holding Yuumei High School's 100th Annual Founders' Day Festival "100 People, 100 Word Speeches" event.
Would presenters one through twenty report immediately to the stage...

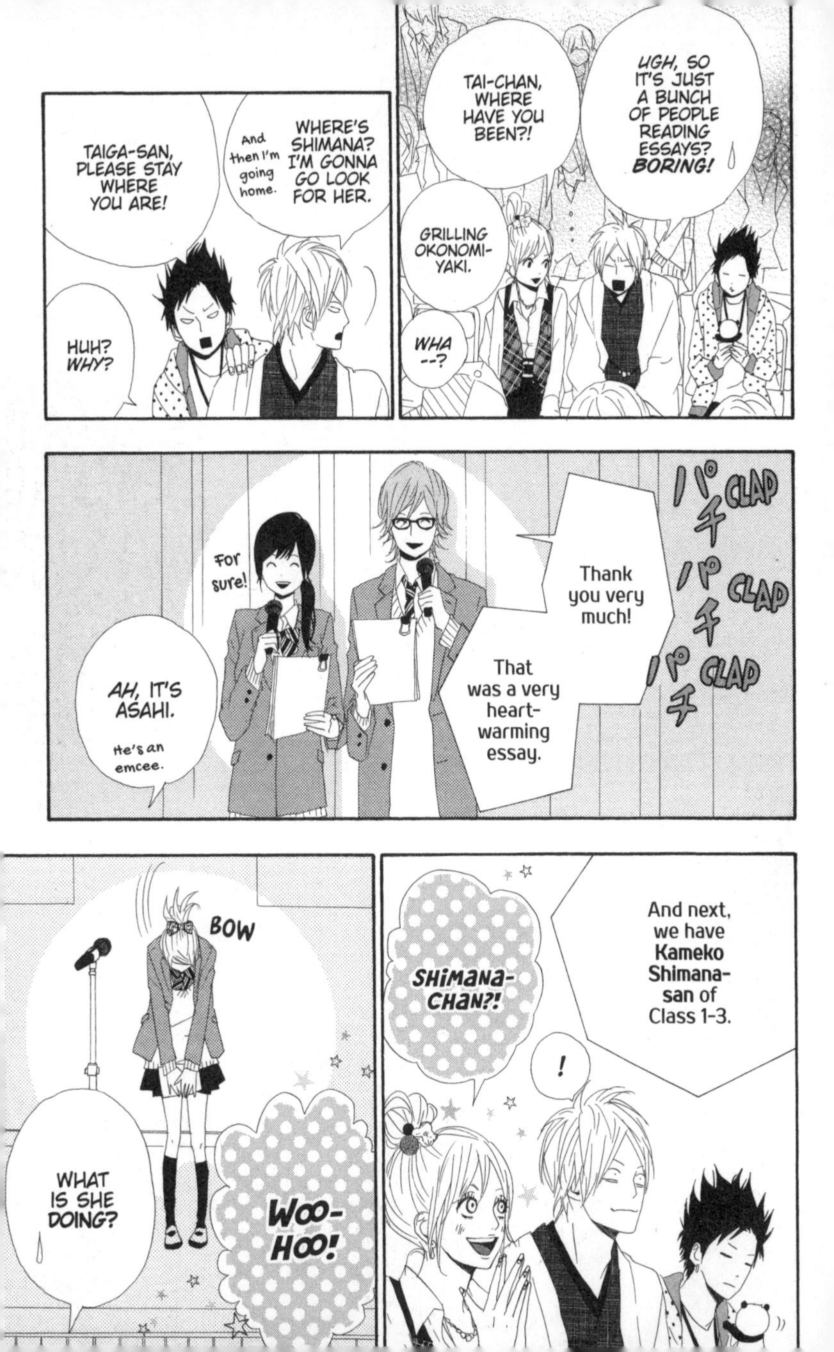
UGH, SO IT'S JUST A BUNCH OF PEOPLE READING ESSAYS? BORING!
TAI-CHAN, WHERE HAVE YOU BEEN?!
GRILLING OKONOMI-YAKI.
WHA --?
WHERE'S SHIMANA? I'M GONNA GO LOOK FOR HER.
And then I'm going home.
TAIGA-SAN, PLEASE STAY WHERE YOU ARE!
HUH? WHY?
パチ CLAP
パチ CLAP
パチ CLAP
Thank you very much!
That was a very heart-warming essay.
For sure!
AH, IT'S ASAHI.
He's an emcee.
And next, we have Kameko Shimana-san of Class 1-3.
SHIMANA-CHAN?!
!
BOW
WOO-HOO!
WHAT IS SHE DOING?

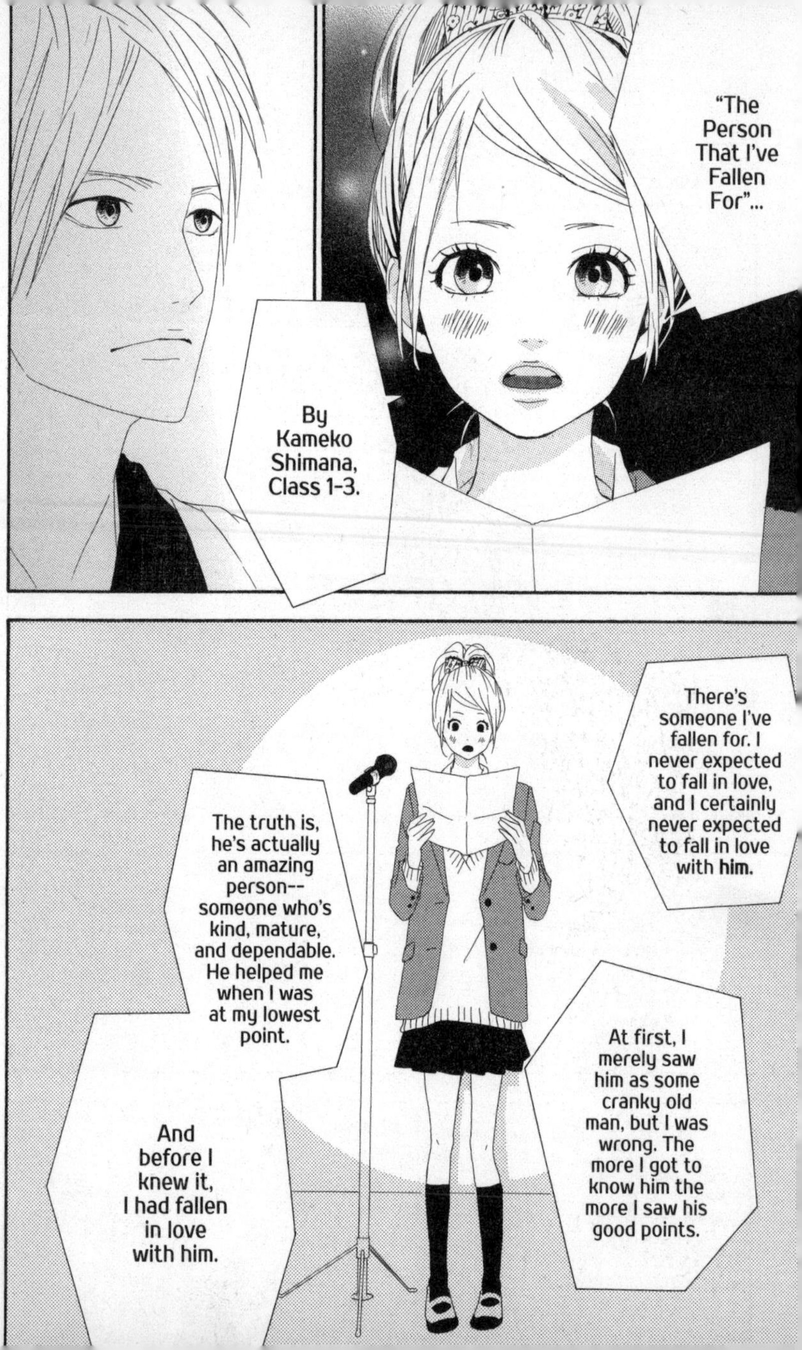
"The Person That I've Fallen For"...
By Kameko Shimana, Class 1-3.
There's someone I've fallen for. I never expected to fall in love, and I certainly never expected to fall in love with **him.**
At first, I merely saw him as some cranky old man, but I was wrong. The more I got to know him the more I saw his good points.
The truth is, he's actually an amazing person--someone who's kind, mature, and dependable. He helped me when I was at my lowest point.
And before I knew it, I had fallen in love with him.

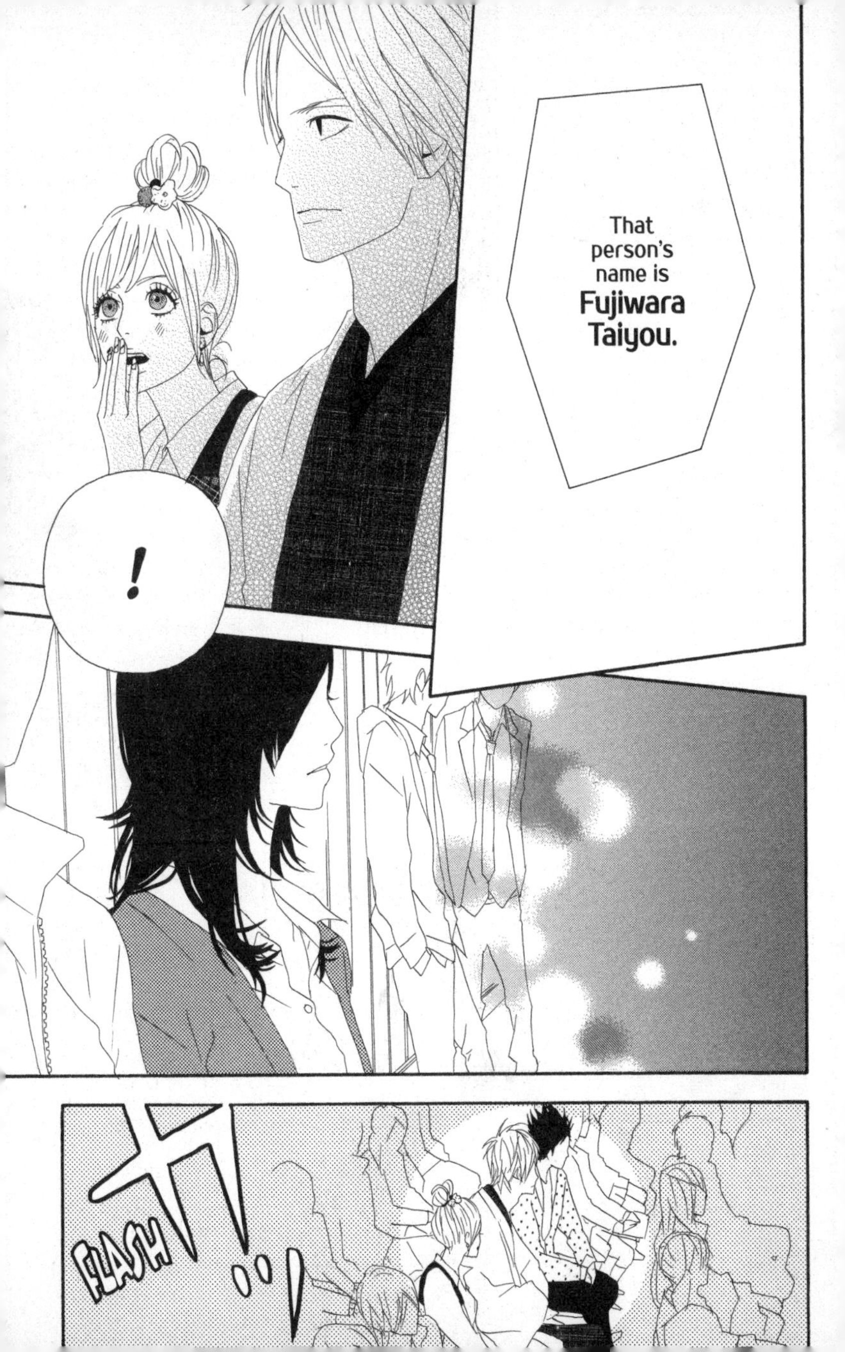
That person's name is Fujiwara Taiyou.
!
FLASH
!!

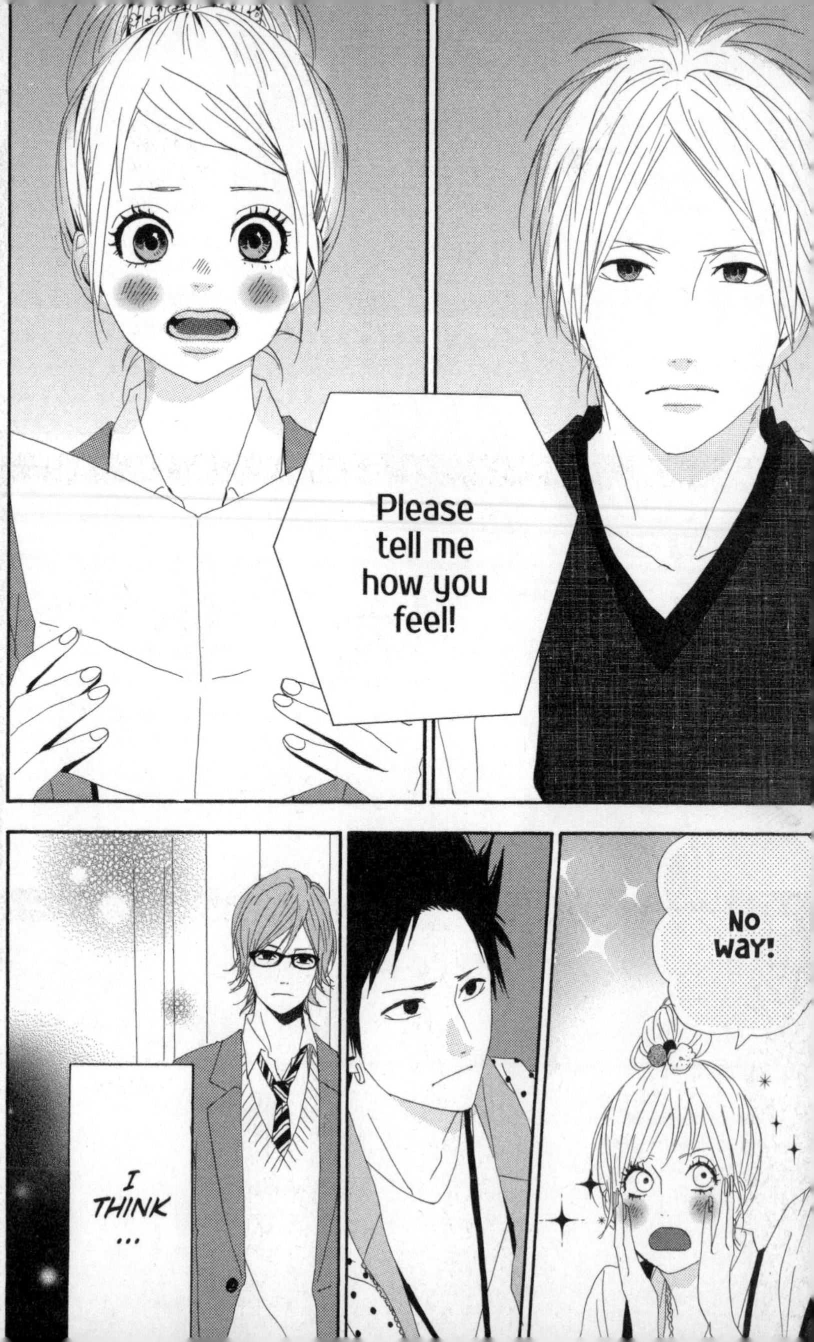
Please tell me how you feel!
No way!
I THINK ...

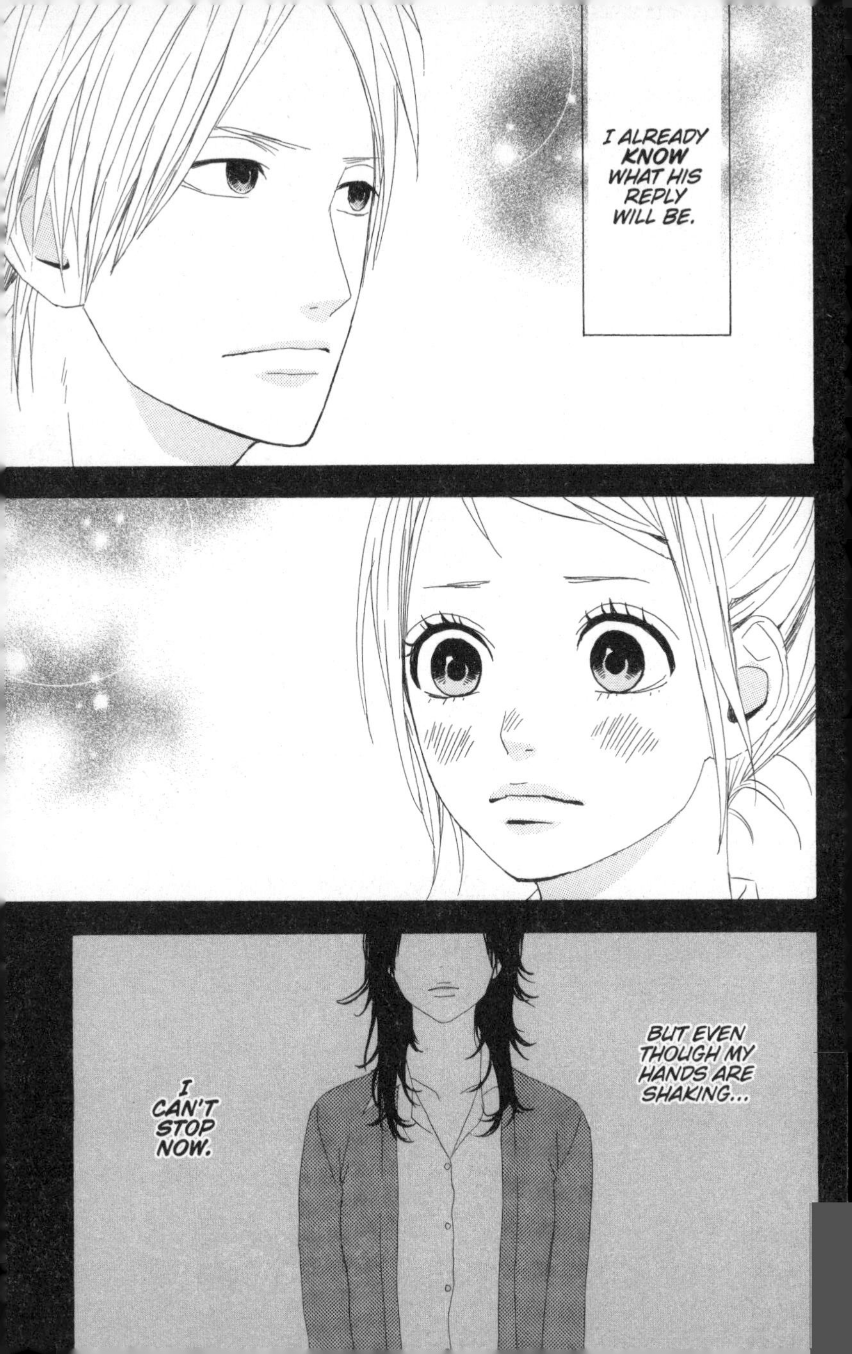
I ALREADY KNOW WHAT HIS REPLY WILL BE.
BUT EVEN THOUGH MY HANDS ARE SHAKING...
I CAN'T STOP NOW.

This is Volume 5, isn't it?!

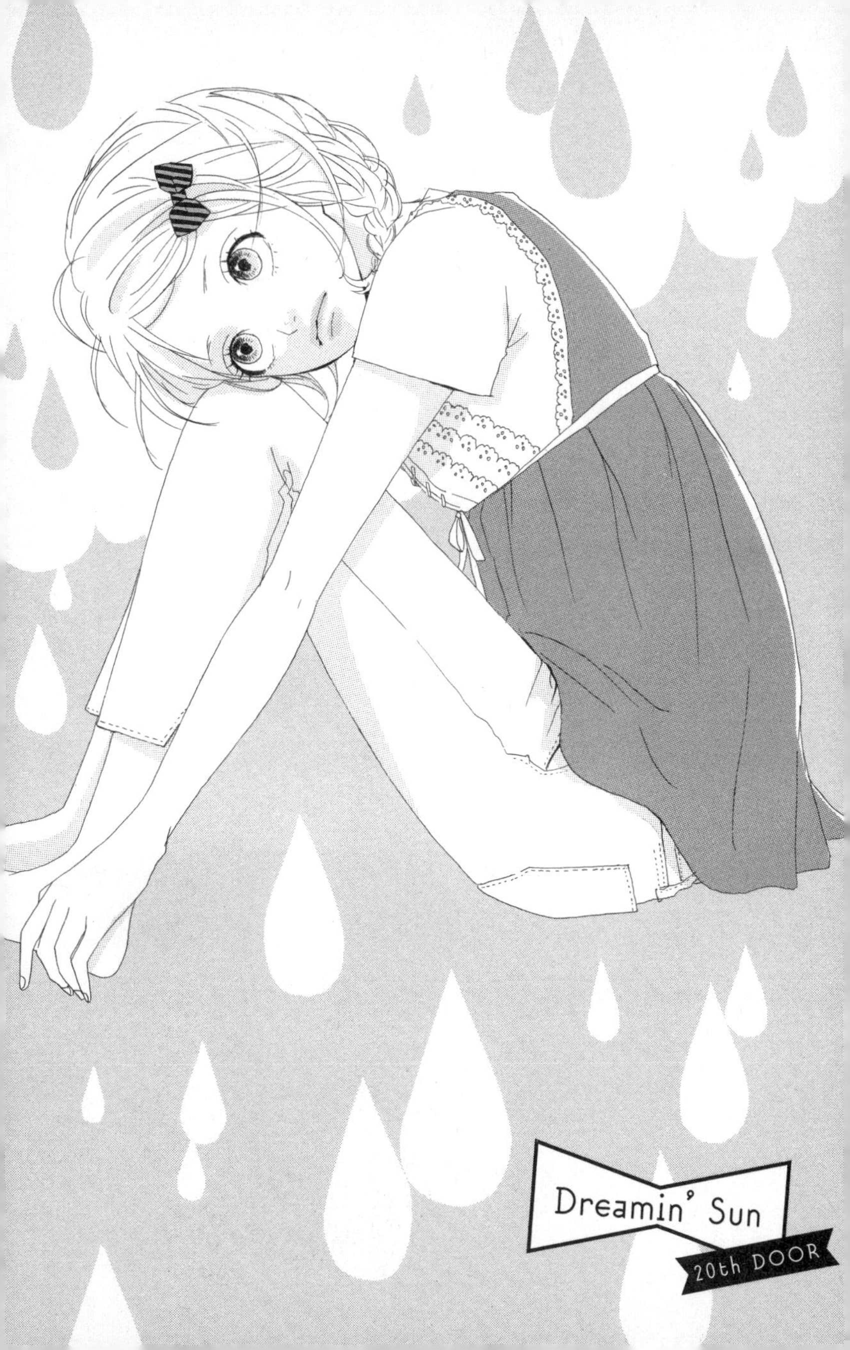
Dreamin' Sun
20th DOOR

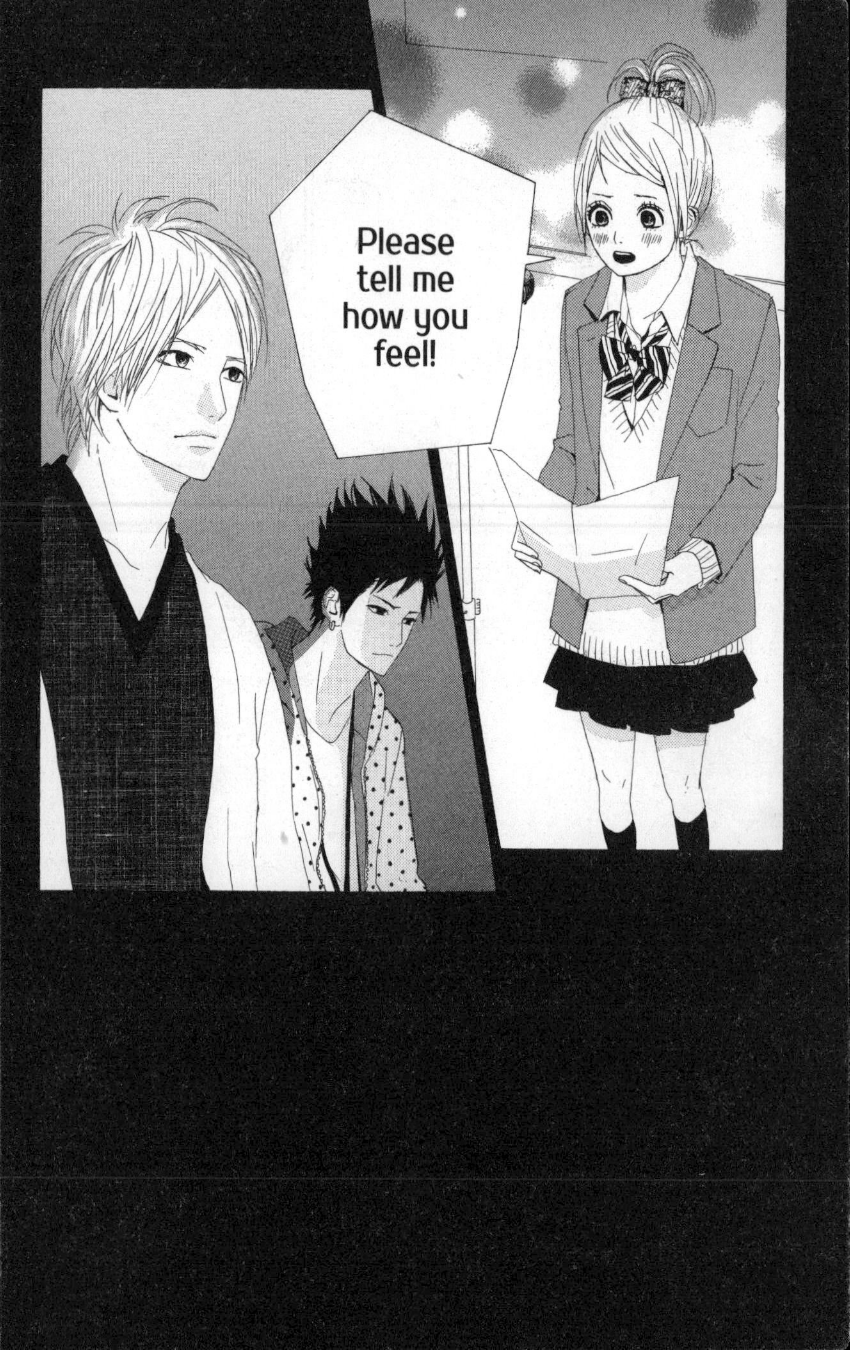
Please tell me how you feel!

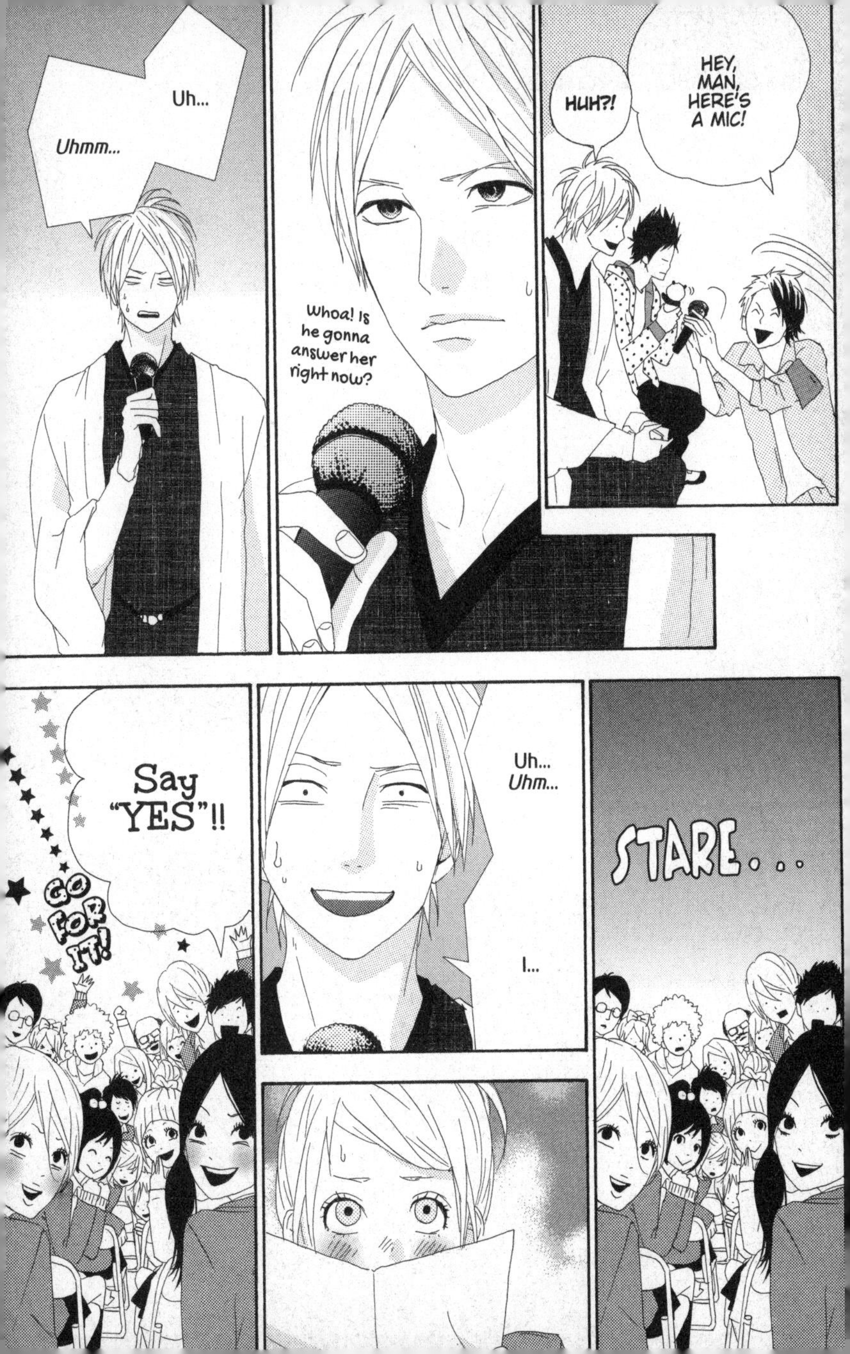
HEY, MAN, HERE'S A MIC!
HUH?!
Whoa! Is he gonna answer her right now?
Uh...
Uhmm...
STARE...
Uh... Uhm...
I...
Say "YES"!!
GO FOR IT!

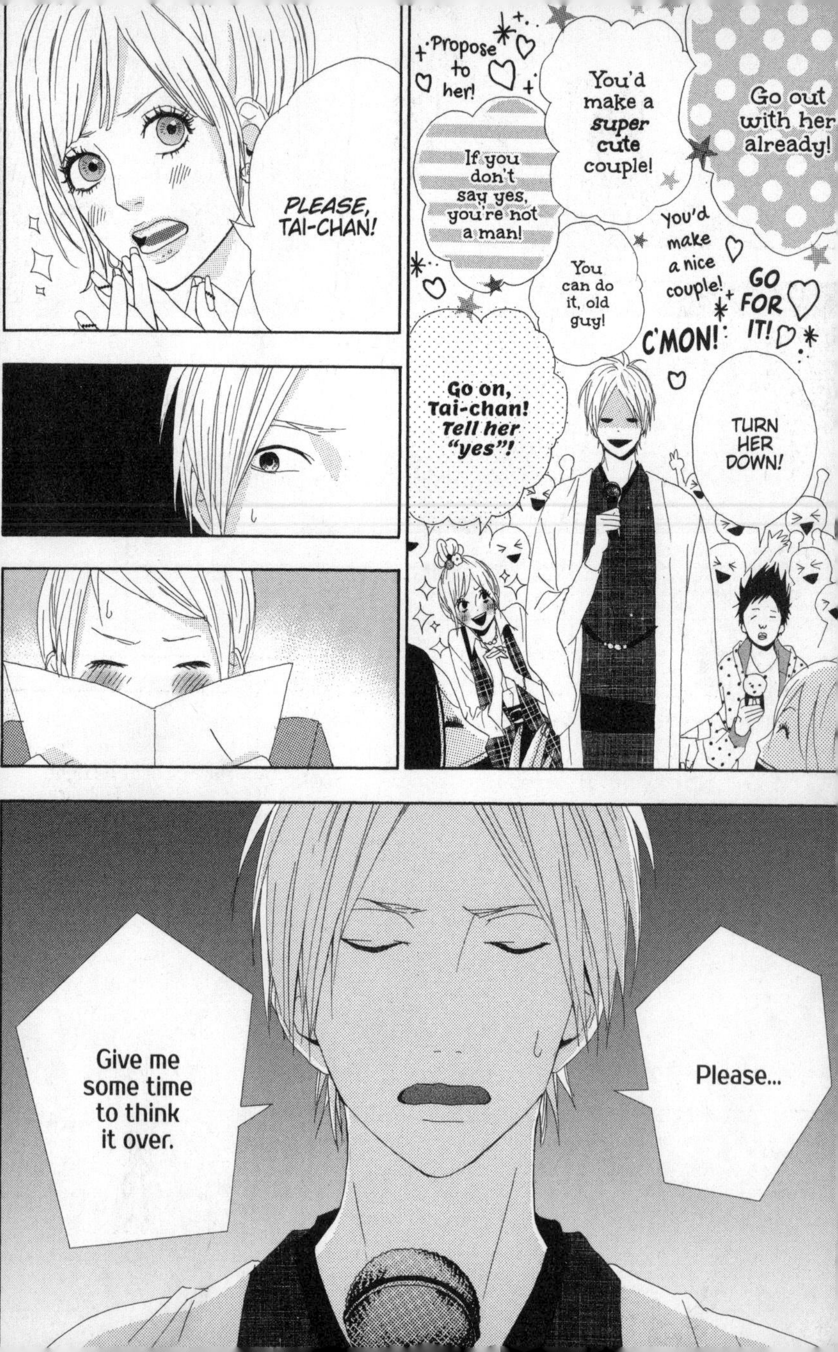
Go out with her already!
You'd make a *super* cute couple!
Propose to her!
If you don't say yes, you're not a man!
You'd make a nice couple!
GO FOR IT!
You can do it, old guy!
C'MON!
TURN HER DOWN!
Go on, Tai-chan! Tell her "yes"!
PLEASE, TAI-CHAN!
Please...
Give me some time to think it over.

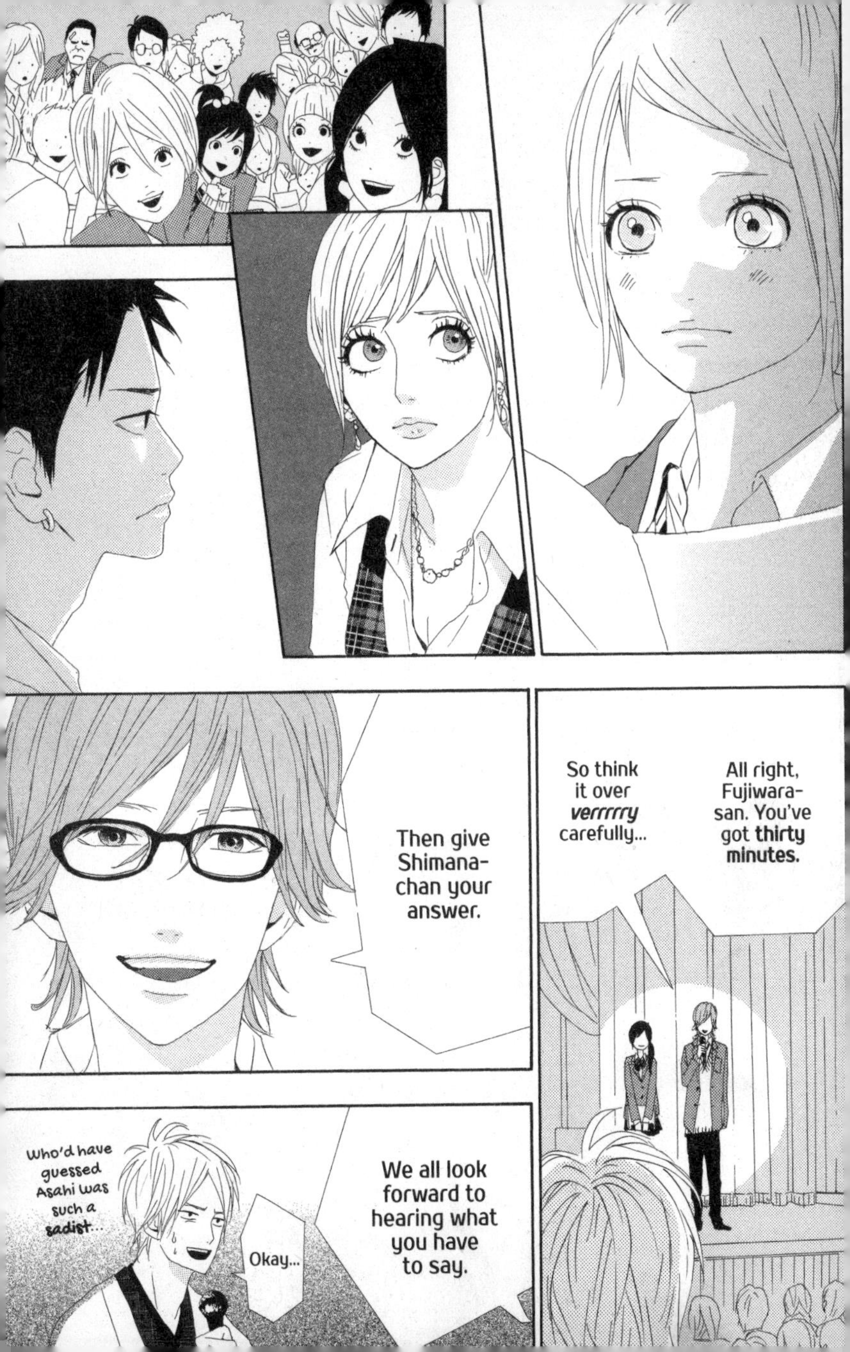
All right, Fujiwara-san. You've got **thirty minutes.**
So think it over ***verrrrrry*** carefully...
Then give Shimana-chan your answer.
We all look forward to hearing what you have to say.
Okay...
Who'd have guessed Asahi was such a **sadist**...

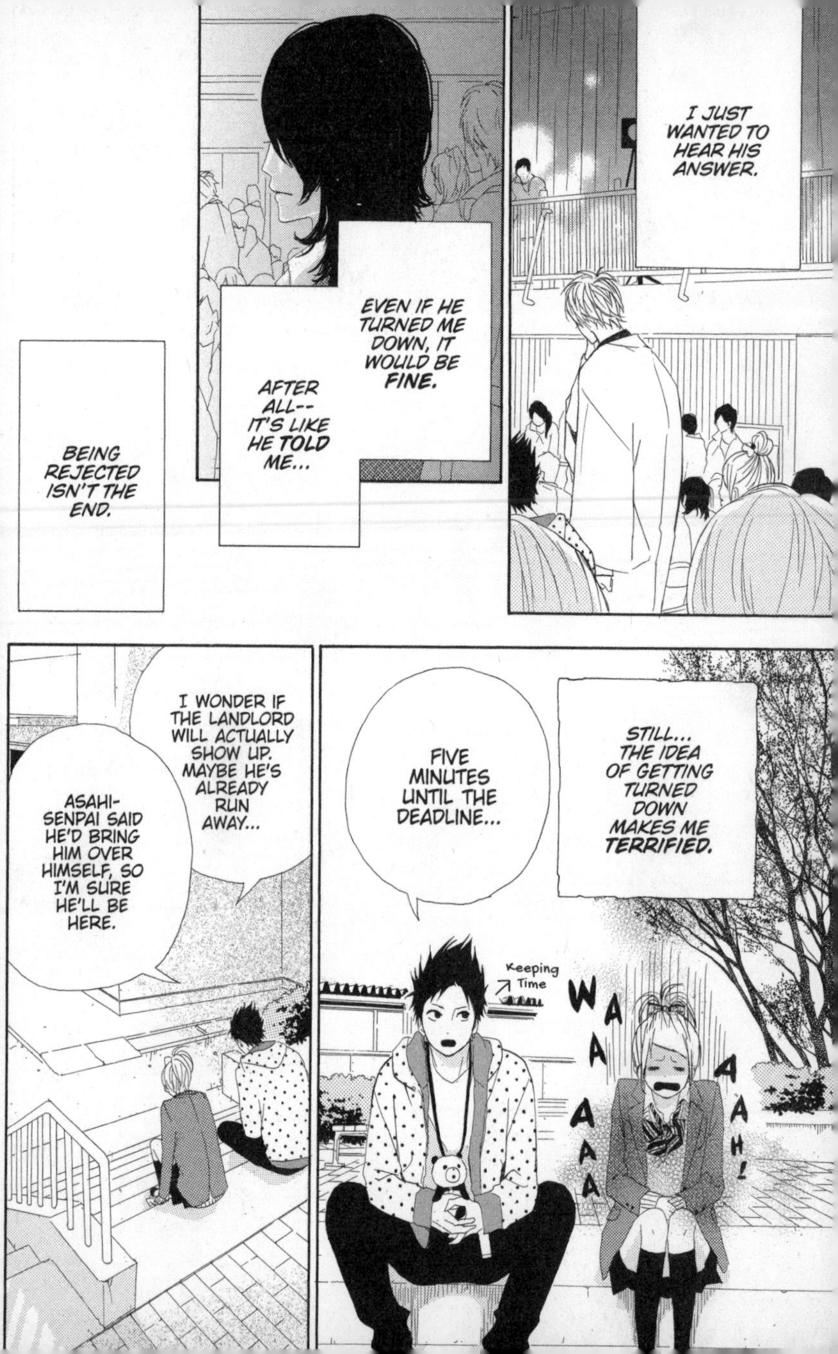
I JUST WANTED TO HEAR HIS ANSWER.
EVEN IF HE TURNED ME DOWN, IT WOULD BE FINE.
AFTER ALL-- IT'S LIKE HE TOLD ME...
BEING REJECTED ISN'T THE END.
STILL... THE IDEA OF GETTING TURNED DOWN MAKES ME TERRIFIED.
FIVE MINUTES UNTIL THE DEADLINE...
Keeping Time
WAAAAAAAAAH!
I WONDER IF THE LANDLORD WILL ACTUALLY SHOW UP. MAYBE HE'S ALREADY RUN AWAY...
ASAHI-SENPAI SAID HE'D BRING HIM OVER HIMSELF, SO I'M SURE HE'LL BE HERE.

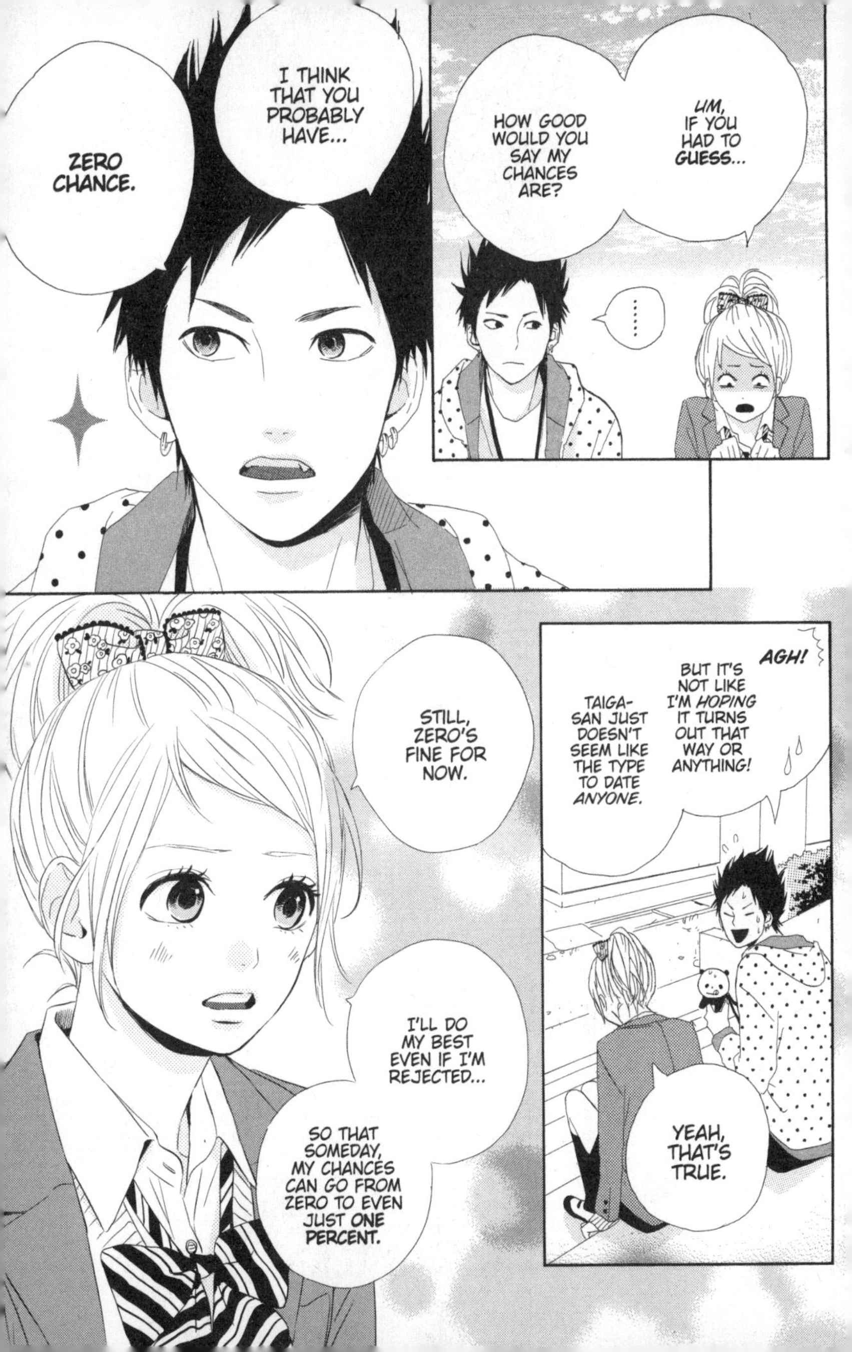
UM, IF YOU HAD TO GUESS...
HOW GOOD WOULD YOU SAY MY CHANCES ARE?
......
I THINK THAT YOU PROBABLY HAVE...
ZERO CHANCE.
AGH!
BUT IT'S NOT LIKE I'M *HOPING* IT TURNS OUT THAT WAY OR ANYTHING!
TAIGA-SAN JUST DOESN'T SEEM LIKE THE TYPE TO DATE *ANYONE*.
YEAH, THAT'S TRUE.
STILL, ZERO'S FINE FOR NOW.
I'LL DO MY BEST EVEN IF I'M REJECTED...
SO THAT SOMEDAY, MY CHANCES CAN GO FROM ZERO TO EVEN JUST ONE PERCENT.

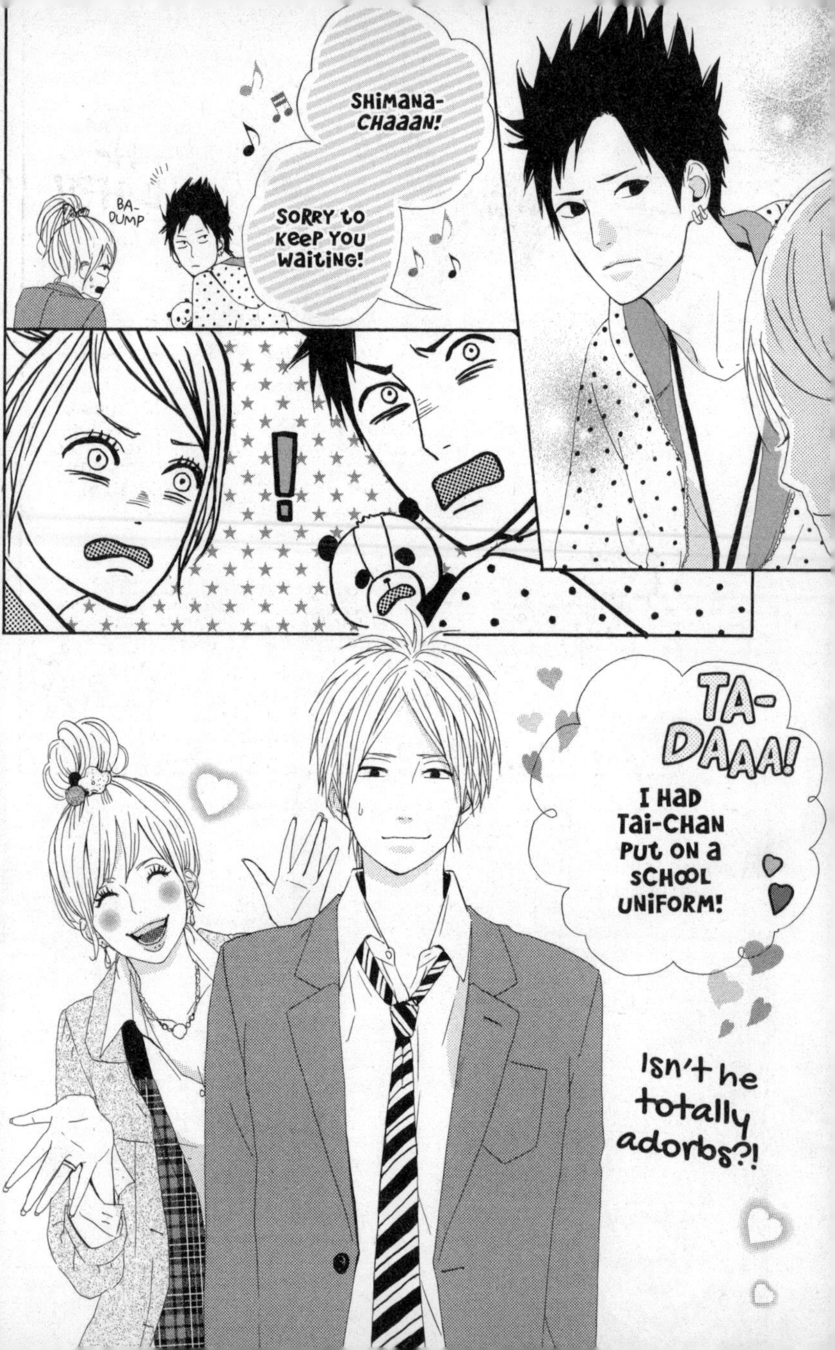
SHIMANA-CHAAAN! SORRY TO KEEP YOU WAITING!
BA-DUMP
!
TA-DAAA! I HAD TAI-CHAN PUT ON A SCHOOL UNIFORM!
Isn't he totally adorbs?!

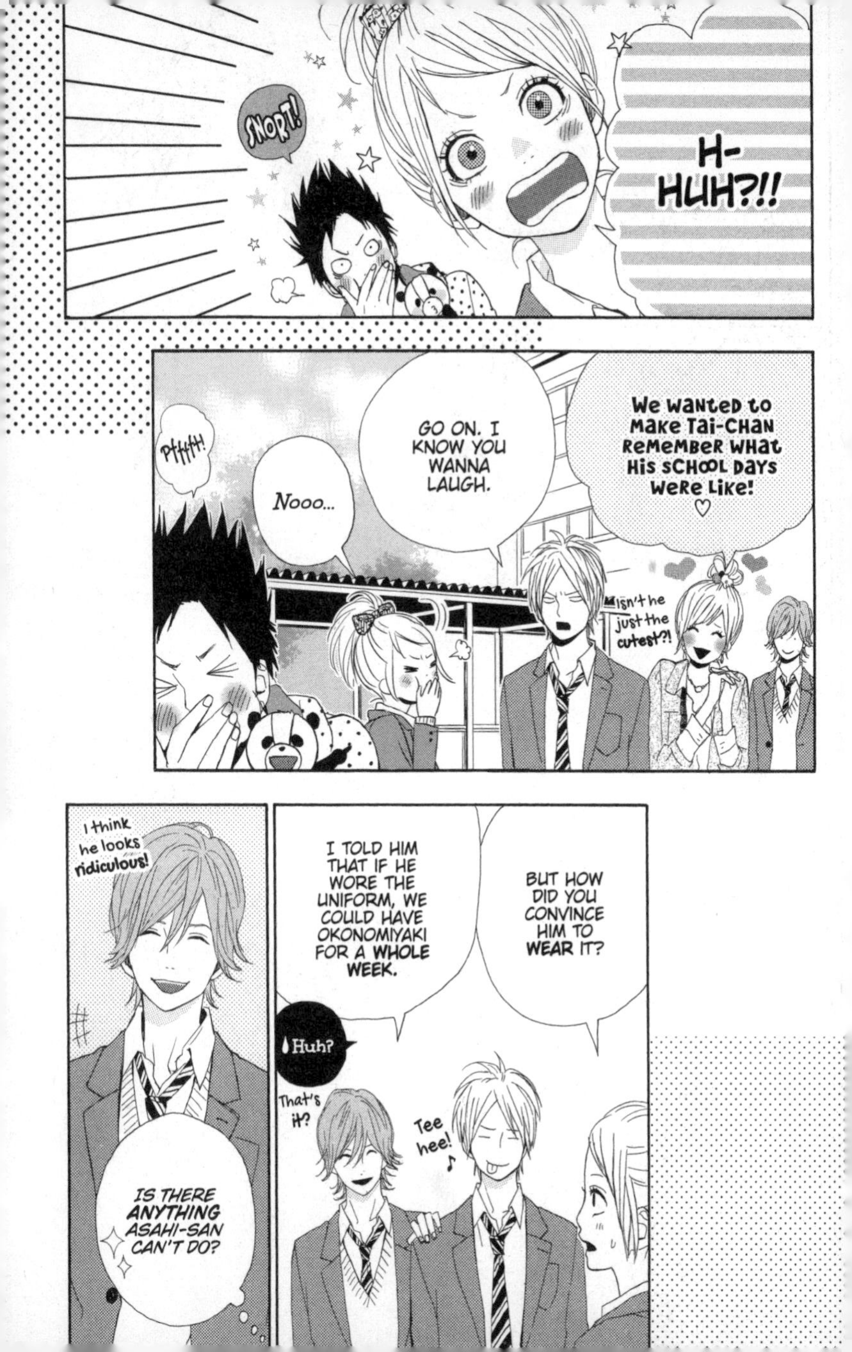
H-HUH?!!
SNORT!
We wanted to make Tai-chan remember what his school days were like! ♡
Isn't he just the cutest?!
GO ON. I KNOW YOU WANNA LAUGH.
Nooo...
Pffft!
BUT HOW DID YOU CONVINCE HIM TO WEAR IT?
I TOLD HIM THAT IF HE WORE THE UNIFORM, WE COULD HAVE OKONOMIYAKI FOR A WHOLE WEEK.
Tee hee! ♪
Huh?
That's it?
I think he looks ridiculous!
IS THERE ANYTHING ASAHI-SAN CAN'T DO?

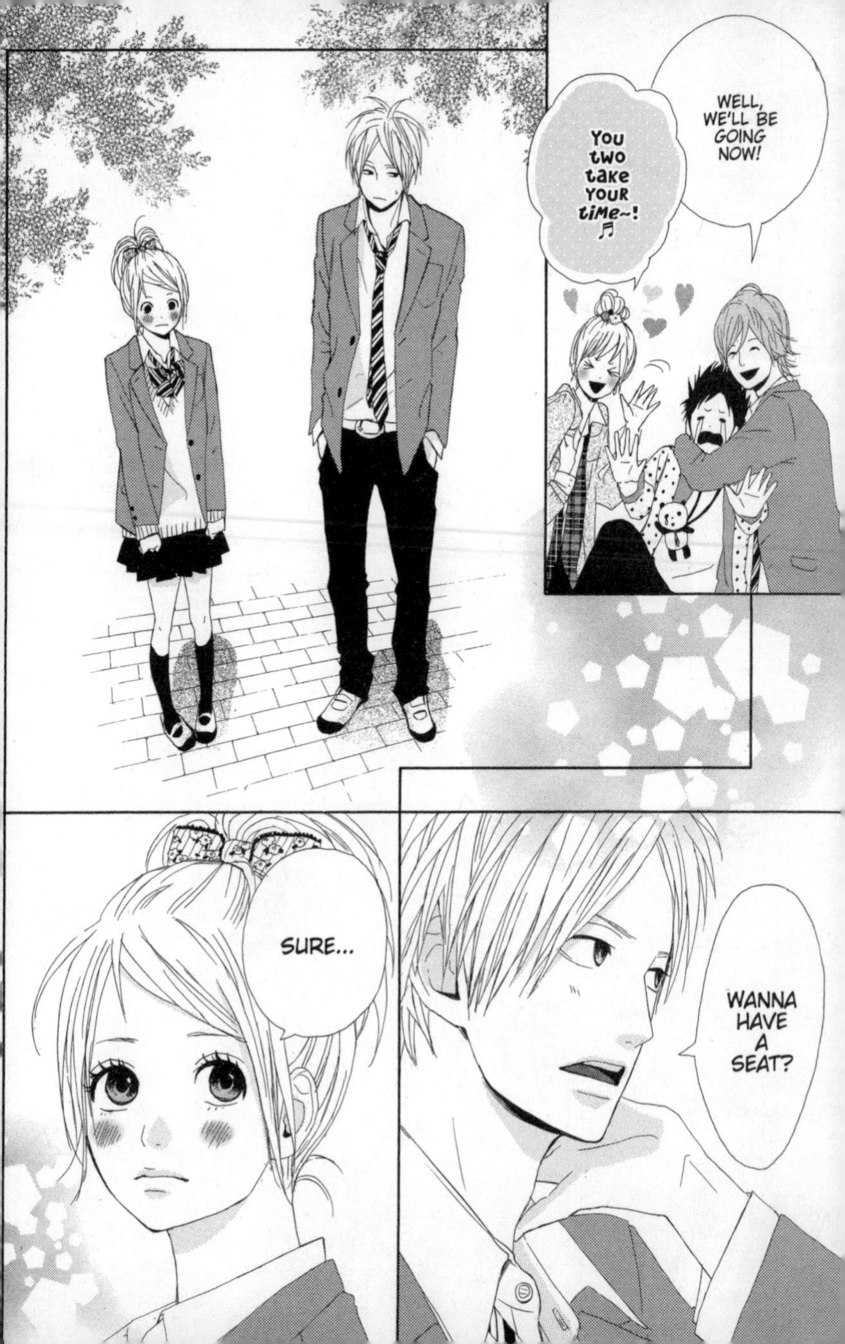
WELL, WE'LL BE GOING NOW!
You two take YOUR time~! ♫
WANNA HAVE A SEAT?
SURE...

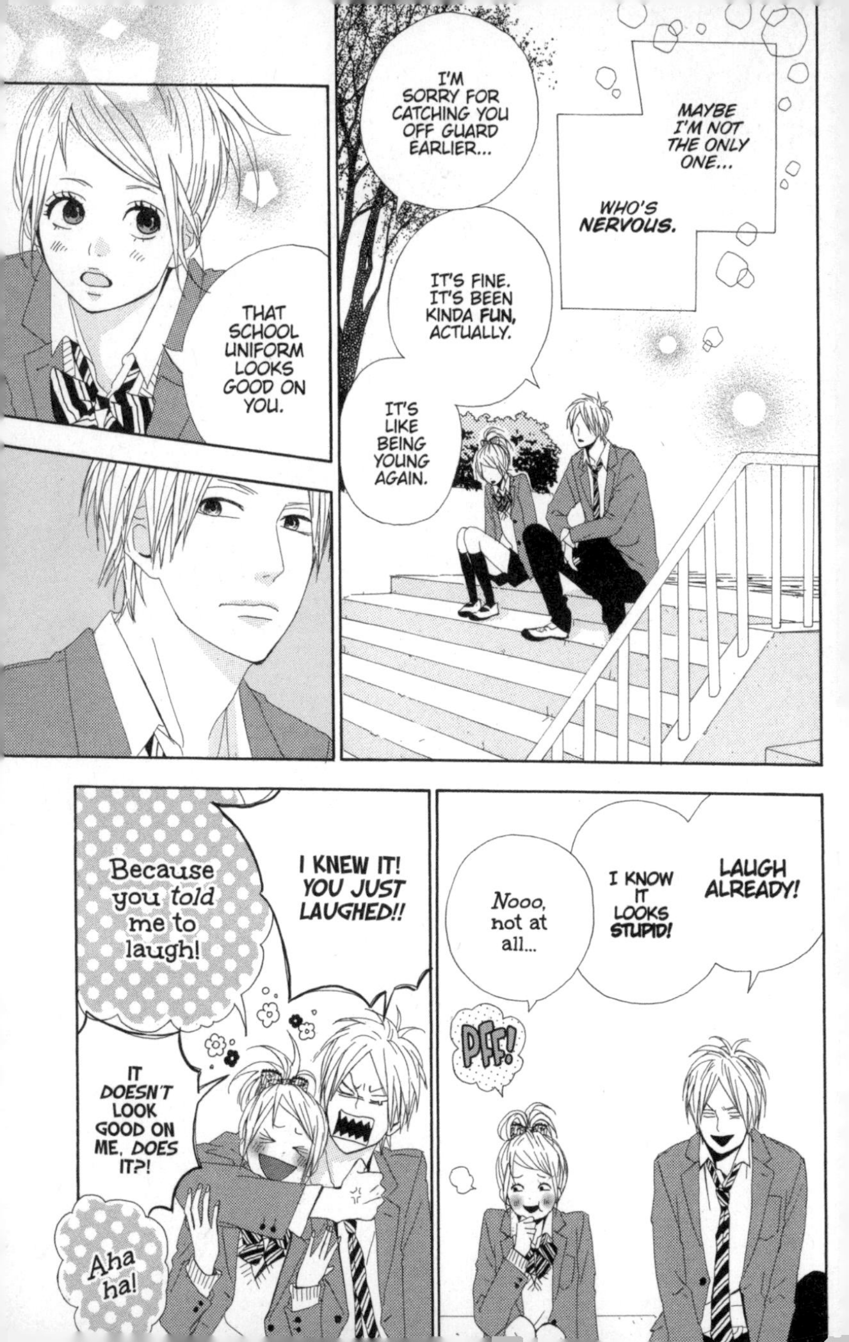
MAYBE I'M NOT THE ONLY ONE...
WHO'S NERVOUS.
I'M SORRY FOR CATCHING YOU OFF GUARD EARLIER...
IT'S FINE. IT'S BEEN KINDA FUN, ACTUALLY.
IT'S LIKE BEING YOUNG AGAIN.
THAT SCHOOL UNIFORM LOOKS GOOD ON YOU.
LAUGH ALREADY!
I KNOW IT LOOKS STUPID!
Nooo, not at all...
PFF!
I KNEW IT! YOU JUST LAUGHED!!
Because you told me to laugh!
IT DOESN'T LOOK GOOD ON ME, DOES IT?!
Aha ha!

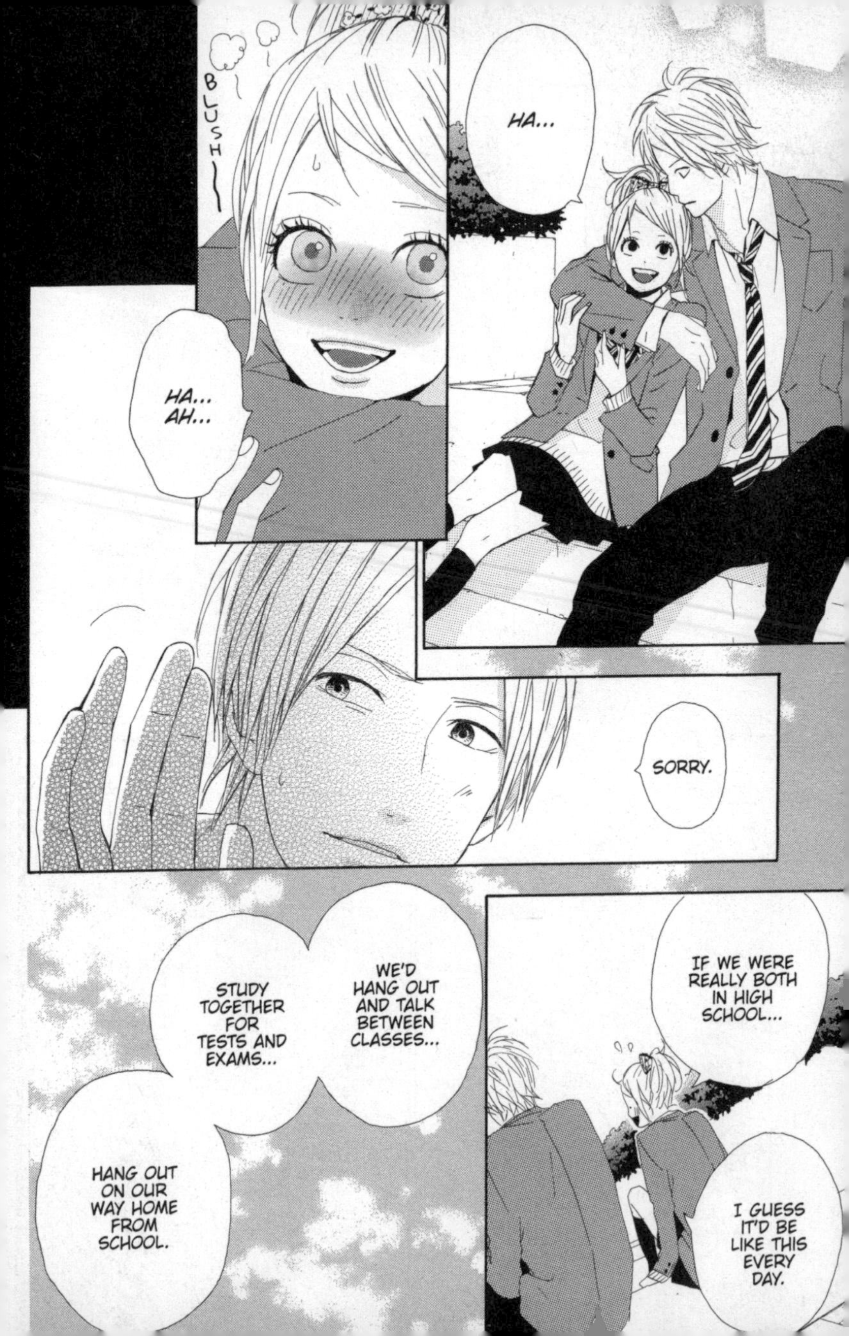
HA...
BLUSH
HA... AH...
SORRY.
IF WE WERE REALLY BOTH IN HIGH SCHOOL...
I GUESS IT'D BE LIKE THIS EVERY DAY.
WE'D HANG OUT AND TALK BETWEEN CLASSES...
STUDY TOGETHER FOR TESTS AND EXAMS...
HANG OUT ON OUR WAY HOME FROM SCHOOL.

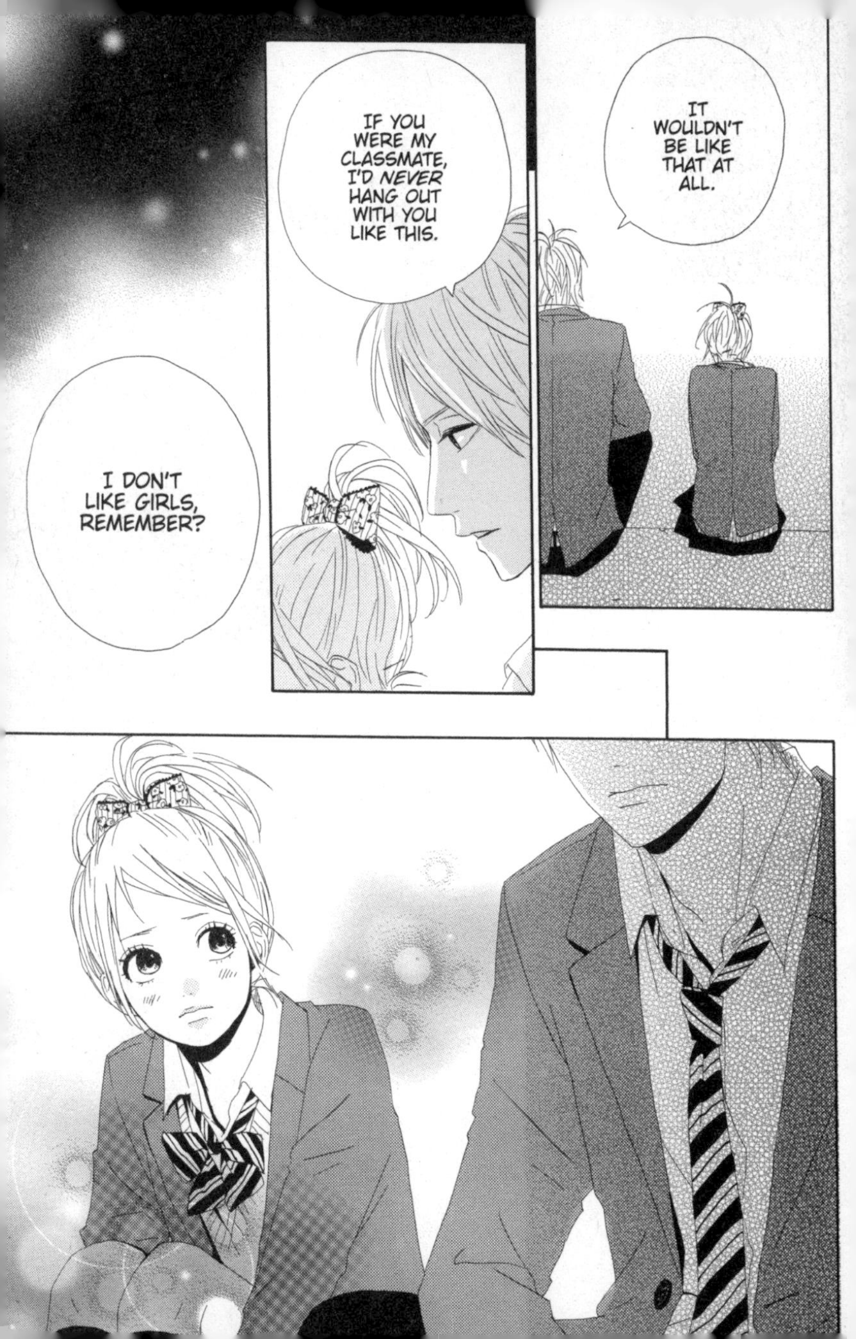
IT WOULDN'T BE LIKE THAT AT ALL.
IF YOU WERE MY CLASSMATE, I'D *NEVER* HANG OUT WITH YOU LIKE THIS.
I DON'T LIKE GIRLS, REMEMBER?

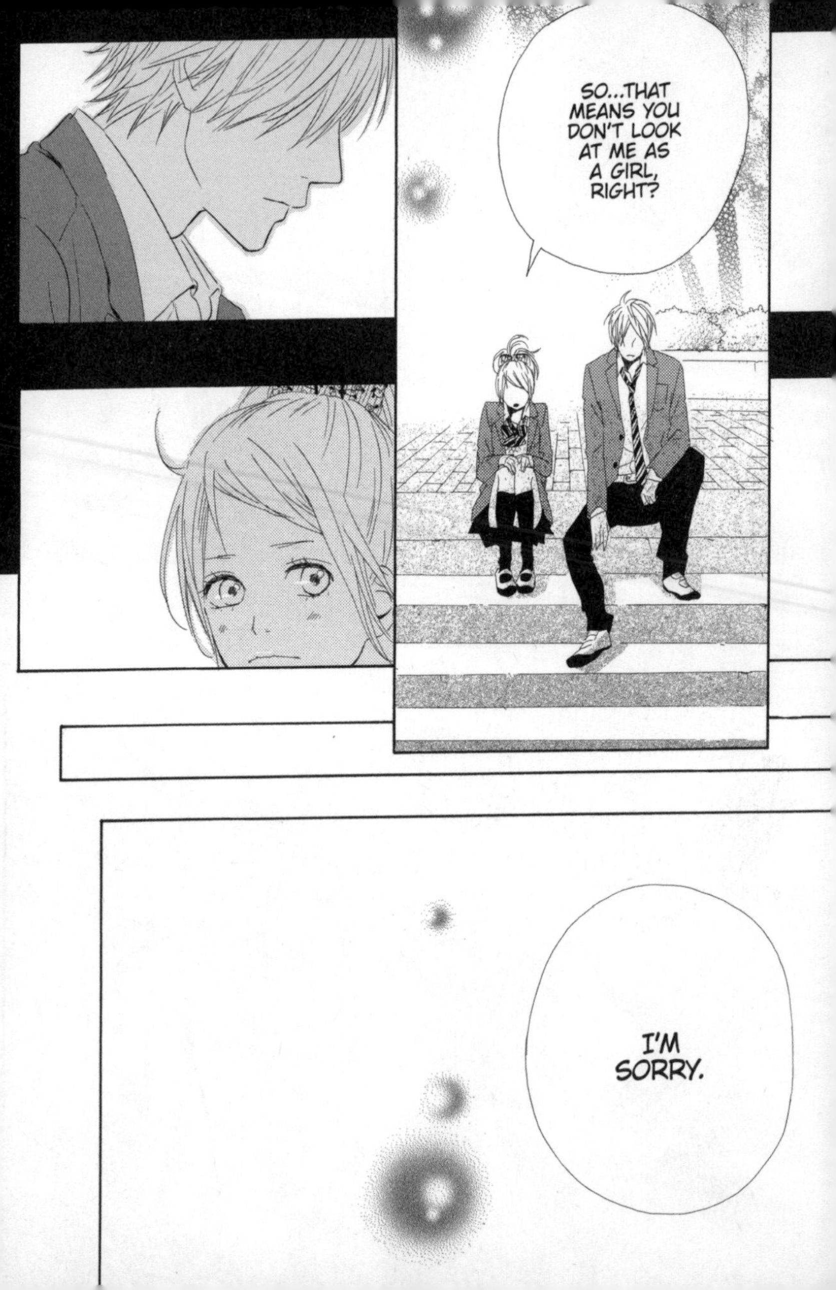
SO...THAT MEANS YOU DON'T LOOK AT ME AS A GIRL, RIGHT?
I'M SORRY.

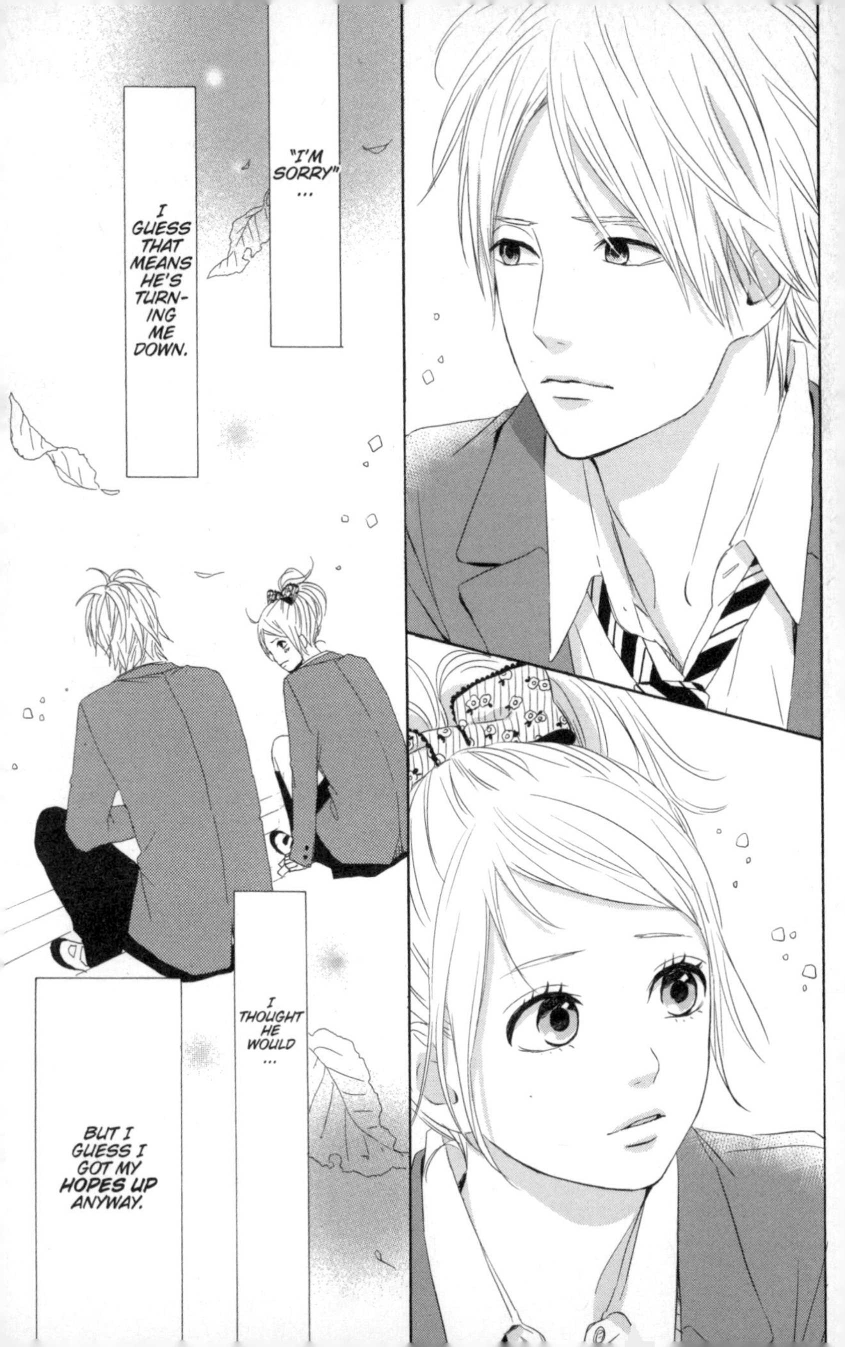
"I'M SORRY" ...
I GUESS THAT MEANS HE'S TURNING ME DOWN.
I THOUGHT HE WOULD ...
BUT I GUESS I GOT MY HOPES UP ANYWAY.

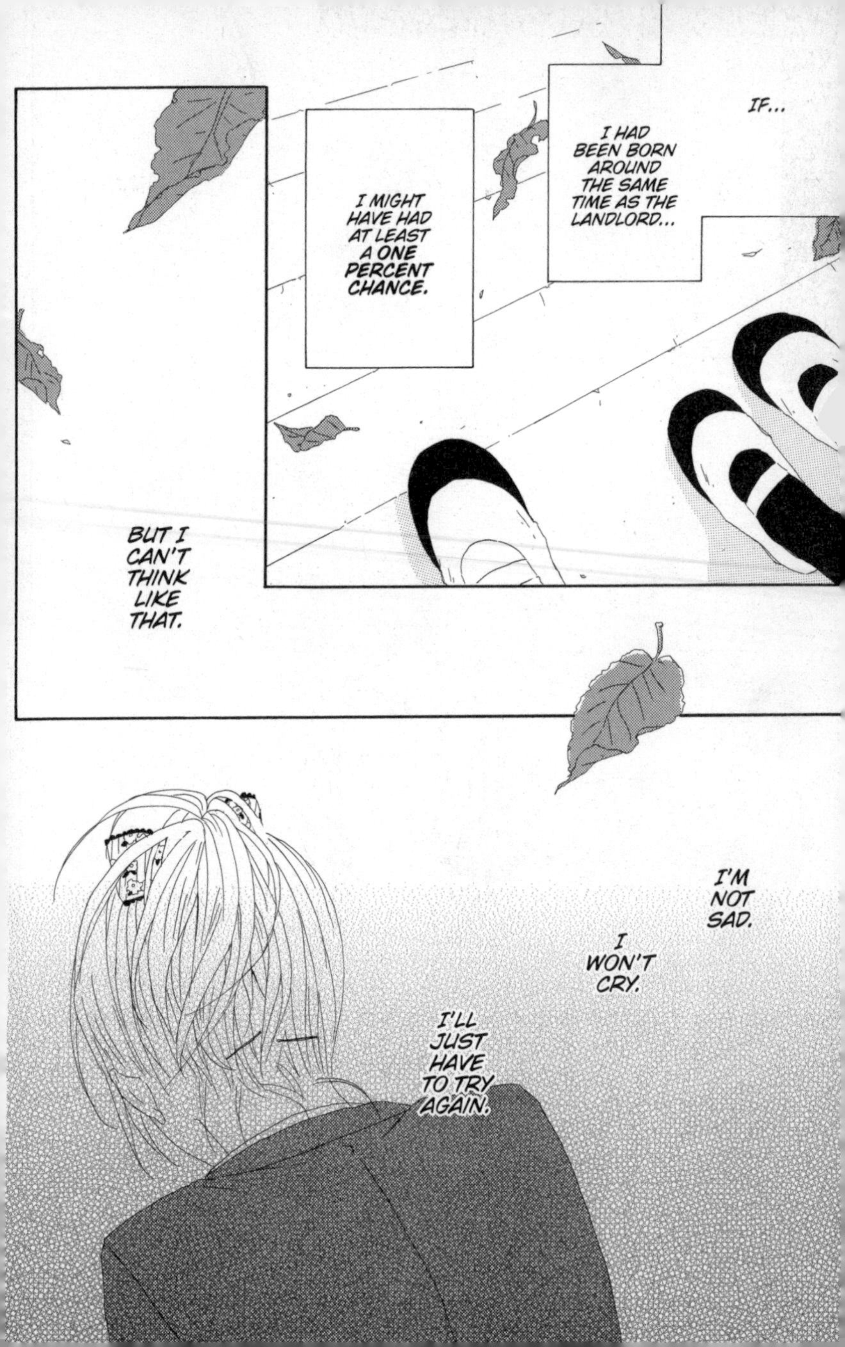
IF...
I HAD BEEN BORN AROUND THE SAME TIME AS THE LANDLORD...
I MIGHT HAVE HAD AT LEAST A ONE PERCENT CHANCE.
BUT I CAN'T THINK LIKE THAT.
I'M NOT SAD.
I WON'T CRY.
I'LL JUST HAVE TO TRY AGAIN.

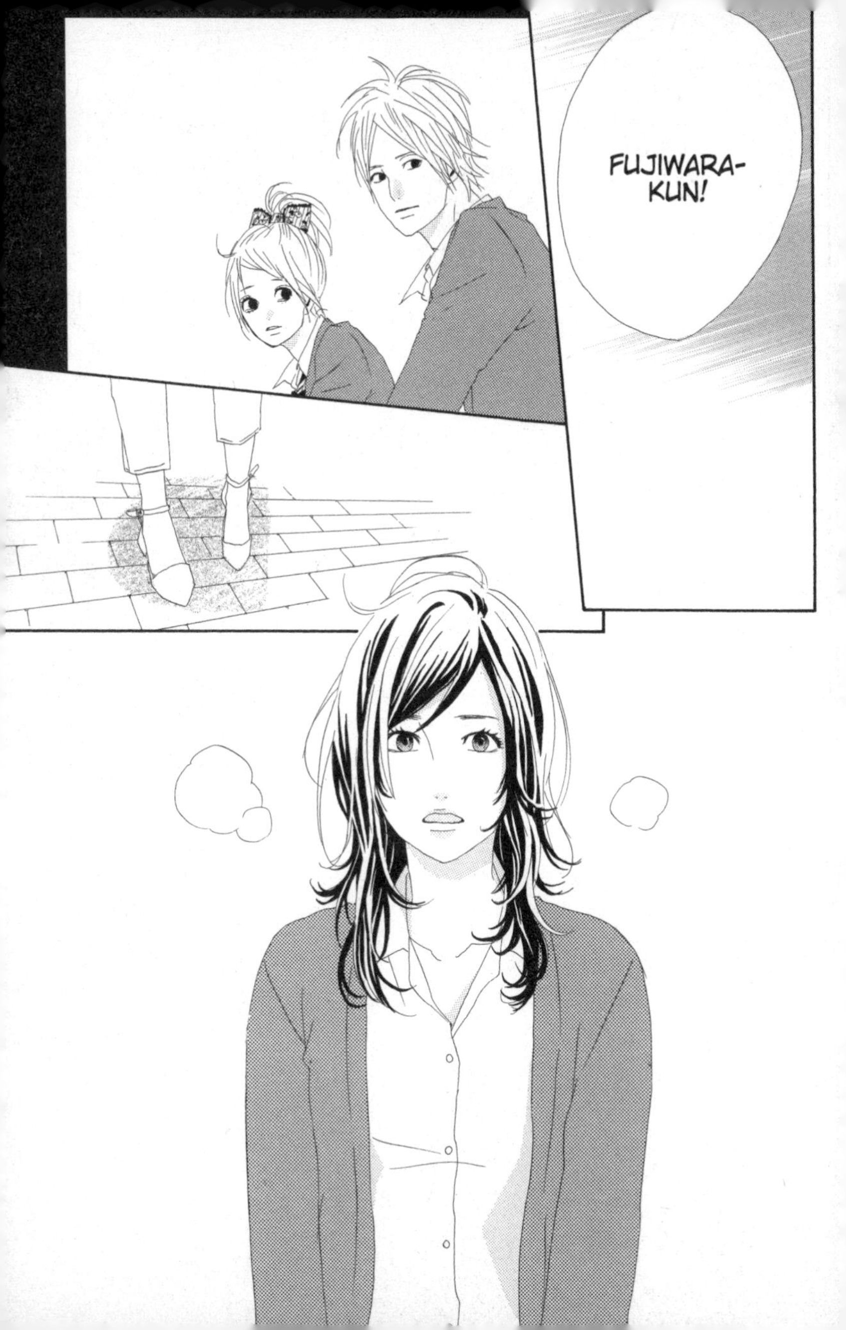
FUJIWARA-KUN!

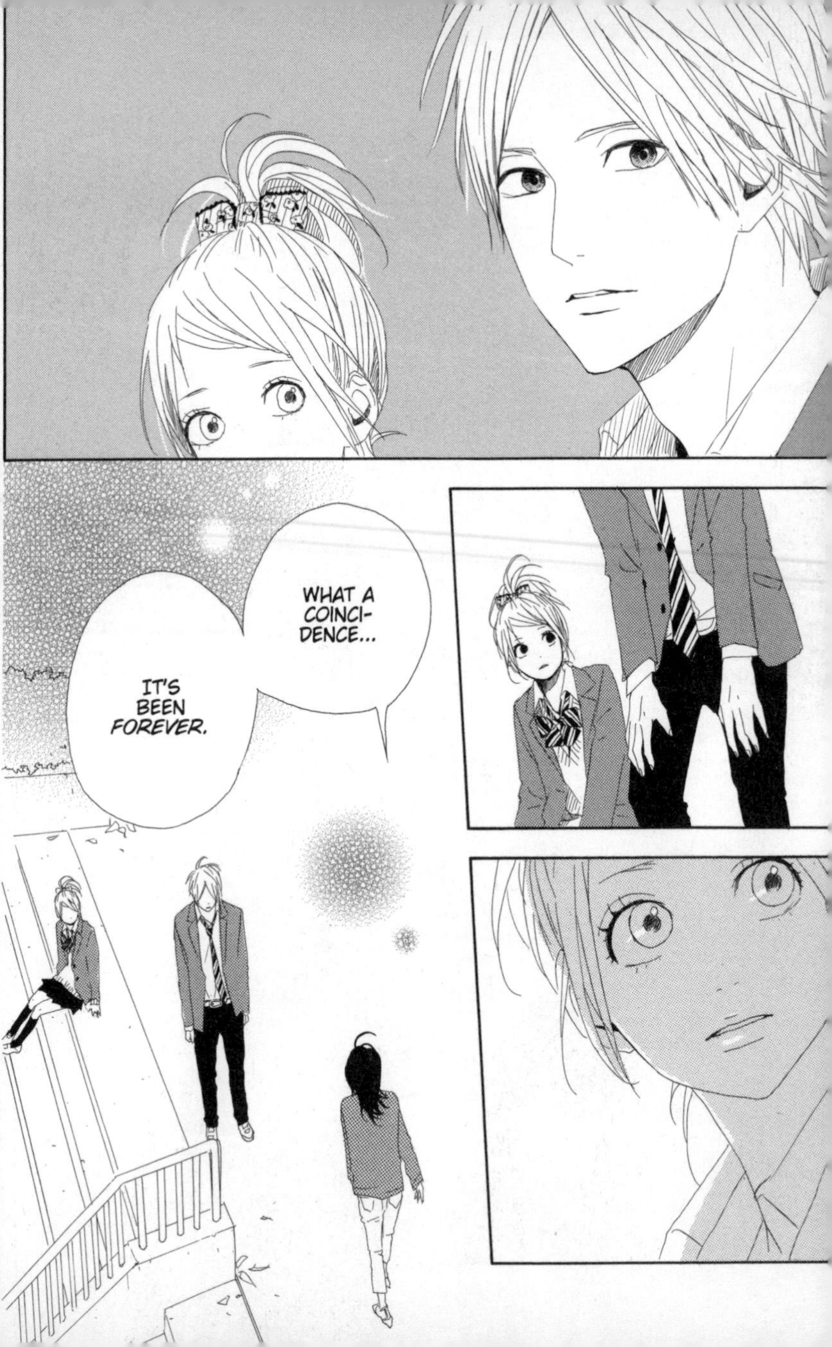
WHAT A COINCI-DENCE...
IT'S BEEN FOREVER.

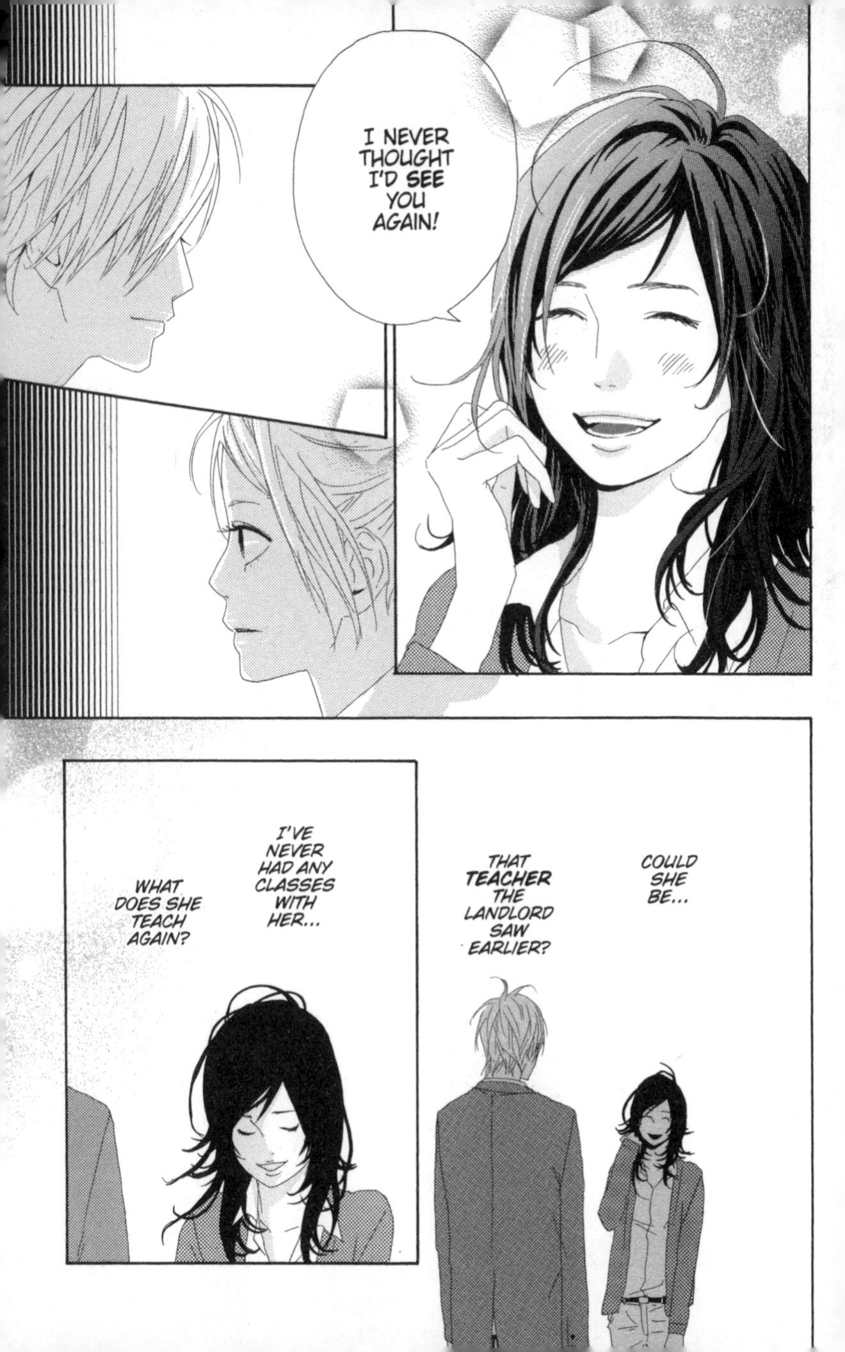
I NEVER THOUGHT I'D SEE YOU AGAIN!
COULD SHE BE...
THAT TEACHER THE LANDLORD SAW EARLIER?
I'VE NEVER HAD ANY CLASSES WITH HER...
WHAT DOES SHE TEACH AGAIN?

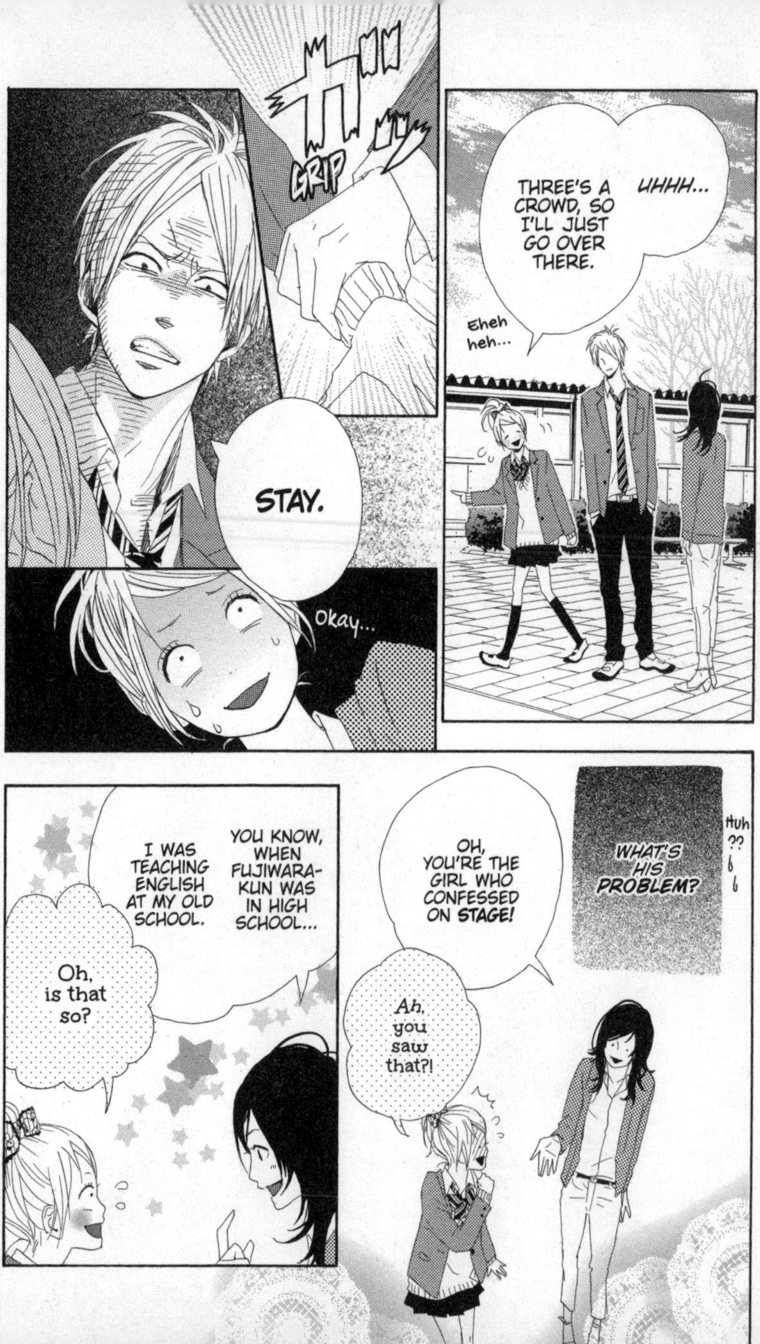
UHHH...
THREE'S A CROWD, SO I'LL JUST GO OVER THERE.
Eheh heh...
GRIP
STAY.
Okay...
Huh??
WHAT'S HIS PROBLEM?
OH, YOU'RE THE GIRL WHO CONFESSED ON STAGE!
Ah, you saw that?!
YOU KNOW, WHEN FUJIWARA-KUN WAS IN HIGH SCHOOL...
I WAS TEACHING ENGLISH AT MY OLD SCHOOL.
Oh, is that so?

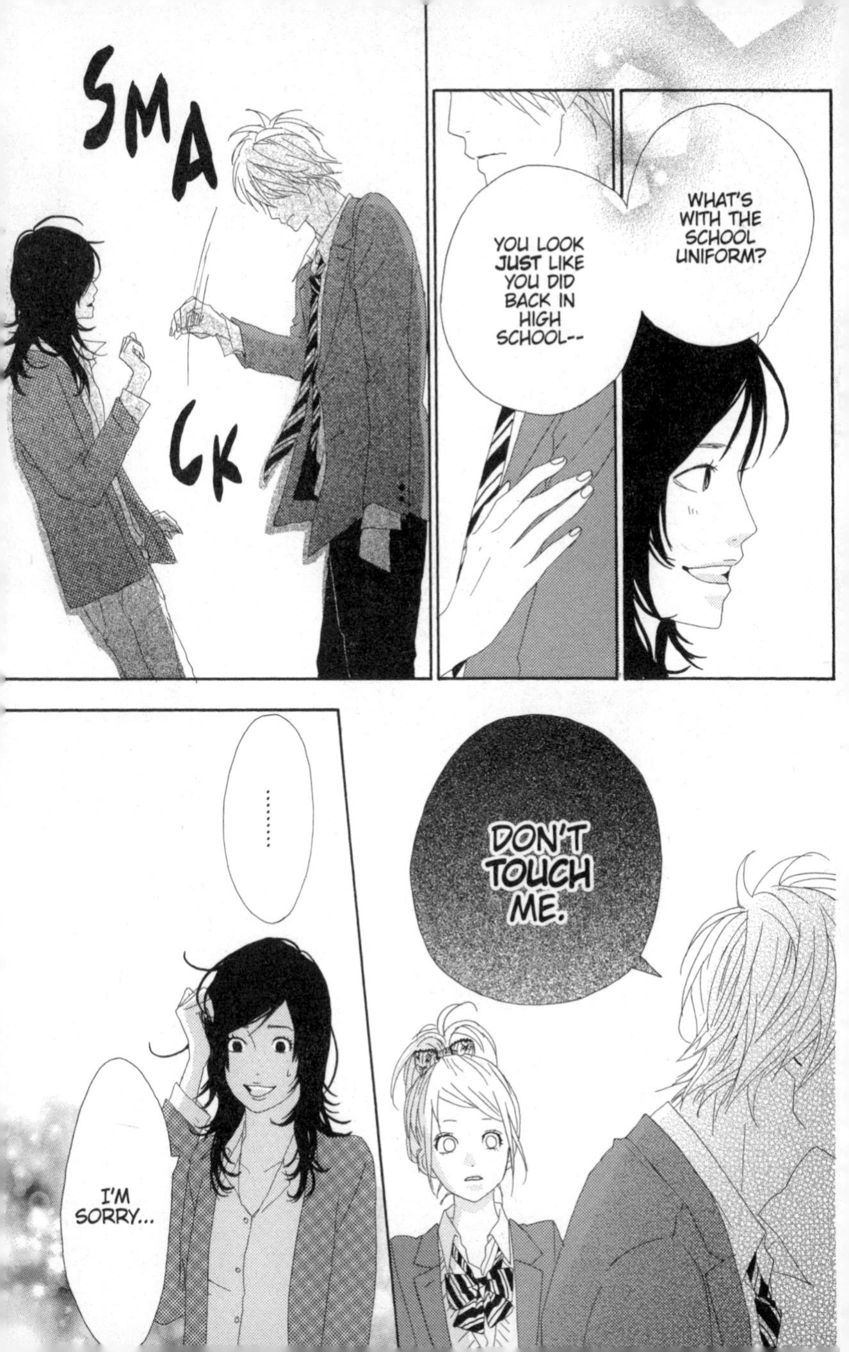
WHAT'S WITH THE SCHOOL UNIFORM?
YOU LOOK JUST LIKE YOU DID BACK IN HIGH SCHOOL--
SMACK
DON'T TOUCH ME.
....
I'M SORRY...

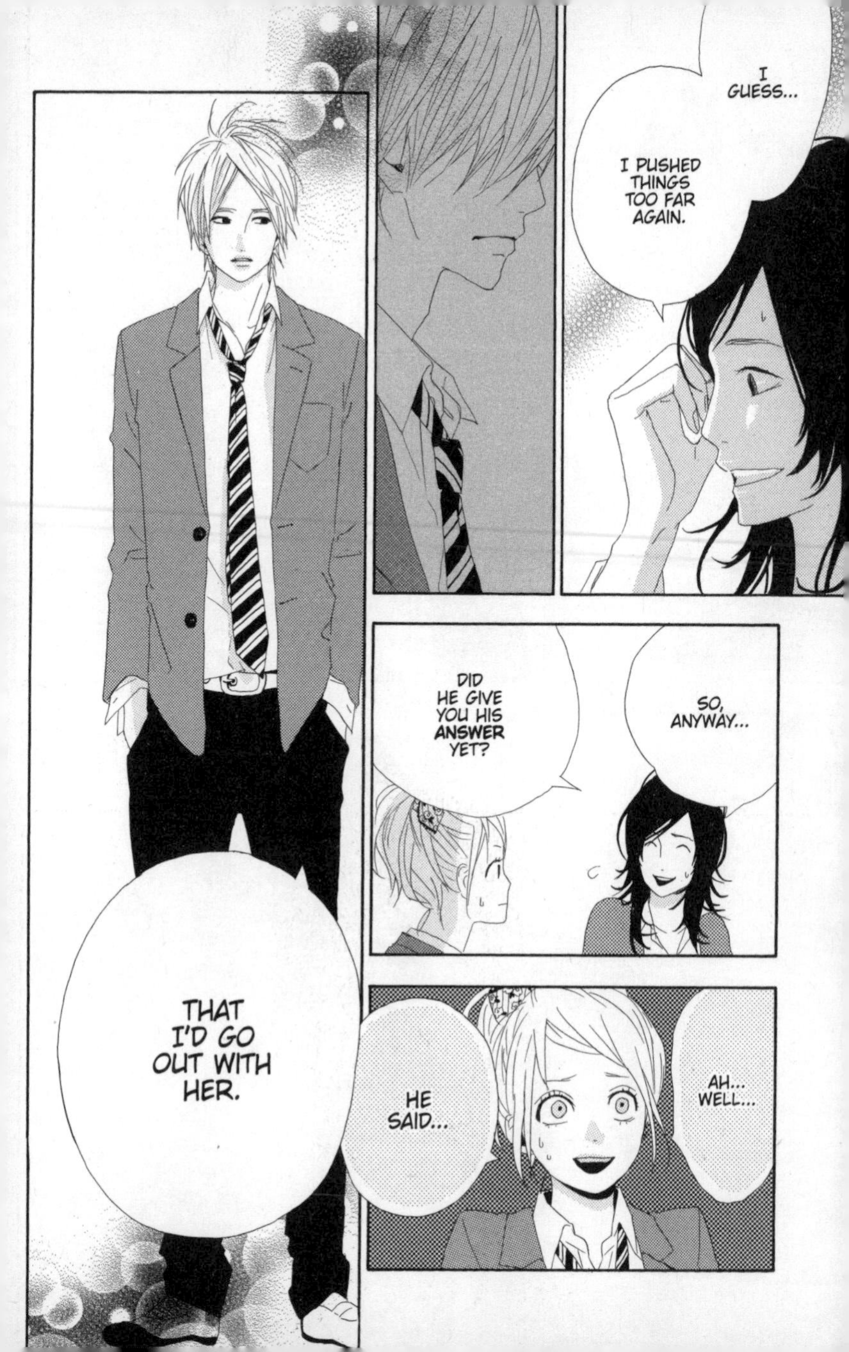

I GUESS...
I PUSHED THINGS TOO FAR AGAIN.
SO, ANYWAY...
DID HE GIVE YOU HIS **ANSWER** YET?
AH... WELL...
HE SAID...
THAT I'D GO OUT WITH HER.

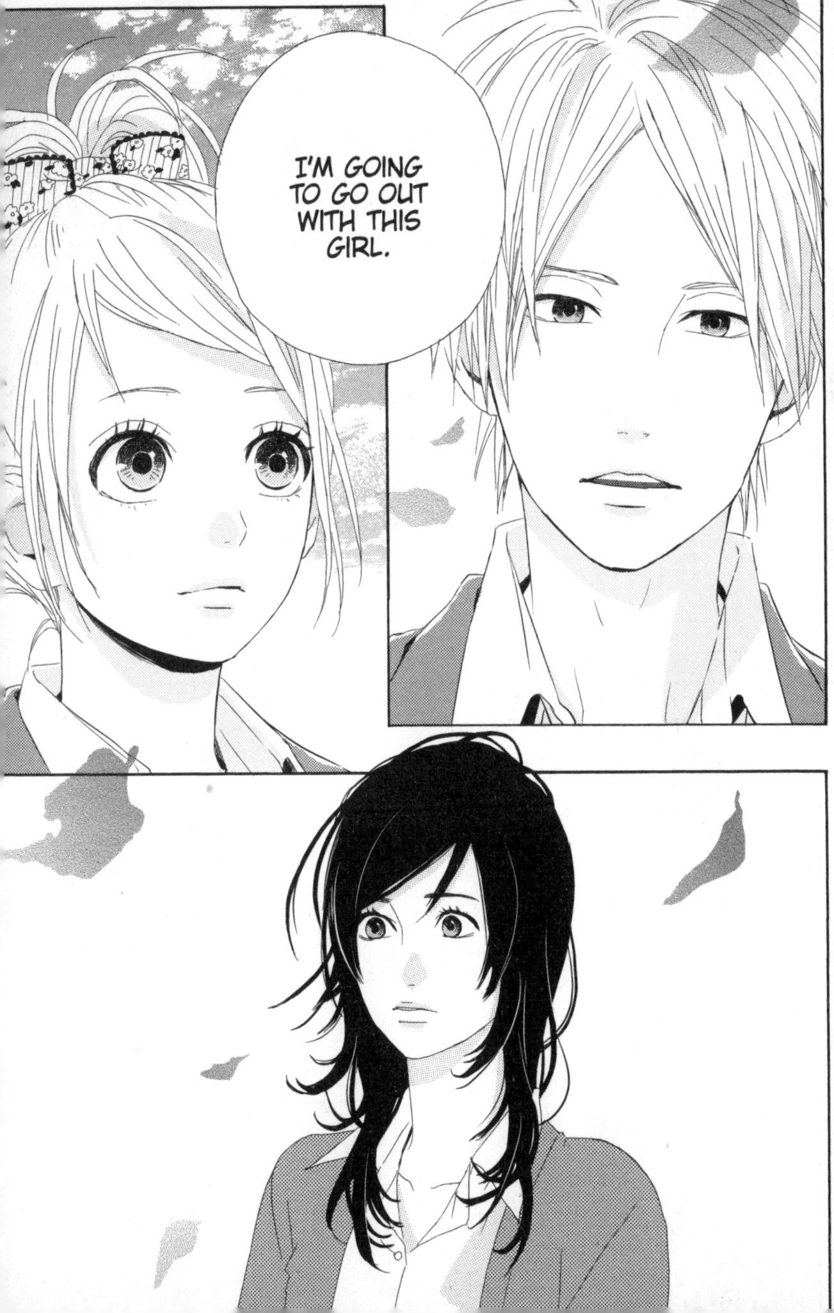
I'M GOING TO GO OUT WITH THIS GIRL.

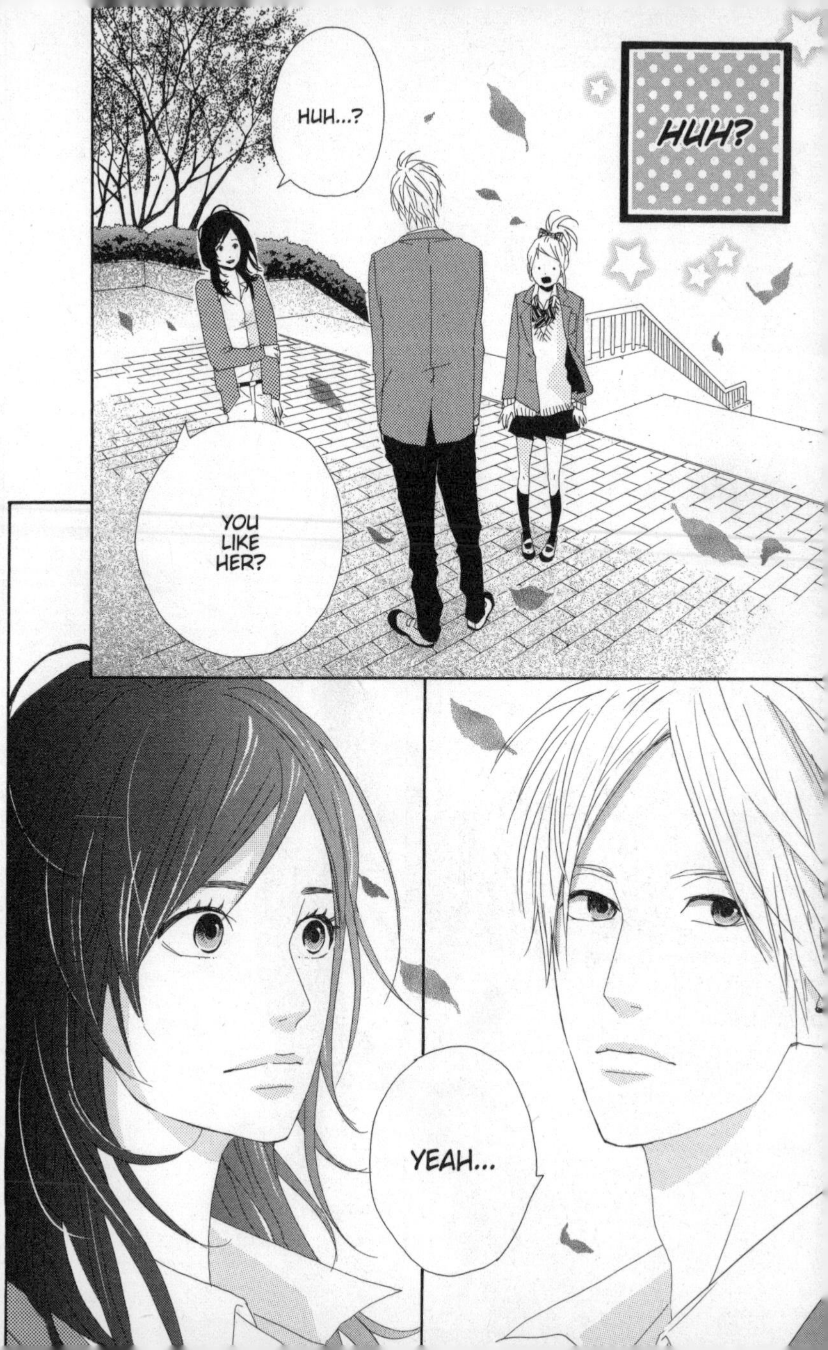
HUH?
HUH...?
YOU LIKE HER?
YEAH...

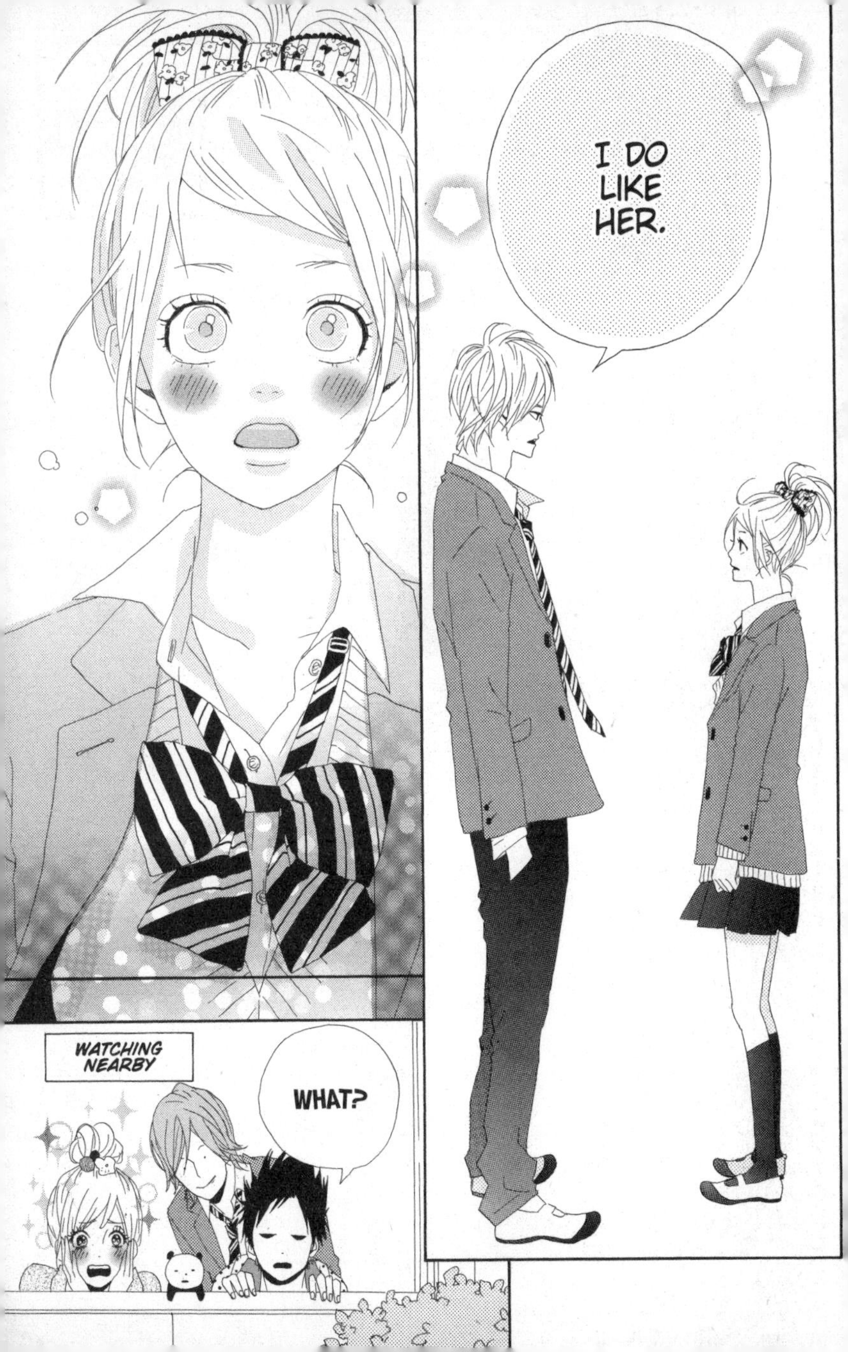
I DO LIKE HER.
WATCHING NEARBY
WHAT?

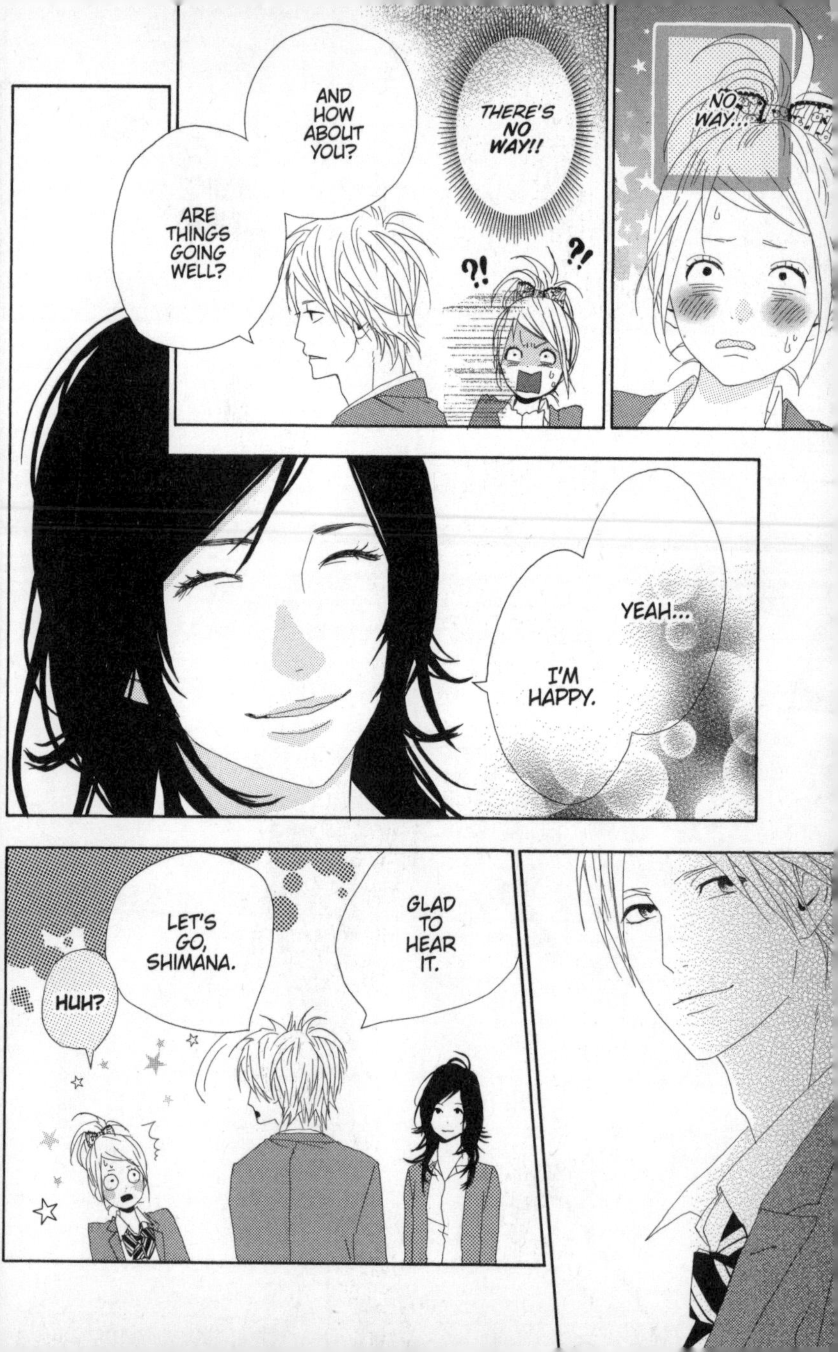
NO WAY...
THERE'S NO WAY!!
?!
?!
AND HOW ABOUT YOU?
ARE THINGS GOING WELL?
YEAH...
I'M HAPPY.
GLAD TO HEAR IT.
LET'S GO, SHIMANA.
HUH?

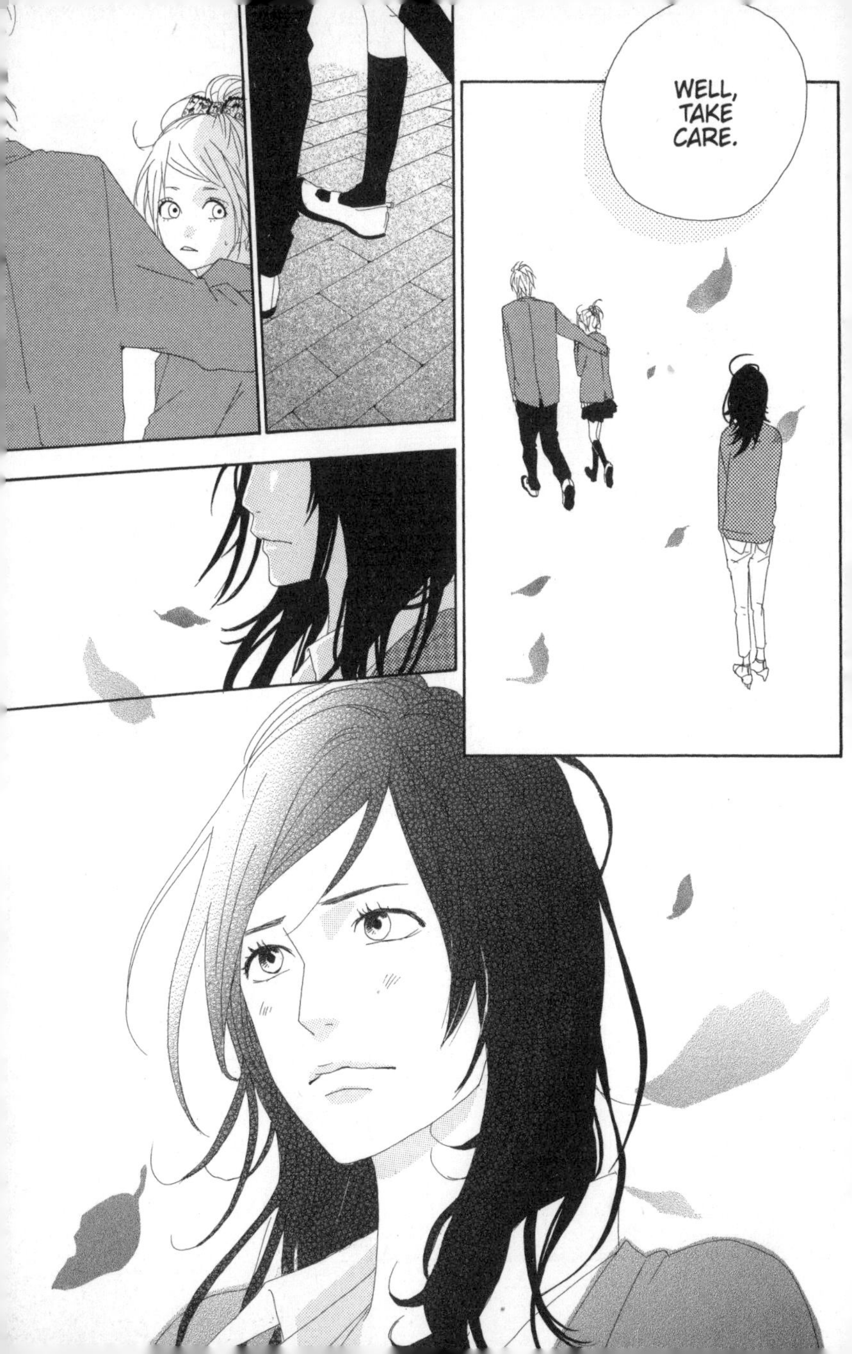
WELL, TAKE CARE.

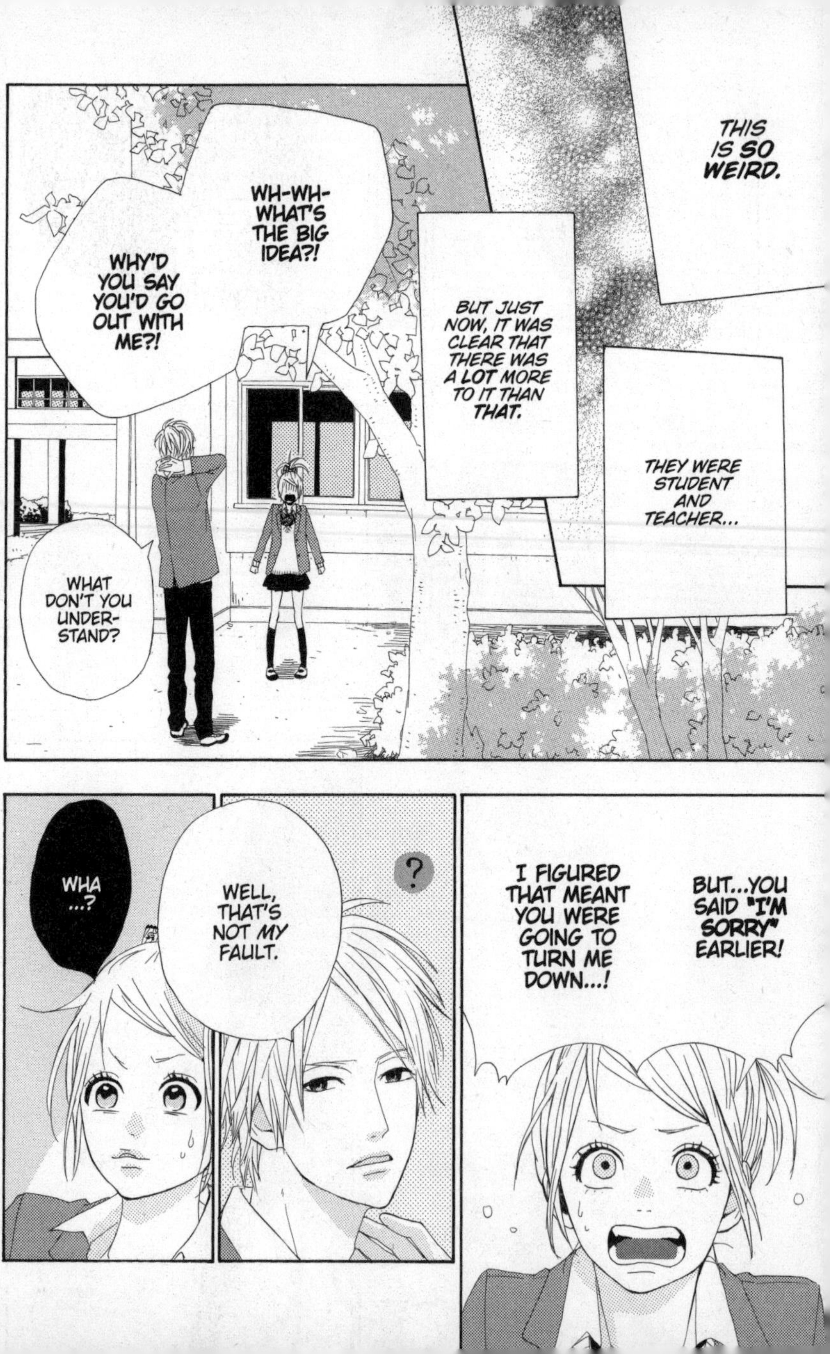
THIS IS SO WEIRD.
THEY WERE STUDENT AND TEACHER...
BUT JUST NOW, IT WAS CLEAR THAT THERE WAS A LOT MORE TO IT THAN THAT.
WH-WH-WHAT'S THE BIG IDEA?!
WHY'D YOU SAY YOU'D GO OUT WITH ME?!
WHAT DON'T YOU UNDERSTAND?
BUT...YOU SAID "I'M SORRY" EARLIER!
I FIGURED THAT MEANT YOU WERE GOING TO TURN ME DOWN...!
WELL, THAT'S NOT MY FAULT.
WHA...?

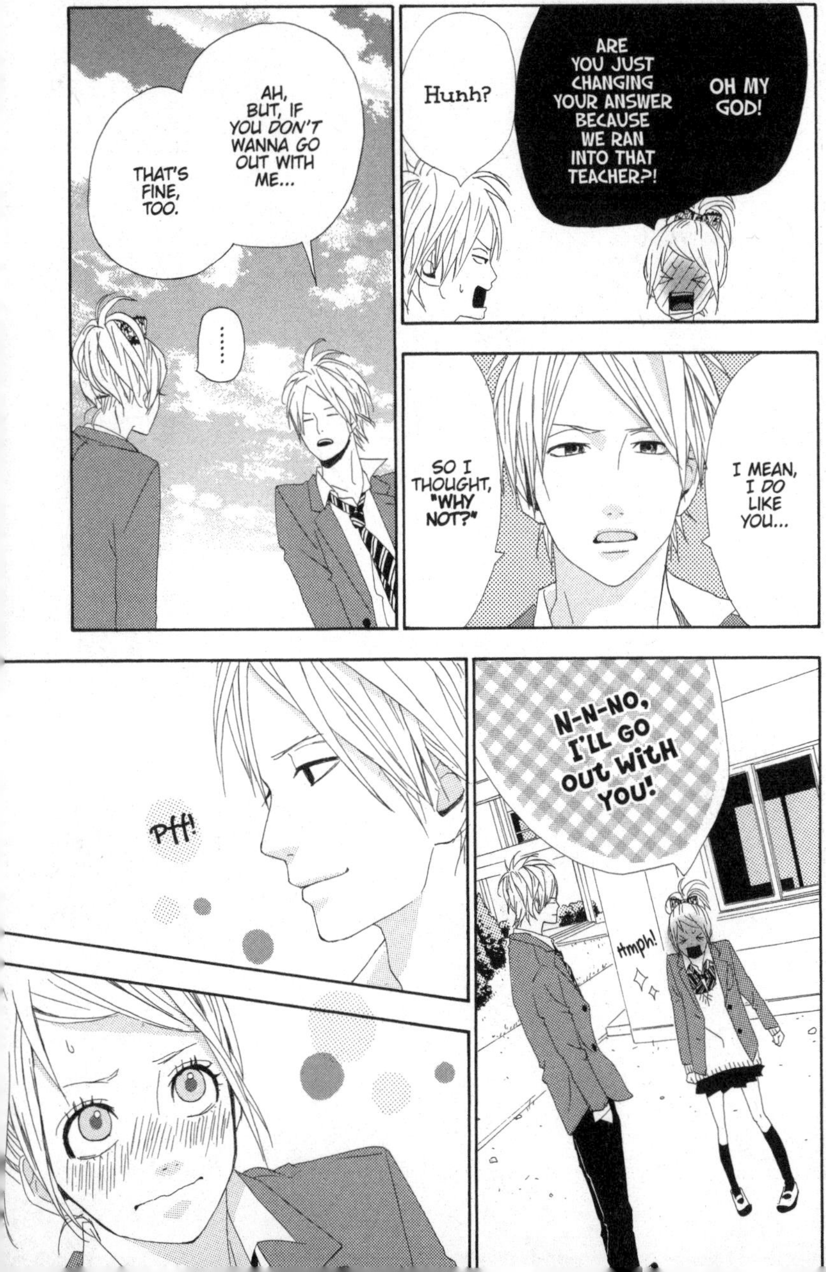
OH MY GOD!
ARE YOU JUST CHANGING YOUR ANSWER BECAUSE WE RAN INTO THAT TEACHER?!
Hunh?
I MEAN, I *DO* LIKE YOU...
SO I THOUGHT, "WHY NOT?"
AH, BUT, IF YOU *DON'T* WANNA GO OUT WITH ME...
THAT'S FINE, TOO.
......
N-N-NO, I'LL GO OUT WITH YOU!
Hmph!
Pff!

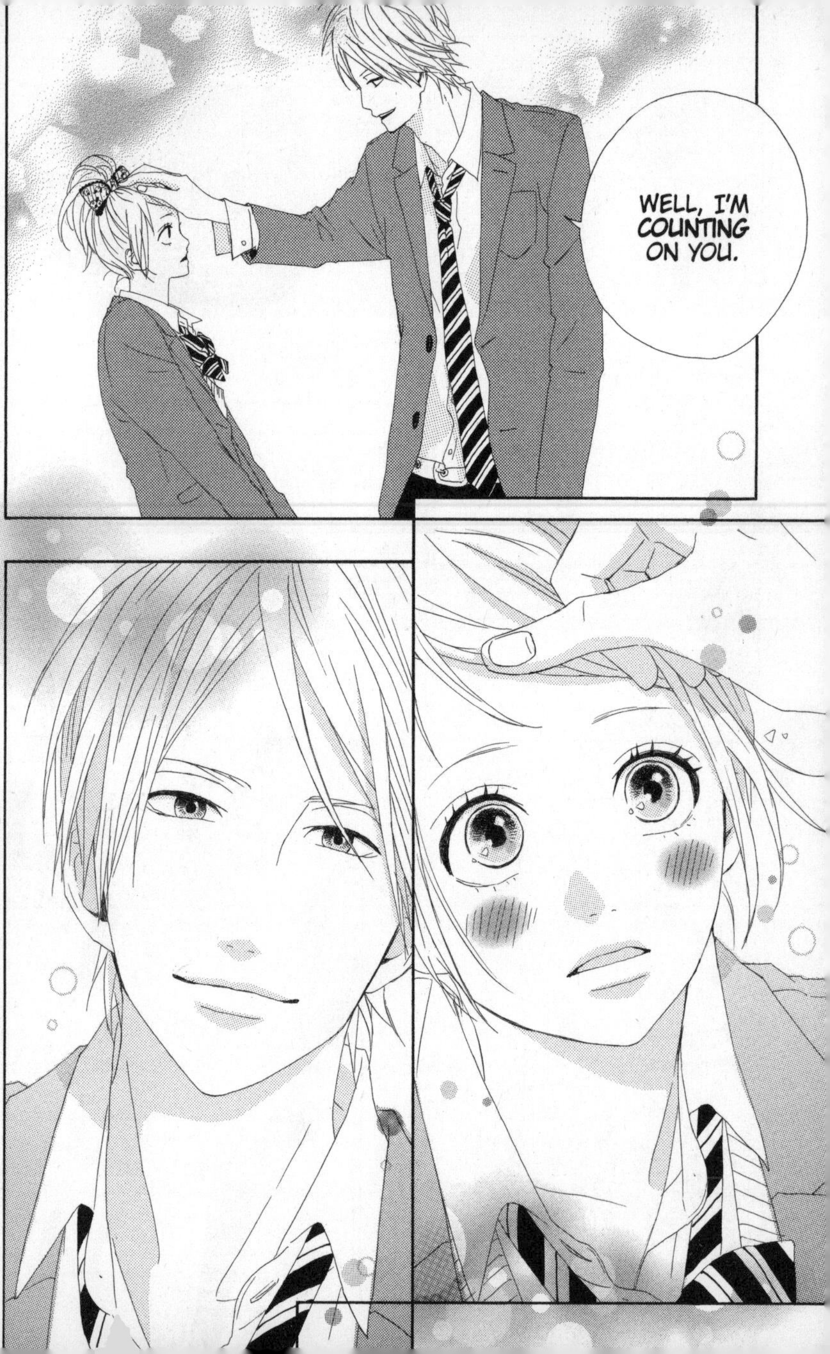
WELL, I'M COUNTING ON YOU.

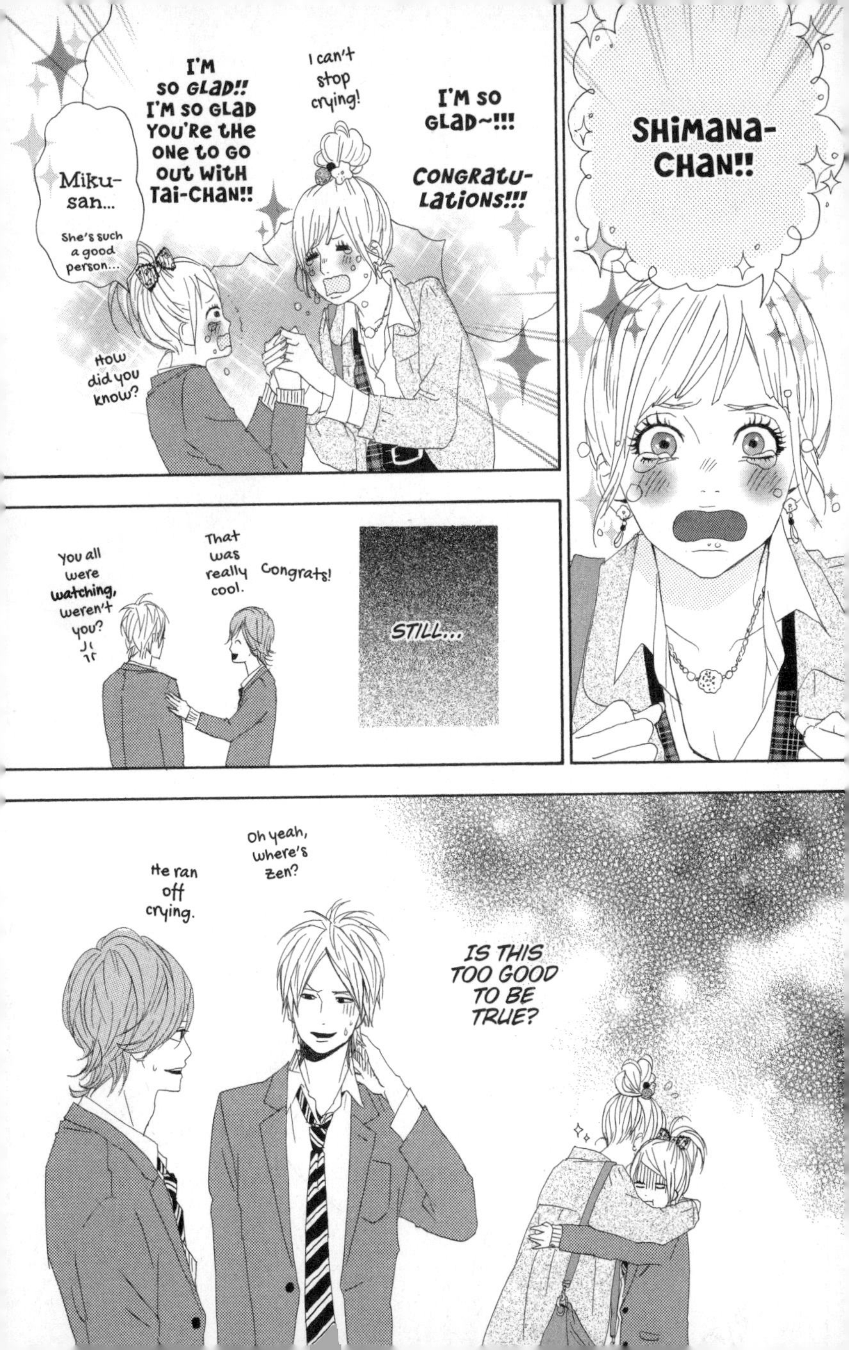
SHIMANA-CHAN!!
I'M SO GLAD~!!!
CONGRATULATIONS!!!
I can't stop crying!
I'M SO GLAD!! I'M SO GLAD YOU'RE THE ONE TO GO OUT WITH TAI-CHAN!!
Miku-san...
She's such a good person...
How did you know?
STILL...
Congrats!
That was really cool.
You all were watching, weren't you?
IS THIS TOO GOOD TO BE TRUE?
Oh yeah, where's Zen?
He ran off crying.

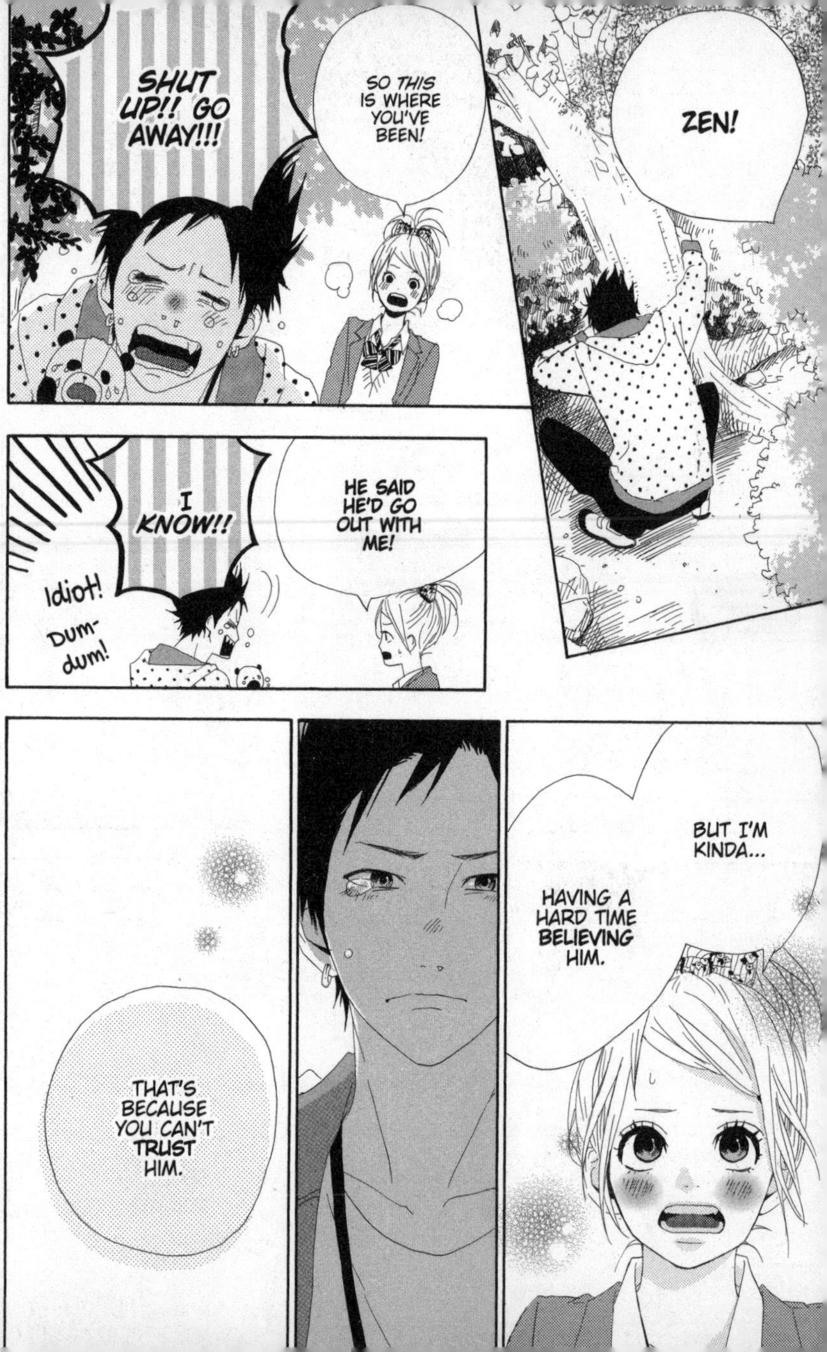
ZEN!
SO THIS IS WHERE YOU'VE BEEN!
SHUT UP!! GO AWAY!!!
HE SAID HE'D GO OUT WITH ME!
I KNOW!!
Idiot!
Dum-dum!
BUT I'M KINDA...
HAVING A HARD TIME BELIEVING HIM.
THAT'S BECAUSE YOU CAN'T TRUST HIM.

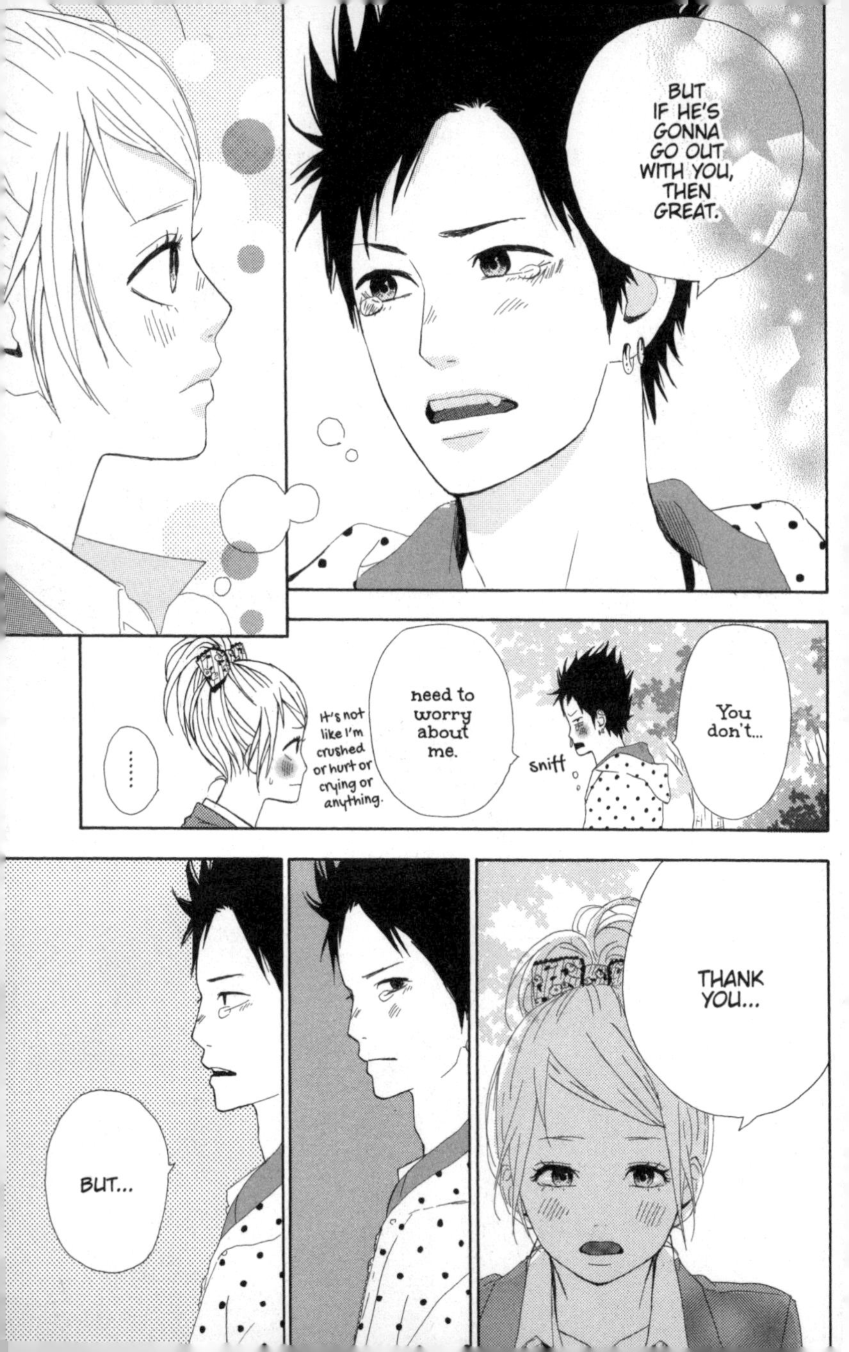
BUT IF HE'S GONNA GO OUT WITH YOU, THEN GREAT.
You don't...
sniff
need to worry about me.
It's not like I'm crushed or hurt or crying or anything.
......
THANK YOU...
BUT...

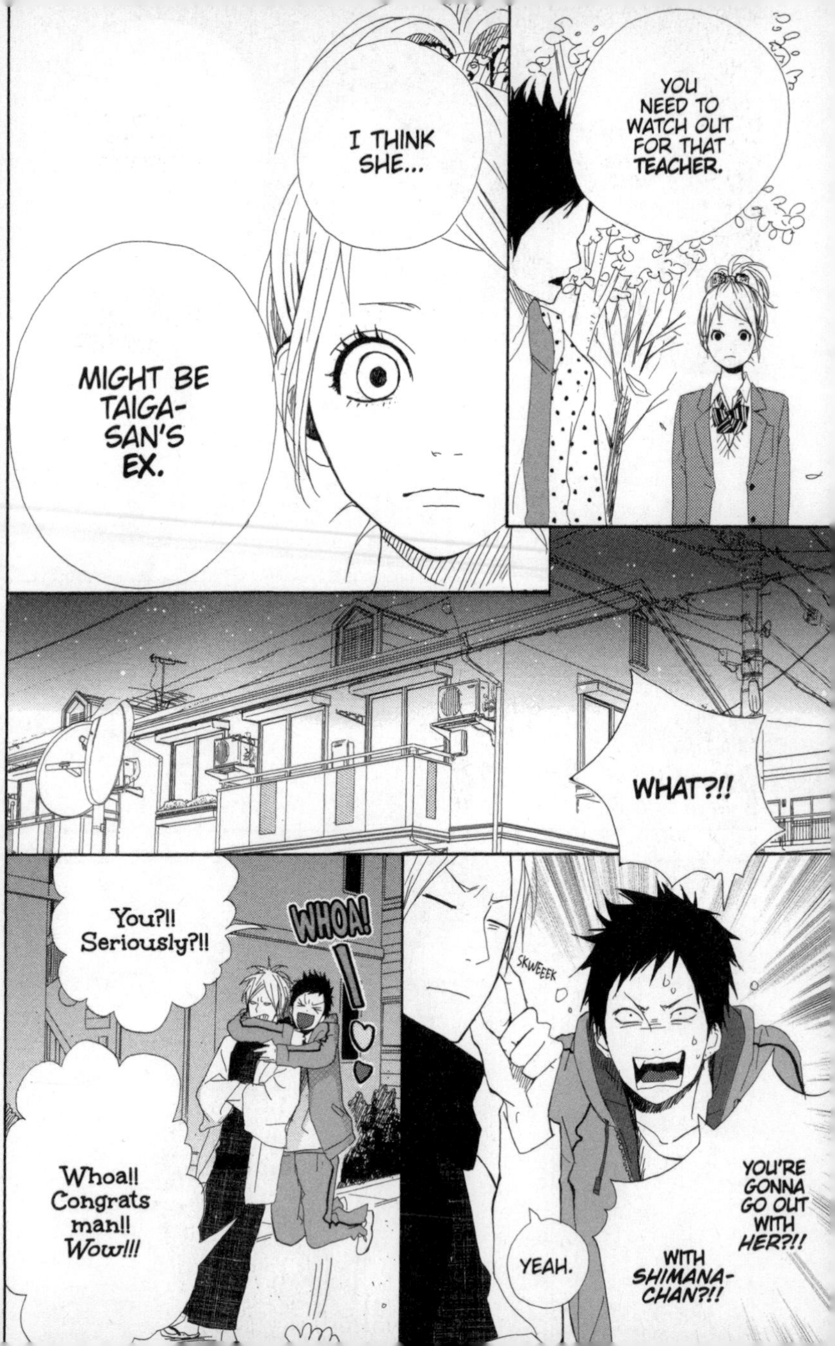
YOU NEED TO WATCH OUT FOR THAT TEACHER.
I THINK SHE...
MIGHT BE TAIGA-SAN'S EX.
WHAT?!!
SKWEEEK
YOU'RE GONNA GO OUT WITH HER?!!
WITH SHIMANA-CHAN?!!
YEAH.
You?!! Seriously?!!
WHOA!
Whoa!! Congrats man!! Wow!!!

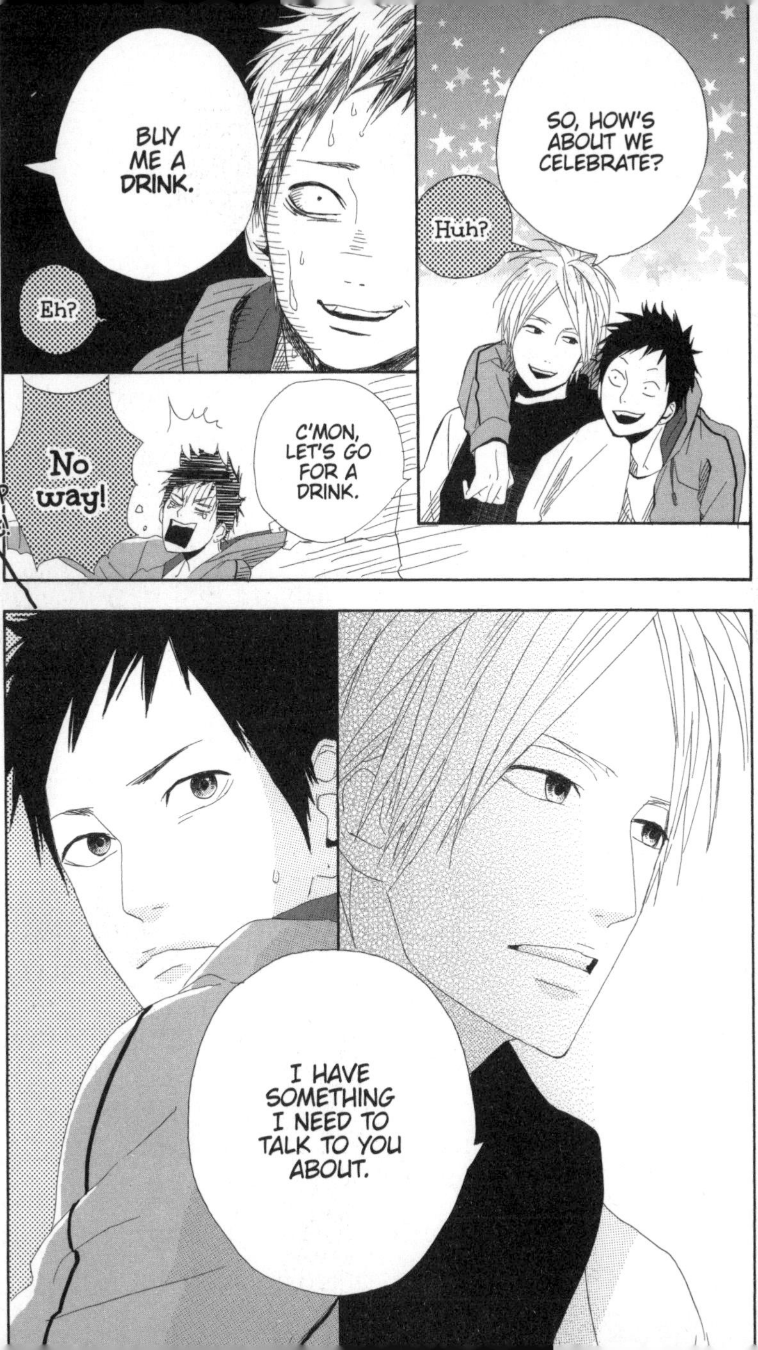
SO, HOW'S ABOUT WE CELEBRATE?
Huh?
BUY ME A DRINK.
Eh?
C'MON, LET'S GO FOR A DRINK.
No way!
HELP ME!
I HAVE SOMETHING I NEED TO TALK TO YOU ABOUT.

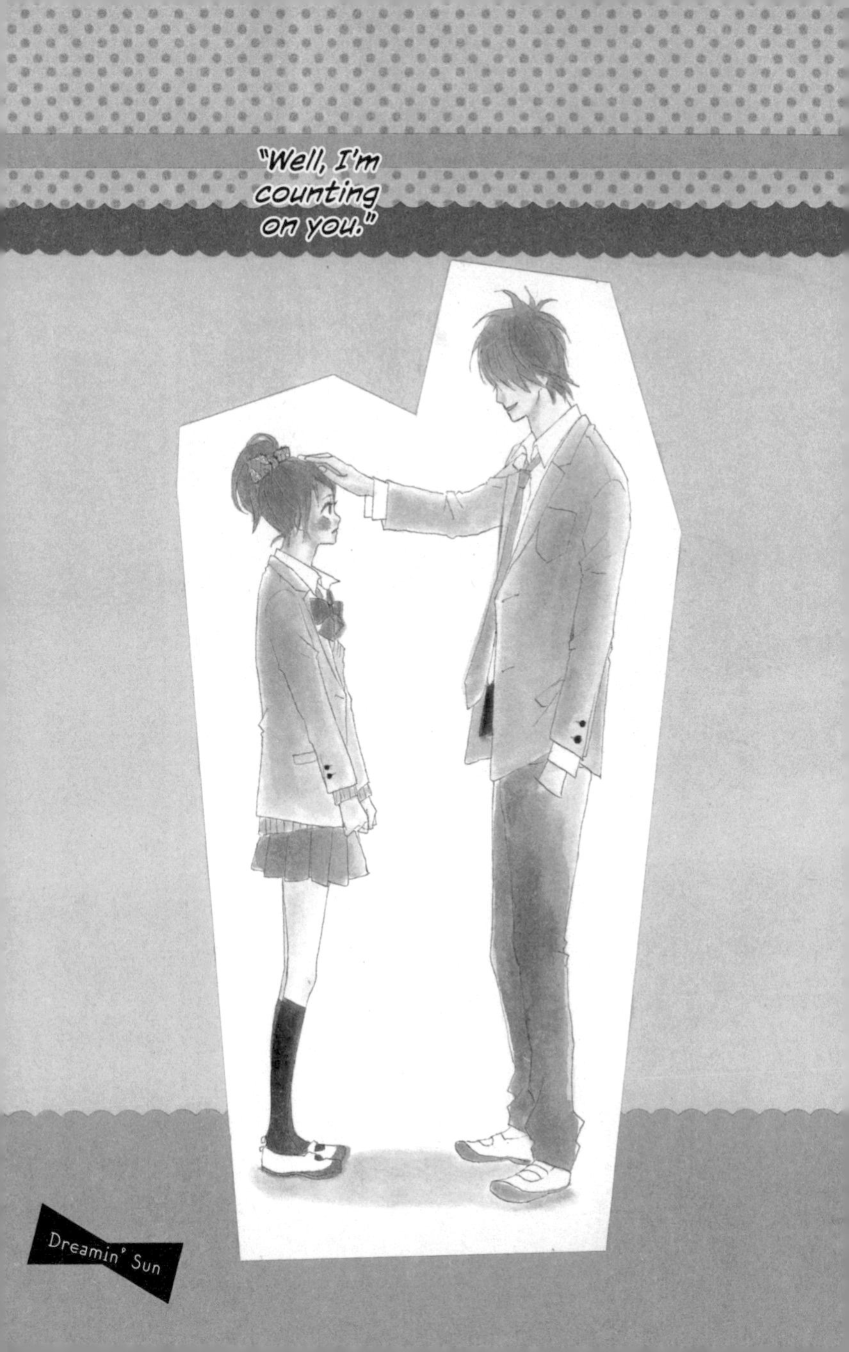
"Well, I'm counting on you."
Dreamin' Sun

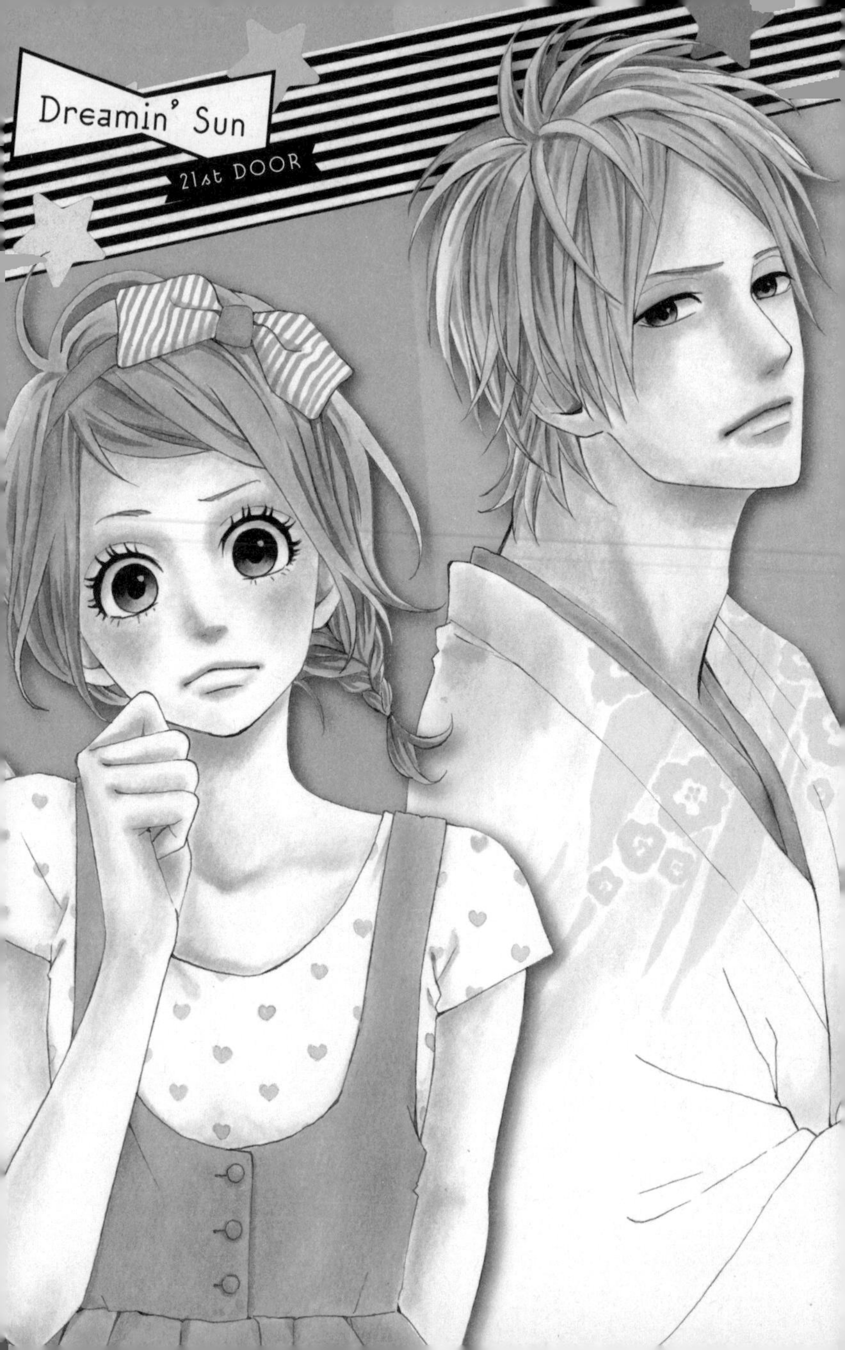
Dreamin' Sun
21st DOOR

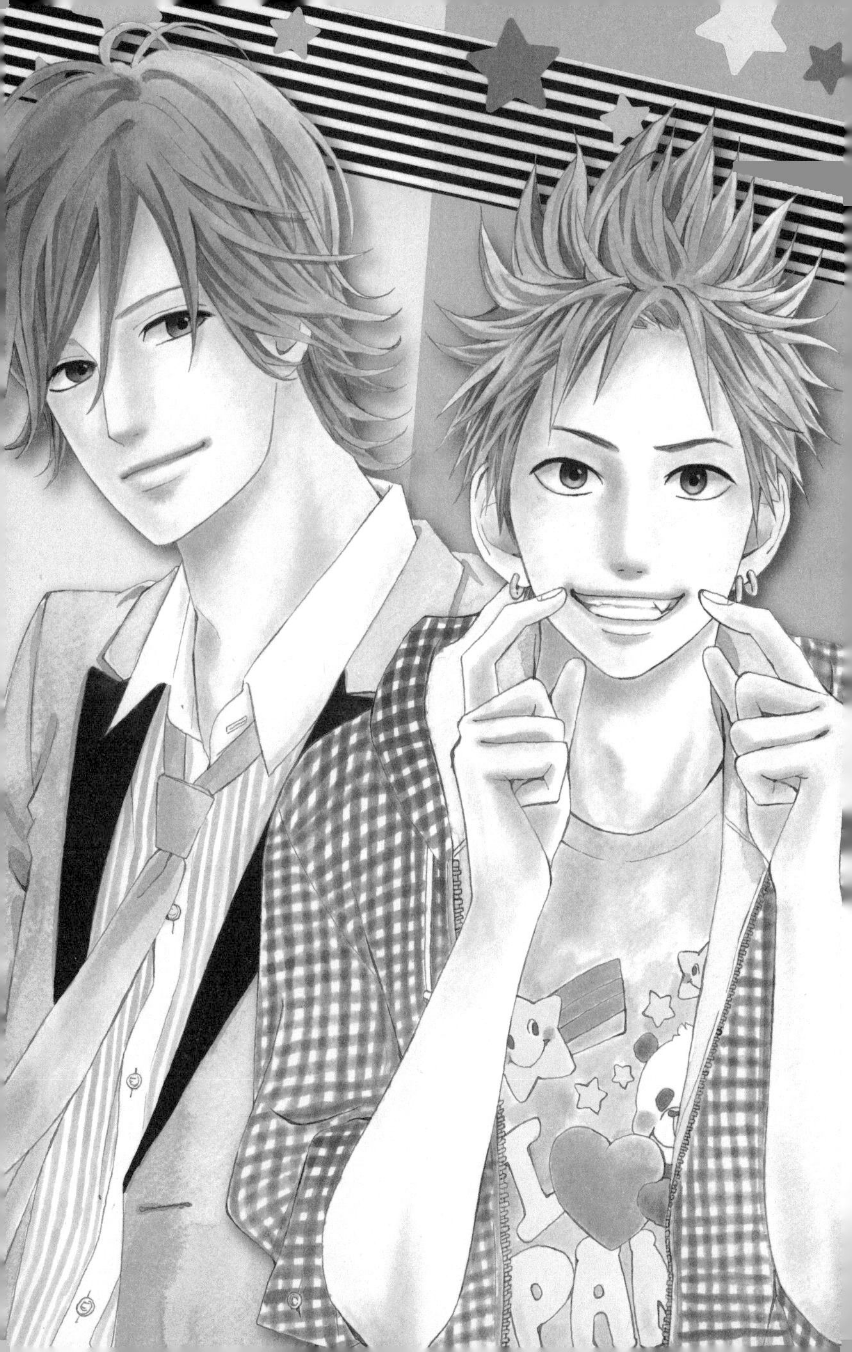

Dreamin'
Sun

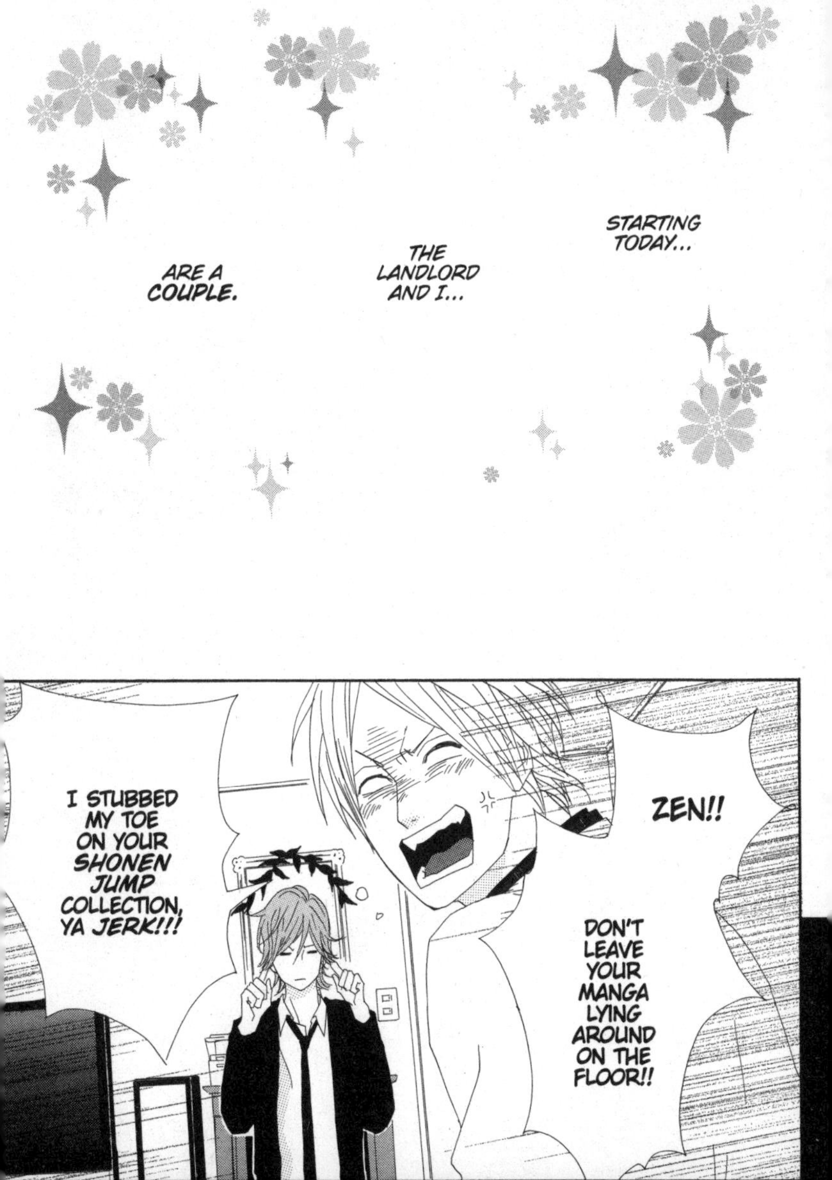
STARTING TODAY...
THE LANDLORD AND I...
ARE A COUPLE.
ZEN!! DON'T LEAVE YOUR MANGA LYING AROUND ON THE FLOOR!!
I STUBBED MY TOE ON YOUR SHONEN JUMP COLLECTION, YA JERK!!!

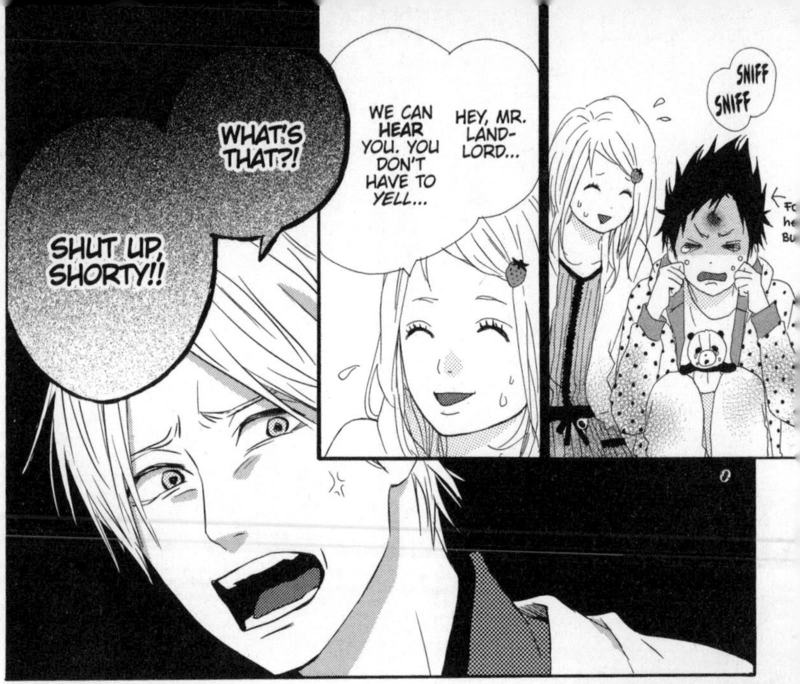
SNIFF SNIFF
HEY, MR. LANDLORD...
WE CAN HEAR YOU. YOU DON'T HAVE TO *YELL*...
WHAT'S THAT?!
SHUT UP, SHORTY!!

Posters: Shaolin..., Kung...

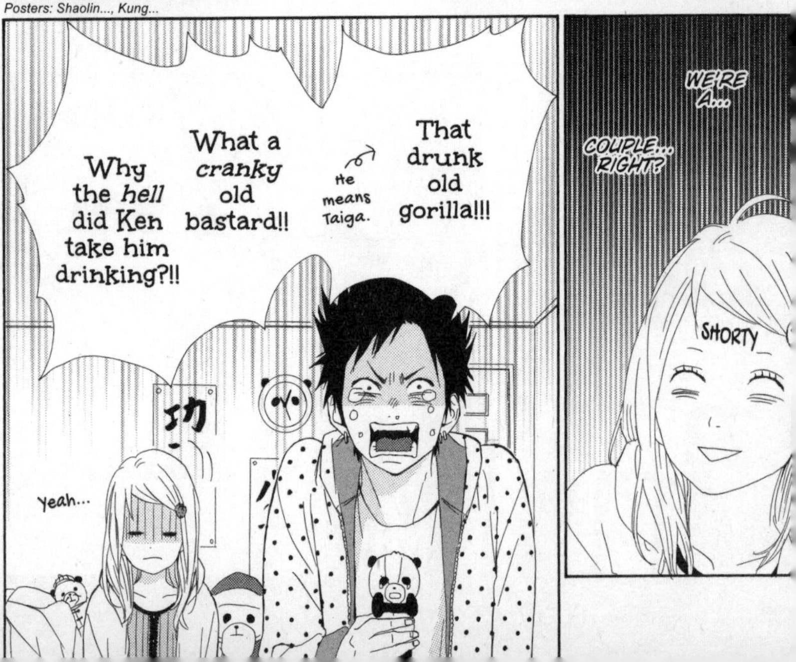
WE'RE A...
COUPLE... RIGHT?
SHORTY
That drunk old gorilla!!!
He means Taiga.
What a *cranky* old bastard!!
Why the *hell* did Ken take him drinking?!!
Yeah...

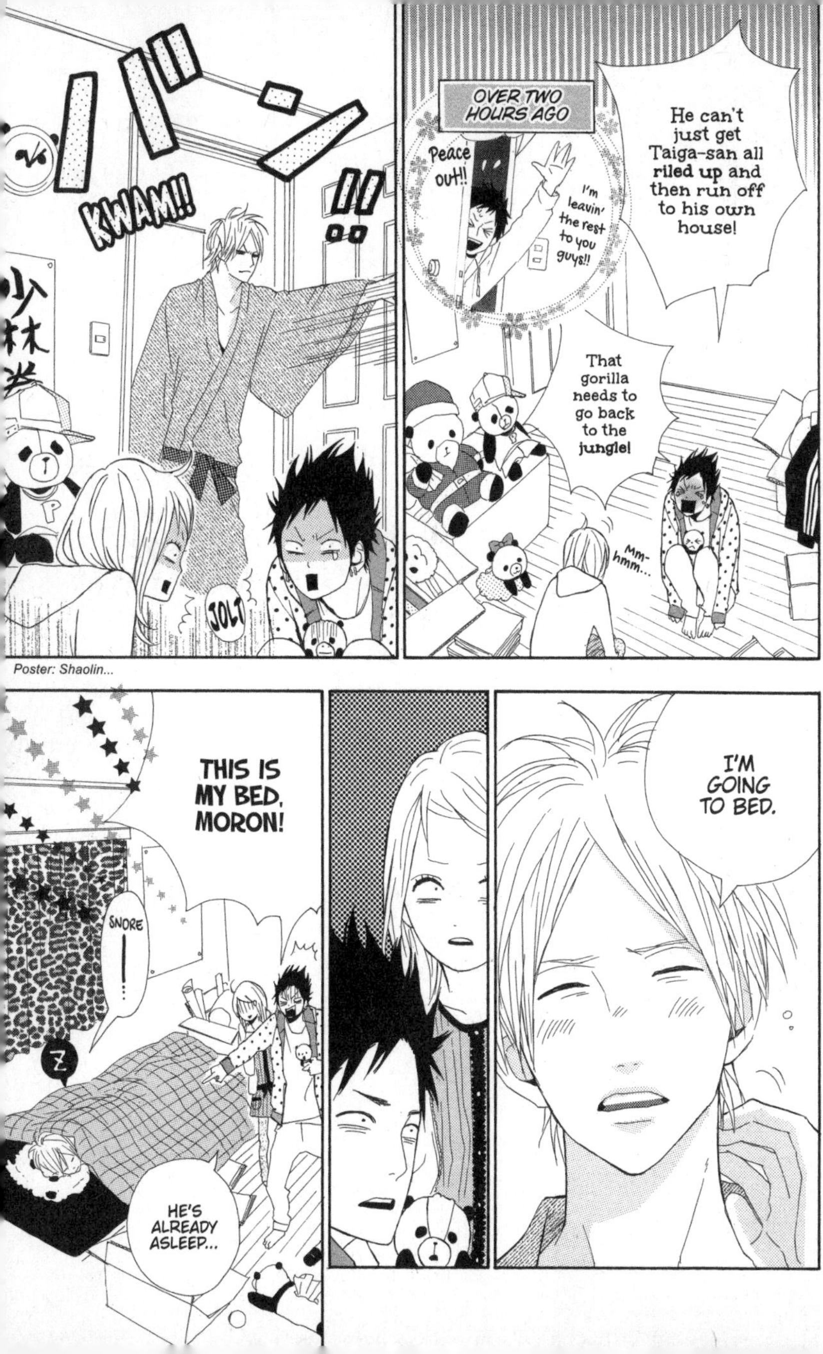
OVER TWO HOURS AGO
Peace out!!
I'm leavin' the rest to you guys!!
He can't just get Taiga-san all riled up and then run off to his own house!
That gorilla needs to go back to the jungle!
Mm-hmm...
KWAM!!
JOLT
I'M GOING TO BED.
THIS IS MY BED, MORON!
SNORE
HE'S ALREADY ASLEEP...

Poster: Shaolin...

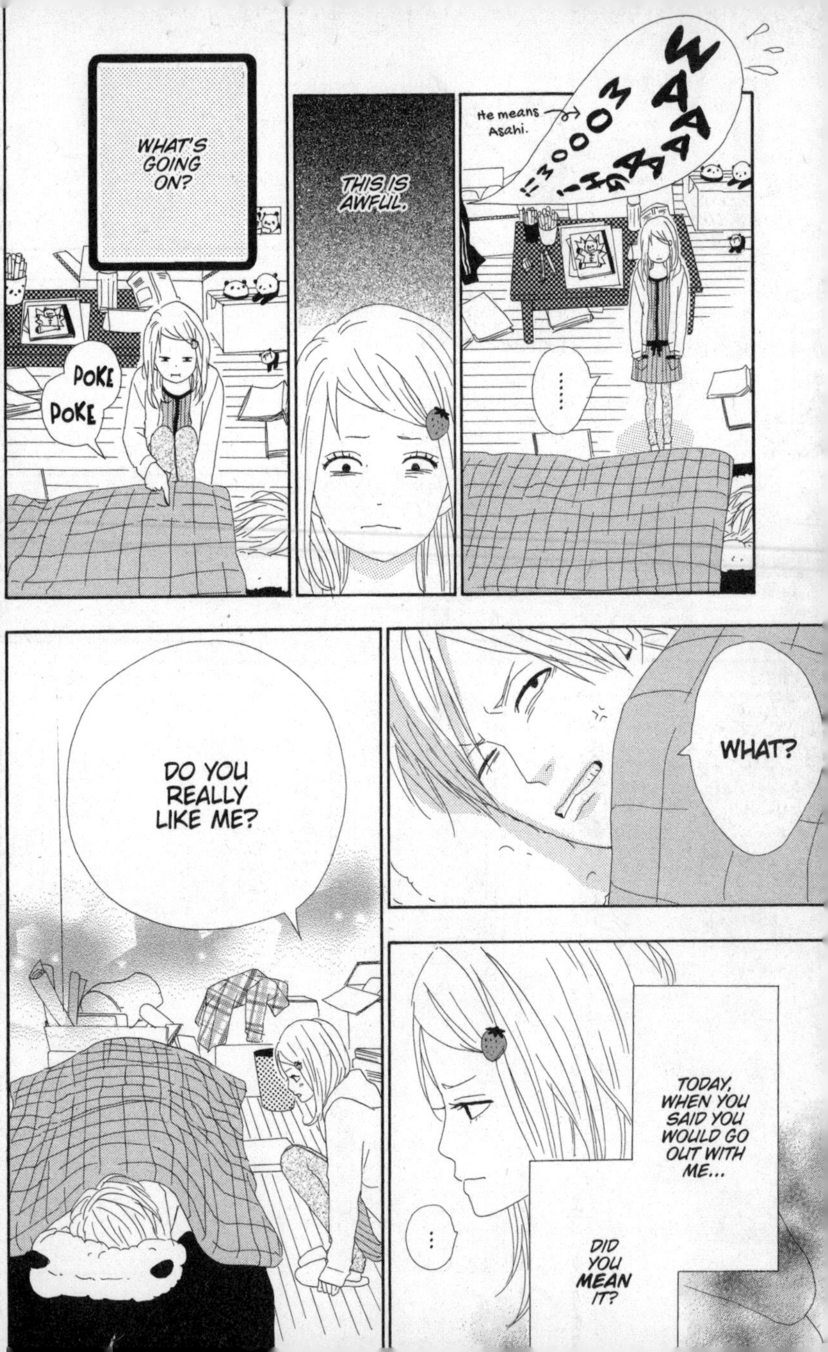

WAAAAGH!
MOOOE!!
He means Asahi.
......
THIS IS AWFUL.
WHAT'S GOING ON?
POKE
POKE
WHAT?
TODAY, WHEN YOU SAID YOU WOULD GO OUT WITH ME...
DID YOU MEAN IT?
...
DO YOU REALLY LIKE ME?

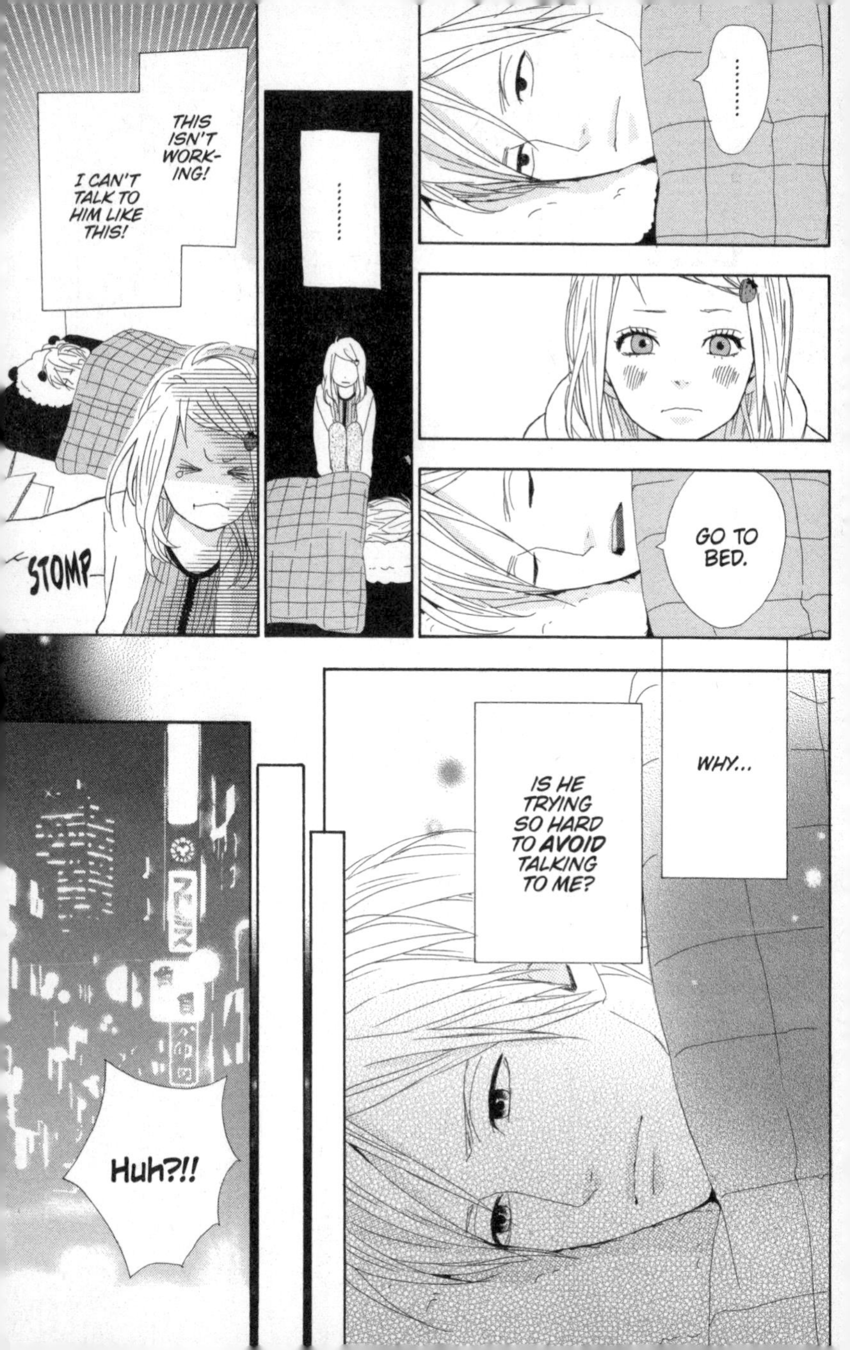
......
GO TO BED.
......
THIS ISN'T WORKING!
I CAN'T TALK TO HIM LIKE THIS!
STOMP
WHY...
IS HE TRYING SO HARD TO AVOID TALKING TO ME?
Huh?!!

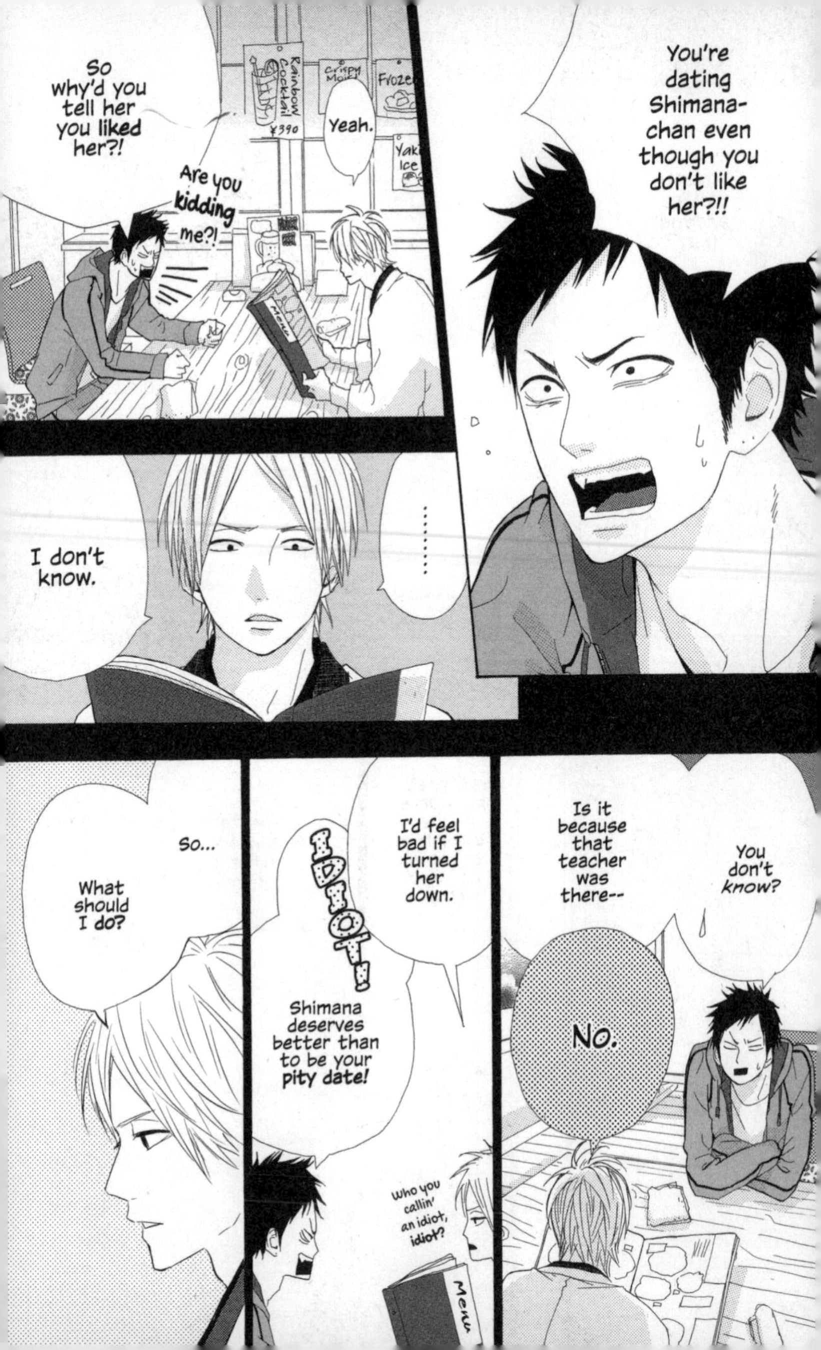
You're dating Shimana-chan even though you don't like her?!!
Rainbow Cocktail
¥390
Yeah.
Are you kidding me?!
So why'd you tell her you liked her?!
Menu
......
I don't know.
You don't know?
Is it because that teacher was there--
NO.
I'd feel bad if I turned her down.
IDIOT!
Shimana deserves better than to be your pity date!
Who you callin' an idiot, idiot?
Menu
So...
What should I do?

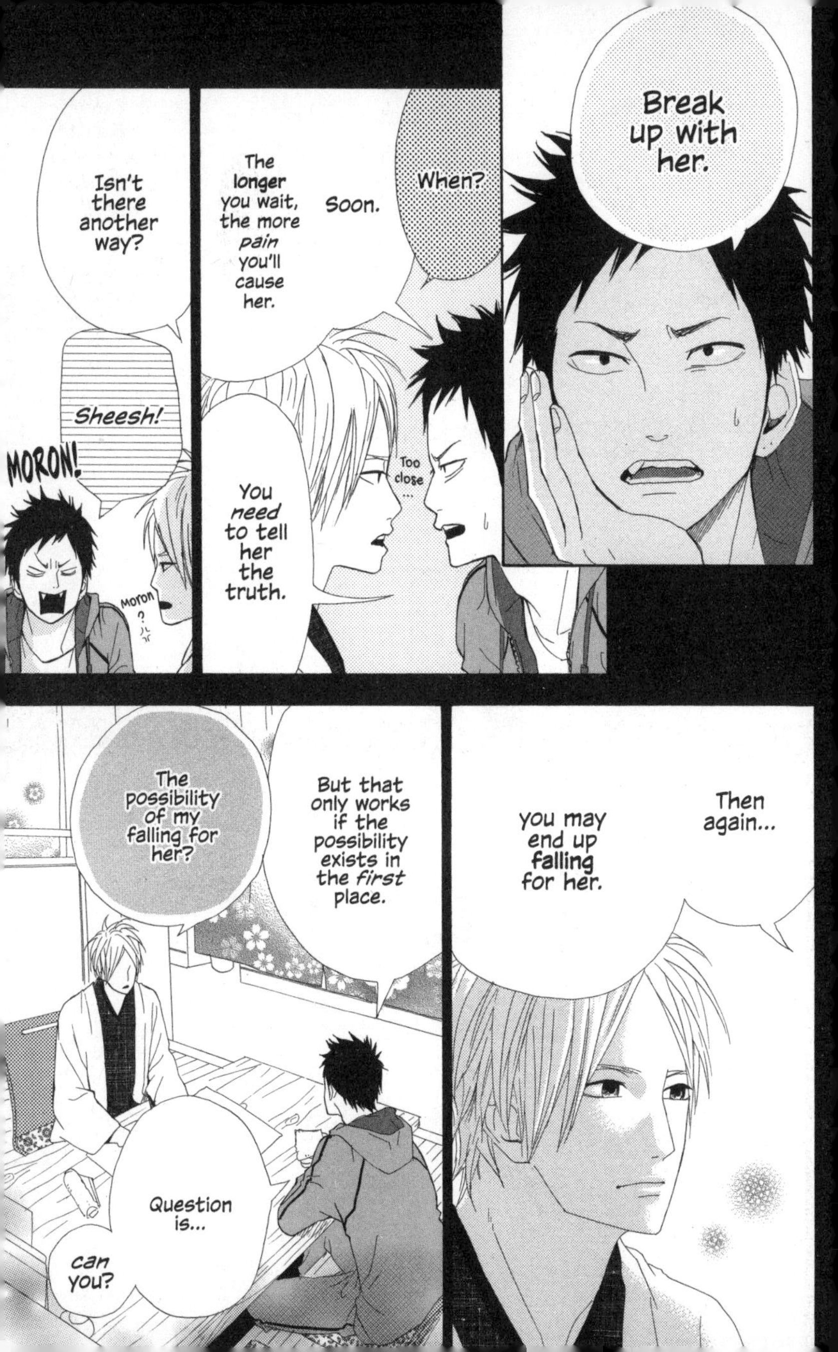
Break up with her.
When?
Soon.
The longer you wait, the more pain you'll cause her.
Too close...
You need to tell her the truth.
Isn't there another way?
Sheesh!
MORON!
Moron?
Then again...
you may end up falling for her.
But that only works if the possibility exists in the first place.
The possibility of my falling for her?
Question is...
can you?

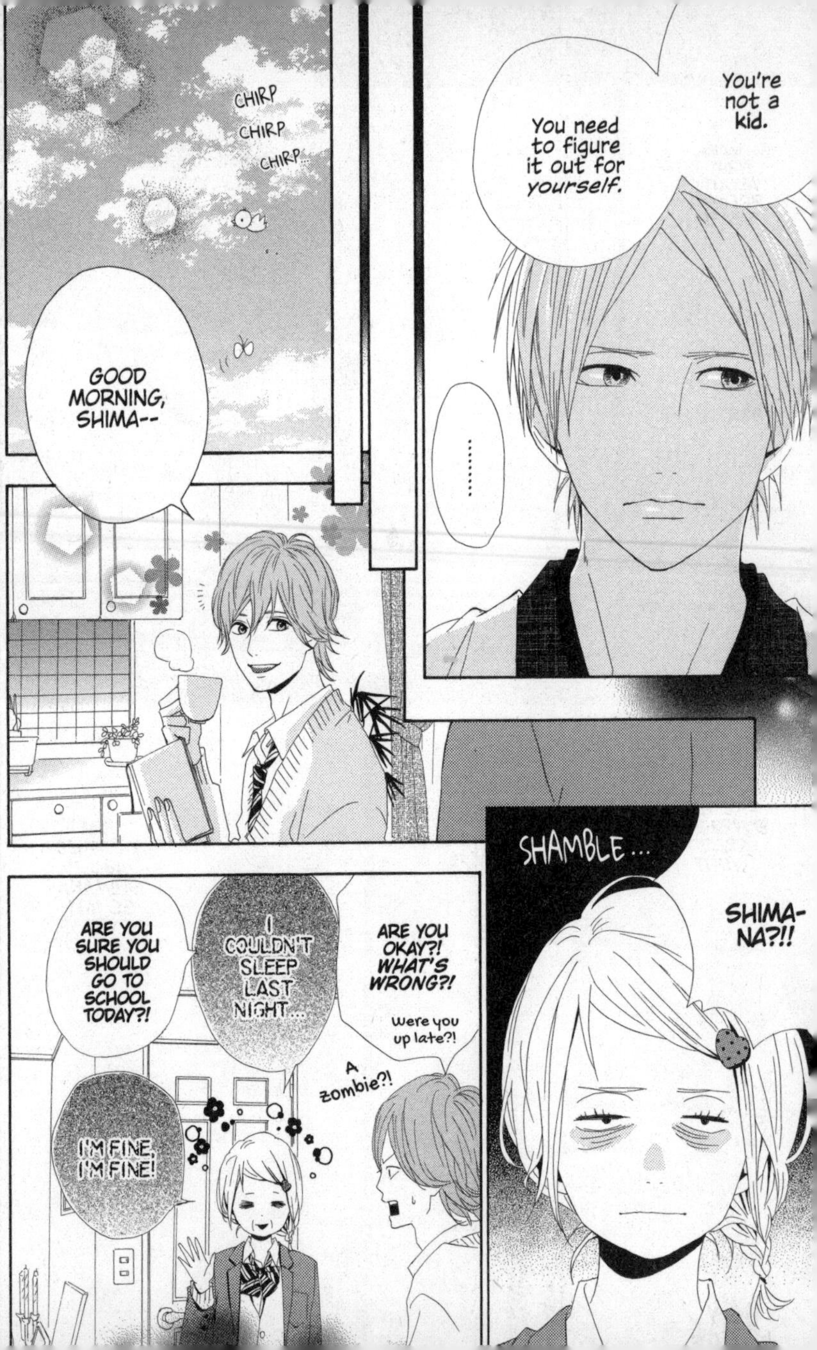
You're not a kid.
You need to figure it out for yourself.
......
CHIRP
CHIRP
CHIRP...
GOOD MORNING, SHIMA--
SHAMBLE...
SHIMA-NA?!!
ARE YOU OKAY?! WHAT'S WRONG?!
Were you up late?!
I COULDN'T SLEEP LAST NIGHT...
ARE YOU SURE YOU SHOULD GO TO SCHOOL TODAY?!
A zombie?!
I'M FINE, I'M FINE!

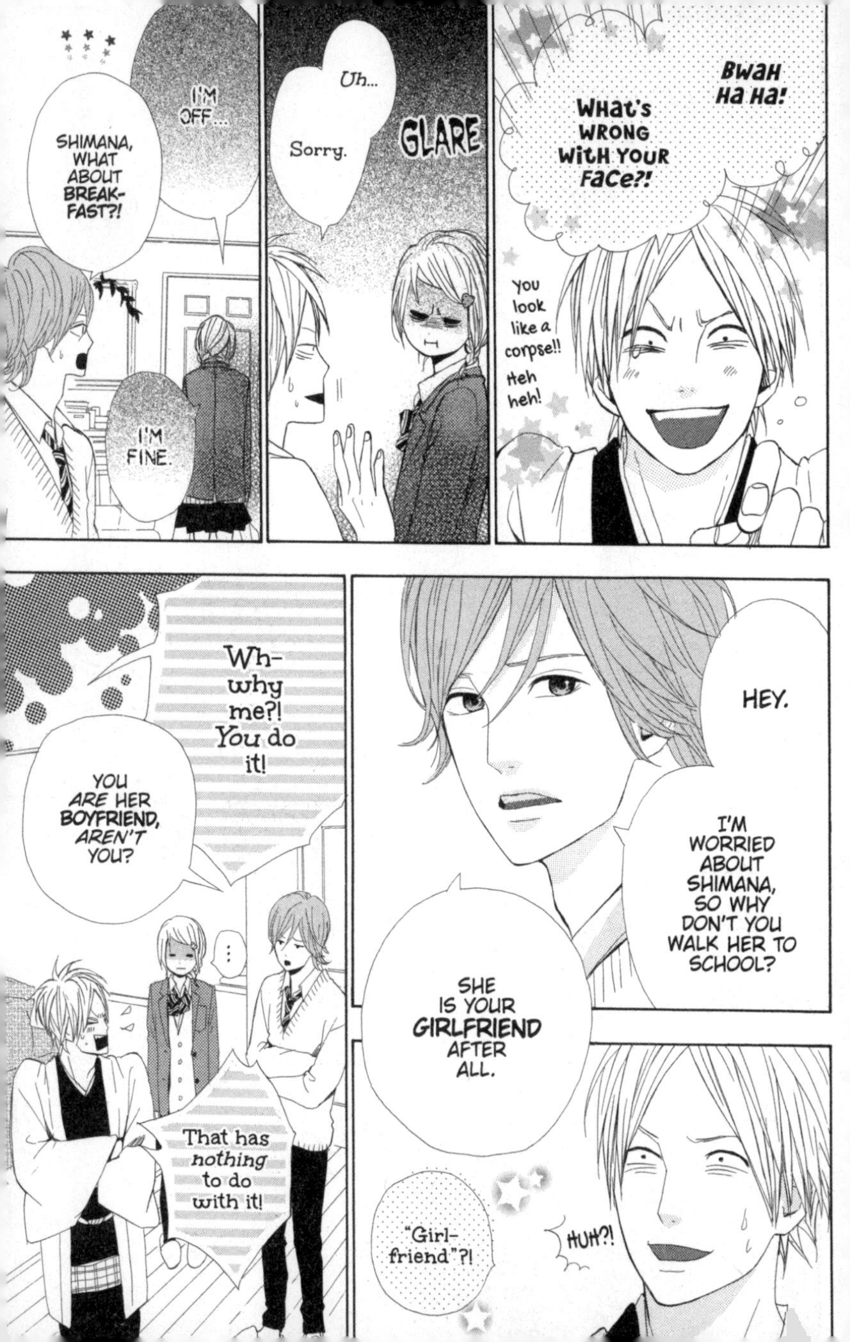
Bwah Ha Ha!
What's wrong with your face?!
You look like a corpse!! Heh heh!
Uh...
Sorry.
GLARE
I'M OFF...
SHIMANA, WHAT ABOUT BREAK-FAST?!
I'M FINE.
HEY.
I'M WORRIED ABOUT SHIMANA, SO WHY DON'T YOU WALK HER TO SCHOOL?
SHE IS YOUR GIRLFRIEND AFTER ALL.
HUH?!
"Girl-friend"?!
Wh-why me?! You do it!
YOU ARE HER BOYFRIEND, AREN'T YOU?
...
That has nothing to do with it!

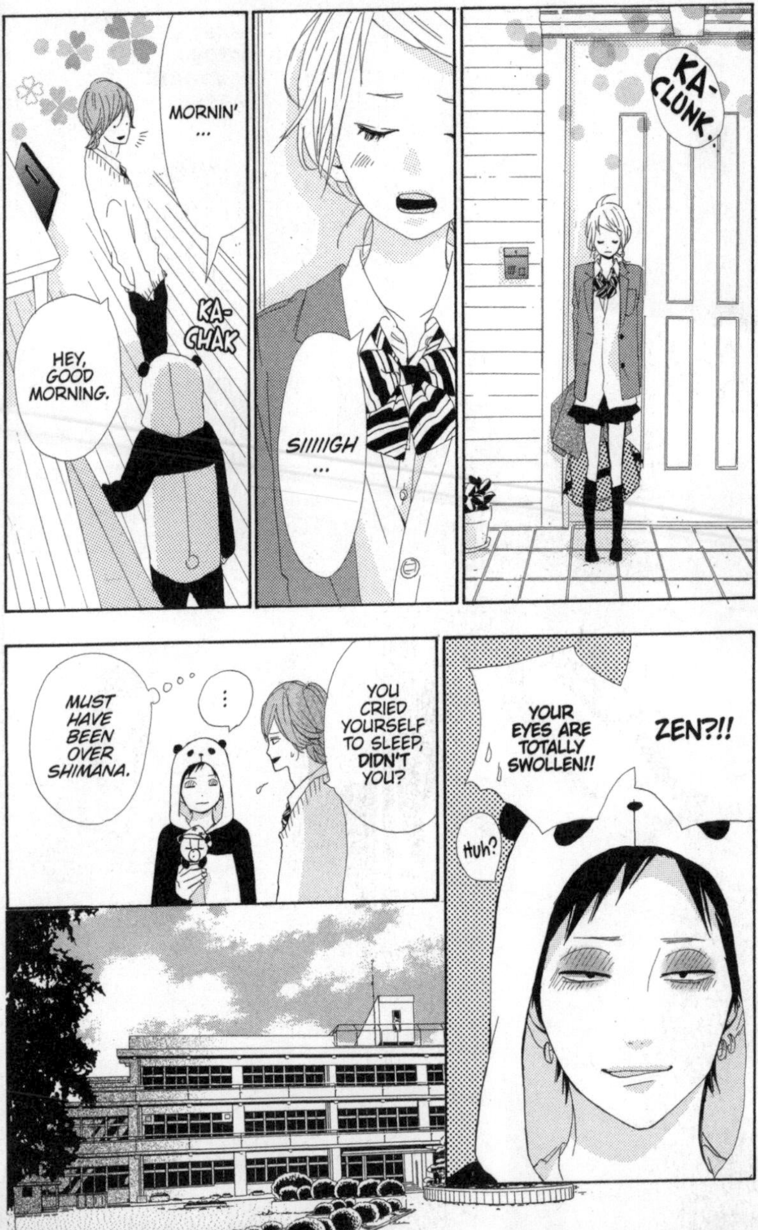
KA-CLUNK.
SIIIIGH ...
MORNIN' ...
KA-CHAK
HEY, GOOD MORNING.
ZEN?!!
YOUR EYES ARE TOTALLY SWOLLEN!!
Huh?
YOU CRIED YOURSELF TO SLEEP, DIDN'T YOU?
...
MUST HAVE BEEN OVER SHIMANA.

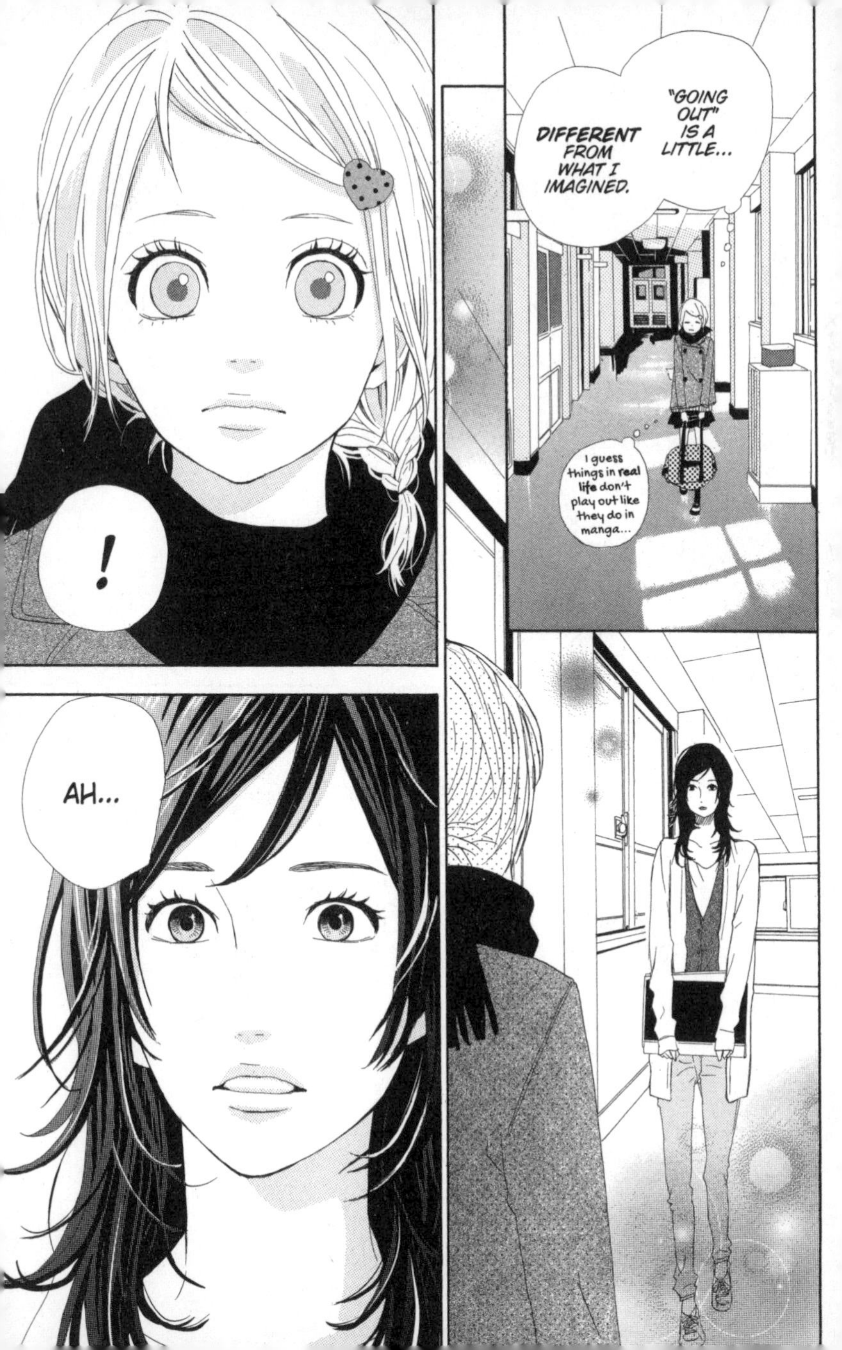
"GOING OUT" IS A LITTLE...
DIFFERENT FROM WHAT I IMAGINED.
I guess things in real life don't play out like they do in manga...
!
AH...

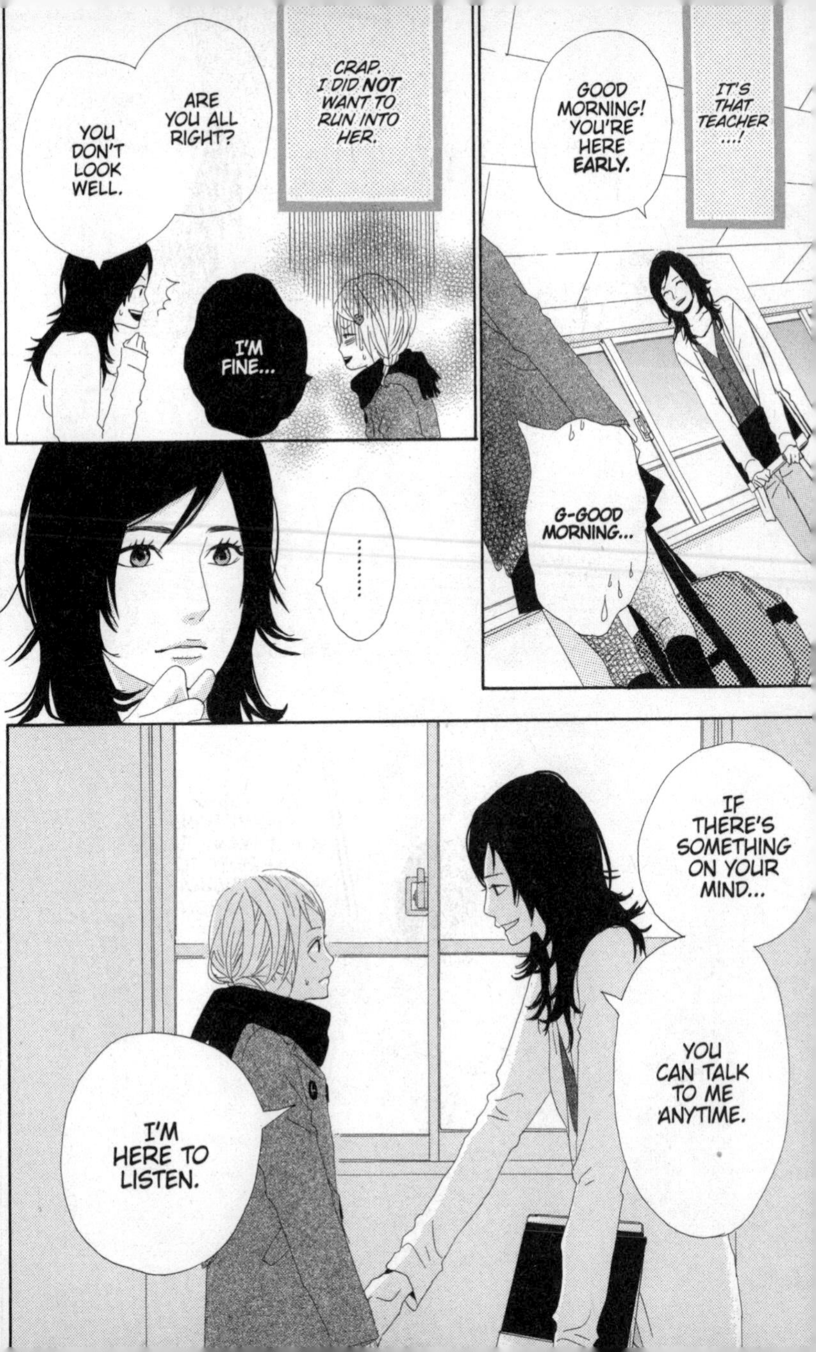
IT'S THAT TEACHER...!
GOOD MORNING! YOU'RE HERE EARLY.
G-GOOD MORNING...
CRAP. I DID NOT WANT TO RUN INTO HER.
ARE YOU ALL RIGHT?
YOU DON'T LOOK WELL.
I'M FINE...
......
IF THERE'S SOMETHING ON YOUR MIND...
YOU CAN TALK TO ME ANYTIME.
I'M HERE TO LISTEN.

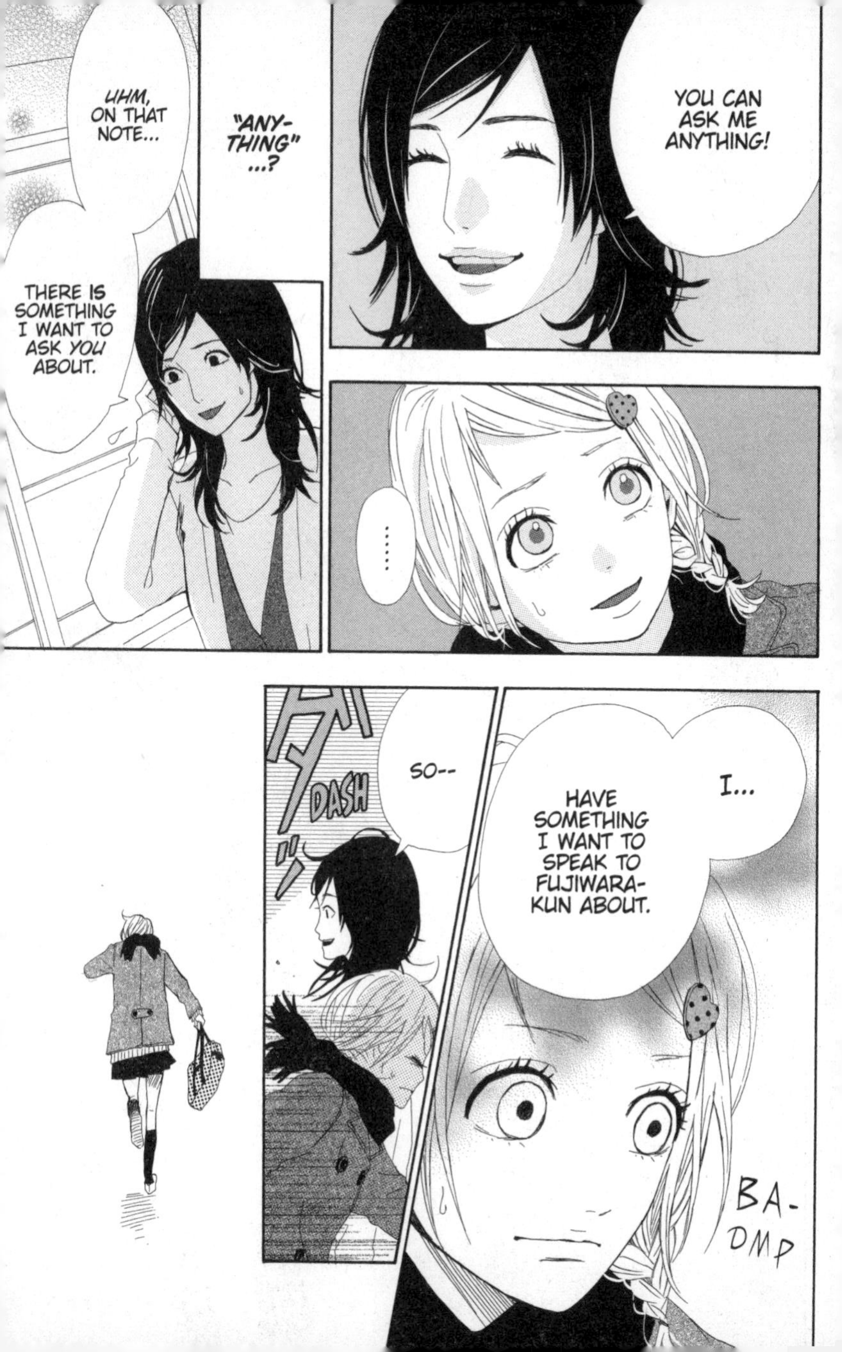
YOU CAN ASK ME ANYTHING!
......
"ANY-THING" ...?
UHM, ON THAT NOTE...
THERE IS SOMETHING I WANT TO ASK *YOU* ABOUT.
I...
HAVE SOMETHING I WANT TO SPEAK TO FUJIWARA-KUN ABOUT.
BA-DMP
SO--
DASH

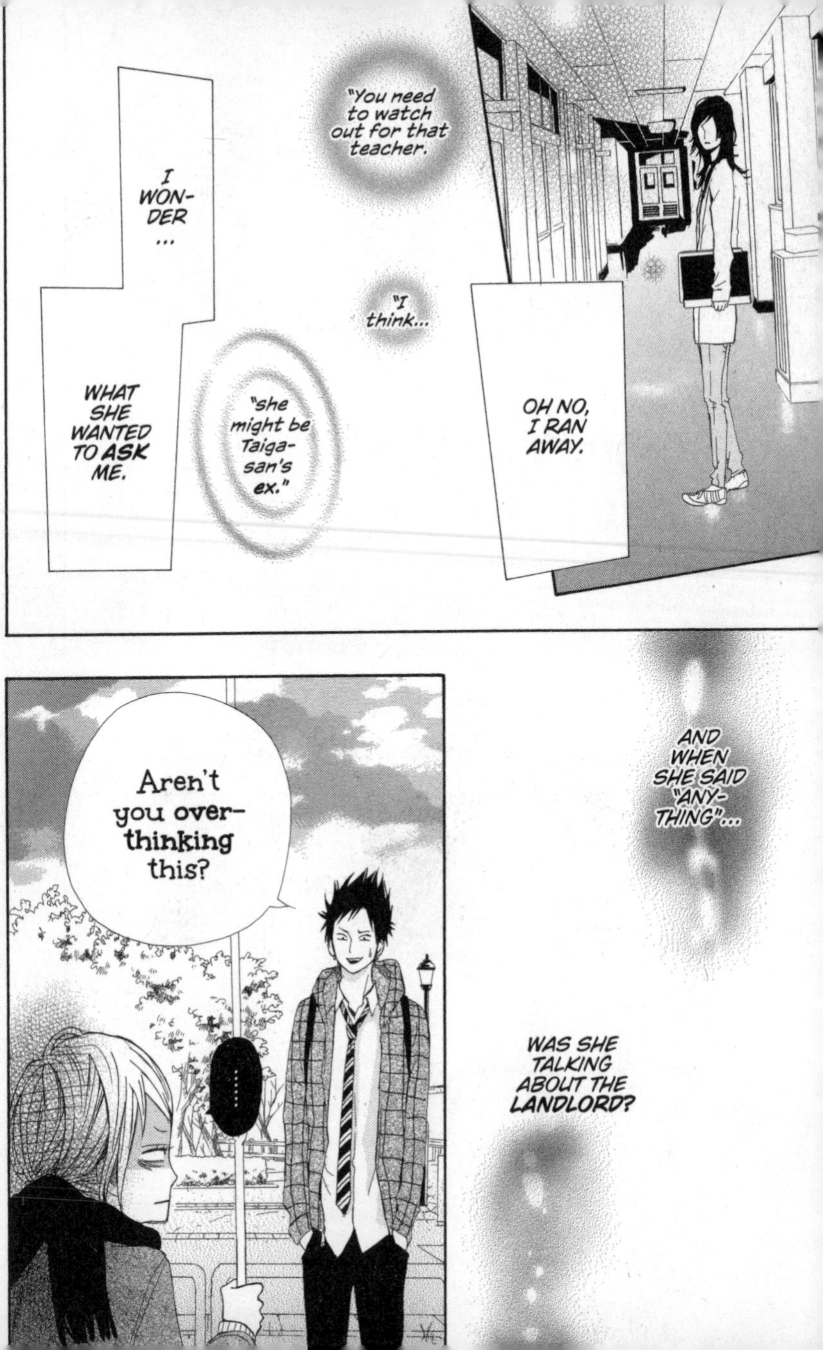
OH NO, I RAN AWAY.
"You need to watch out for that teacher.
"I think...
"she might be Taiga-san's ex."
I WONDER...
WHAT SHE WANTED TO ASK ME.
AND WHEN SHE SAID "ANY-THING"...
WAS SHE TALKING ABOUT THE LANDLORD?
Aren't you over-thinking this?
......

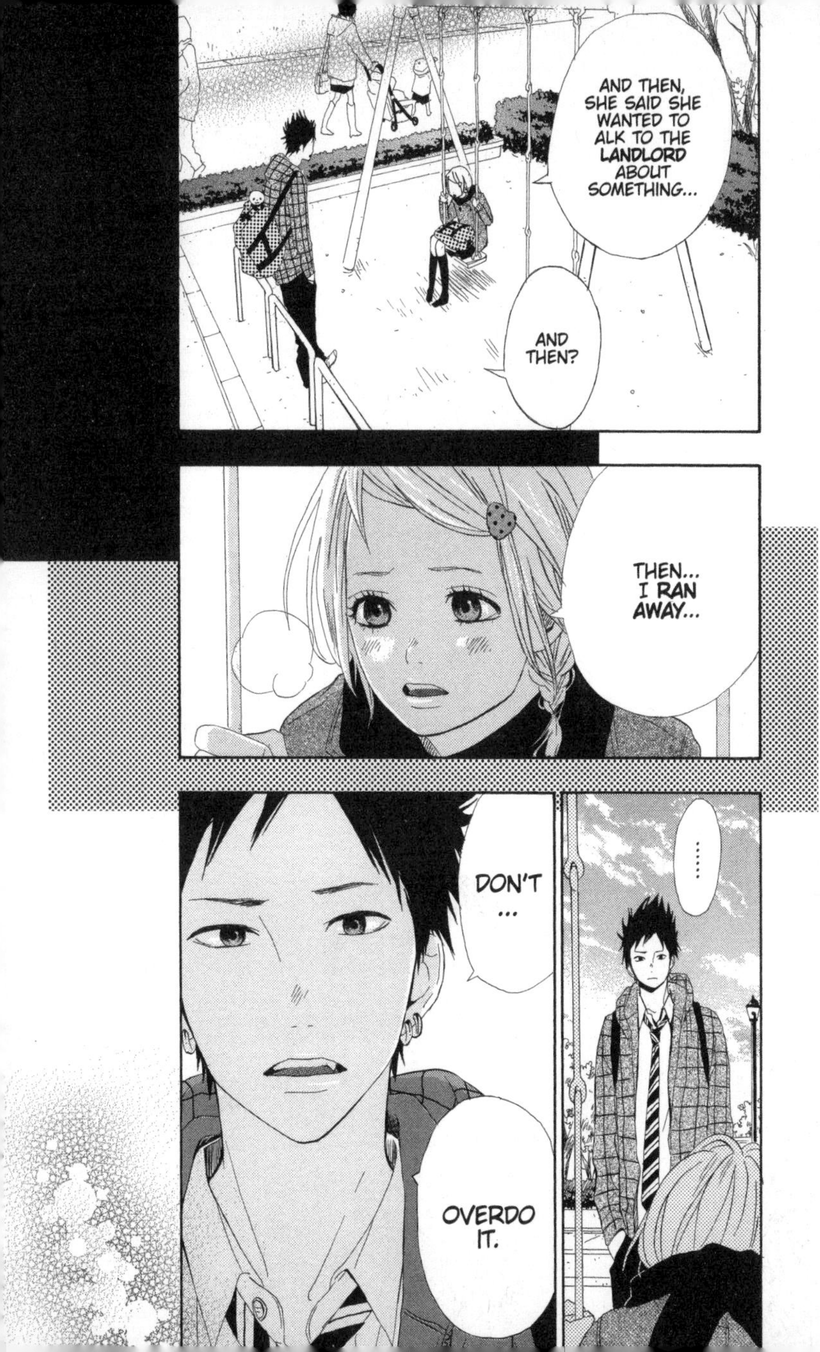
AND THEN, SHE SAID SHE WANTED TO ALK TO THE LANDLORD ABOUT SOMETHING...
AND THEN?
THEN... I RAN AWAY...
......
DON'T ...
OVERDO IT.

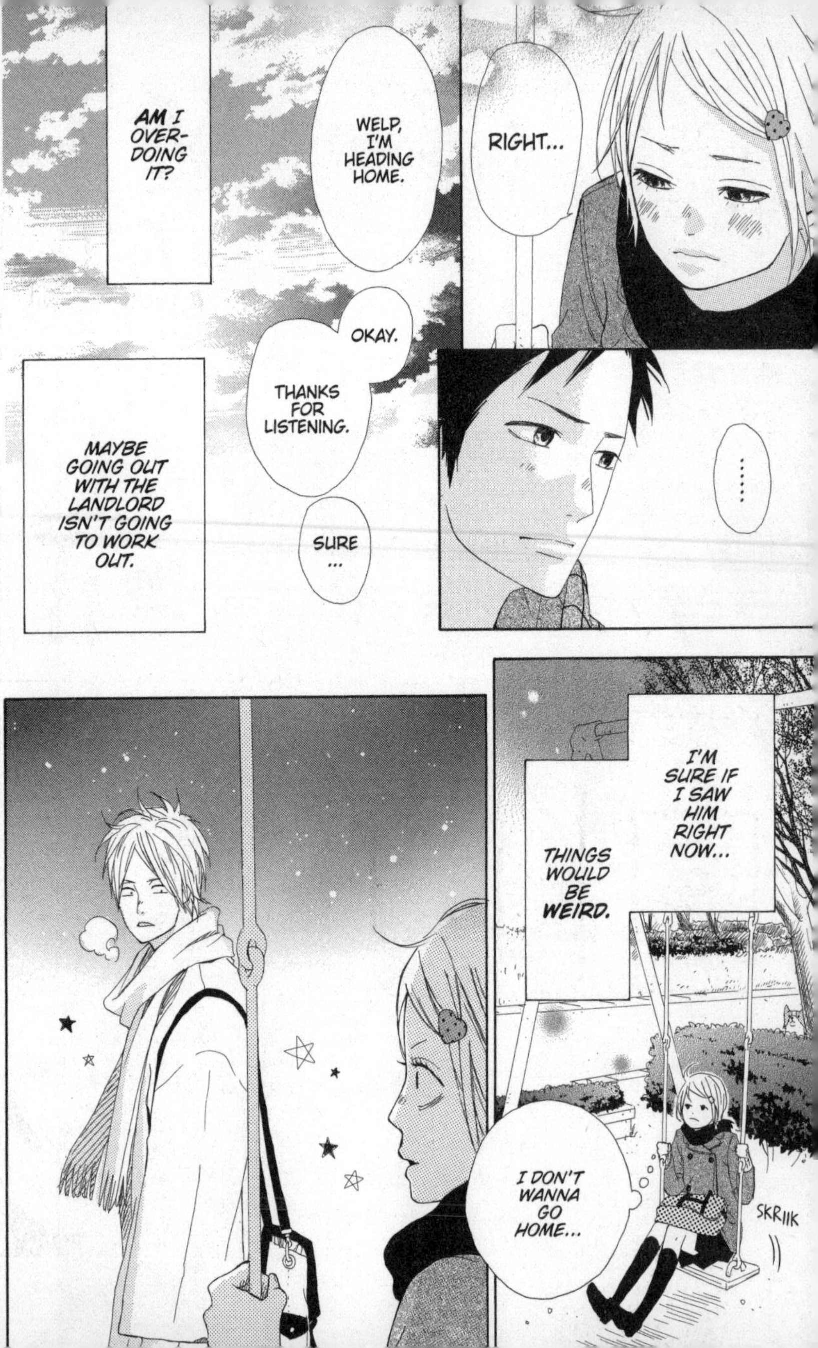
RIGHT...
......
WELP, I'M HEADING HOME.
AM I OVER-DOING IT?
OKAY.
THANKS FOR LISTENING.
SURE...
MAYBE GOING OUT WITH THE LANDLORD ISN'T GOING TO WORK OUT.
I'M SURE IF I SAW HIM RIGHT NOW...
THINGS WOULD BE WEIRD.
I DON'T WANNA GO HOME...
SKRIIK

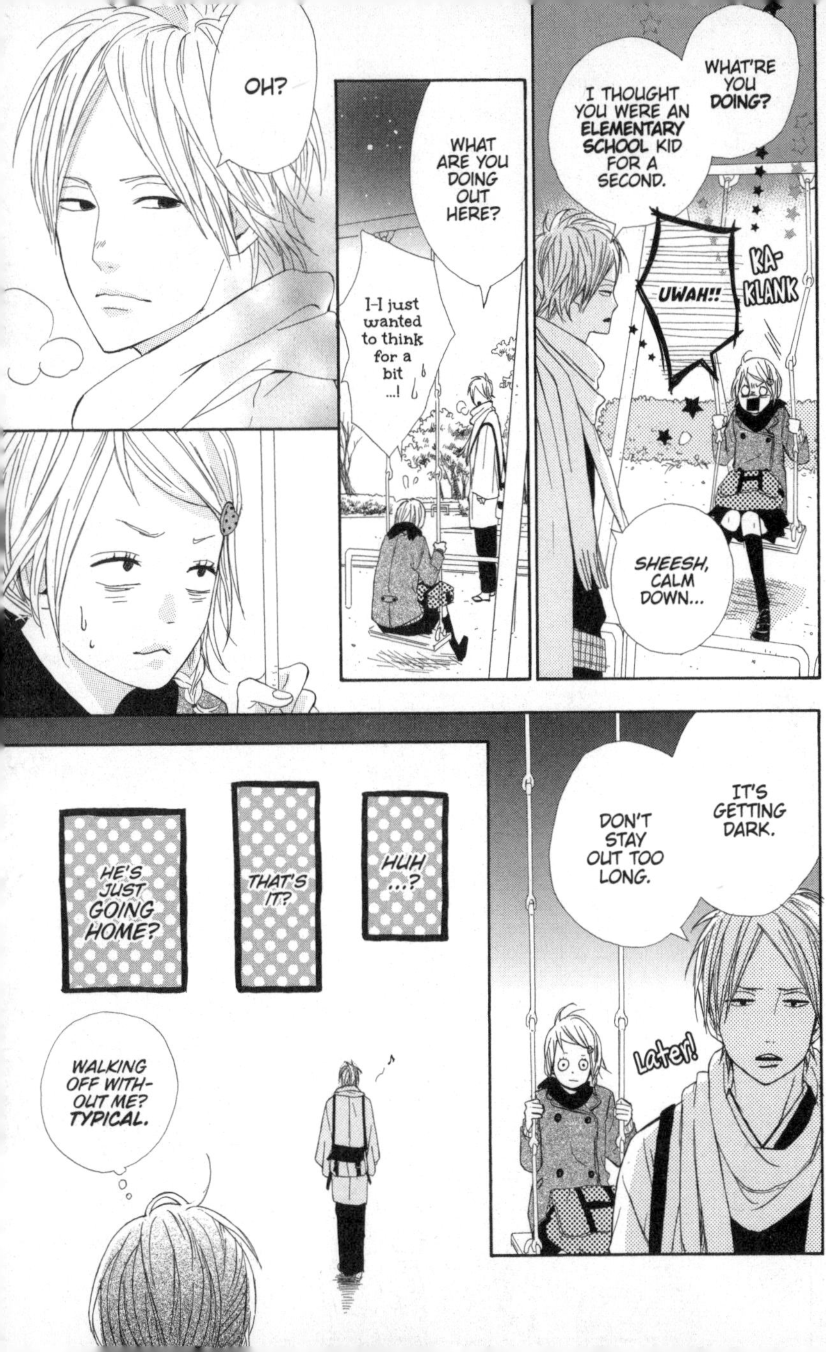
WHAT'RE YOU DOING?
I THOUGHT YOU WERE AN ELEMENTARY SCHOOL KID FOR A SECOND.
KA-KLANK
UWAH!!
SHEESH, CALM DOWN...
WHAT ARE YOU DOING OUT HERE?
I-I just wanted to think for a bit ...!
OH?
IT'S GETTING DARK.
DON'T STAY OUT TOO LONG.
Later!
HUH ...?
THAT'S IT?
HE'S JUST GOING HOME?
WALKING OFF WITH-OUT ME? TYPICAL.

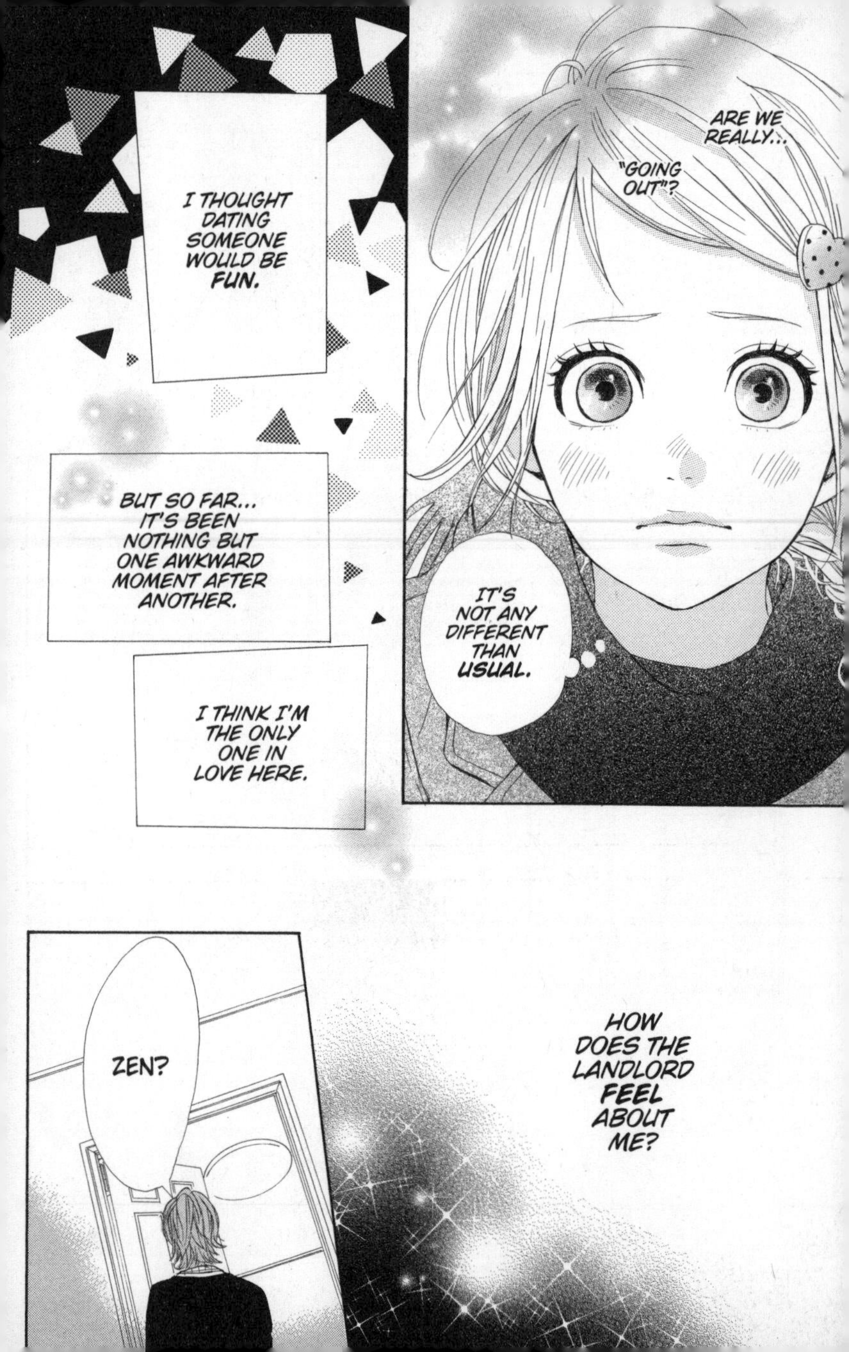
ARE WE REALLY...
"GOING OUT"?
IT'S NOT ANY DIFFERENT THAN USUAL.
I THOUGHT DATING SOMEONE WOULD BE FUN.
BUT SO FAR... IT'S BEEN NOTHING BUT ONE AWKWARD MOMENT AFTER ANOTHER.
I THINK I'M THE ONLY ONE IN LOVE HERE.
HOW DOES THE LANDLORD FEEL ABOUT ME?
ZEN?

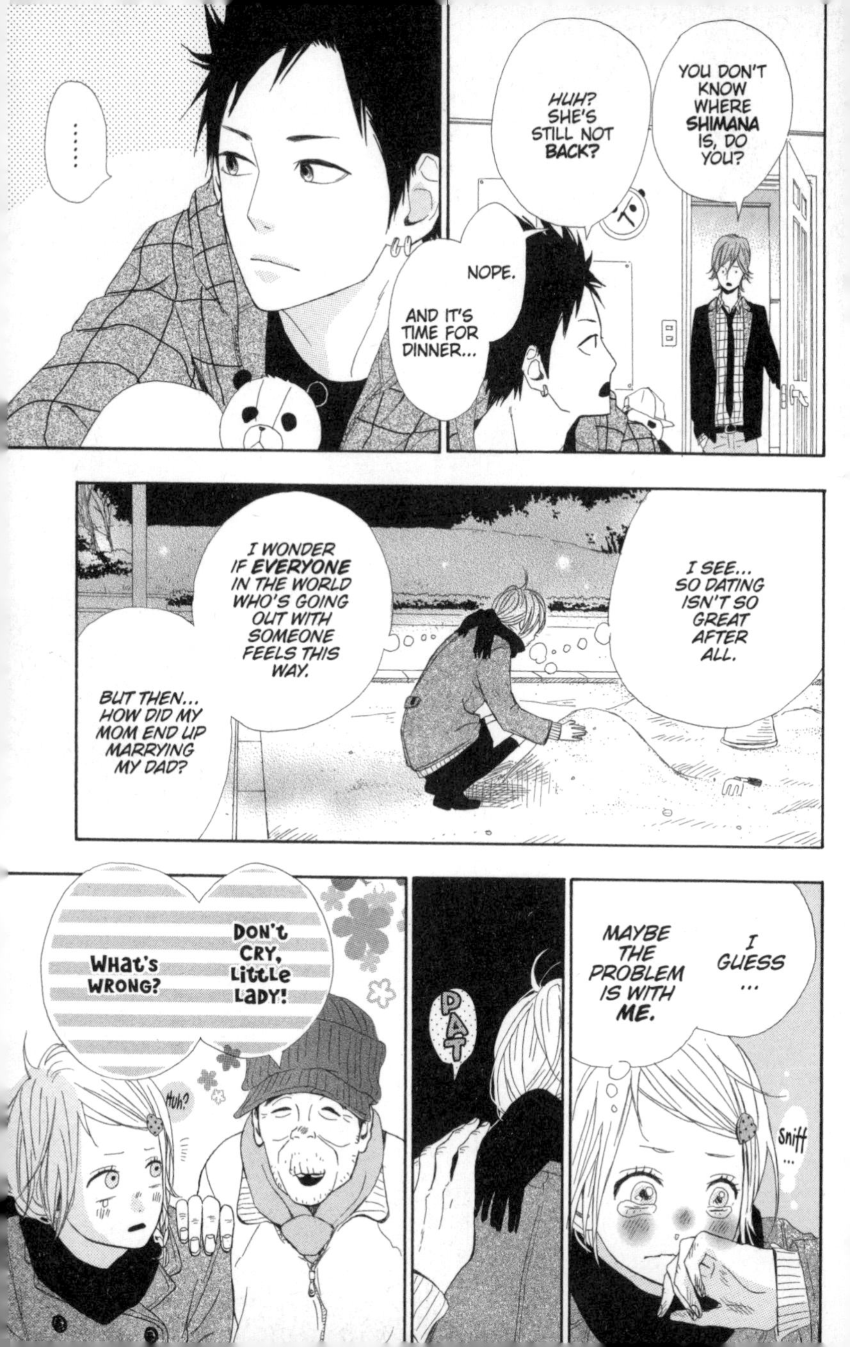
YOU DON'T KNOW WHERE SHIMANA IS, DO YOU?
HUH? SHE'S STILL NOT BACK?
NOPE.
AND IT'S TIME FOR DINNER...
......
I SEE... SO DATING ISN'T SO GREAT AFTER ALL.
I WONDER IF EVERYONE IN THE WORLD WHO'S GOING OUT WITH SOMEONE FEELS THIS WAY.
BUT THEN... HOW DID MY MOM END UP MARRYING MY DAD?
I GUESS...
MAYBE THE PROBLEM IS WITH ME.
Sniff...
PAT
Don't cry, little lady!
What's wrong?
Huh?

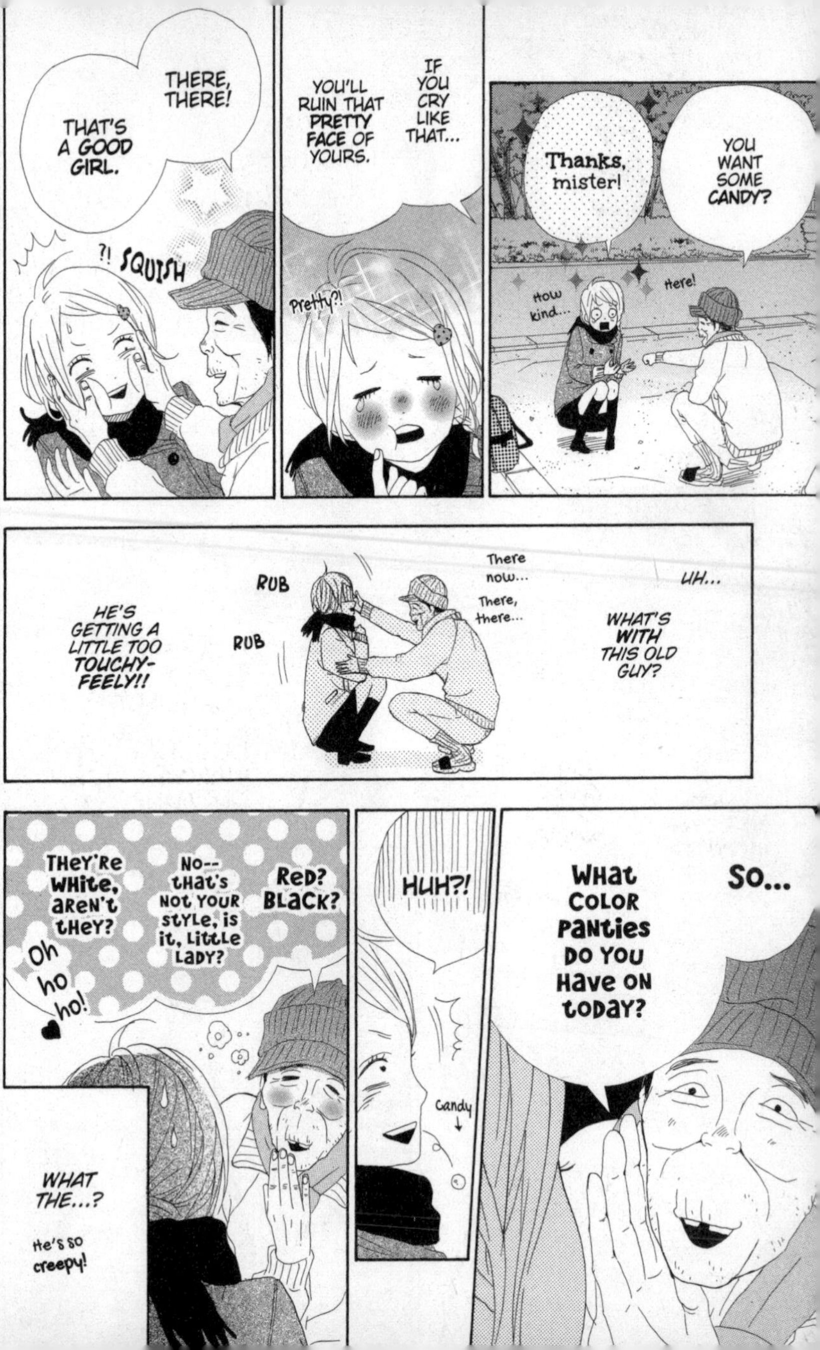
YOU WANT SOME CANDY?
Thanks, mister!
Here!
How kind...
IF YOU CRY LIKE THAT...
YOU'LL RUIN THAT PRETTY FACE OF YOURS.
Pretty?!
THERE, THERE!
THAT'S A GOOD GIRL.
?!
SQUISH
UH...
WHAT'S WITH THIS OLD GUY?
There now...
There, there...
RUB
RUB
HE'S GETTING A LITTLE TOO TOUCHY-FEELY!!
SO...
WHAT COLOR PANTIES DO YOU HAVE ON TODAY?
HUH?!
Candy
Red? Black?
No--that's not your style, is it, little lady?
They're white, aren't they?
Oh ho ho!
WHAT THE...?
He's so creepy!

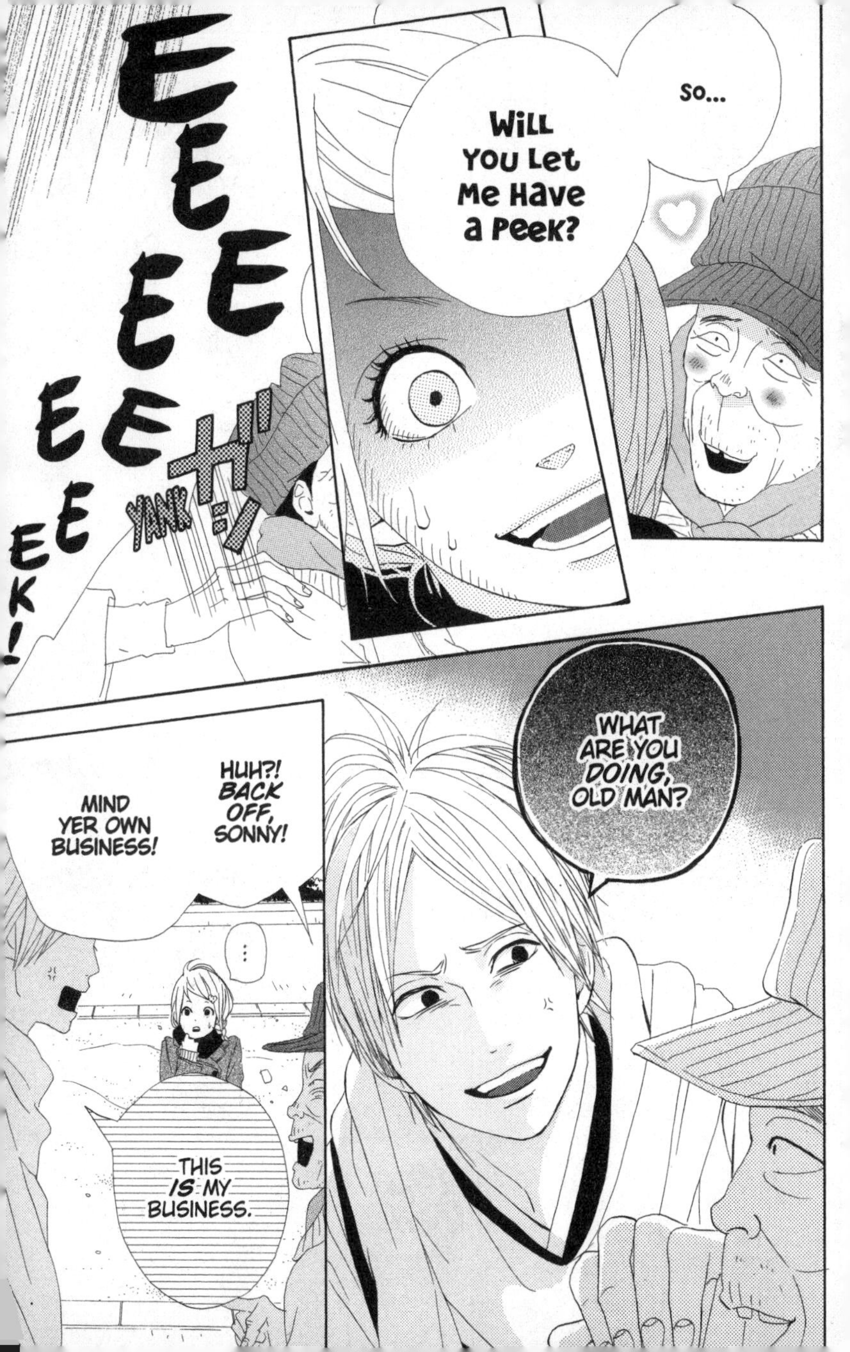

SO...
WILL YOU LET ME HAVE A PEEK?
EEEEEEEEK!
YANK
WHAT ARE YOU DOING, OLD MAN?
HUH?! BACK OFF, SONNY!
MIND YER OWN BUSINESS!
...
THIS IS MY BUSINESS.

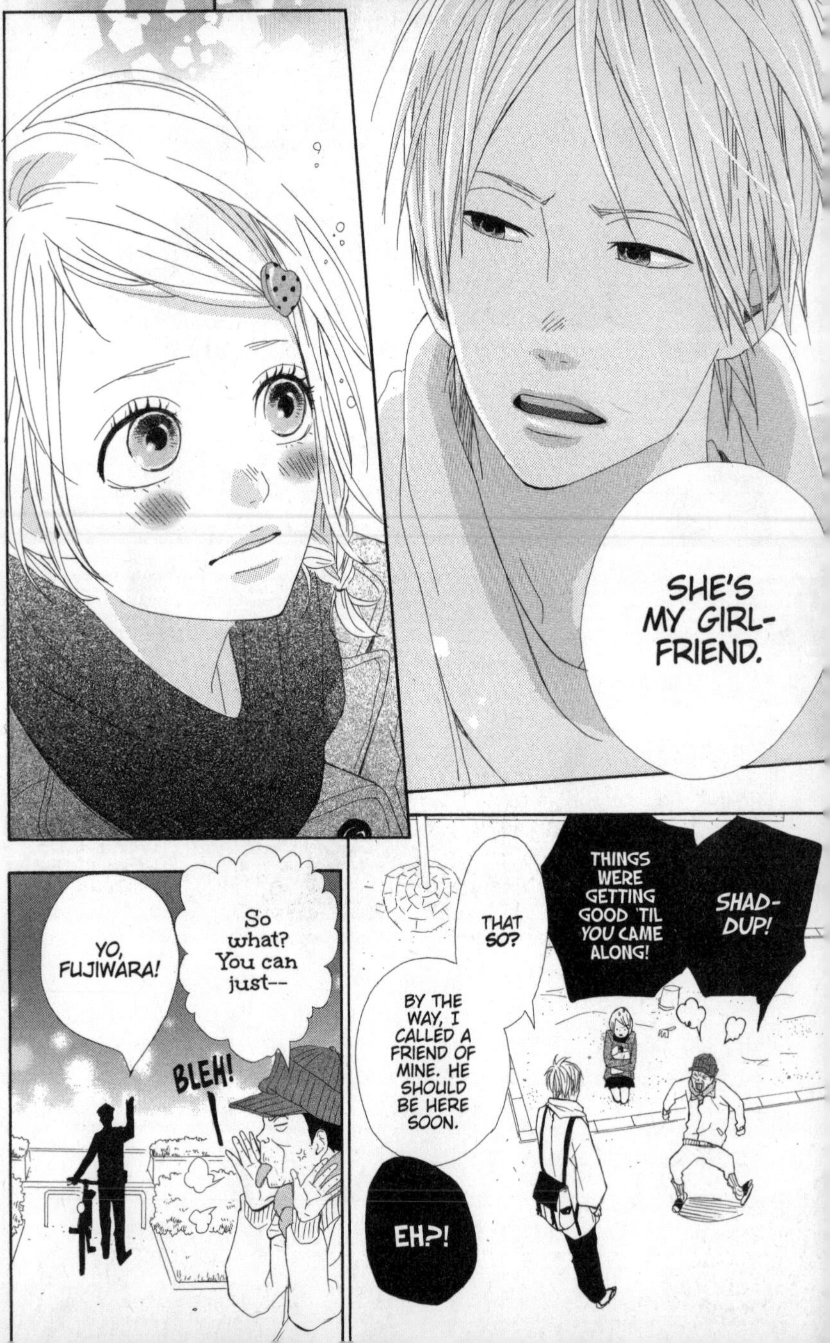
SHE'S MY GIRL-FRIEND.
SHAD-DUP!
THINGS WERE GETTING GOOD 'TIL YOU CAME ALONG!
THAT SO?
BY THE WAY, I CALLED A FRIEND OF MINE. HE SHOULD BE HERE SOON.
EH?!
So what? You can just--
YO, FUJIWARA!
BLEH!

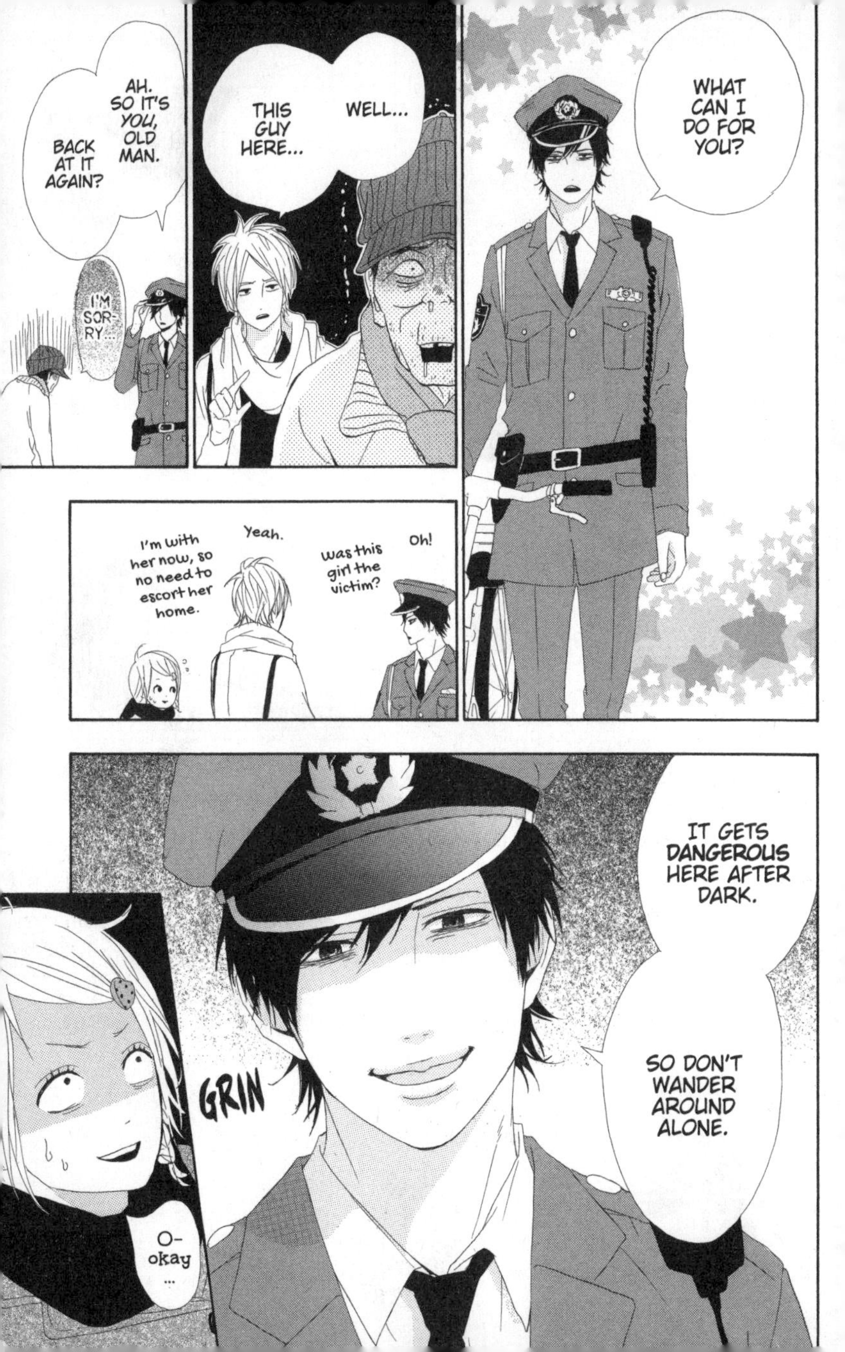
WHAT CAN I DO FOR YOU?
WELL...
THIS GUY HERE...
AH. SO IT'S YOU, OLD MAN.
BACK AT IT AGAIN?
I'M SOR-RY...
Oh!
Was this girl the victim?
Yeah.
I'm with her now, so no need to escort her home.
IT GETS DANGEROUS HERE AFTER DARK.
SO DON'T WANDER AROUND ALONE.
GRIN
O-okay...

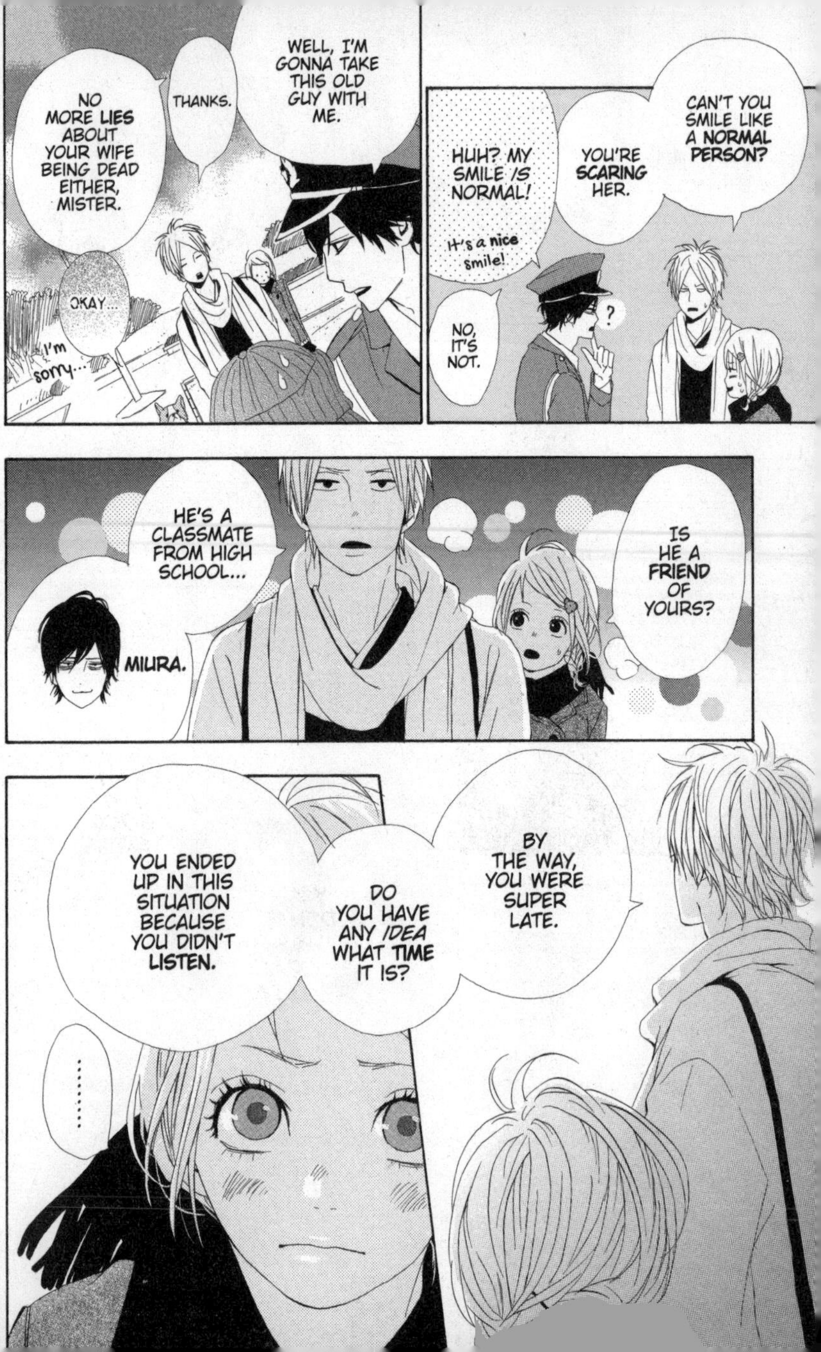
CAN'T YOU SMILE LIKE A NORMAL PERSON?
YOU'RE SCARING HER.
HUH? MY SMILE IS NORMAL!
It's a nice smile!
NO, IT'S NOT.
?
WELL, I'M GONNA TAKE THIS OLD GUY WITH ME.
THANKS.
NO MORE LIES ABOUT YOUR WIFE BEING DEAD EITHER, MISTER.
OKAY...
I'm sorry...
IS HE A FRIEND OF YOURS?
HE'S A CLASSMATE FROM HIGH SCHOOL...
MIURA.
BY THE WAY, YOU WERE SUPER LATE.
DO YOU HAVE ANY IDEA WHAT TIME IT IS?
YOU ENDED UP IN THIS SITUATION BECAUSE YOU DIDN'T LISTEN.
......

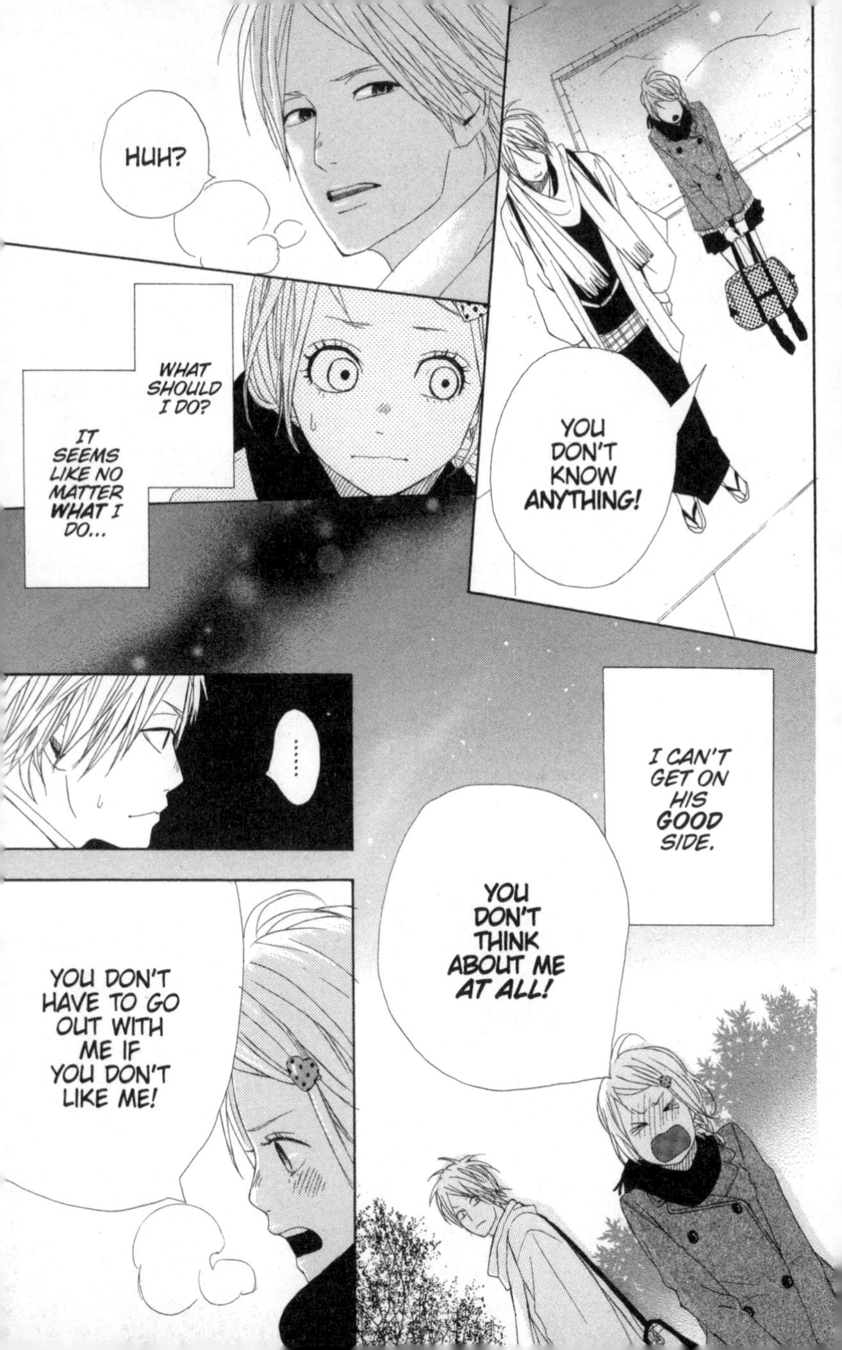
YOU DON'T KNOW ANYTHING!
HUH?
WHAT SHOULD I DO?
IT SEEMS LIKE NO MATTER WHAT I DO...
I CAN'T GET ON HIS GOOD SIDE.
YOU DON'T THINK ABOUT ME AT ALL!
......
YOU DON'T HAVE TO GO OUT WITH ME IF YOU DON'T LIKE ME!

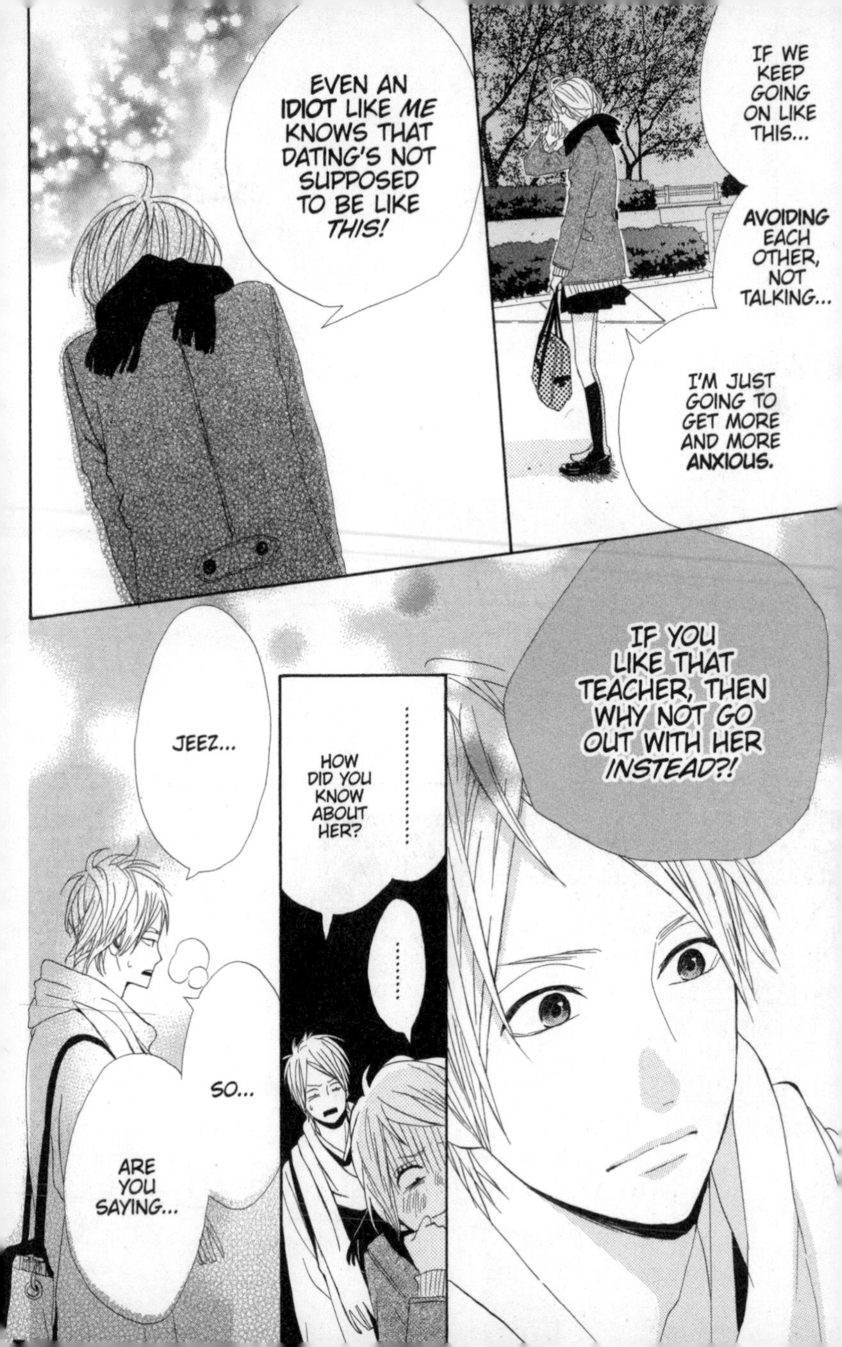
IF WE KEEP GOING ON LIKE THIS...
AVOIDING EACH OTHER, NOT TALKING...
I'M JUST GOING TO GET MORE AND MORE ANXIOUS.
EVEN AN IDIOT LIKE *ME* KNOWS THAT DATING'S NOT SUPPOSED TO BE LIKE *THIS!*
IF YOU LIKE THAT TEACHER, THEN WHY NOT GO OUT WITH HER *INSTEAD?!*
......
HOW DID YOU KNOW ABOUT HER?
......
JEEZ...
SO...
ARE YOU SAYING...

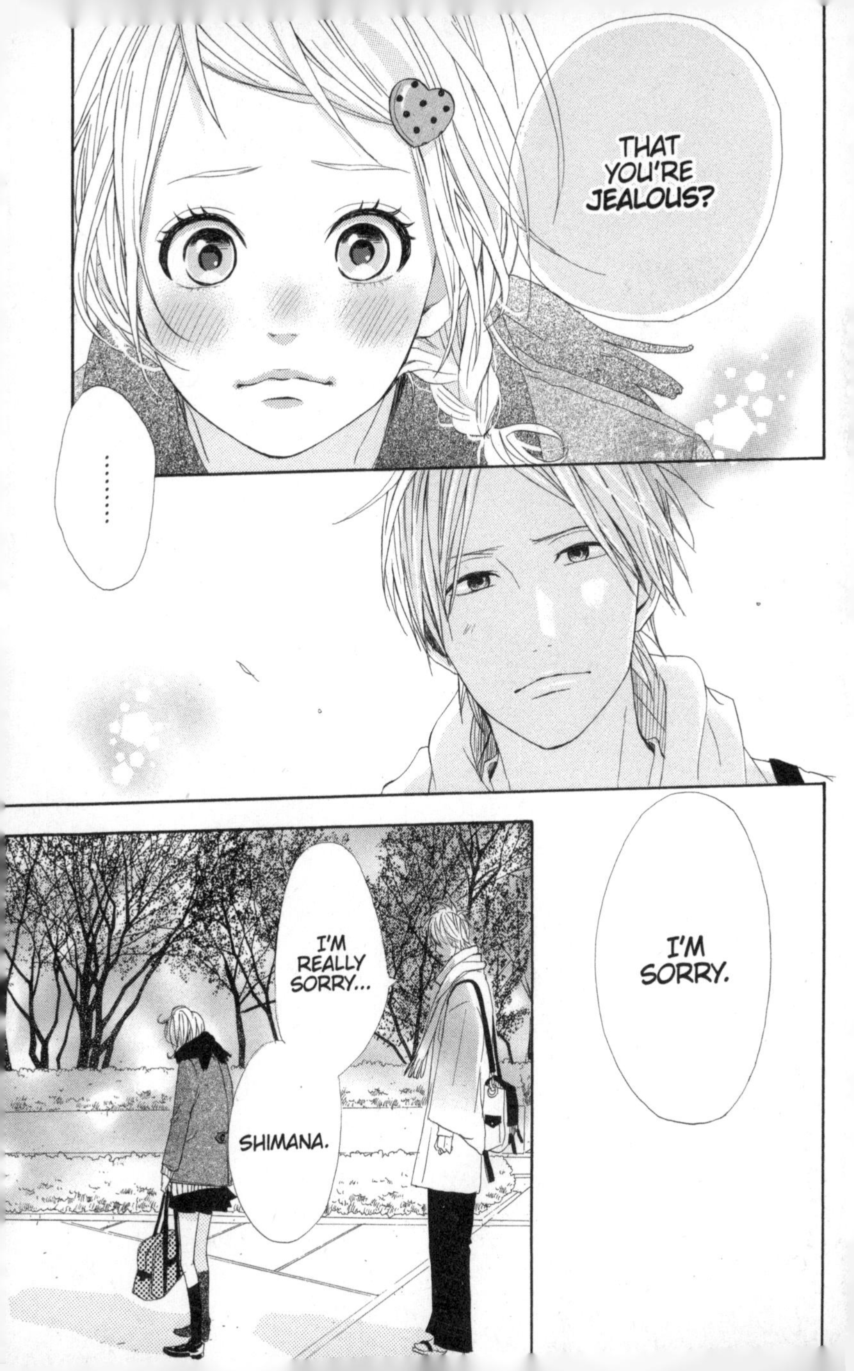
THAT YOU'RE JEALOUS?
......
I'M SORRY.
I'M REALLY SORRY...
SHIMANA.

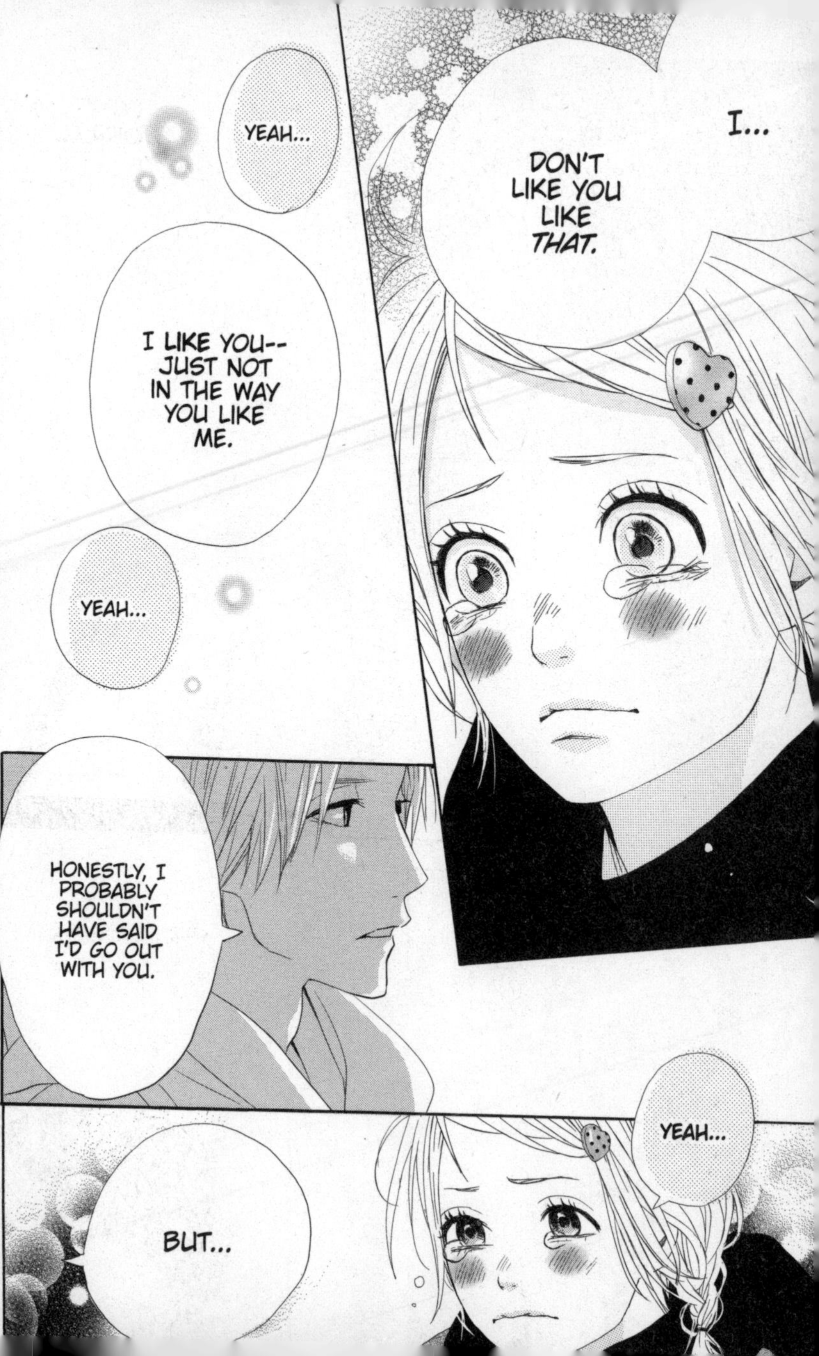
I...
DON'T LIKE YOU LIKE *THAT.*
YEAH...
I LIKE YOU-- JUST NOT IN THE WAY YOU LIKE ME.
YEAH...
HONESTLY, I PROBABLY SHOULDN'T HAVE SAID I'D GO OUT WITH YOU.
YEAH...
BUT...

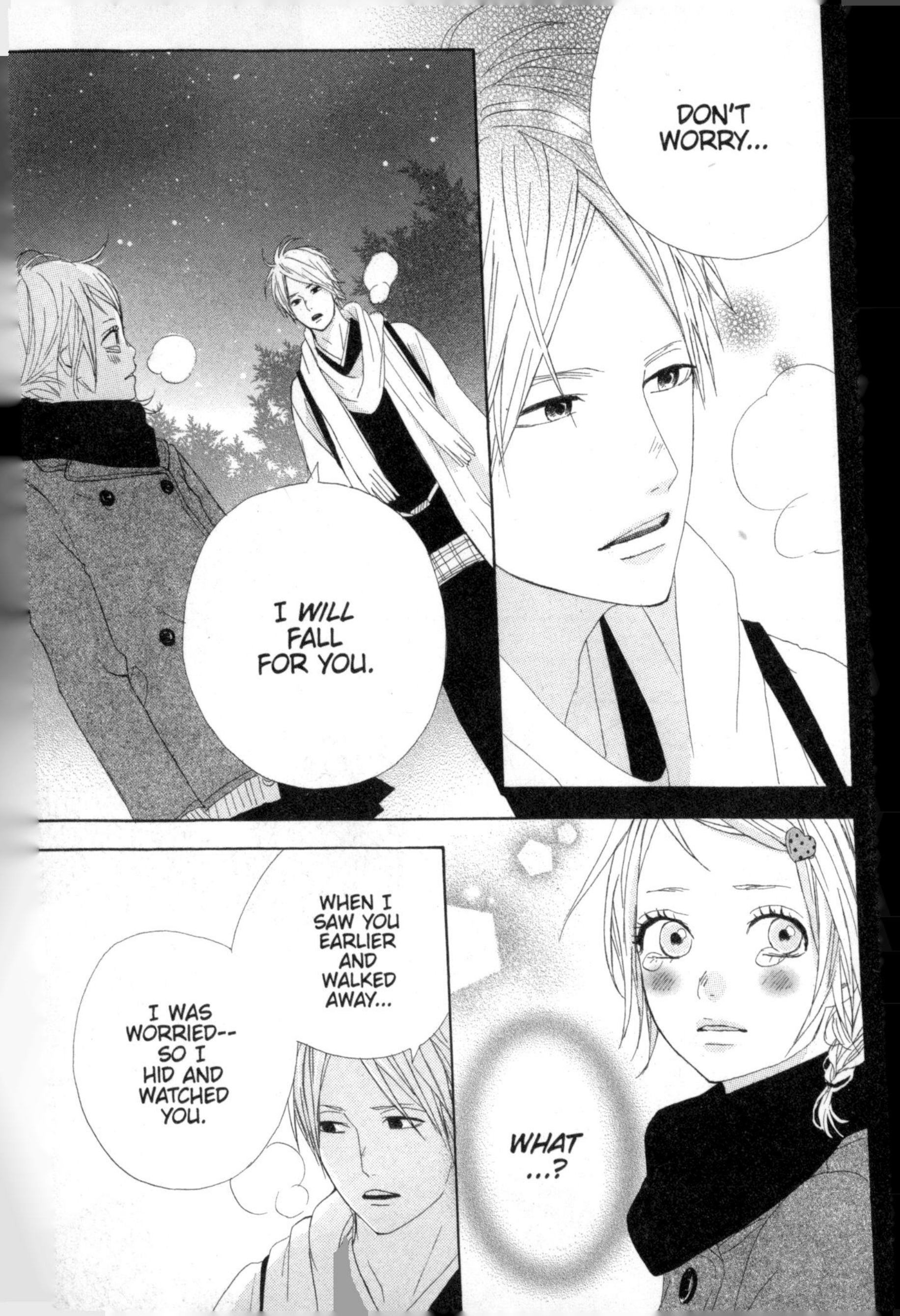
DON'T WORRY...
I *WILL* FALL FOR YOU.
WHAT ...?
WHEN I SAW YOU EARLIER AND WALKED AWAY...
I WAS WORRIED-- SO I HID AND WATCHED YOU.

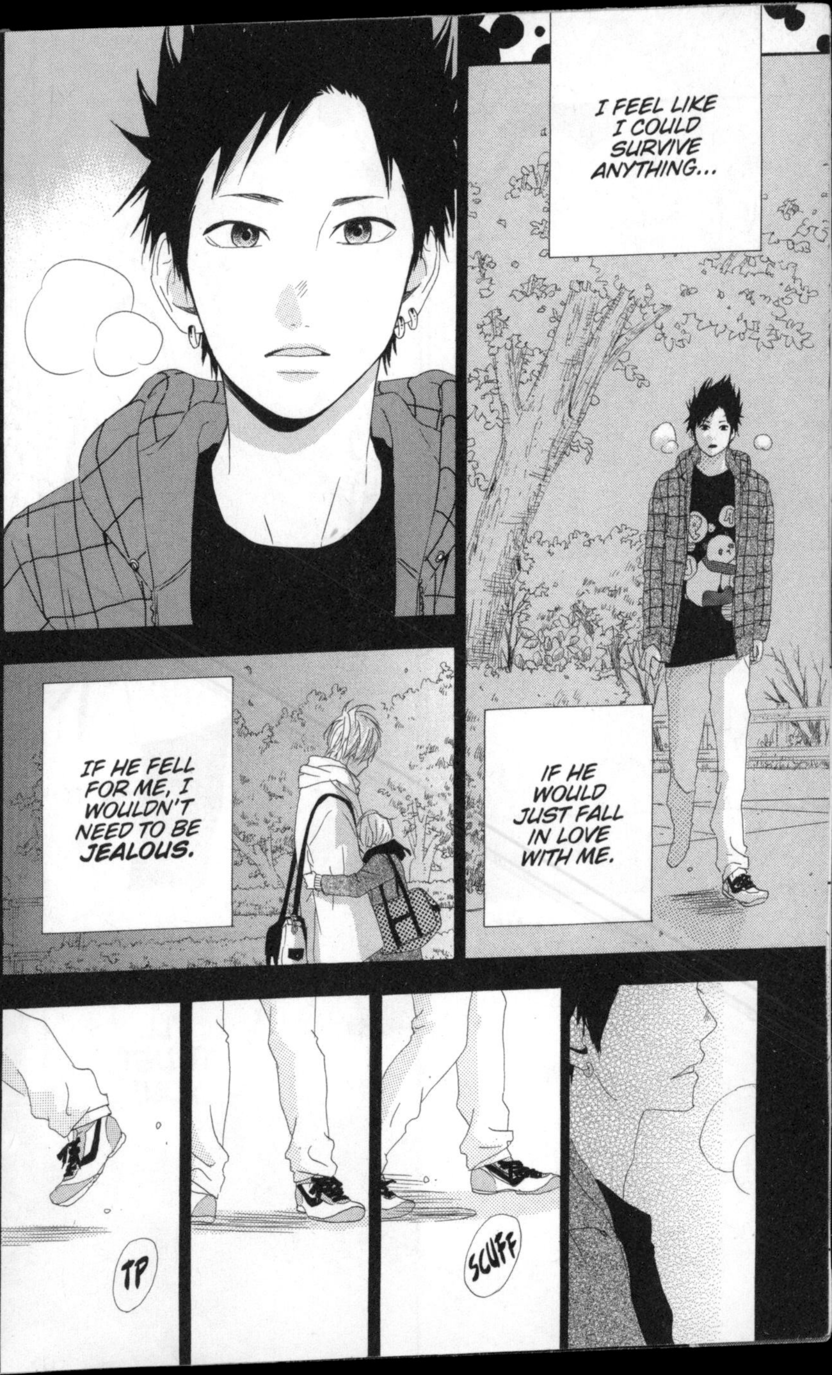
I FEEL LIKE I COULD SURVIVE ANYTHING...
IF HE WOULD JUST FALL IN LOVE WITH ME.
IF HE FELL FOR ME, I WOULDN'T NEED TO BE JEALOUS.
SCUFF
TP

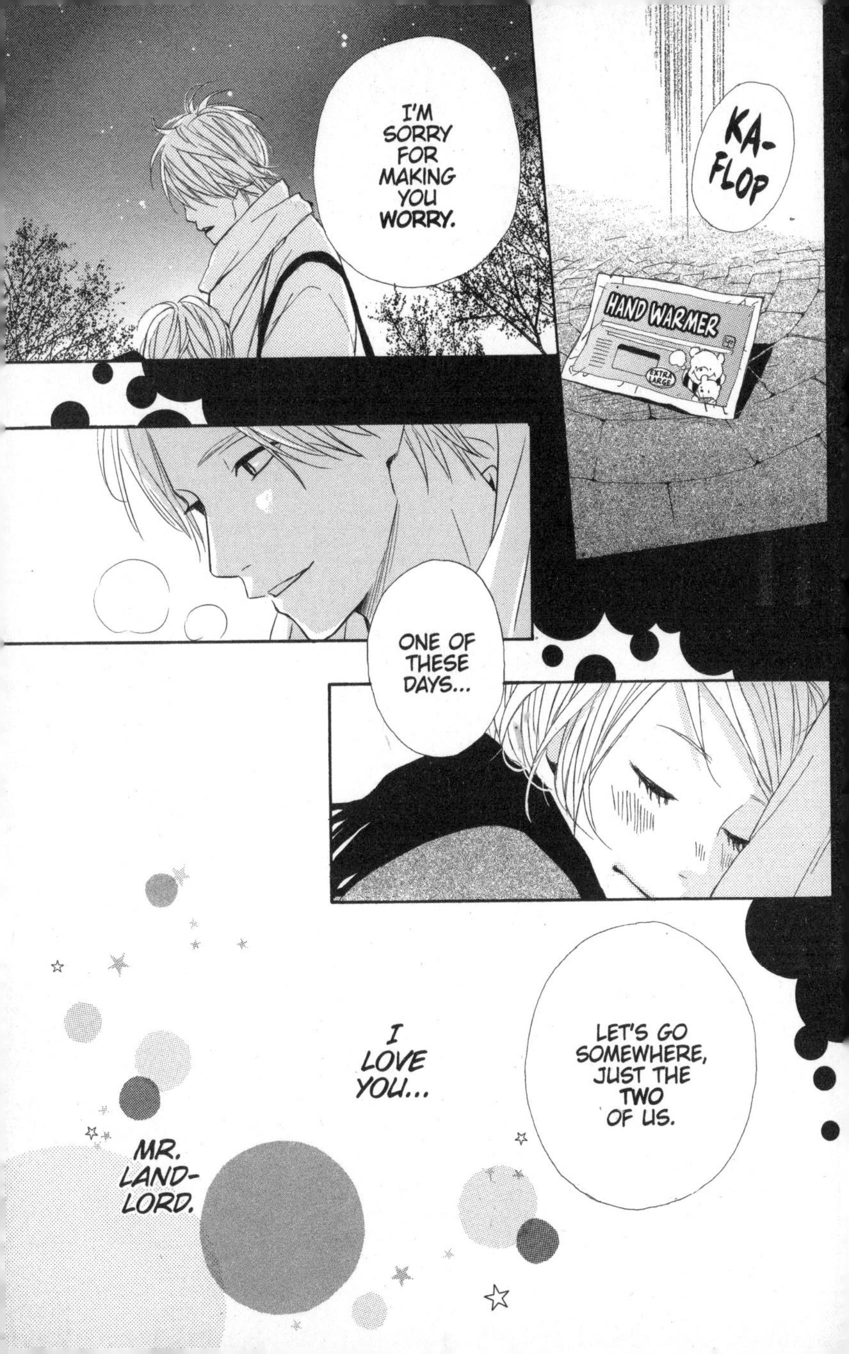
KA-FLOP
HAND WARMER
EXTRA LARGE
I'M SORRY FOR MAKING YOU WORRY.
ONE OF THESE DAYS...
LET'S GO SOMEWHERE, JUST THE TWO OF US.
I LOVE YOU...
MR. LANDLORD.

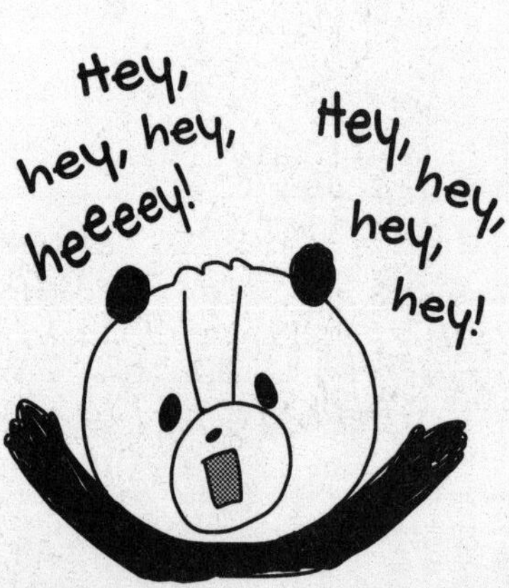
Hey, hey, hey, heeeey!
Hey, hey, hey, hey!

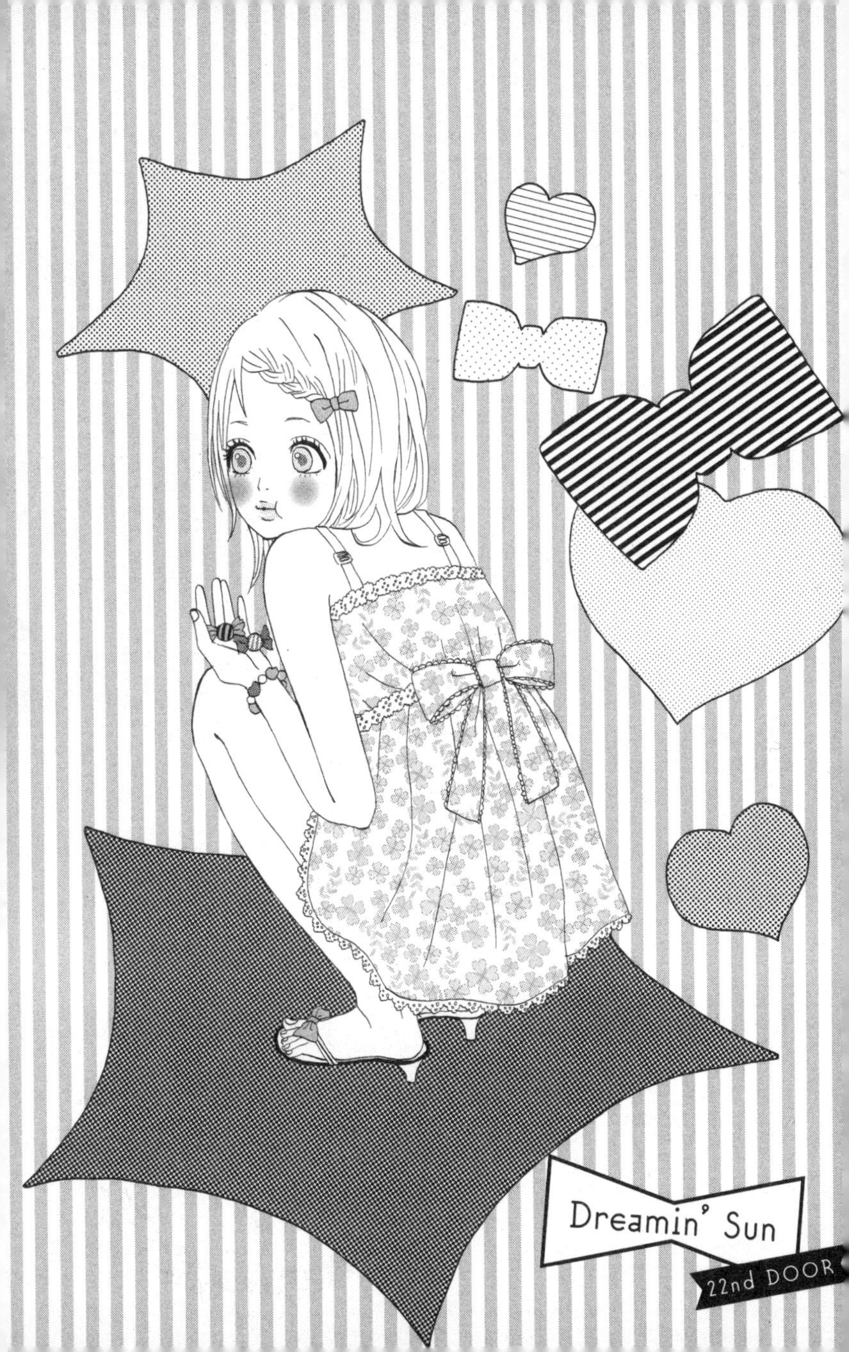
Dreamin' Sun
22nd DOOR

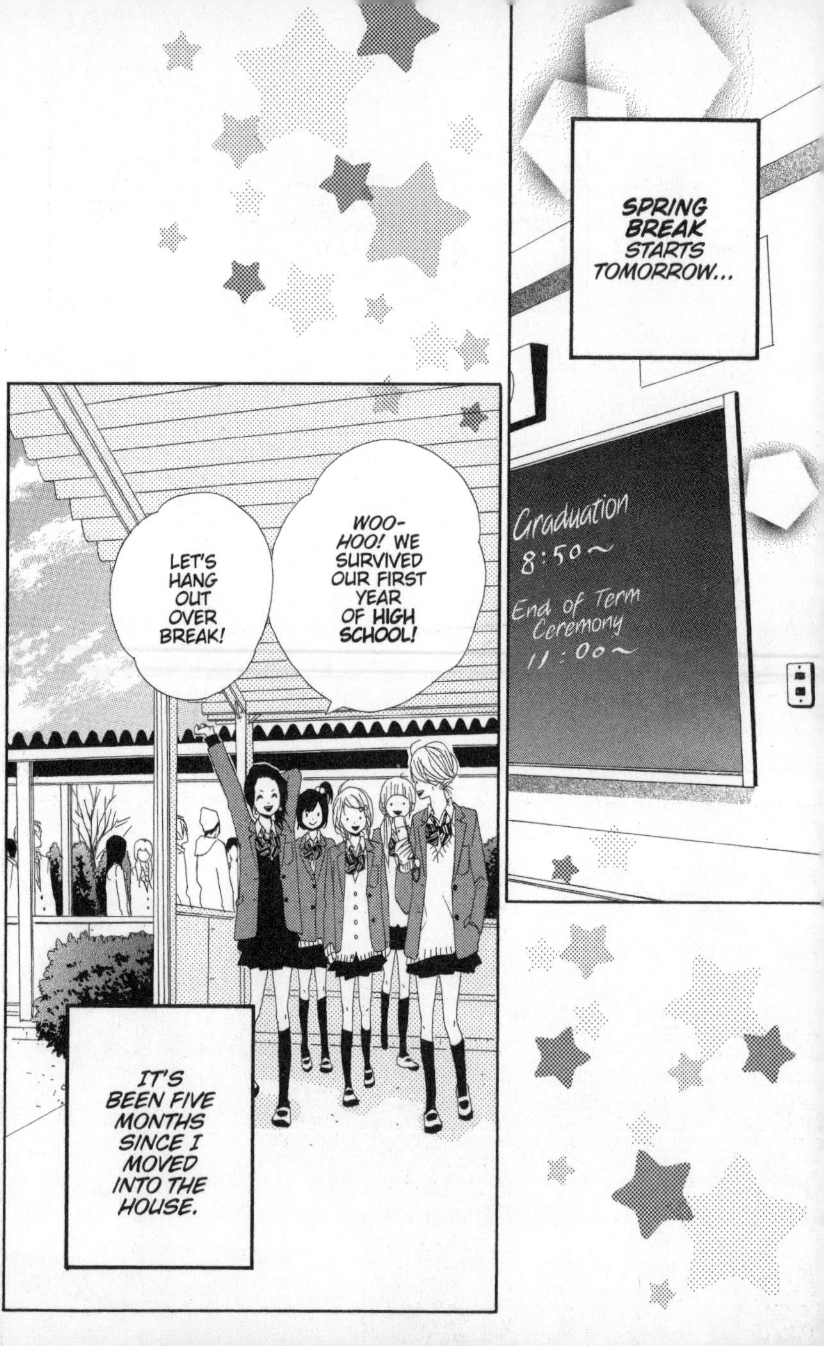
SPRING BREAK STARTS TOMORROW...
Graduation 8:50~
End of Term Ceremony 11:00~
WOO-HOO! WE SURVIVED OUR FIRST YEAR OF HIGH SCHOOL!
LET'S HANG OUT OVER BREAK!
IT'S BEEN FIVE MONTHS SINCE I MOVED INTO THE HOUSE.

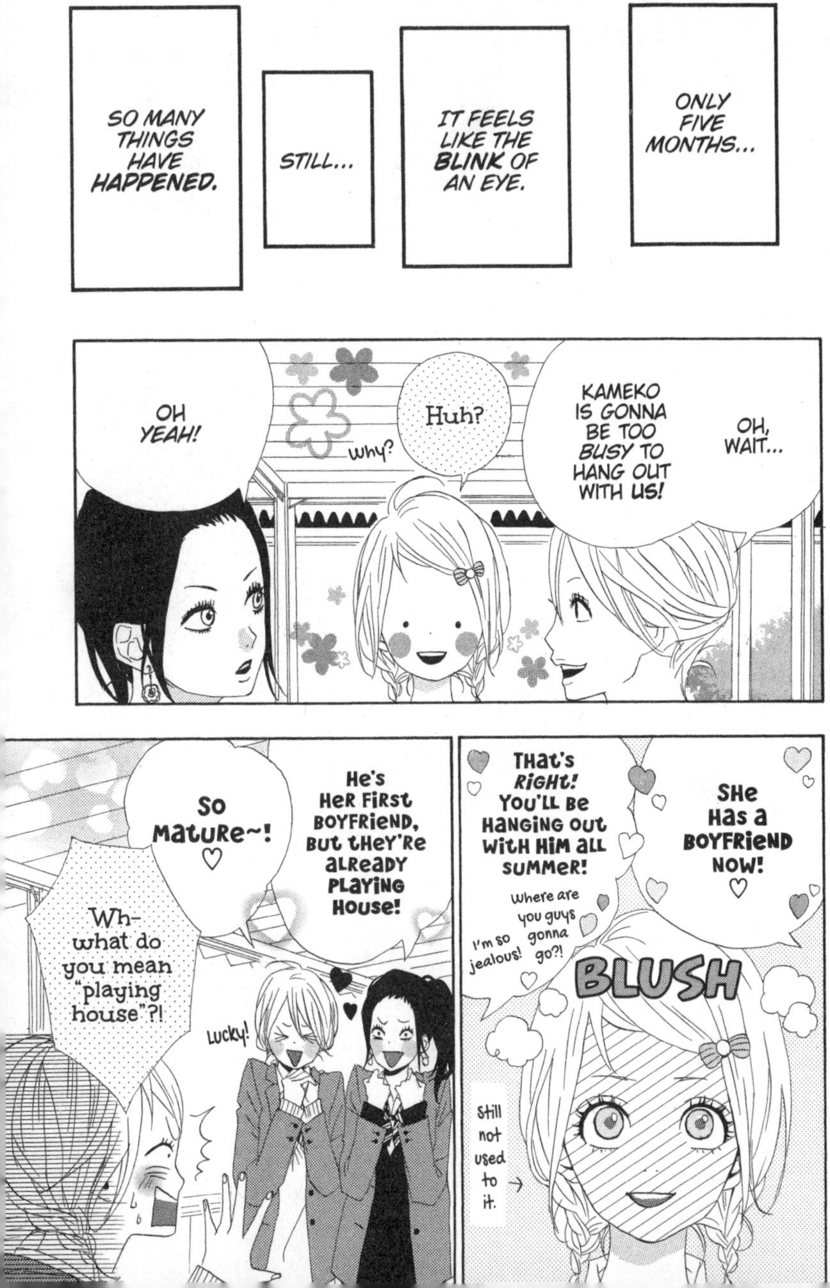
ONLY FIVE MONTHS...
IT FEELS LIKE THE BLINK OF AN EYE.
STILL...
SO MANY THINGS HAVE HAPPENED.
OH, WAIT...
KAMEKO IS GONNA BE TOO BUSY TO HANG OUT WITH US!
Huh?
why?
OH YEAH!
SHE HAS A BOYFRIEND NOW! ♡
THAT'S RIGHT! YOU'LL BE HANGING OUT WITH HIM ALL SUMMER!
Where are you guys gonna go?!
I'm so jealous!
BLUSH
Still not used to it. →
HE'S HER FIRST BOYFRIEND, BUT THEY'RE ALREADY PLAYING HOUSE!
SO MATURE~! ♡
Wh- what do you mean "playing house"?!
LUCKY!

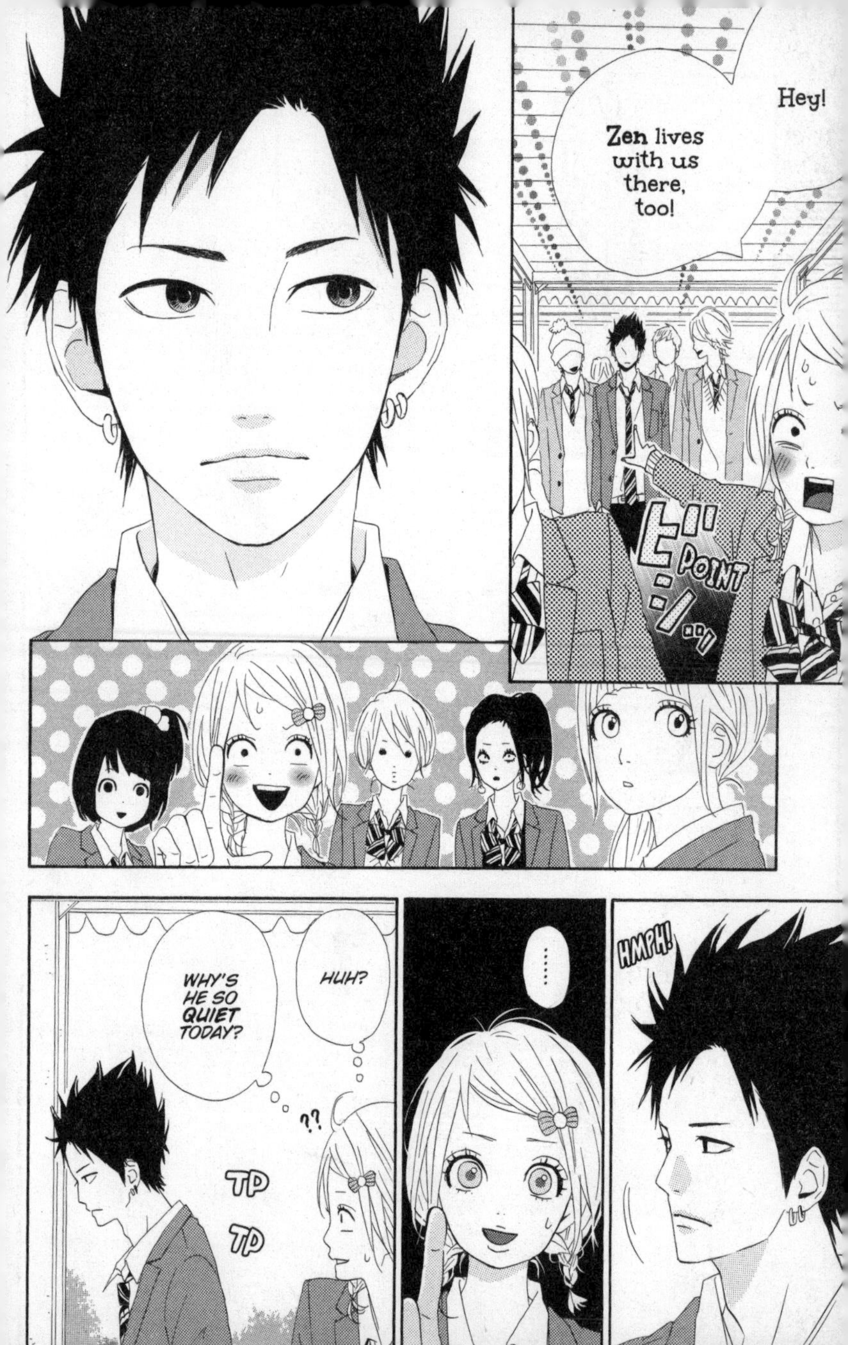
Hey!
Zen lives with us there, too!
POINT
HMPH!
......
HUH?
WHY'S HE SO QUIET TODAY?
??
TP
TP

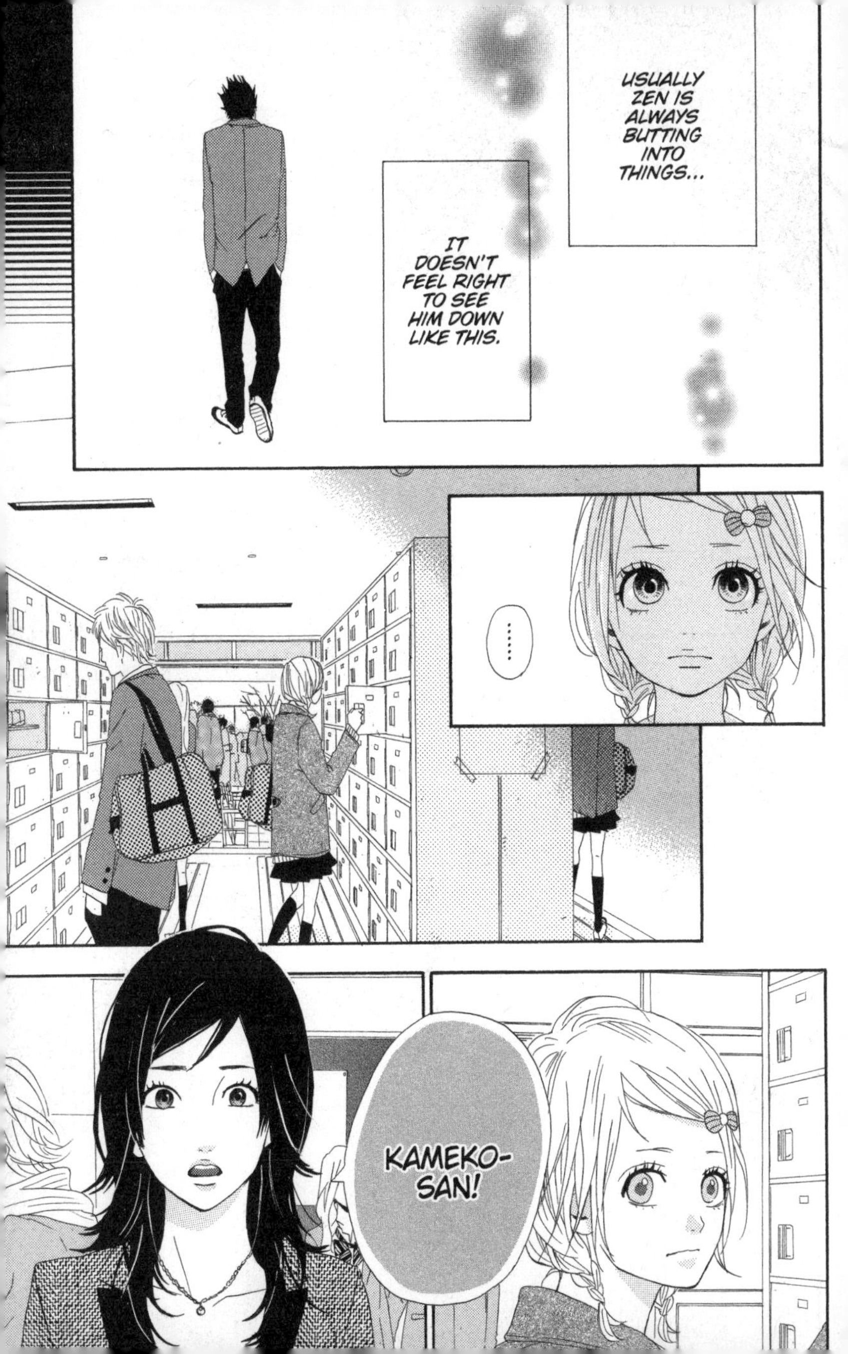
USUALLY ZEN IS ALWAYS BUTTING INTO THINGS...
IT DOESN'T FEEL RIGHT TO SEE HIM DOWN LIKE THIS.
......
KAMEKO-SAN!

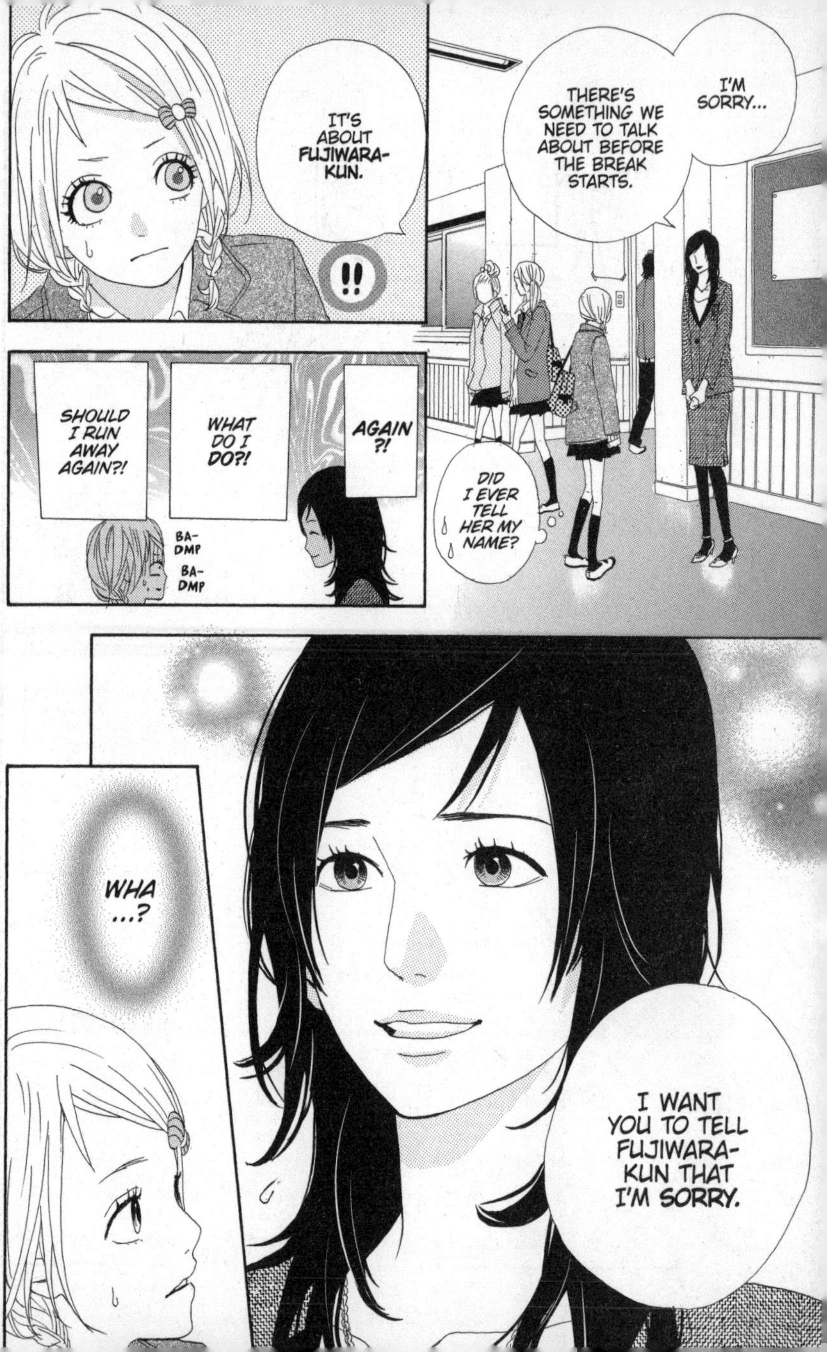
I'M SORRY...
THERE'S SOMETHING WE NEED TO TALK ABOUT BEFORE THE BREAK STARTS.
DID I EVER TELL HER MY NAME?
IT'S ABOUT FUJIWARA-KUN.
!!
AGAIN?!
WHAT DO I DO?!
SHOULD I RUN AWAY AGAIN?!
BA-DMP BA-DMP
I WANT YOU TO TELL FUJIWARA-KUN THAT I'M SORRY.
WHA...?

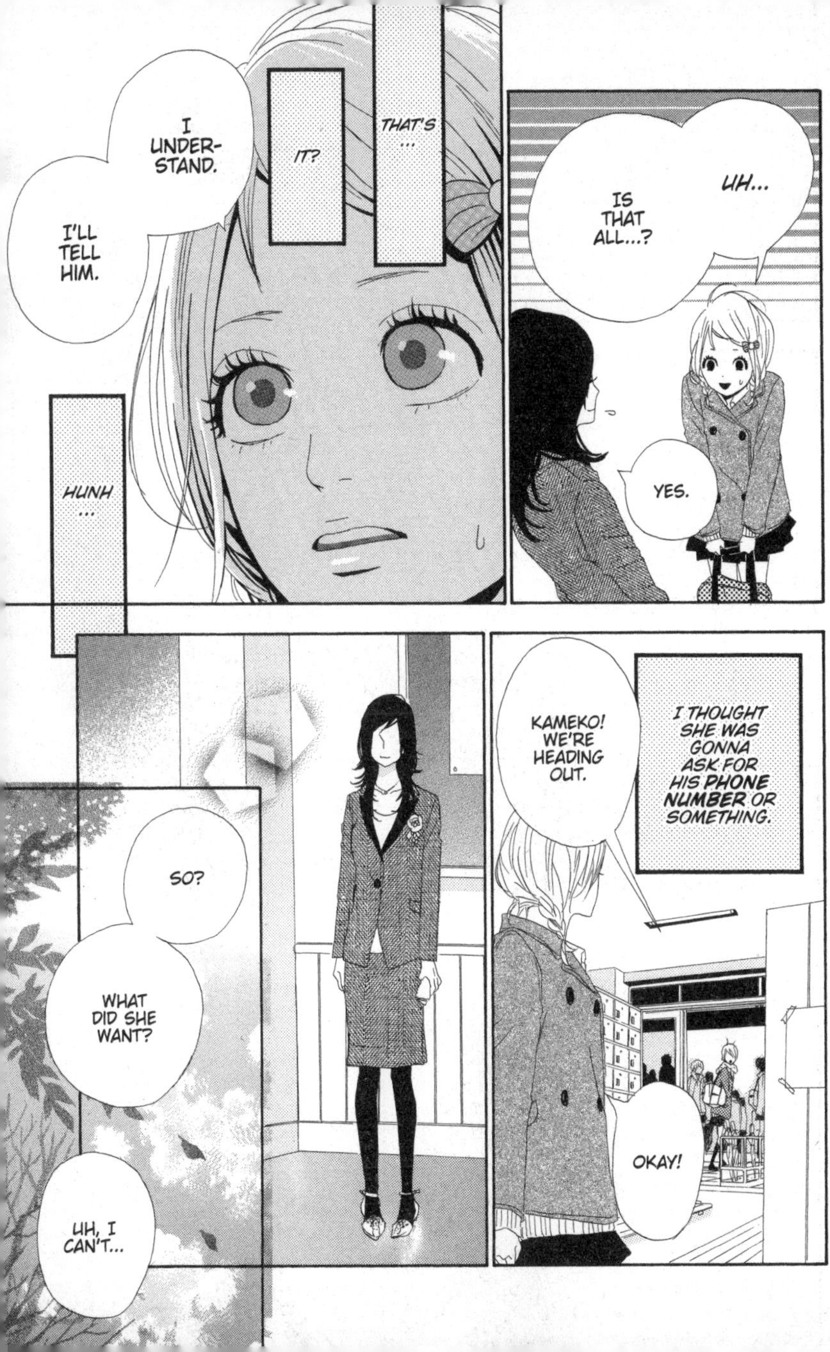
UH...
IS THAT ALL...?
YES.
THAT'S...
IT?
I UNDERSTAND.
I'LL TELL HIM.
HUNH...
I THOUGHT SHE WAS GONNA ASK FOR HIS **PHONE NUMBER** OR SOMETHING.
KAMEKO! WE'RE HEADING OUT.
OKAY!
SO?
WHAT DID SHE WANT?
UH, I CAN'T...

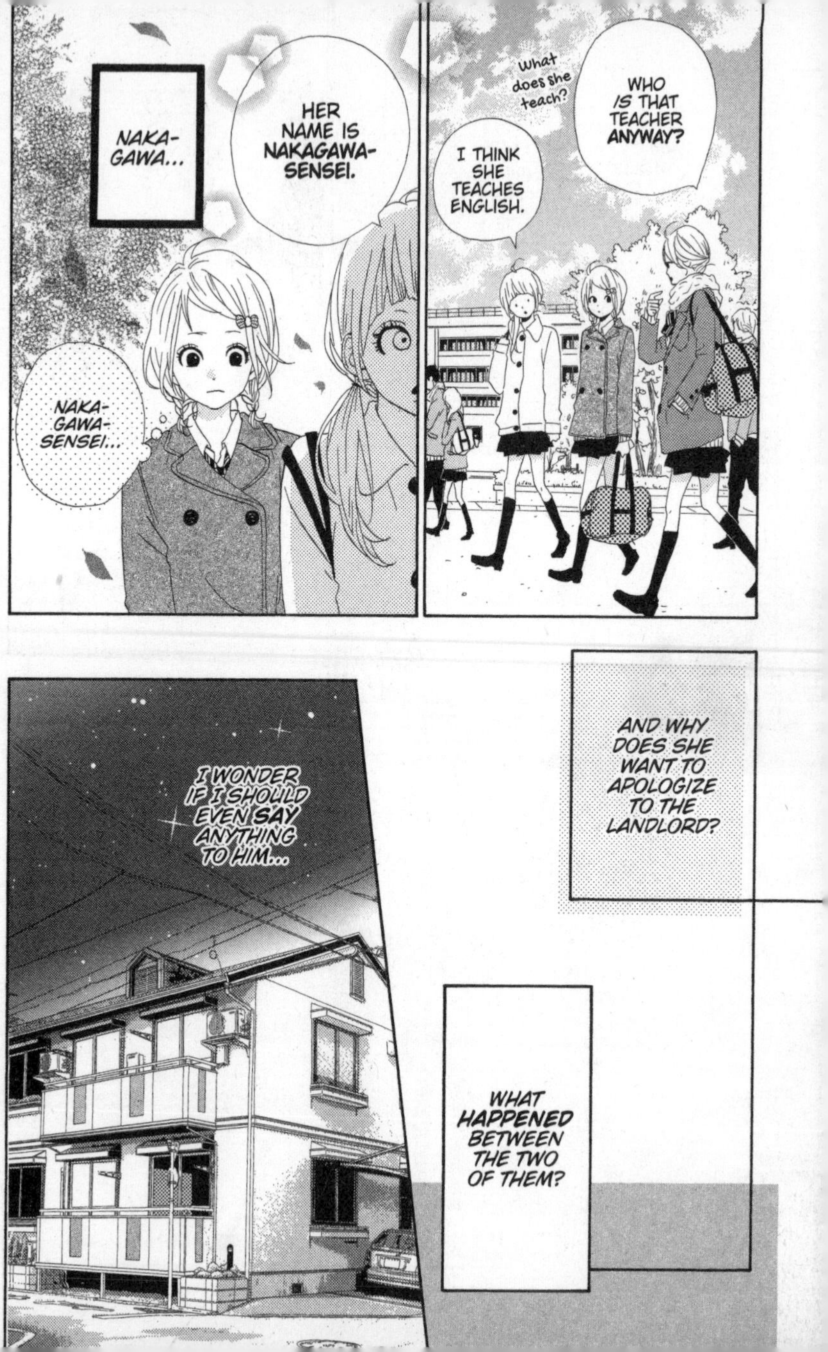
WHO IS THAT TEACHER ANYWAY?
What does she teach?
I THINK SHE TEACHES ENGLISH.
HER NAME IS NAKAGAWA-SENSEI.
NAKA-GAWA...
NAKA-GAWA-SENSEI...
AND WHY DOES SHE WANT TO APOLOGIZE TO THE LANDLORD?
WHAT HAPPENED BETWEEN THE TWO OF THEM?
I WONDER IF I SHOULD EVEN SAY ANYTHING TO HIM...

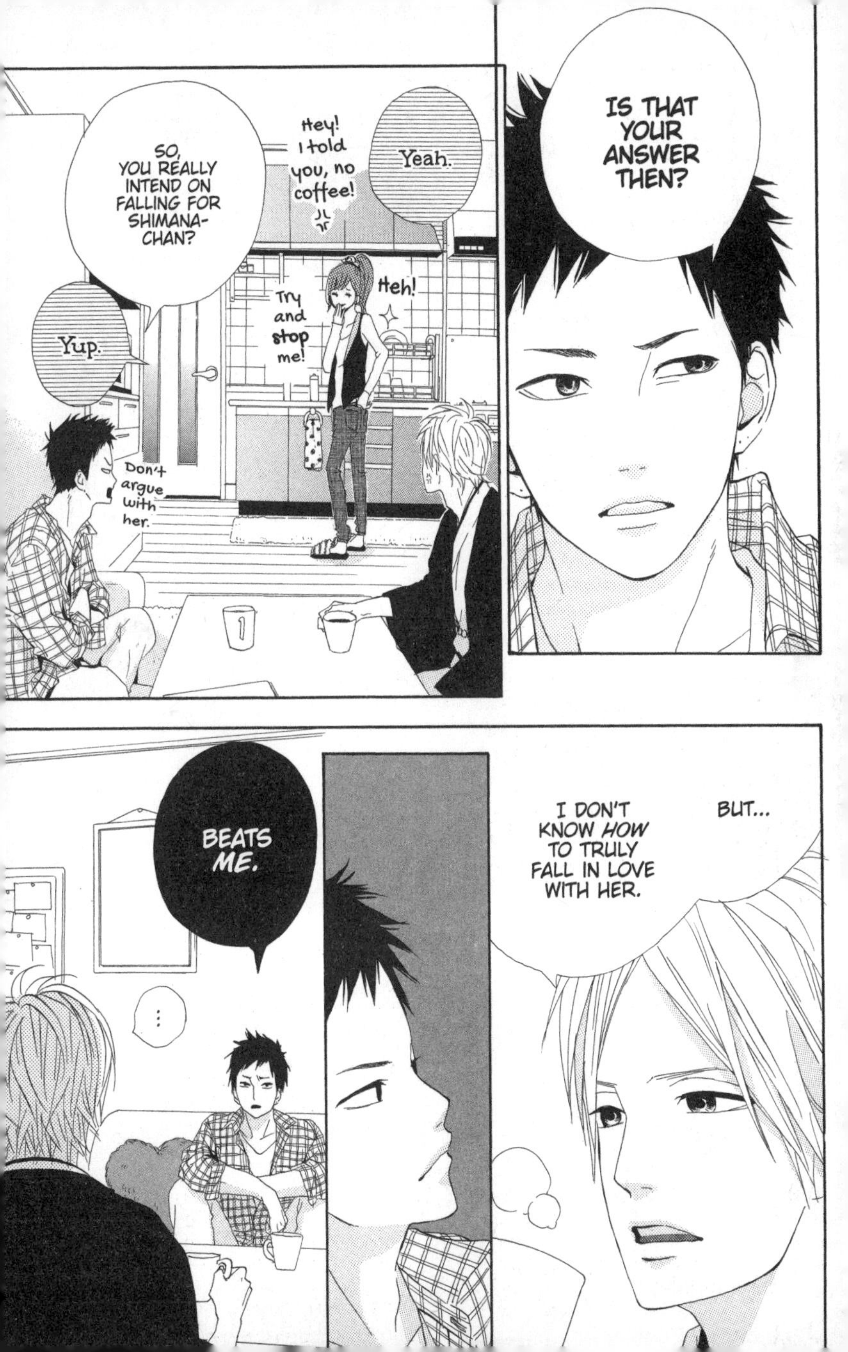
IS THAT YOUR ANSWER THEN?
Yeah.
Hey! I told you, no coffee!
SO, YOU REALLY INTEND ON FALLING FOR SHIMANA-CHAN?
Heh!
Try and stop me!
Yup.
Don't argue with her.
BUT...
I DON'T KNOW *HOW* TO TRULY FALL IN LOVE WITH HER.
BEATS *ME.*
...

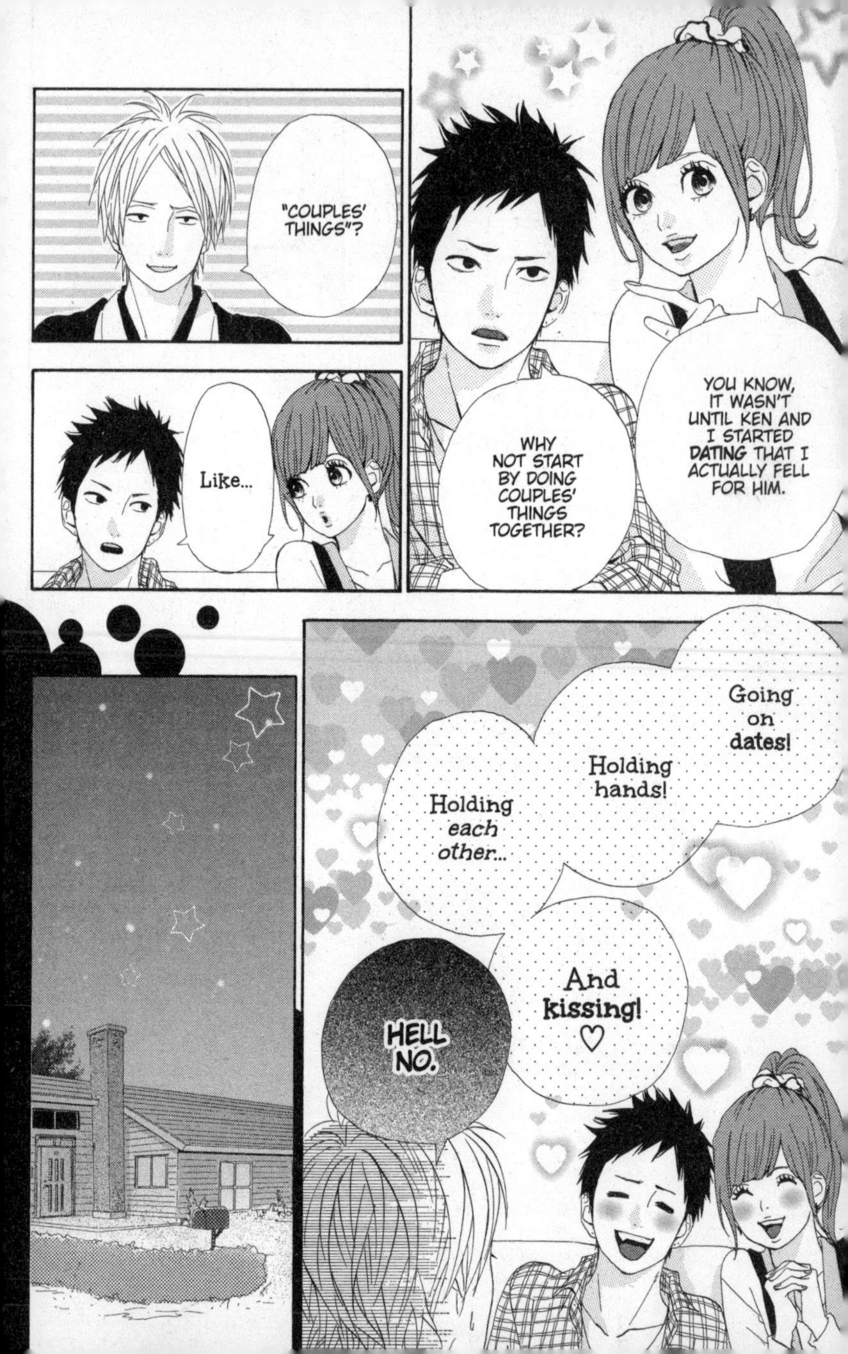
YOU KNOW, IT WASN'T UNTIL KEN AND I STARTED DATING THAT I ACTUALLY FELL FOR HIM.
WHY NOT START BY DOING COUPLES' THINGS TOGETHER?
"COUPLES' THINGS"?
Like...
Going on dates!
Holding hands!
Holding each other...
And kissing! ♡
HELL NO.

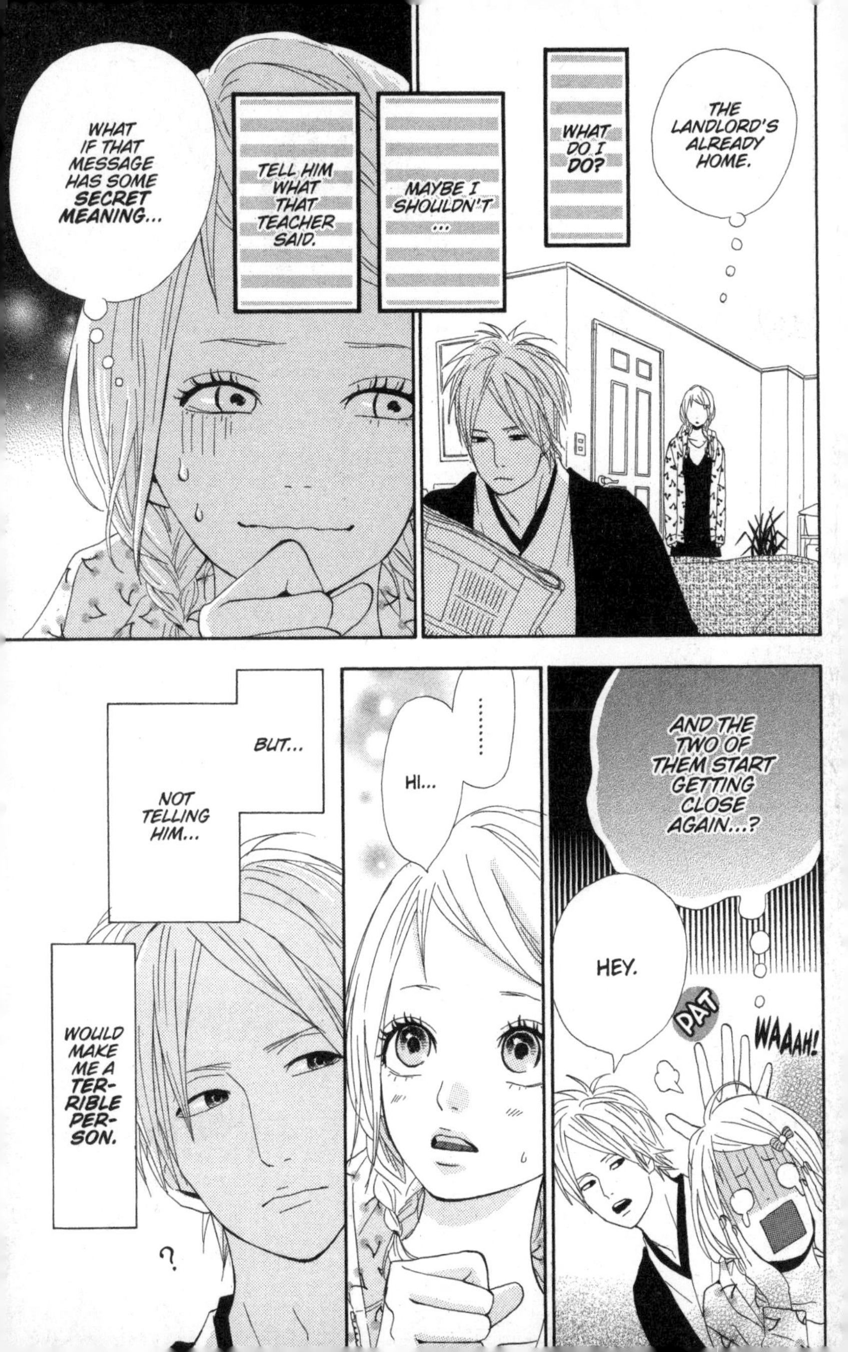
THE LANDLORD'S ALREADY HOME.
WHAT DO I DO?
MAYBE I SHOULDN'T ...
TELL HIM WHAT THAT TEACHER SAID.
WHAT IF THAT MESSAGE HAS SOME SECRET MEANING...
AND THE TWO OF THEM START GETTING CLOSE AGAIN...?
HEY.
PAT
WAAAH!
......
HI...
BUT...
NOT TELLING HIM...
WOULD MAKE ME A TER-RIBLE PER-SON.
?

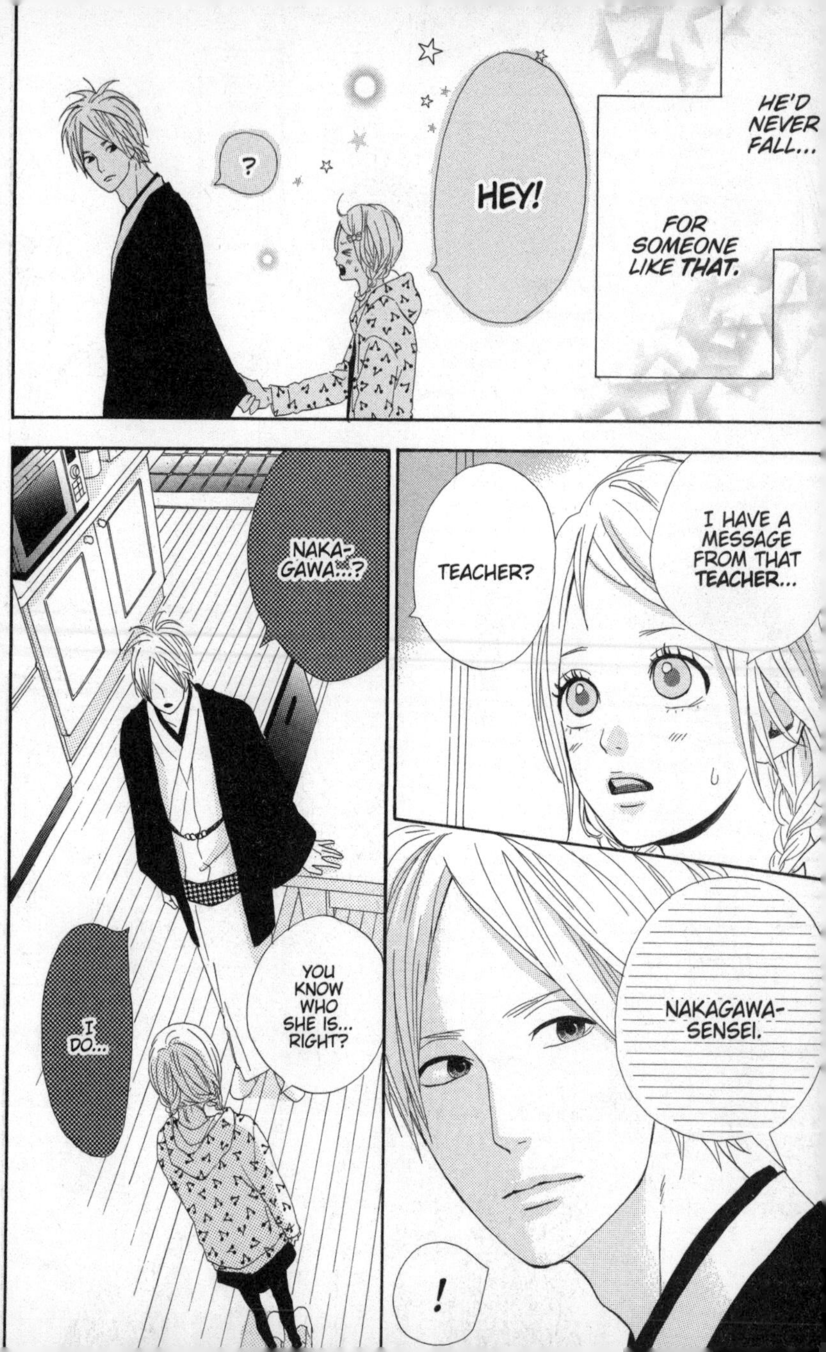
HE'D NEVER FALL...
FOR SOMEONE LIKE THAT.
HEY!
?
I HAVE A MESSAGE FROM THAT TEACHER...
TEACHER?
NAKAGAWA-SENSEI.
!
NAKA-GAWA...?
YOU KNOW WHO SHE IS... RIGHT?
I DO...

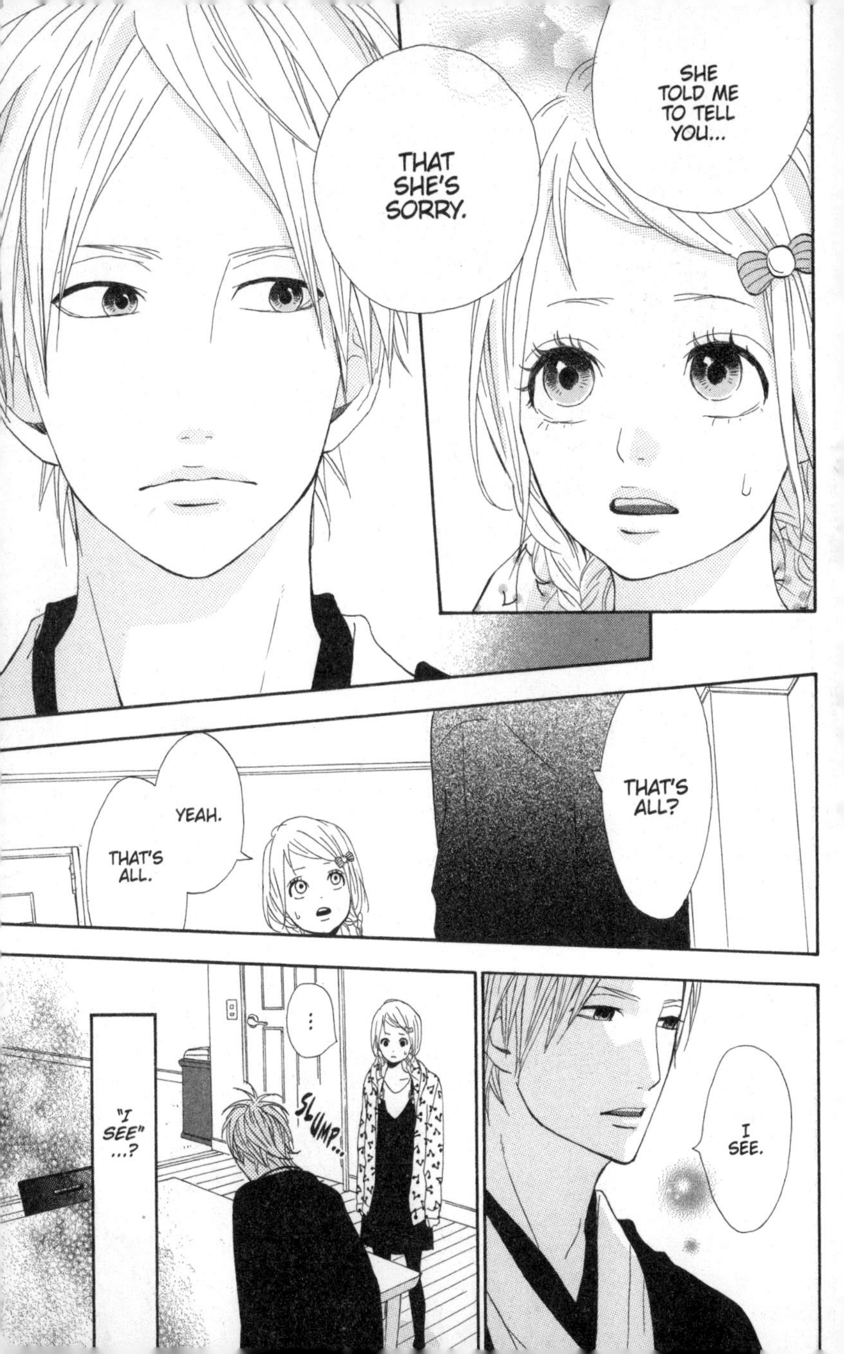
SHE TOLD ME TO TELL YOU...
THAT SHE'S SORRY.
THAT'S ALL?
YEAH.
THAT'S ALL.
I SEE.
...
SLUMP...
"I SEE" ...?

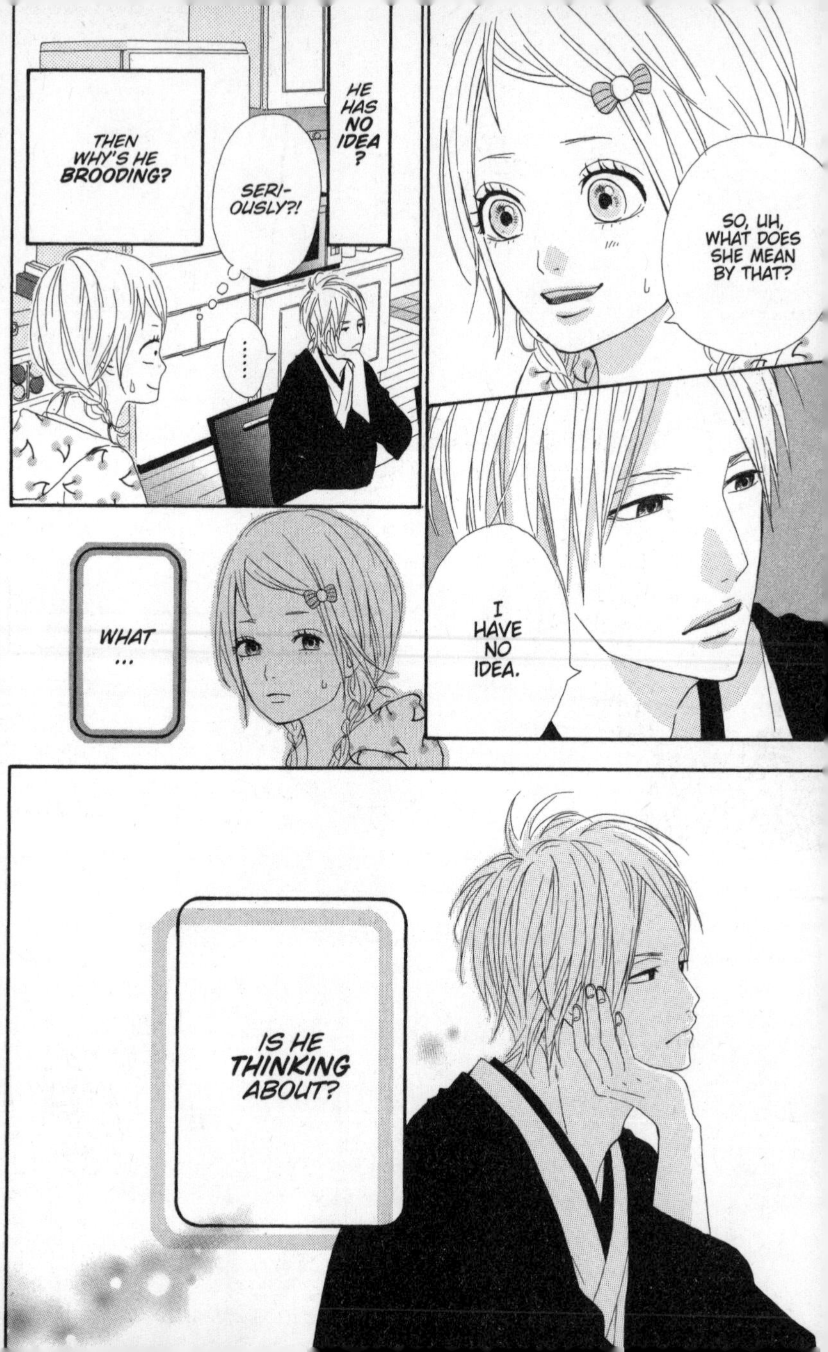

SO, UH, WHAT DOES SHE MEAN BY THAT?
I HAVE NO IDEA.
HE HAS NO IDEA?
SERI-OUSLY?!
THEN WHY'S HE BROODING?
......
WHAT ...
IS HE THINKING ABOUT?

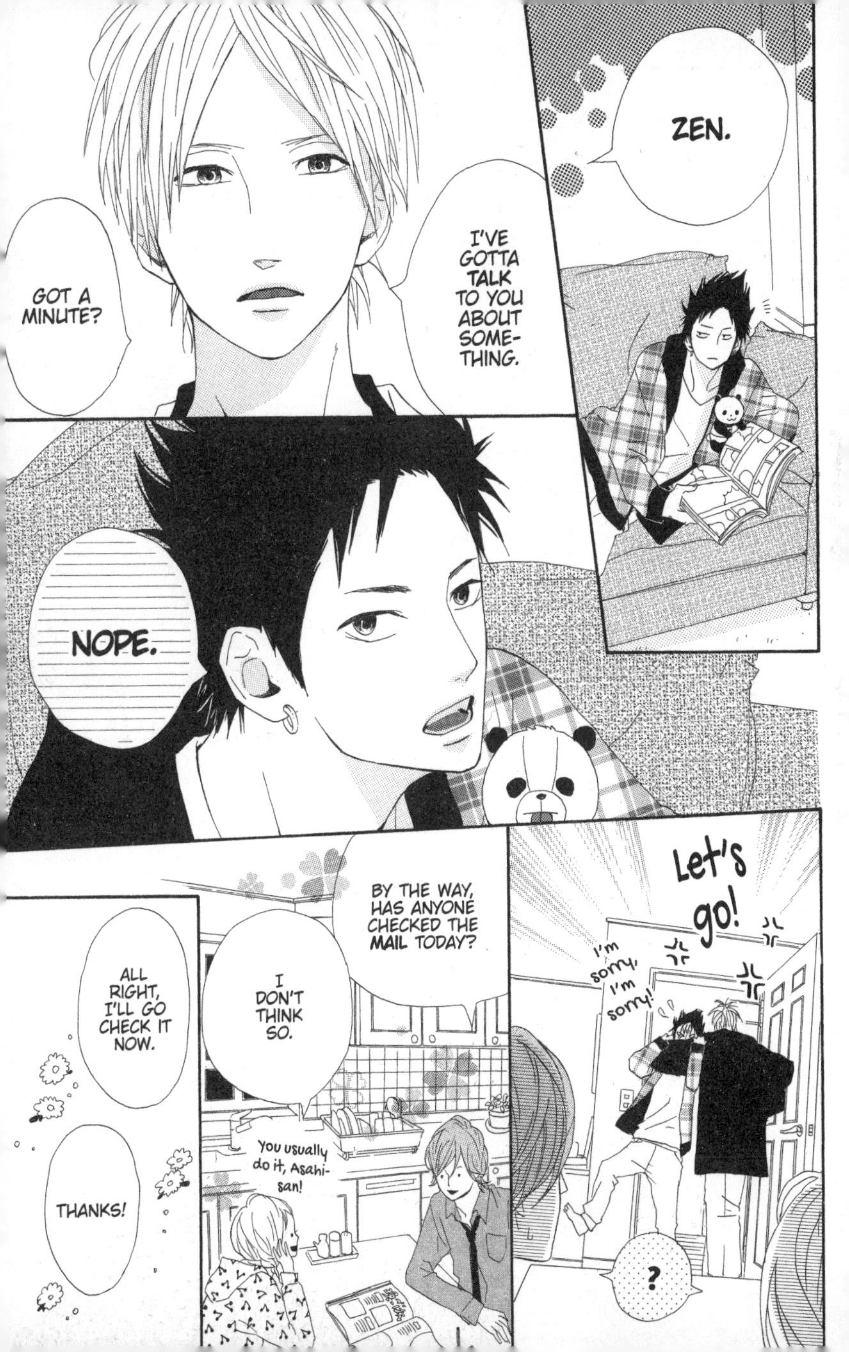
ZEN.
I'VE GOTTA TALK TO YOU ABOUT SOME-THING.
GOT A MINUTE?
NOPE.
Let's go!
I'm sorry, I'm sorry!
?
BY THE WAY, HAS ANYONE CHECKED THE MAIL TODAY?
I DON'T THINK SO.
You usually do it, Asahi-san!
ALL RIGHT, I'LL GO CHECK IT NOW.
THANKS!

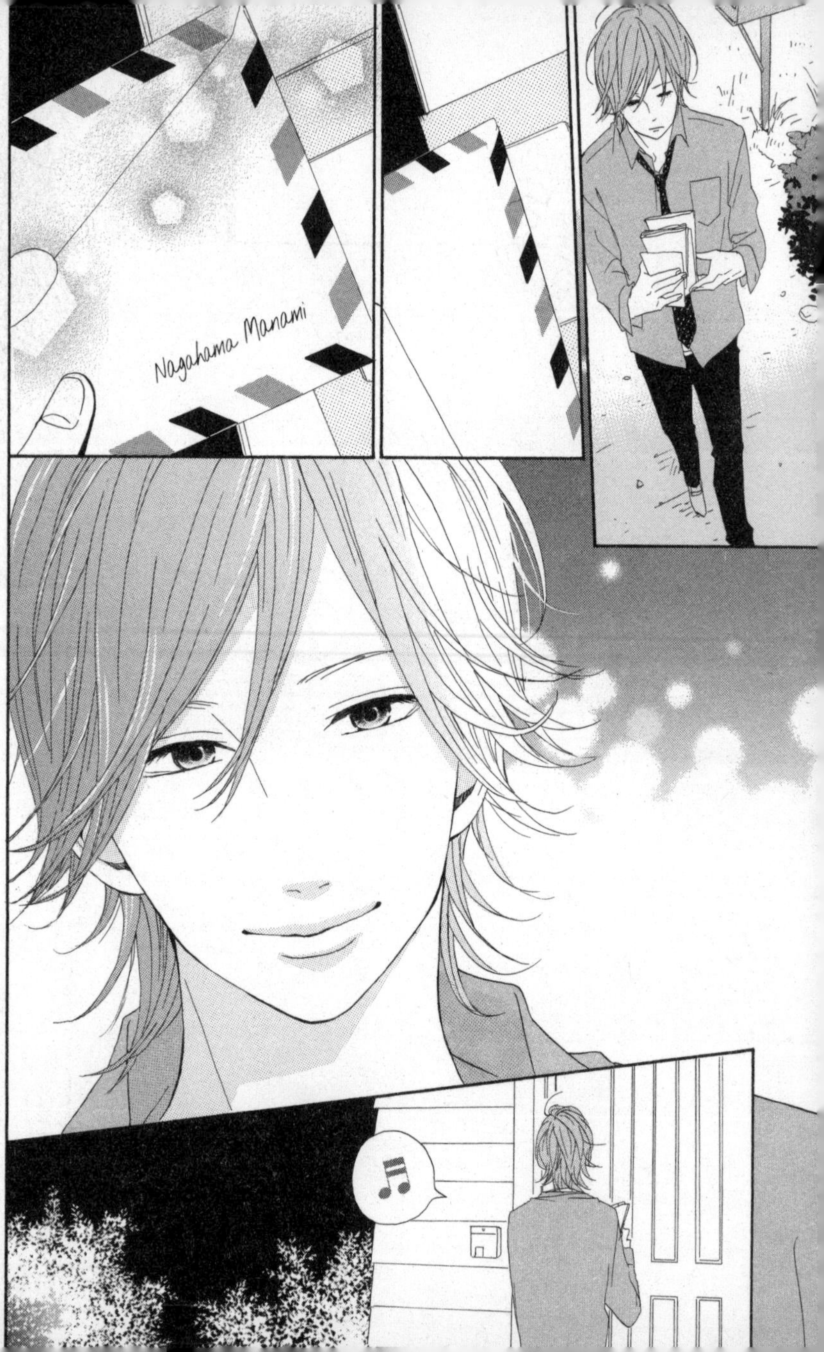
Nagahama Manami

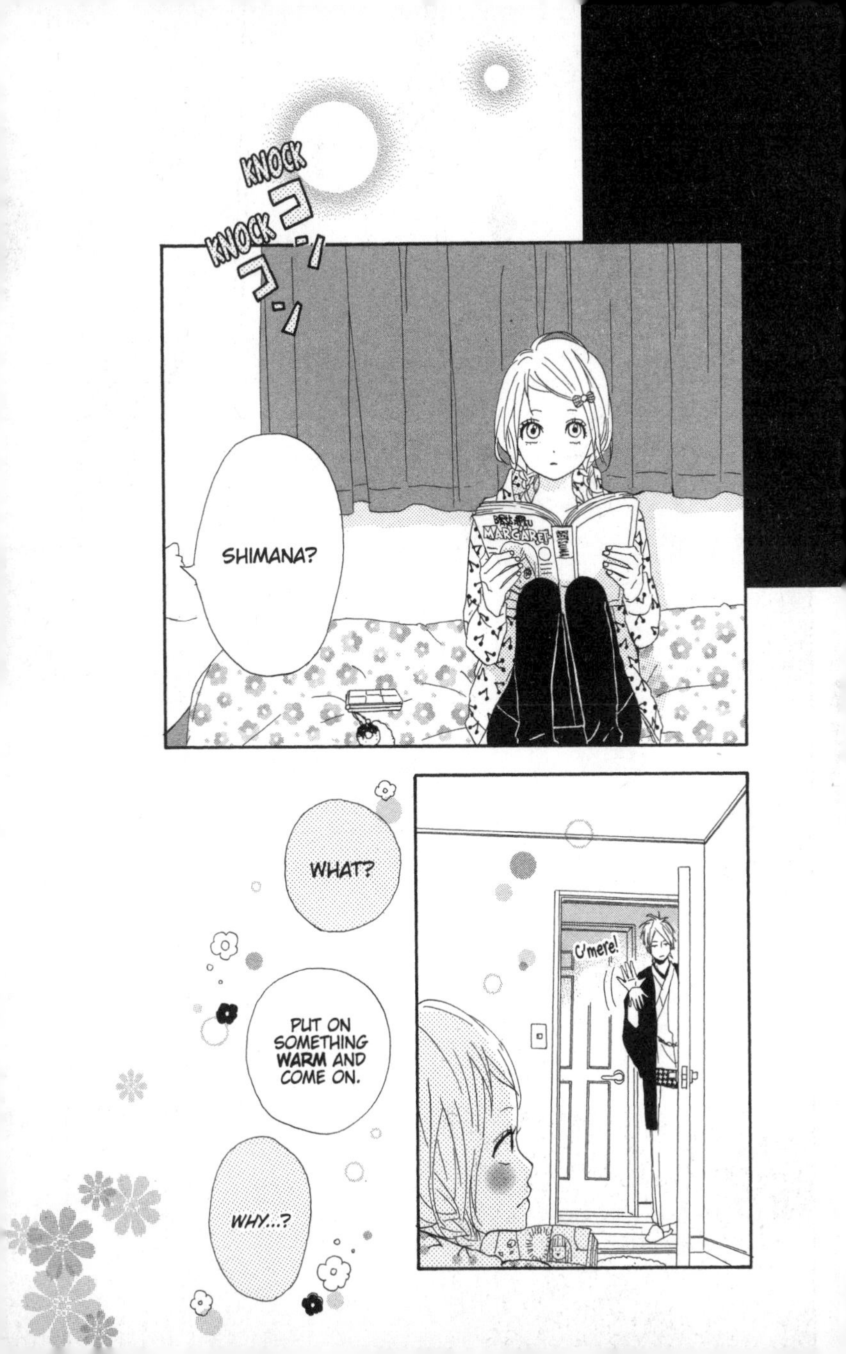
KNOCK
KNOCK
SHIMANA?
MARGARET
WHAT?
C'mere!
PUT ON SOMETHING WARM AND COME ON.
WHY...?

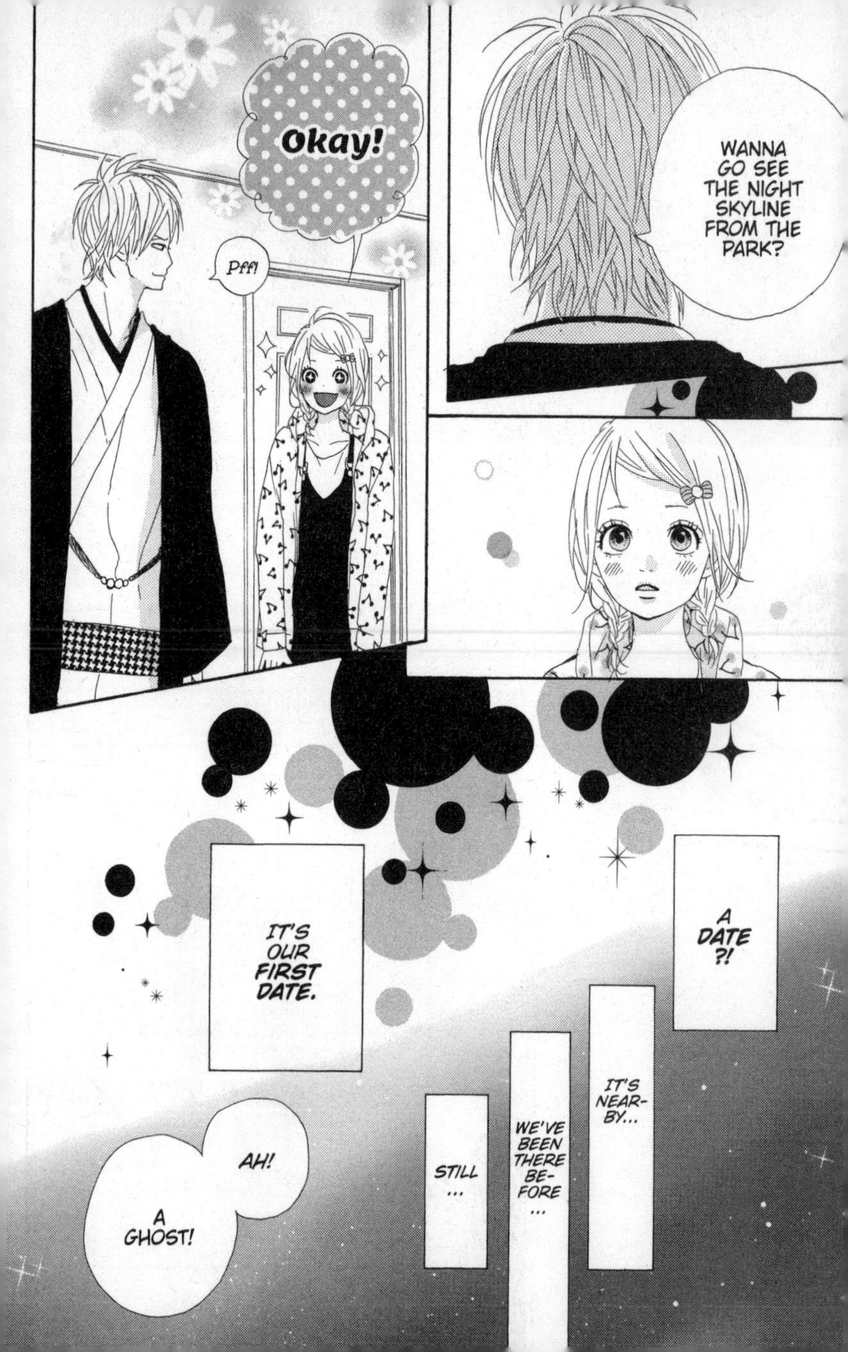
WANNA GO SEE THE NIGHT SKYLINE FROM THE PARK?
Okay!
Pff!
A DATE?!
IT'S NEARBY...
WE'VE BEEN THERE BEFORE...
STILL...
IT'S OUR FIRST DATE.
AH! A GHOST!

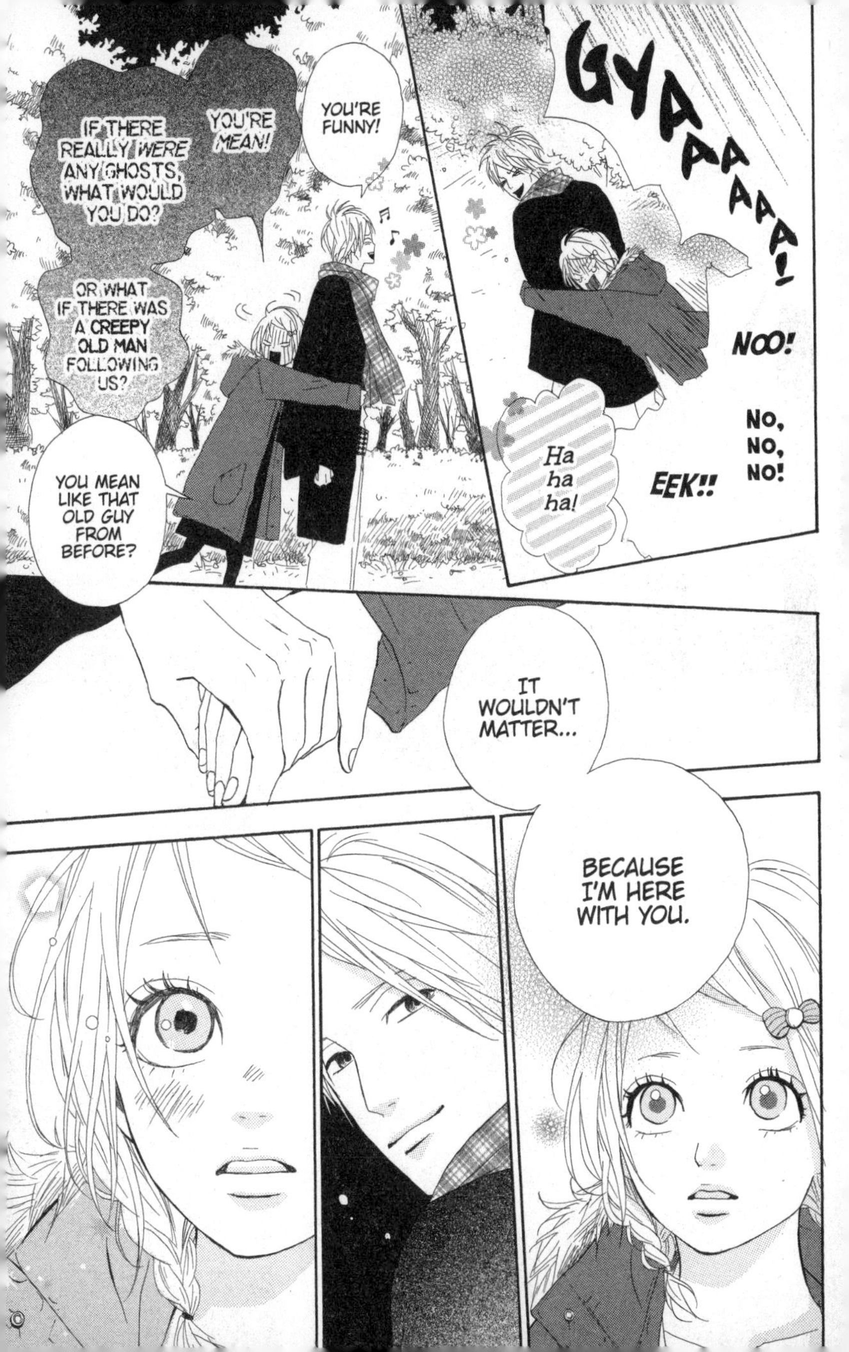
GYAAAAA!
NOO!
NO, NO, NO!
EEK!!
Ha ha ha!
YOU'RE FUNNY!
YOU'RE MEAN!
IF THERE REALLY WERE ANY GHOSTS, WHAT WOULD YOU DO?
OR WHAT IF THERE WAS A CREEPY OLD MAN FOLLOWING US?
YOU MEAN LIKE THAT OLD GUY FROM BEFORE?
IT WOULDN'T MATTER...
BECAUSE I'M HERE WITH YOU.

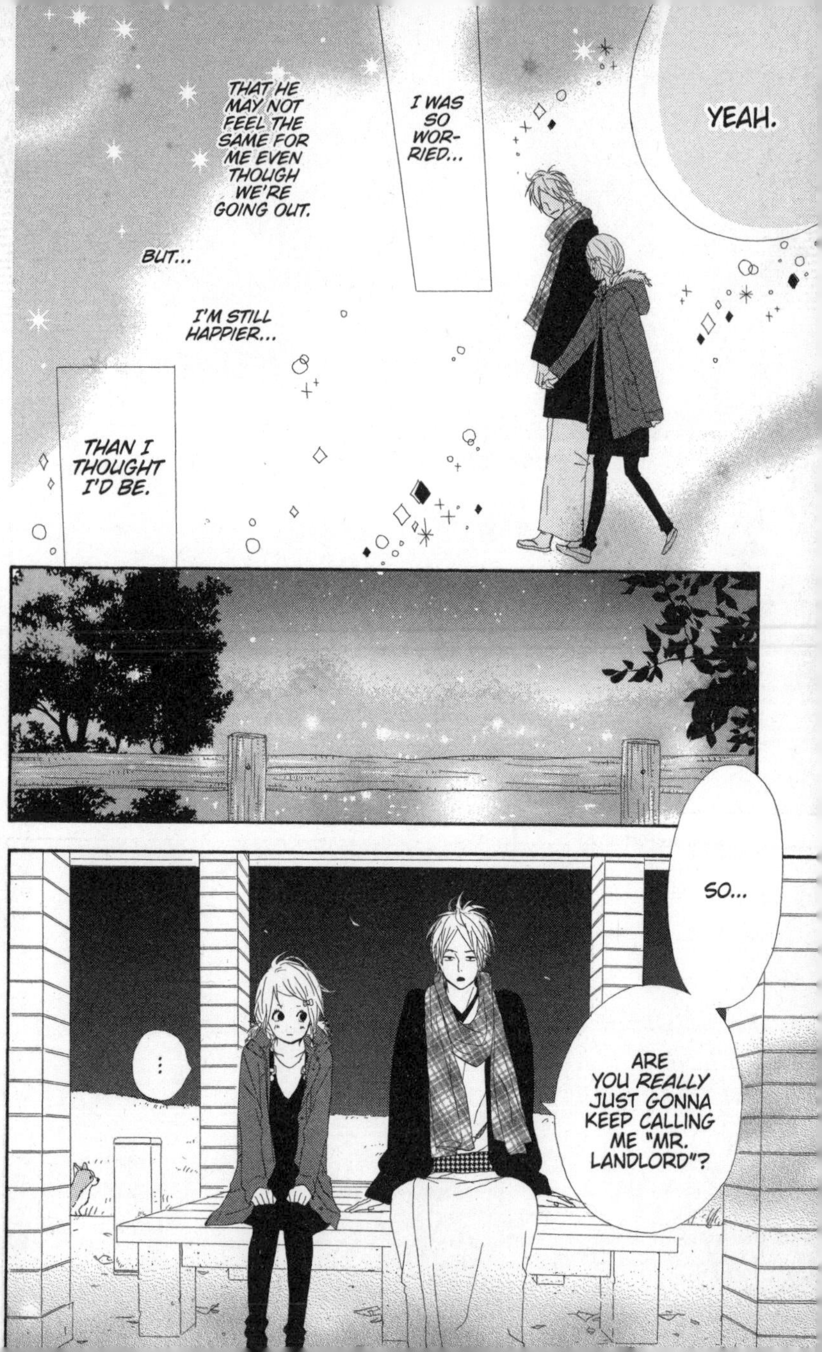
YEAH.
I WAS SO WORRIED...
THAT HE MAY NOT FEEL THE SAME FOR ME EVEN THOUGH WE'RE GOING OUT.
BUT...
I'M STILL HAPPIER...
THAN I THOUGHT I'D BE.
SO...
ARE YOU REALLY JUST GONNA KEEP CALLING ME "MR. LANDLORD"?
...

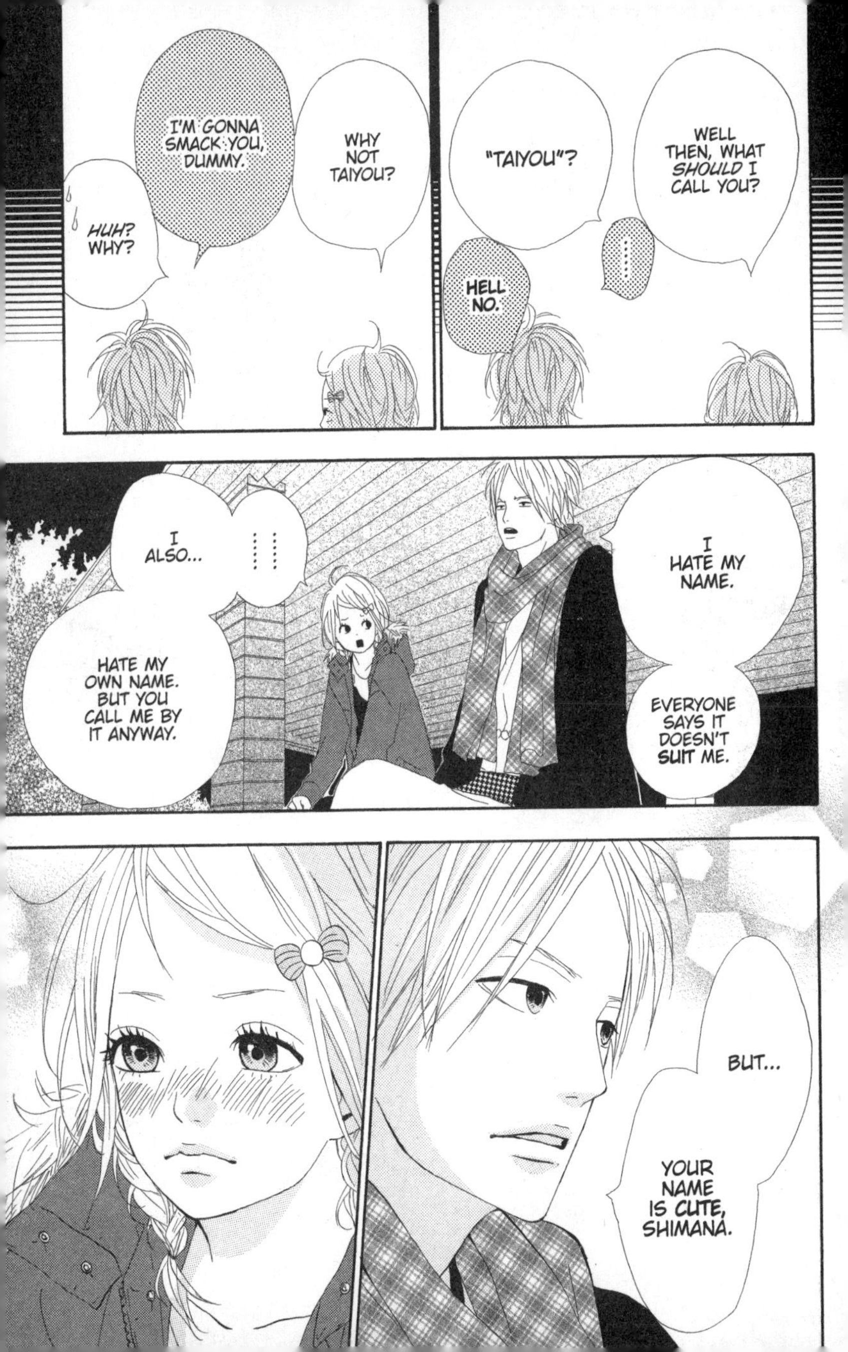
WELL THEN, WHAT *SHOULD* I CALL YOU?
......
"TAIYOU"?
HELL NO.
WHY NOT TAIYOU?
I'M GONNA SMACK YOU, DUMMY.
HUH? WHY?
I HATE MY NAME.
EVERYONE SAYS IT DOESN'T SUIT ME.
......
I ALSO...
HATE MY OWN NAME. BUT YOU CALL ME BY IT ANYWAY.
BUT...
YOUR NAME IS CUTE, SHIMANA.

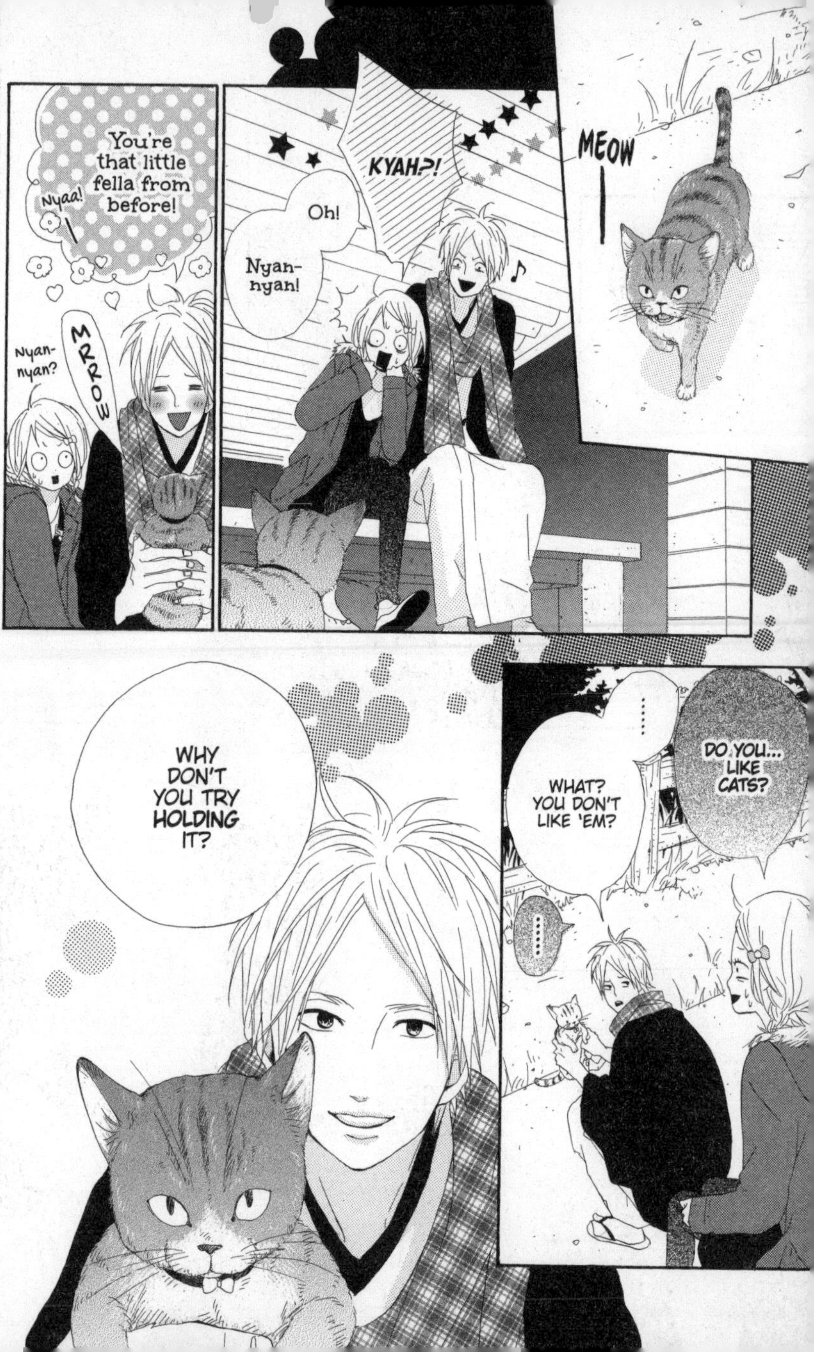
MEOW
KYAH?!
Oh!
Nyan-nyan!
You're that little fella from before!
Nyaa!
MRROW
Nyan-nyan?
DO YOU... LIKE CATS?
......
WHAT? YOU DON'T LIKE 'EM?
......
WHY DON'T YOU TRY HOLDING IT?

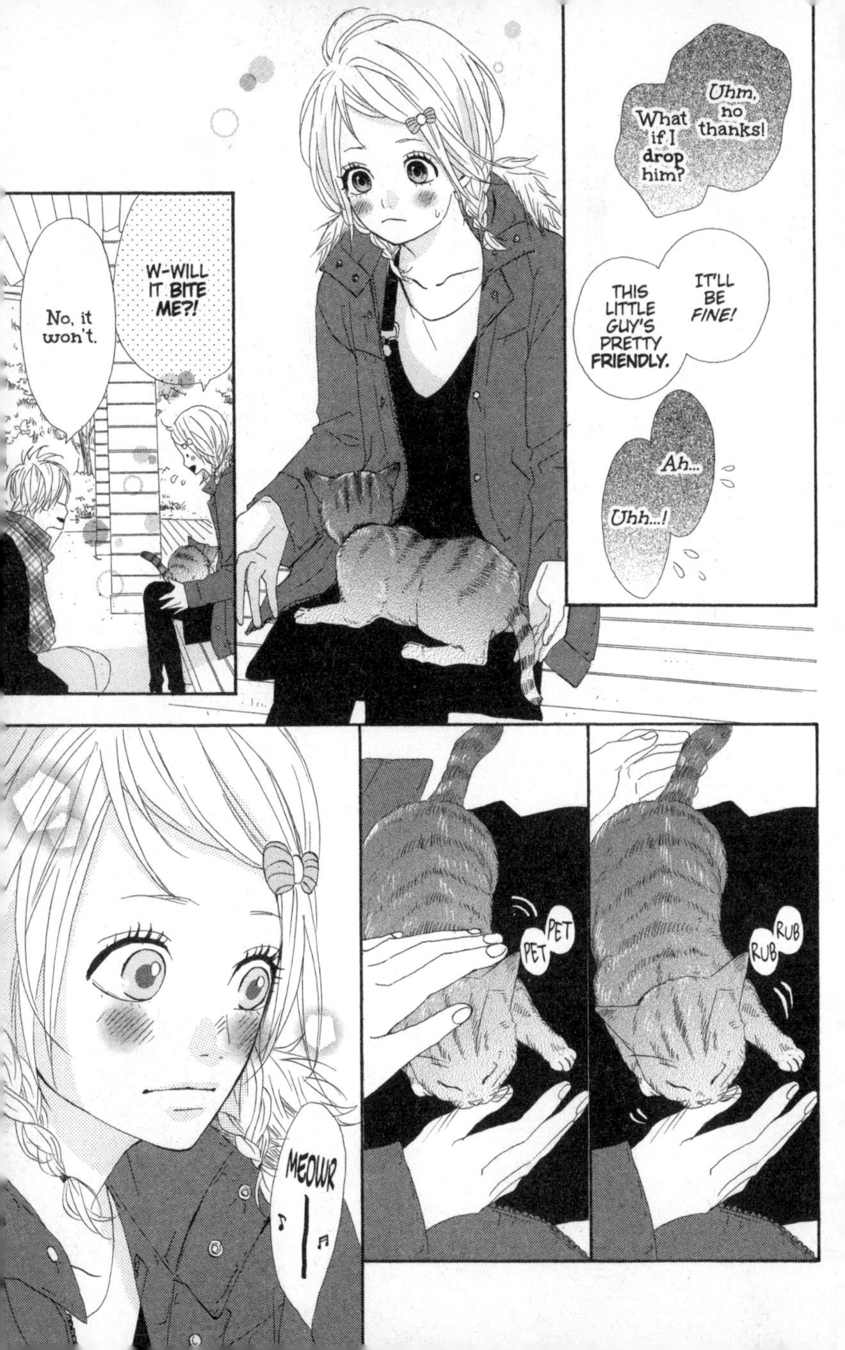
Uhm, no thanks!
What if I drop him?
IT'LL BE FINE!
THIS LITTLE GUY'S PRETTY FRIENDLY.
Ah...
Uhh...!
W-WILL IT BITE ME?!
No, it won't.
RUB RUB
PET PET
MEOWR

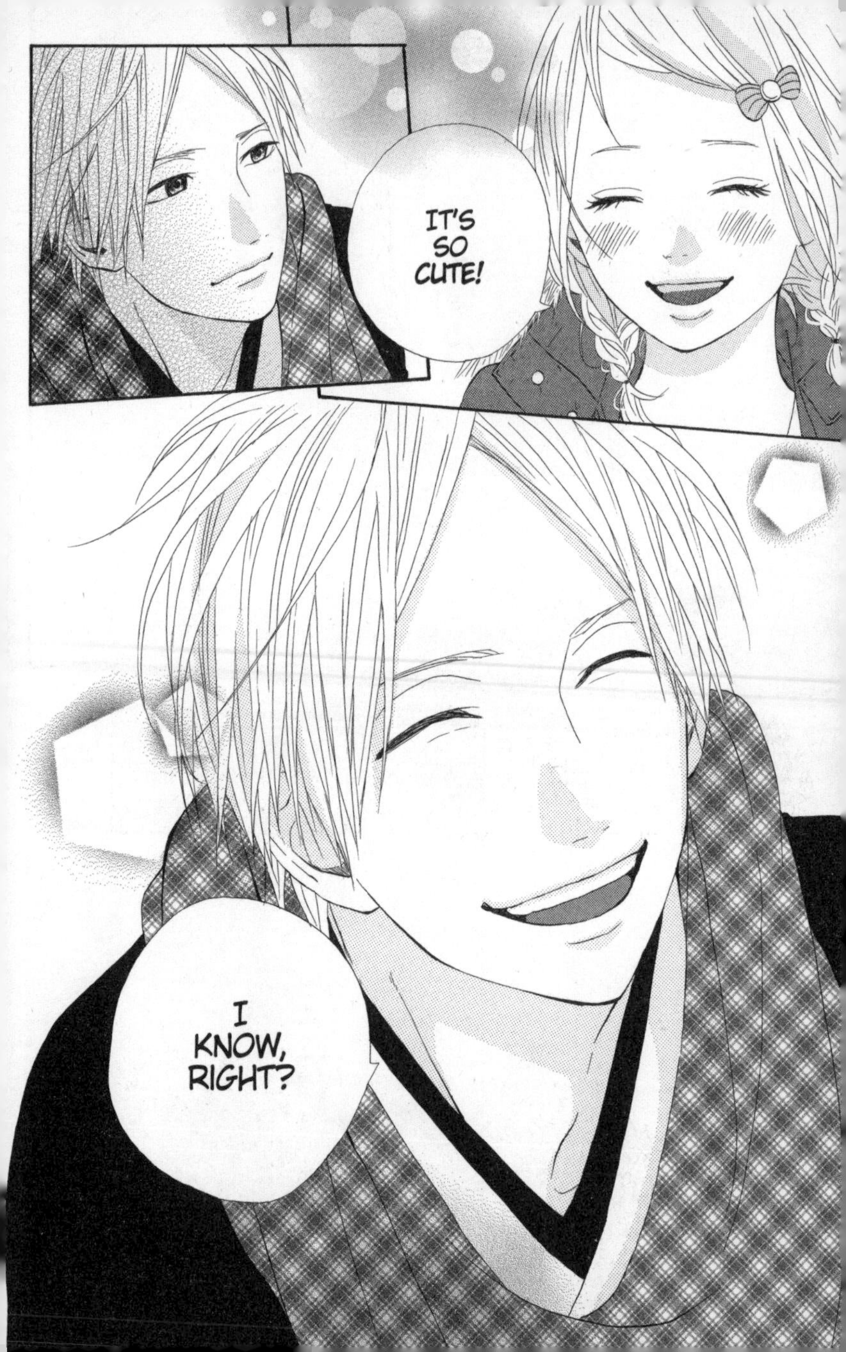
IT'S SO CUTE!
I KNOW, RIGHT?

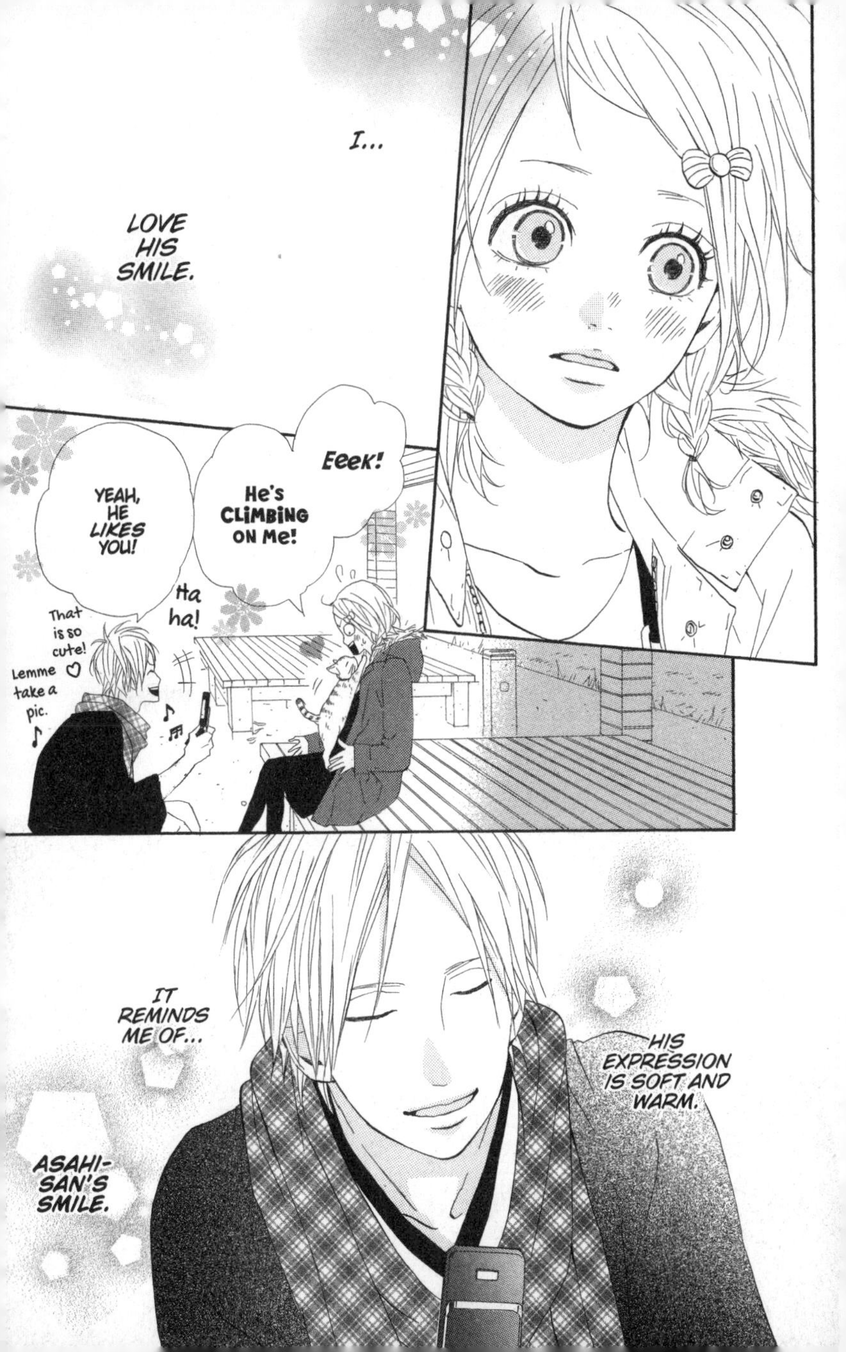
I...
LOVE HIS SMILE.
Eeek!
He's CLIMBING ON ME!
Ha ha!
YEAH, HE LIKES YOU!
That is so cute! Lemme ♡ take a pic. ♪
HIS EXPRESSION IS SOFT AND WARM.
IT REMINDS ME OF...
ASAHI-SAN'S SMILE.

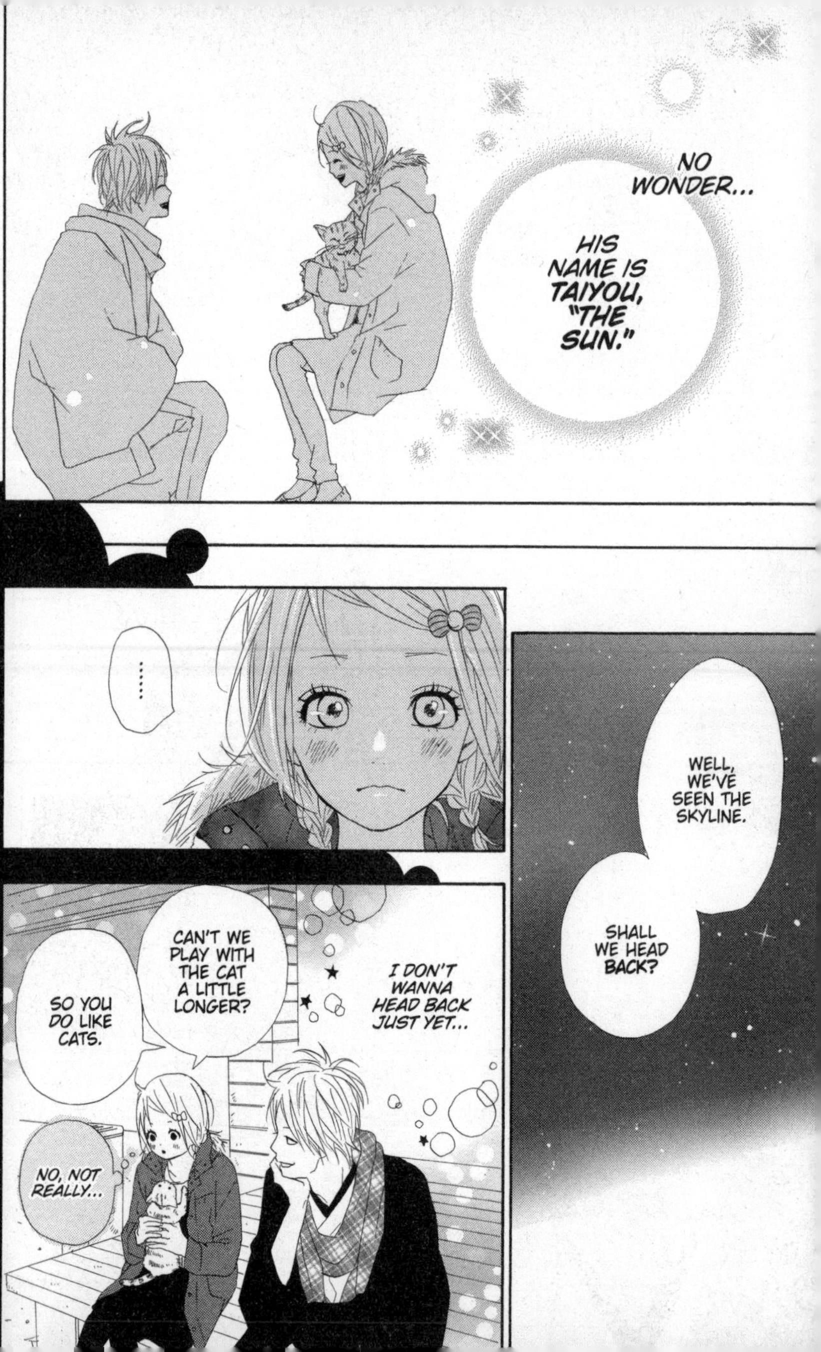
NO WONDER...
HIS NAME IS TAIYOU, "THE SUN."
WELL, WE'VE SEEN THE SKYLINE.
SHALL WE HEAD BACK?
......
I DON'T WANNA HEAD BACK JUST YET...
CAN'T WE PLAY WITH THE CAT A LITTLE LONGER?
SO YOU DO LIKE CATS.
NO, NOT REALLY...

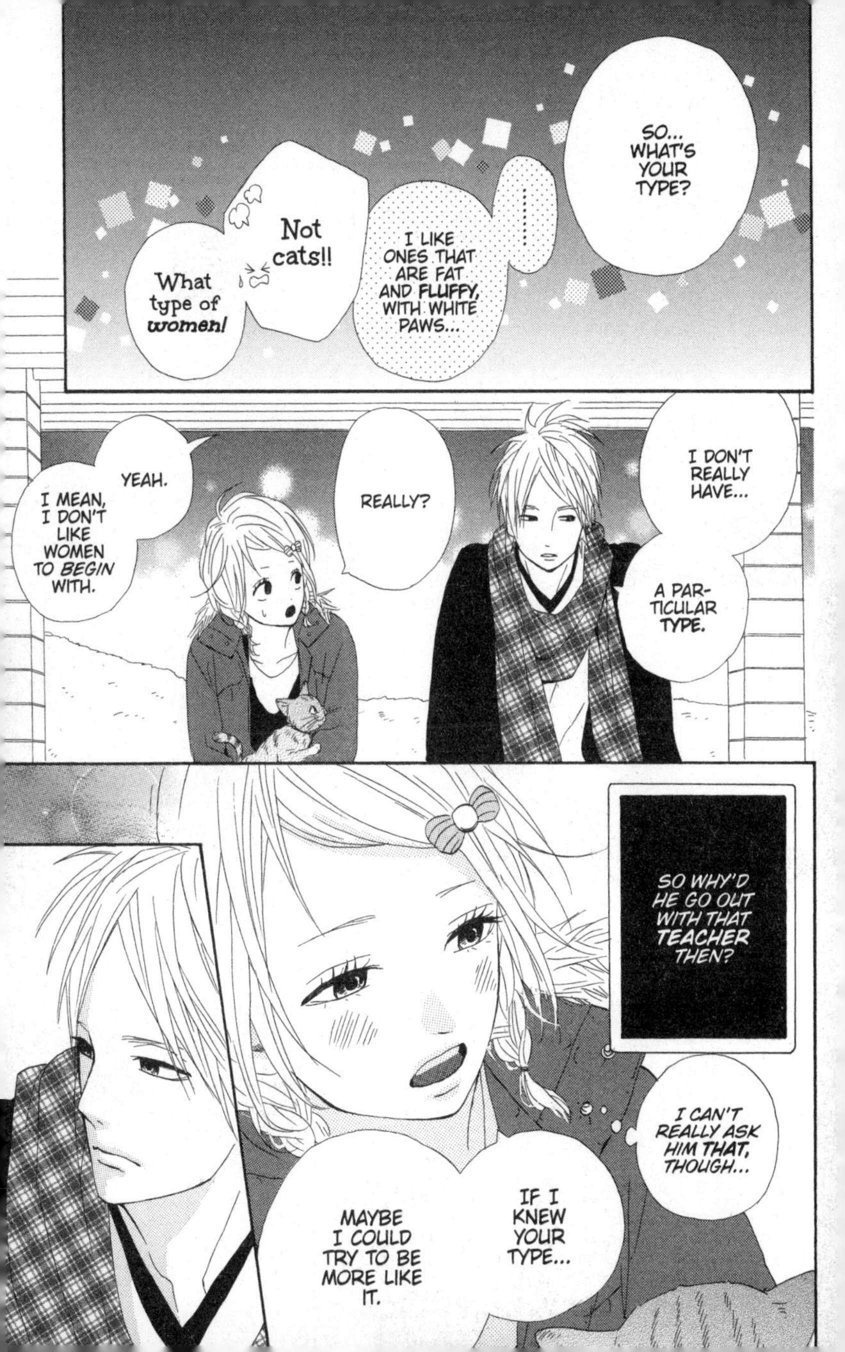
SO... WHAT'S YOUR TYPE?
......
I LIKE ONES THAT ARE FAT AND FLUFFY, WITH WHITE PAWS...
Not cats!!
What type of women!
I DON'T REALLY HAVE...
A PARTICULAR TYPE.
REALLY?
YEAH.
I MEAN, I DON'T LIKE WOMEN TO BEGIN WITH.
SO WHY'D HE GO OUT WITH THAT TEACHER THEN?
I CAN'T REALLY ASK HIM THAT, THOUGH...
IF I KNEW YOUR TYPE...
MAYBE I COULD TRY TO BE MORE LIKE IT.

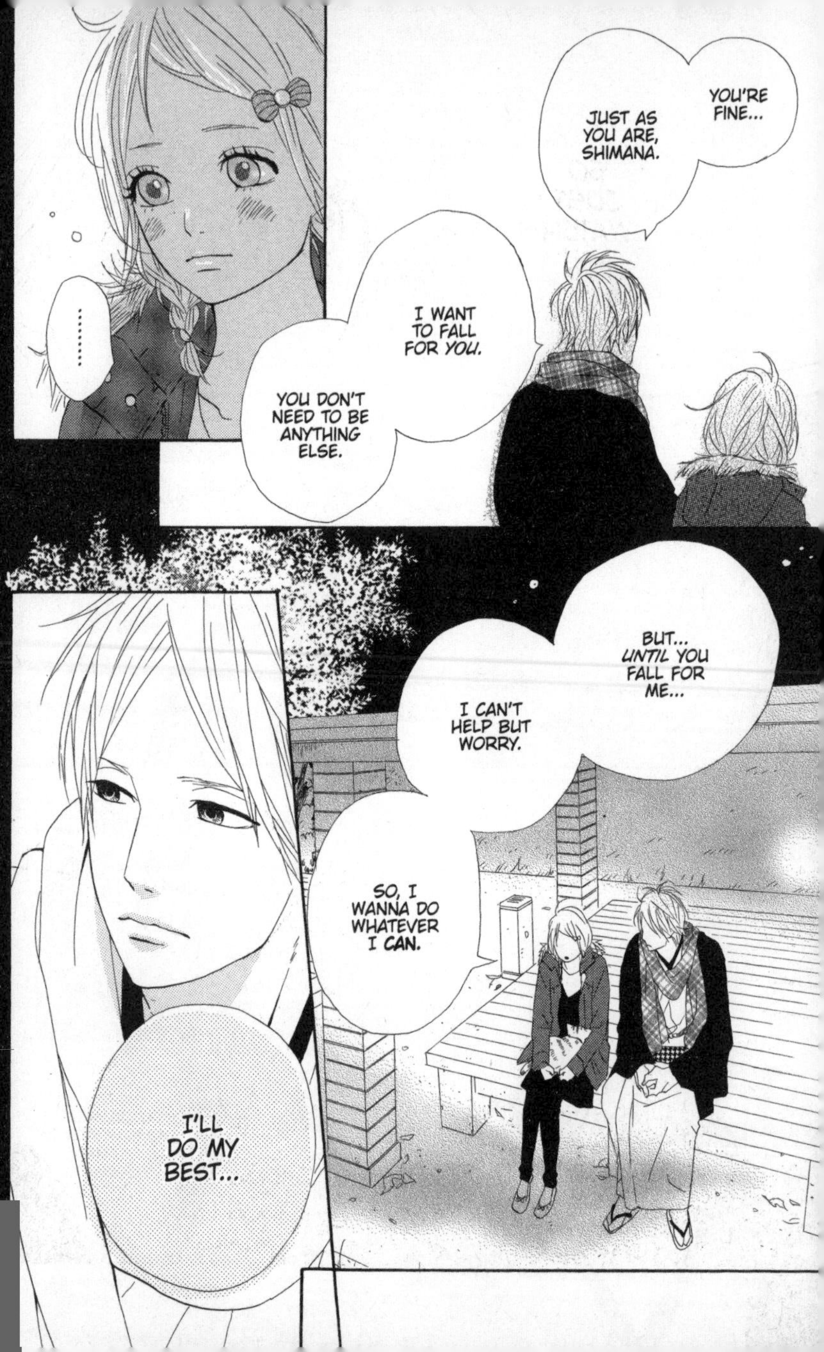
YOU'RE FINE...
JUST AS YOU ARE, SHIMANA.
I WANT TO FALL FOR *YOU.*
YOU DON'T NEED TO BE ANYTHING ELSE.
......
BUT... *UNTIL* YOU FALL FOR ME...
I CAN'T HELP BUT WORRY.
SO, I WANNA DO WHATEVER I CAN.
I'LL DO MY BEST...

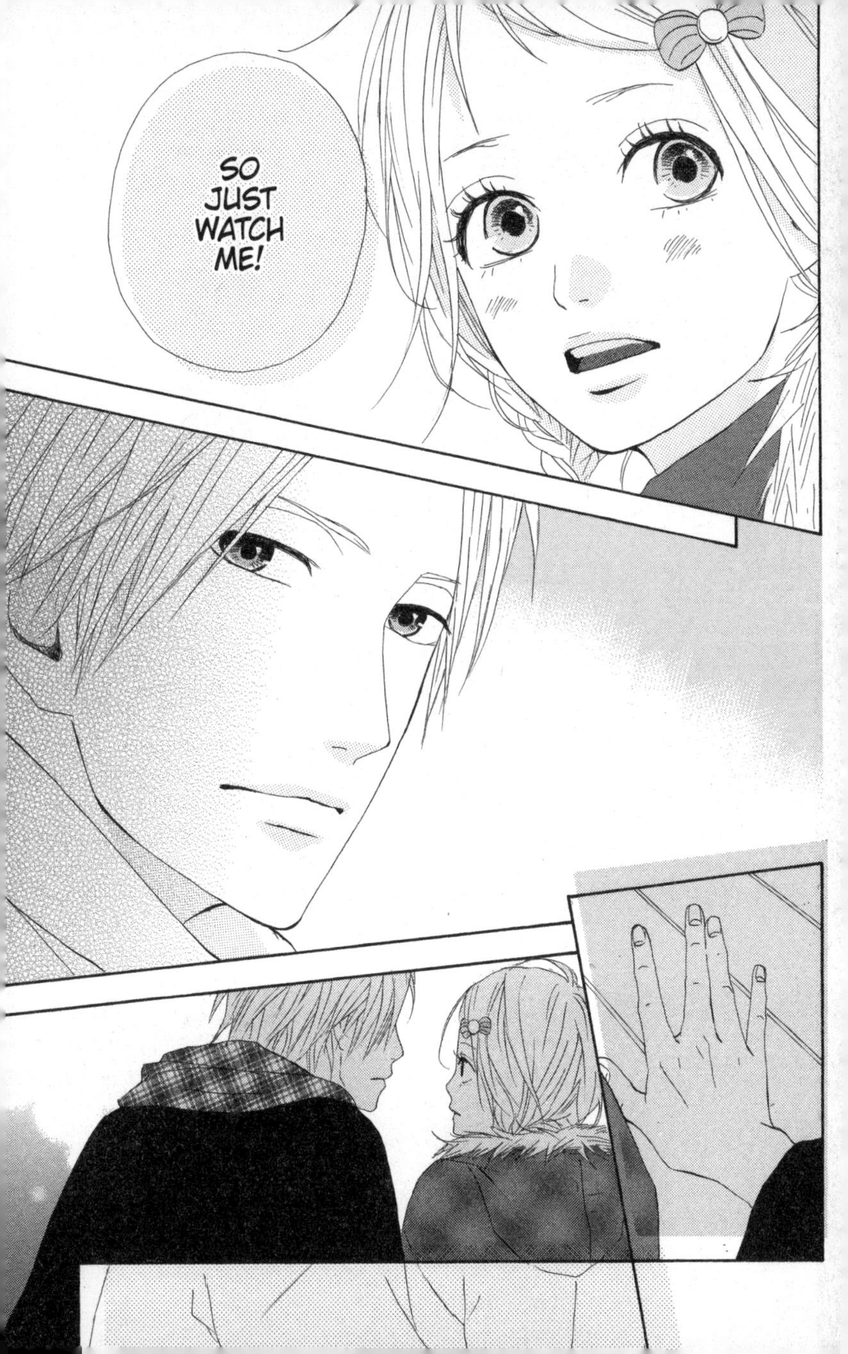
SO JUST WATCH ME!

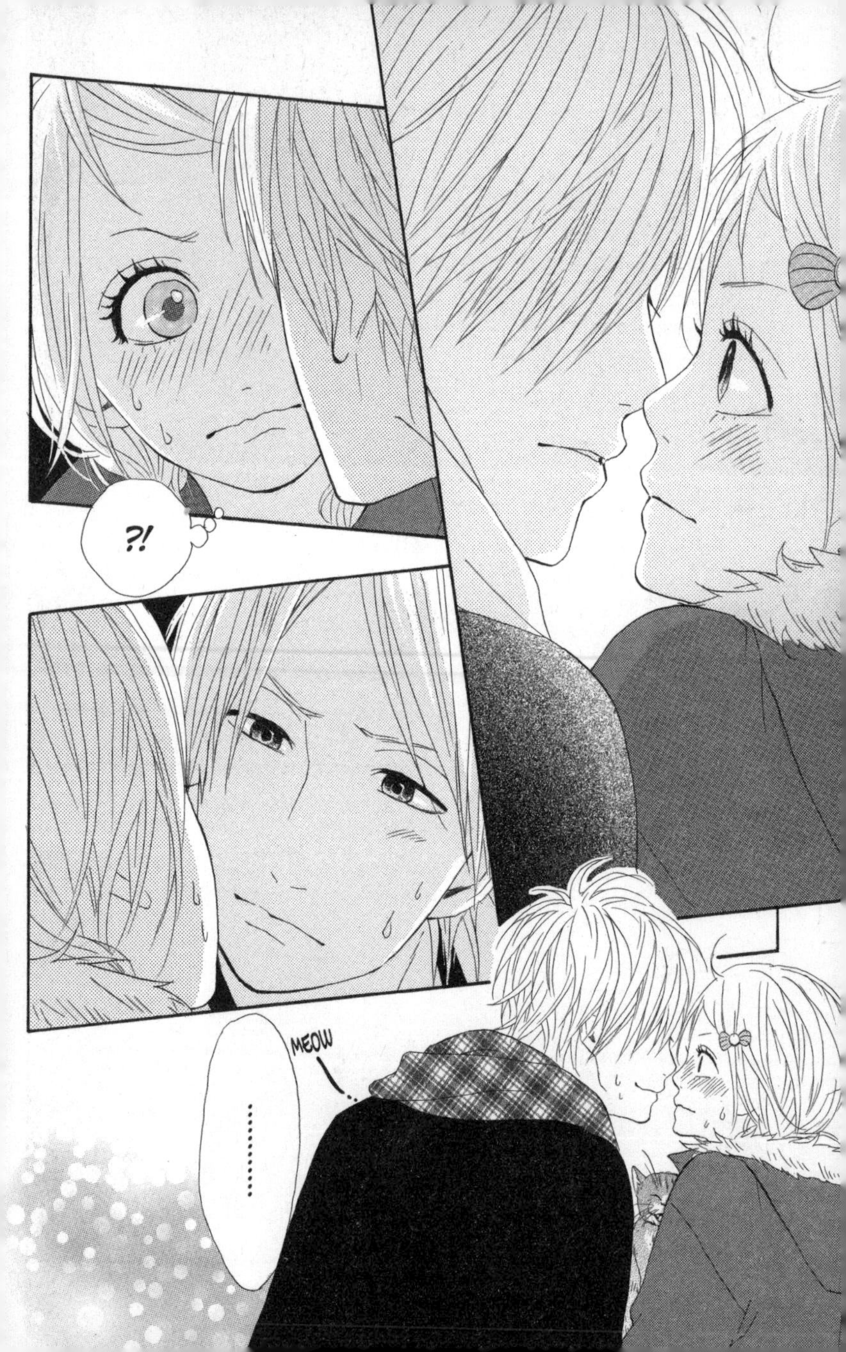
?!
MEOW
......

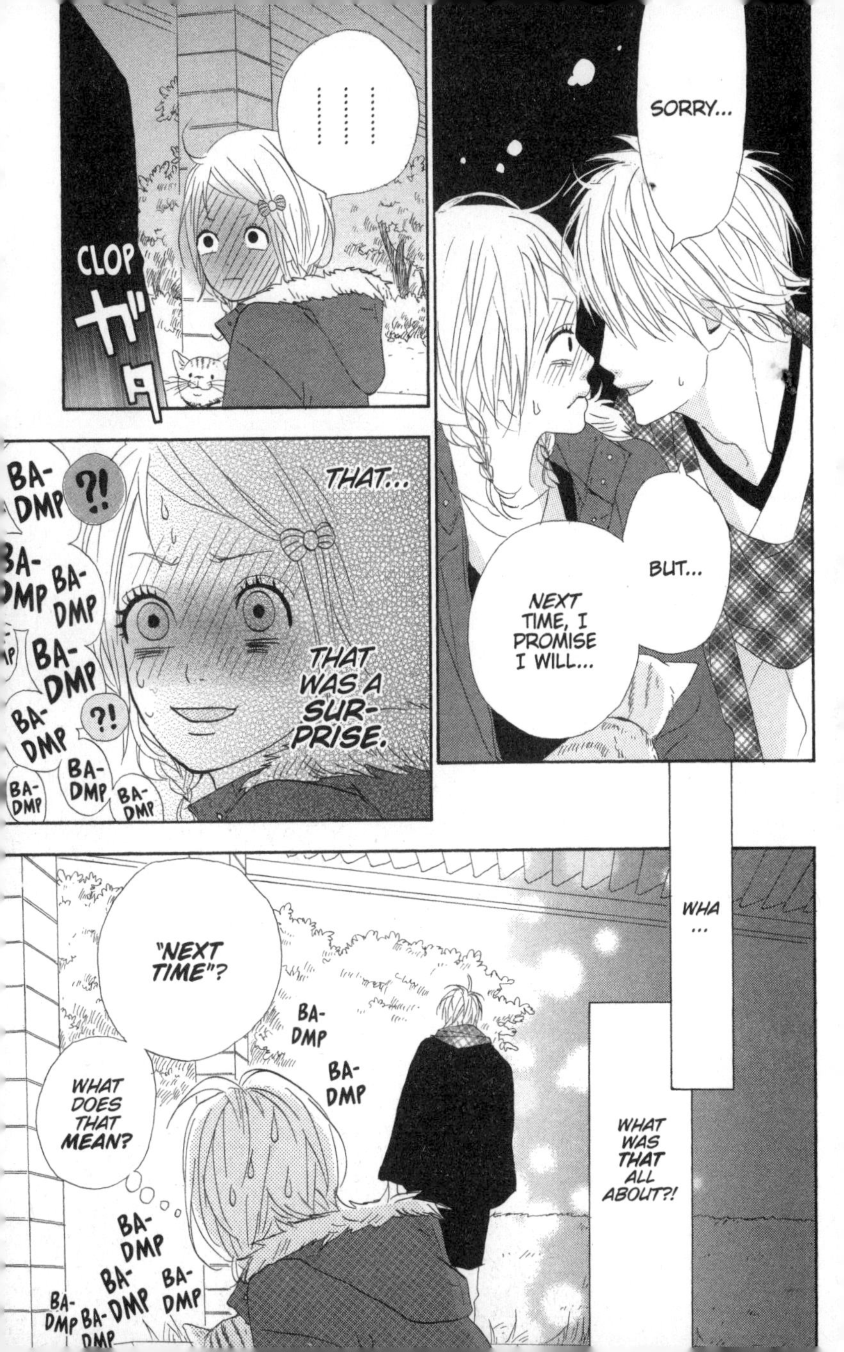
SORRY...
BUT...
NEXT TIME, I PROMISE I WILL...
CLOP
ガタ
THAT...
THAT WAS A SURPRISE.
BA-DMP
?!
BA-DMP
BA-DMP
BA-DMP
BA-DMP
?!
BA-DMP
BA-DMP
BA-DMP
WHA...
WHAT WAS THAT ALL ABOUT?!
"NEXT TIME"?
WHAT DOES THAT MEAN?
BA-DMP
BA-DMP
BA-DMP
BA-DMP
BA-DMP
BA-DMP
BA-DMP

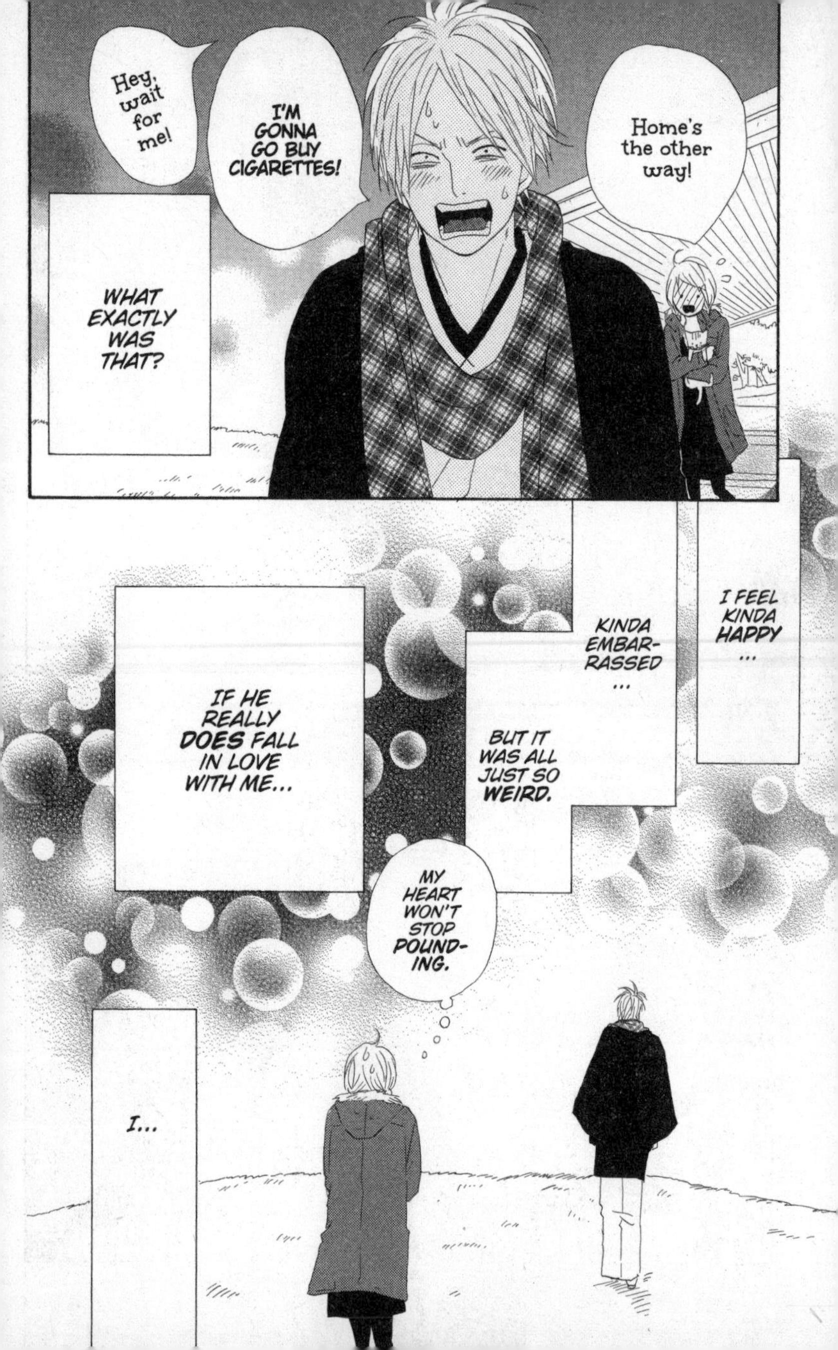
Home's the other way!
I'M GONNA GO BUY CIGARETTES!
Hey, wait for me!
WHAT EXACTLY WAS THAT?
I FEEL KINDA HAPPY...
KINDA EMBARRASSED...
BUT IT WAS ALL JUST SO WEIRD.
IF HE REALLY DOES FALL IN LOVE WITH ME...
MY HEART WON'T STOP POUNDING.
I...

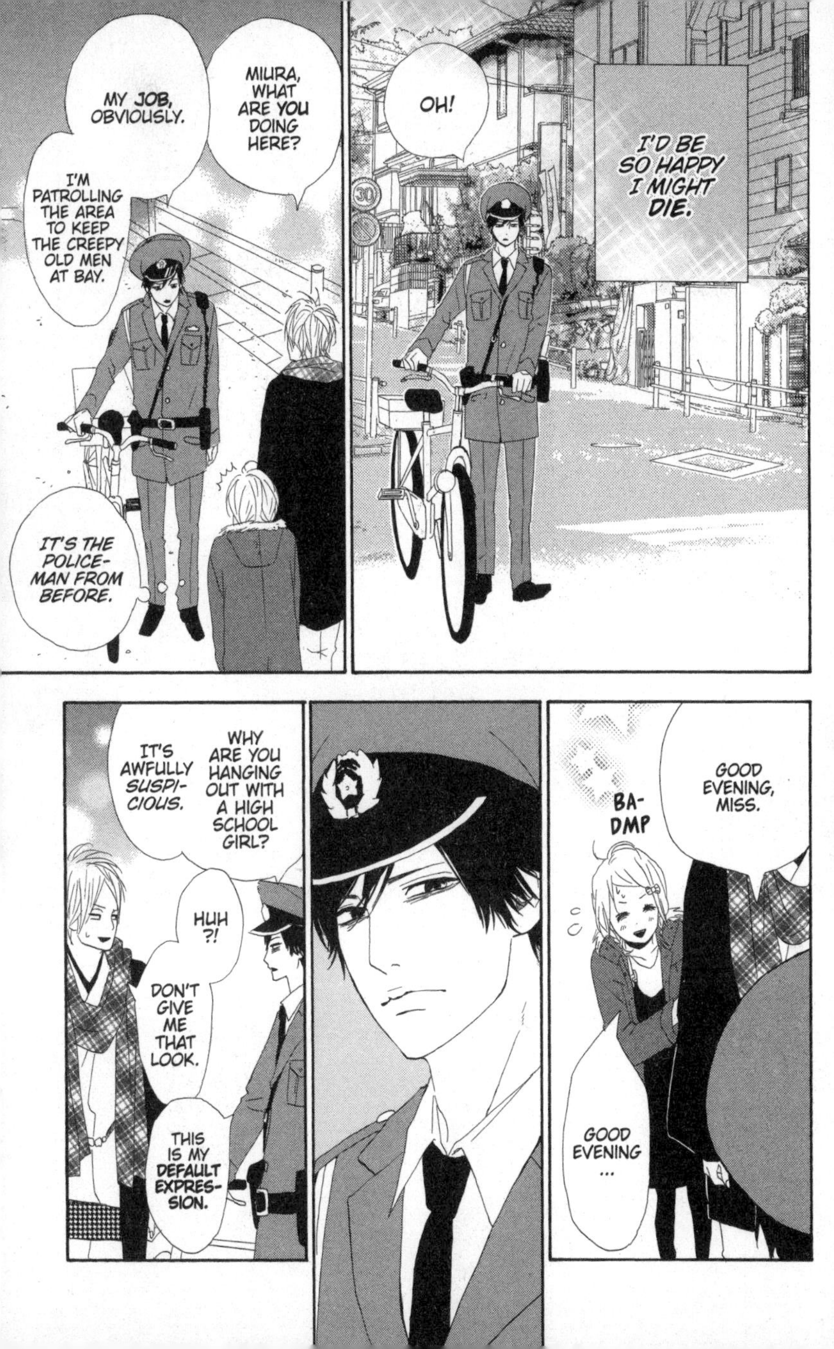
I'D BE SO HAPPY I MIGHT DIE.
OH!
MIURA, WHAT ARE YOU DOING HERE?
MY JOB, OBVIOUSLY.
I'M PATROLLING THE AREA TO KEEP THE CREEPY OLD MEN AT BAY.
IT'S THE POLICEMAN FROM BEFORE.
GOOD EVENING, MISS.
BA-DMP
GOOD EVENING...
WHY ARE YOU HANGING OUT WITH A HIGH SCHOOL GIRL?
IT'S AWFULLY SUSPICIOUS.
HUH?!
DON'T GIVE ME THAT LOOK.
THIS IS MY DEFAULT EXPRESSION.

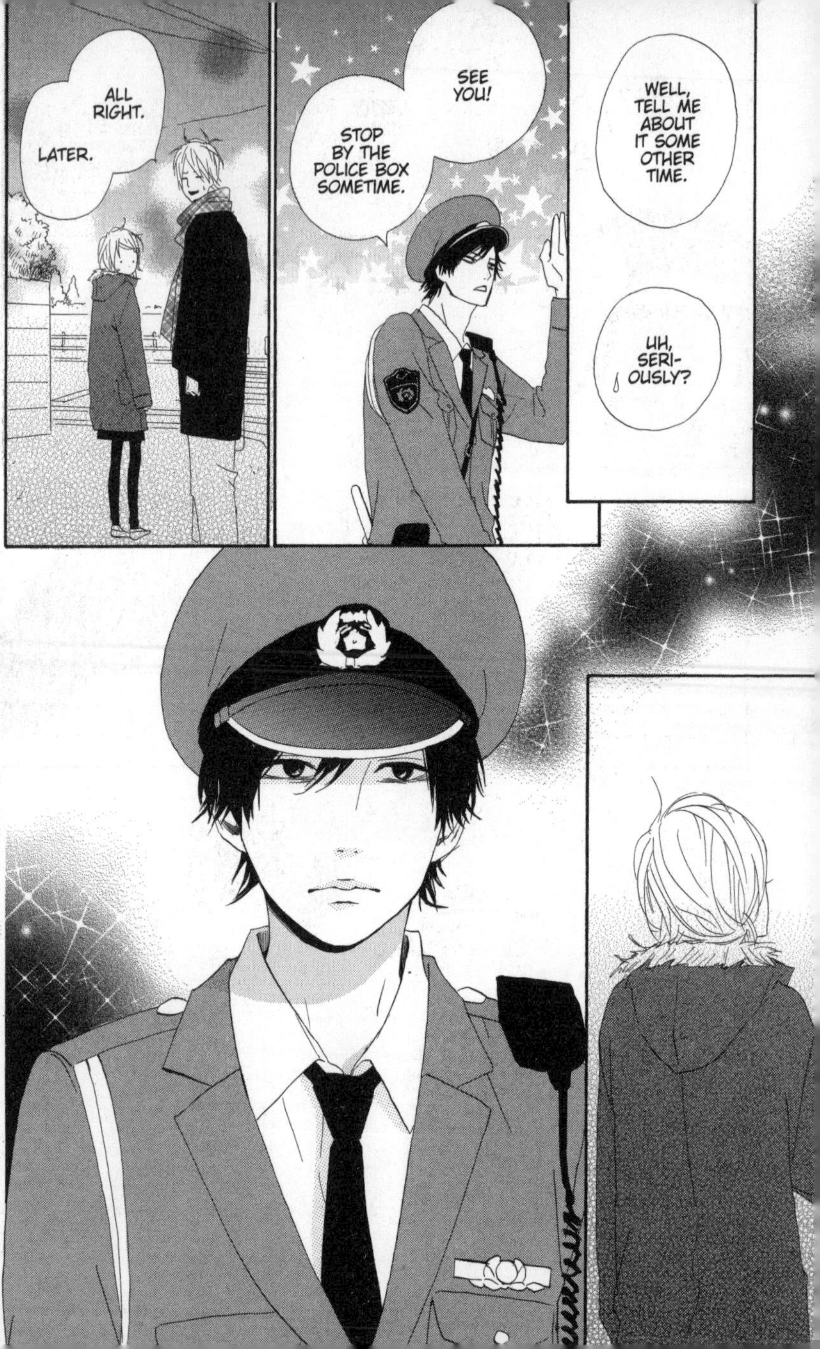
WELL, TELL ME ABOUT IT SOME OTHER TIME.
UH, SERI-OUSLY?
SEE YOU!
STOP BY THE POLICE BOX SOMETIME.
ALL RIGHT.
LATER.

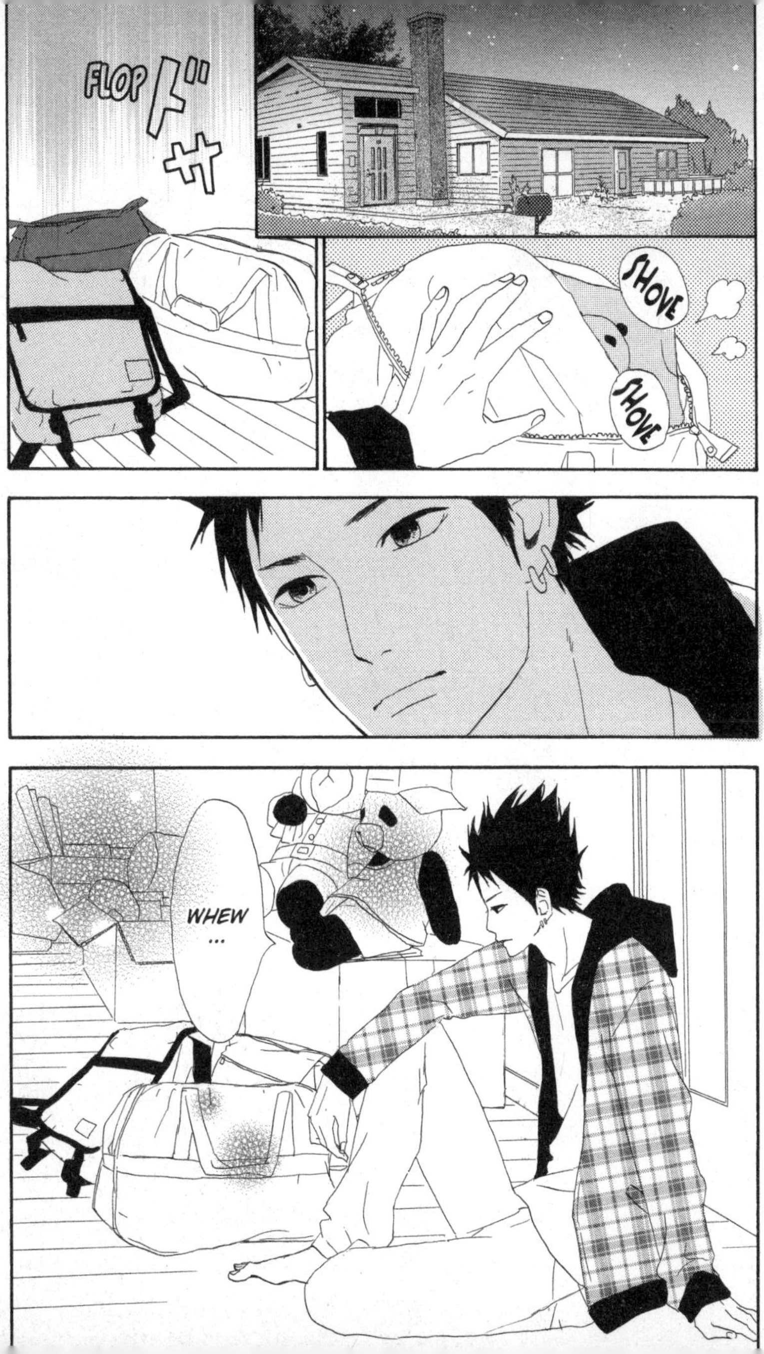
SHOVE
SHOVE
FLOP ドサ
WHEW ...

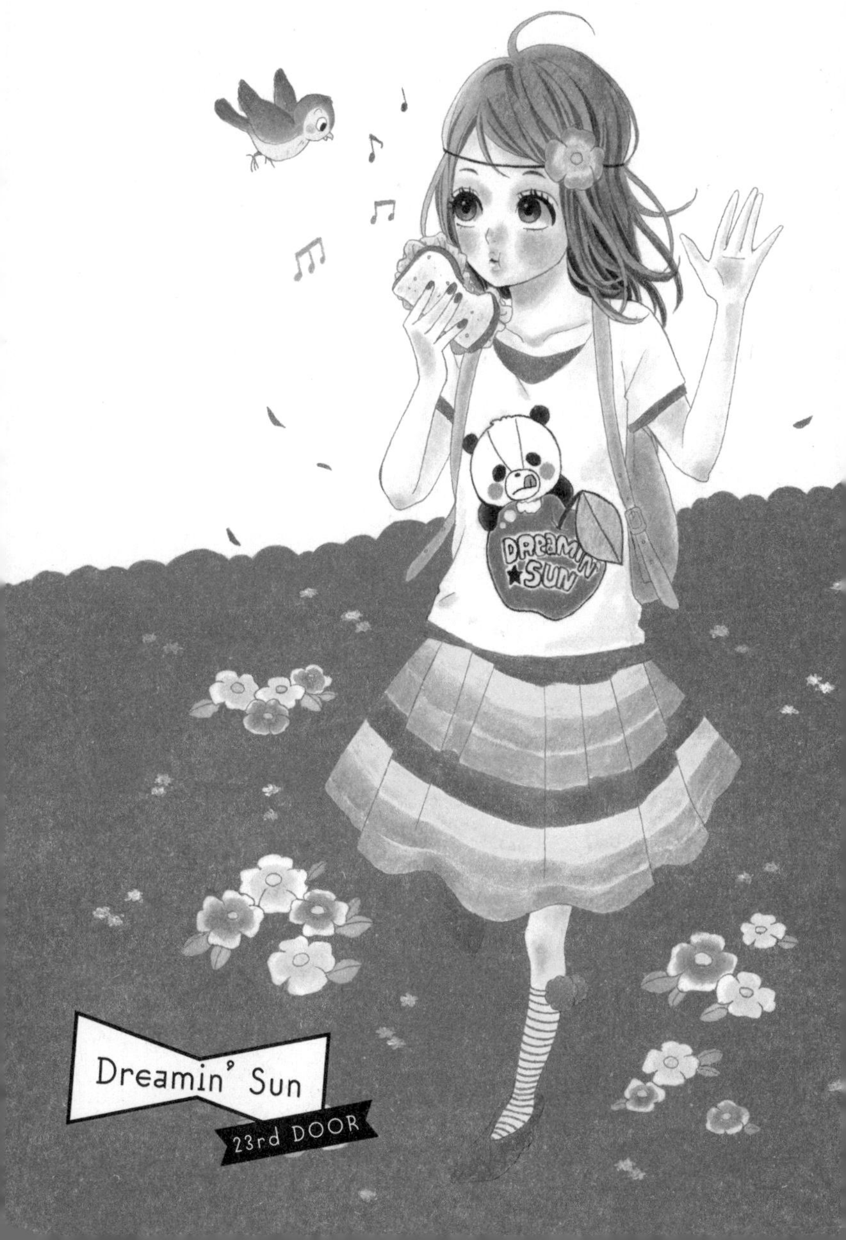
DREAMIN' ★SUN
Dreamin' Sun
23rd DOOR

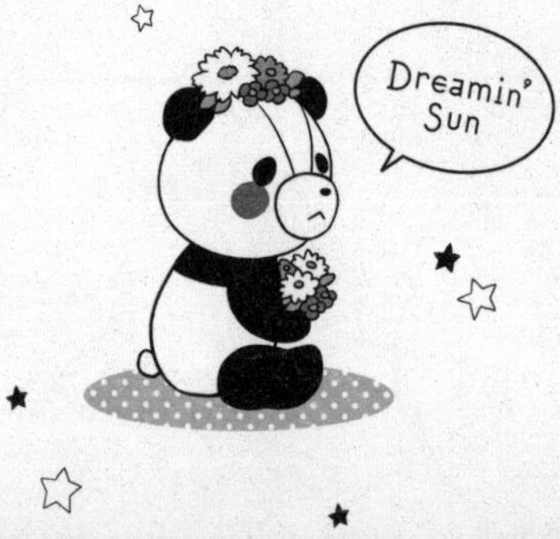
Dreamin' Sun

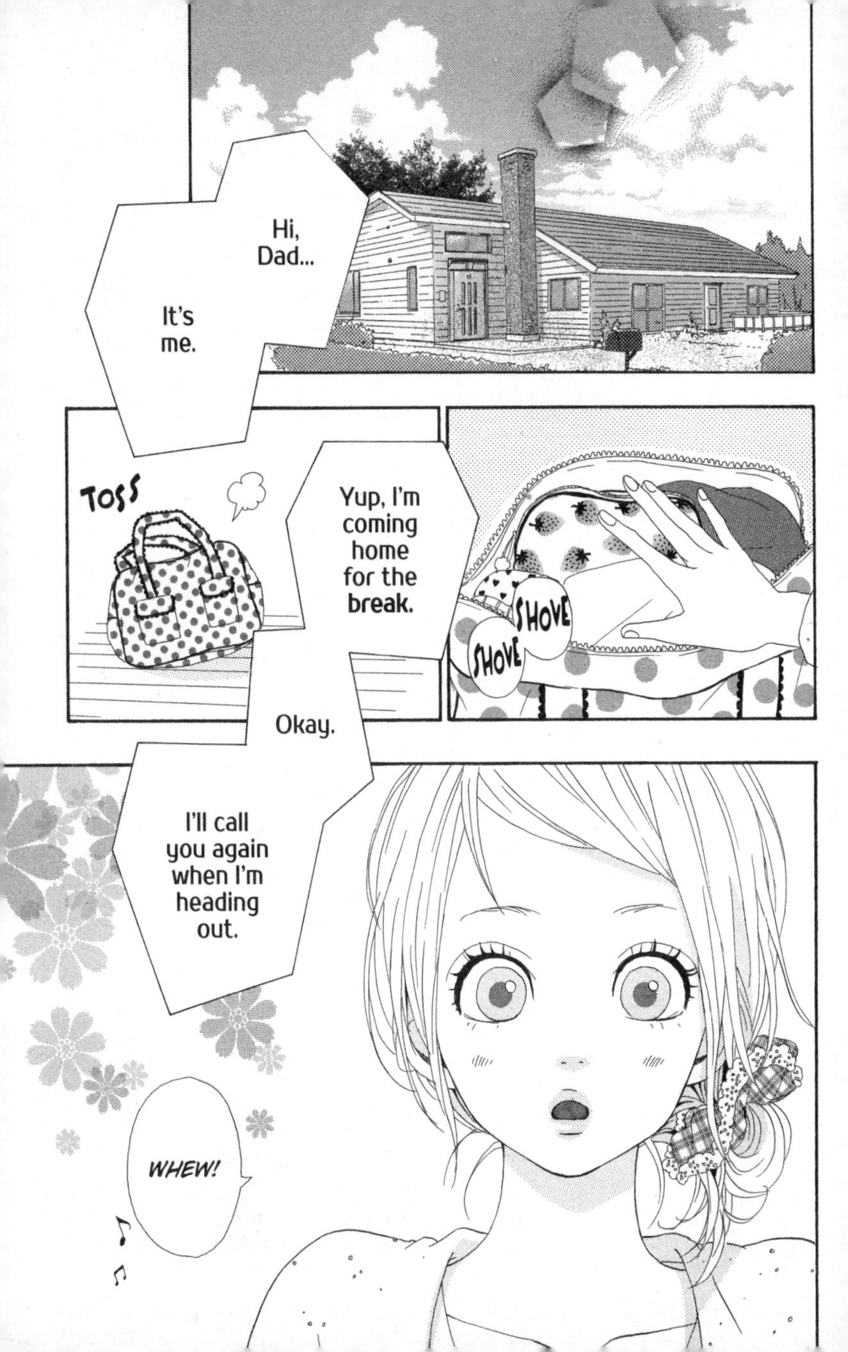
Hi, Dad...
It's me.
Yup, I'm coming home for the break.
SHOVE
SHOVE
TOSS
Okay.
I'll call you again when I'm heading out.
WHEW!

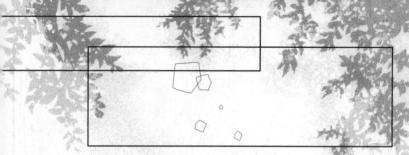

WELL...

I'M GONNA HEAD OUT.

ZEN, YOU LEAVING ALREADY?

THAT'S A *LOT* OF BAGS FOR A SHORT VISIT!

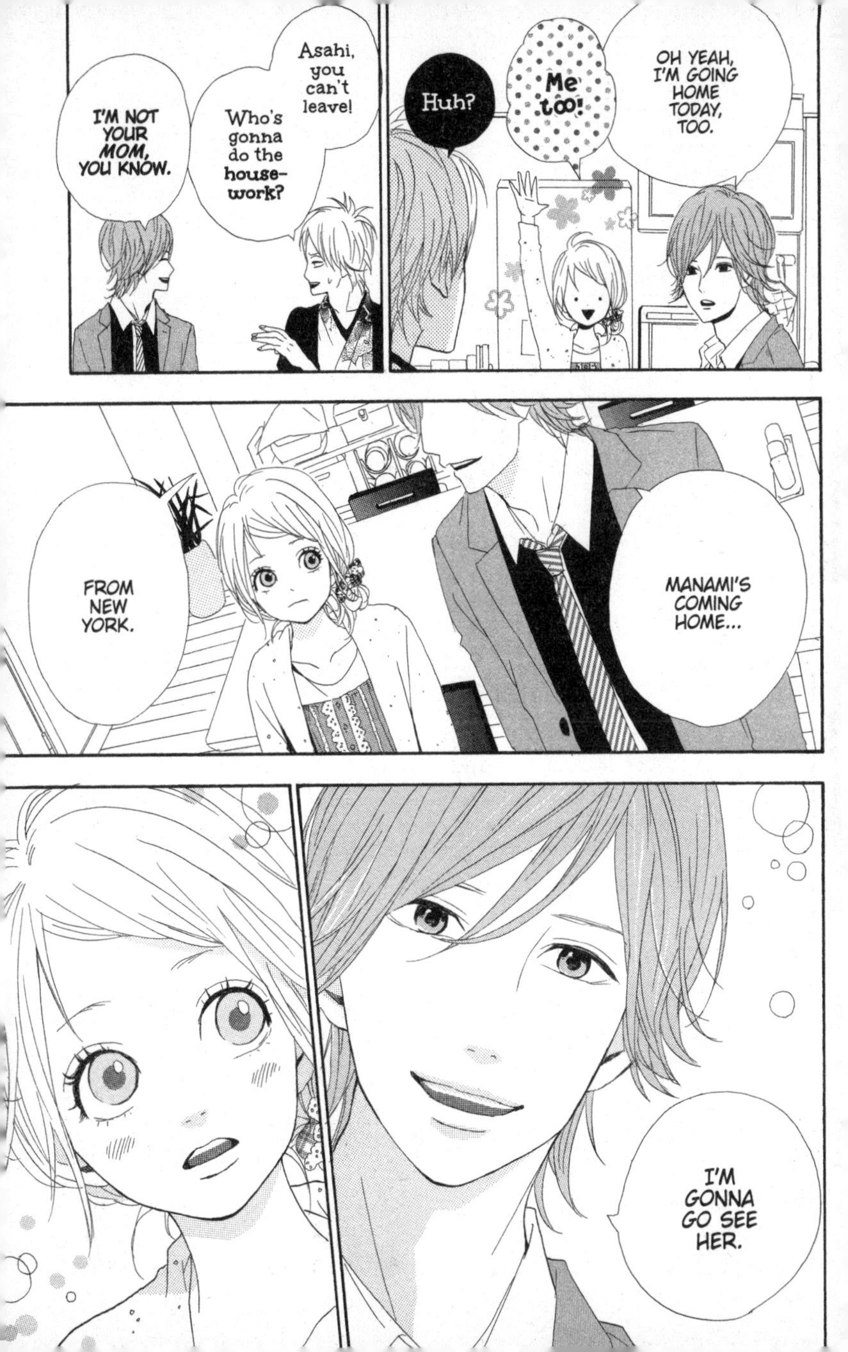
OH YEAH, I'M GOING HOME TODAY, TOO.
Me too!
Huh?
Asahi, you can't leave!
Who's gonna do the housework?
I'M NOT YOUR MOM, YOU KNOW.
MANAMI'S COMING HOME...
FROM NEW YORK.
I'M GONNA GO SEE HER.

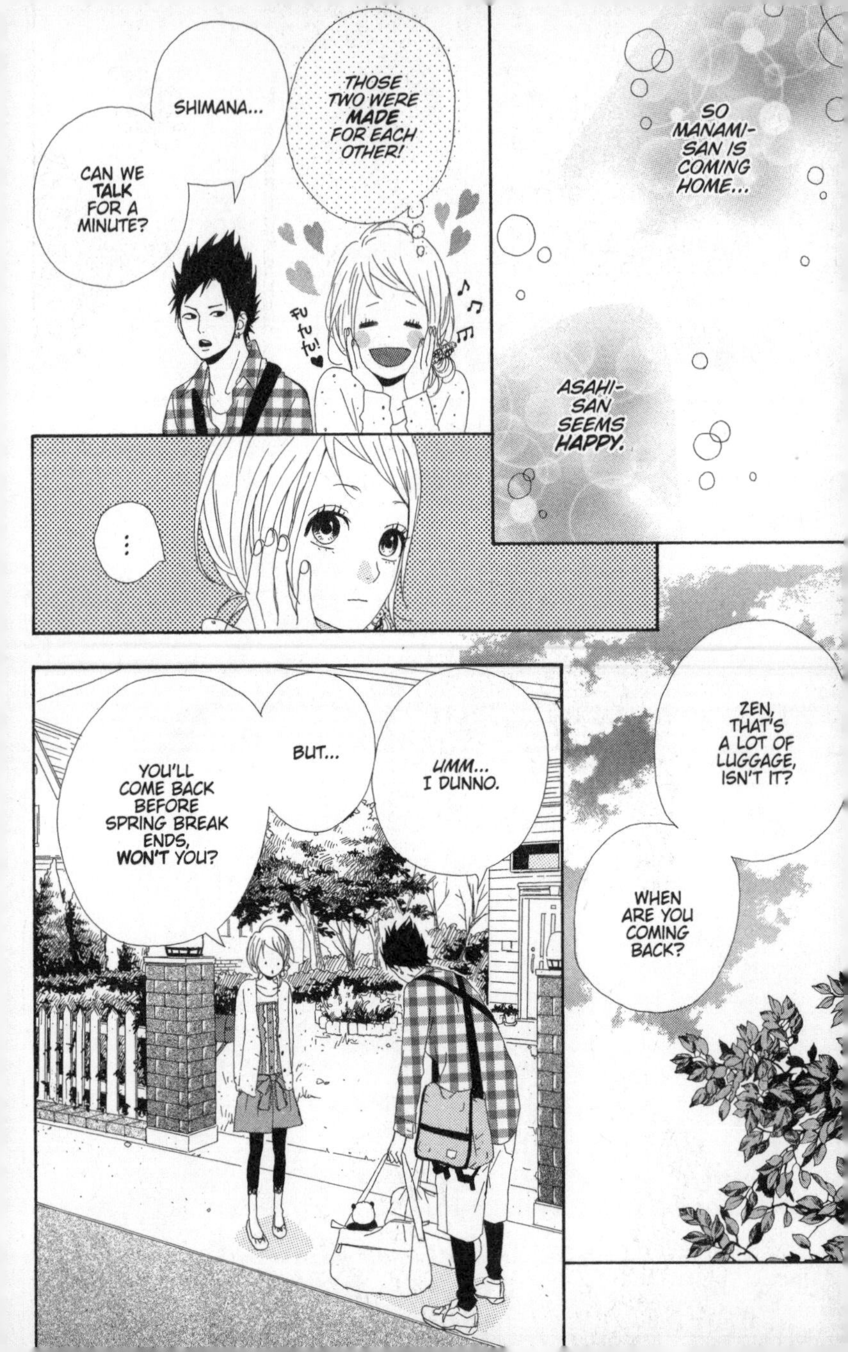
SO MANAMI-SAN IS COMING HOME...
ASAHI-SAN SEEMS HAPPY.
THOSE TWO WERE MADE FOR EACH OTHER!
SHIMANA...
CAN WE TALK FOR A MINUTE?
FU FU FU!
...
ZEN, THAT'S A LOT OF LUGGAGE, ISN'T IT?
WHEN ARE YOU COMING BACK?
UMM... I DUNNO.
BUT...
YOU'LL COME BACK BEFORE SPRING BREAK ENDS, WON'T YOU?

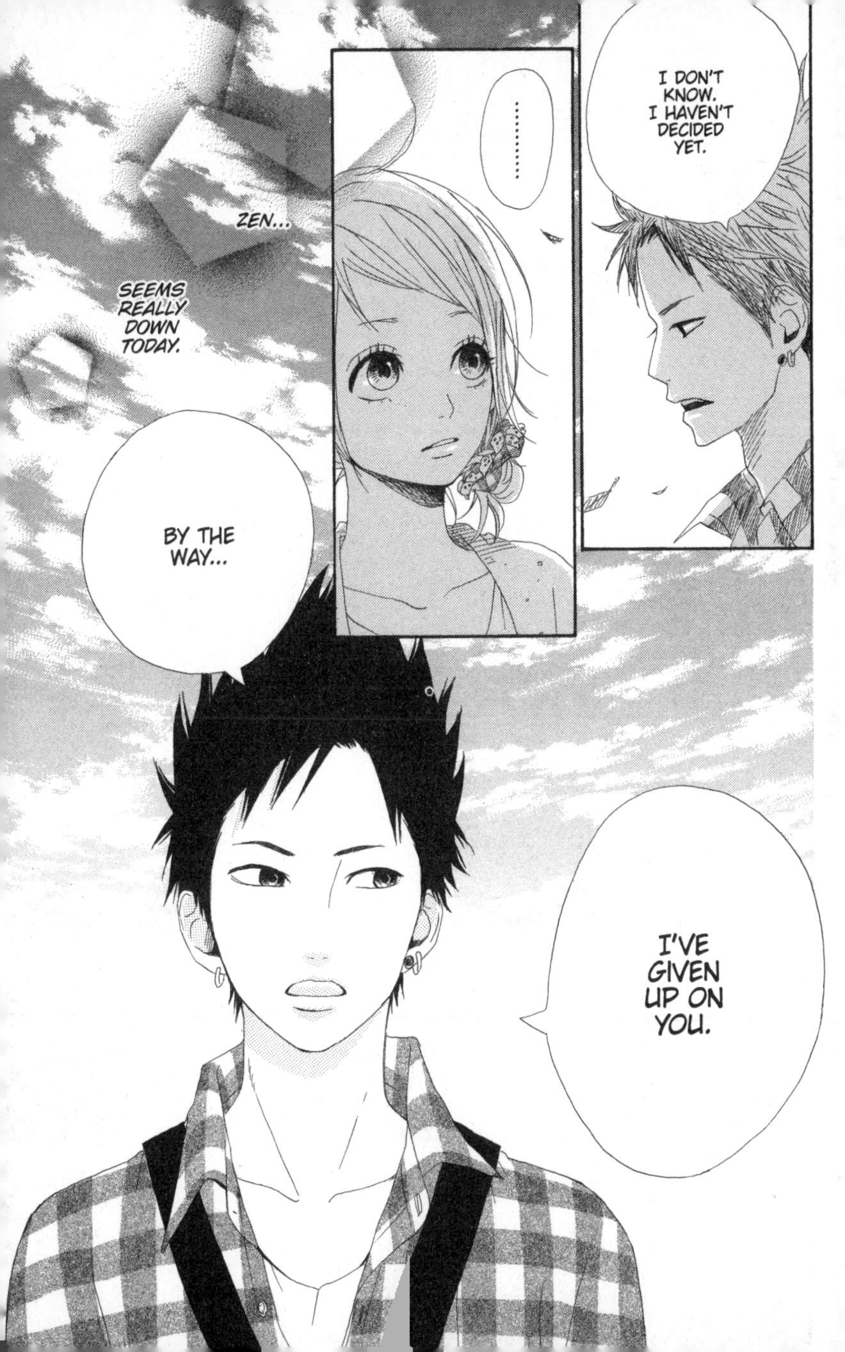
I DON'T KNOW. I HAVEN'T DECIDED YET.
……
ZEN...
SEEMS REALLY DOWN TODAY.
BY THE WAY...
I'VE GIVEN UP ON YOU.

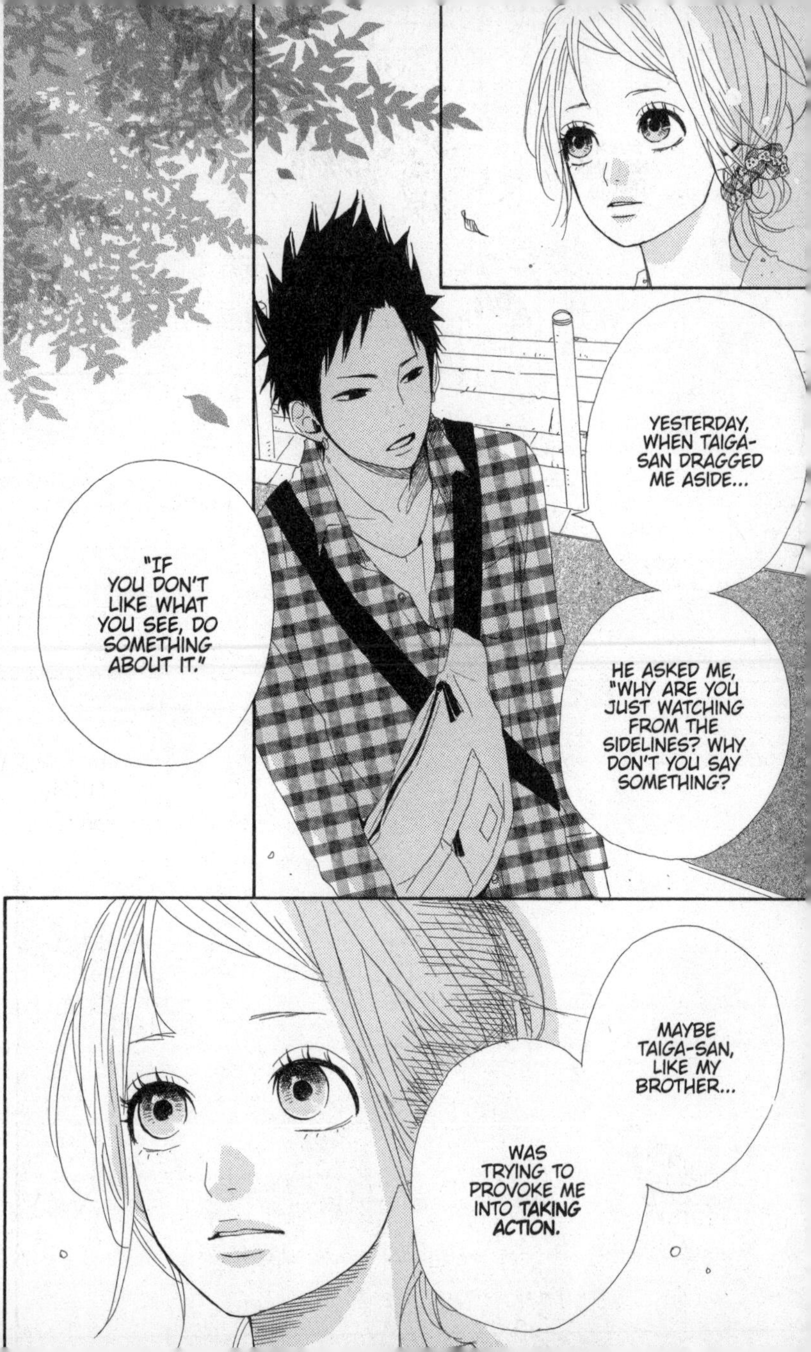
YESTERDAY, WHEN TAIGA-SAN DRAGGED ME ASIDE...
HE ASKED ME, "WHY ARE YOU JUST WATCHING FROM THE SIDELINES? WHY DON'T YOU SAY SOMETHING?
"IF YOU DON'T LIKE WHAT YOU SEE, DO SOMETHING ABOUT IT."
MAYBE TAIGA-SAN, LIKE MY BROTHER...
WAS TRYING TO PROVOKE ME INTO TAKING ACTION.

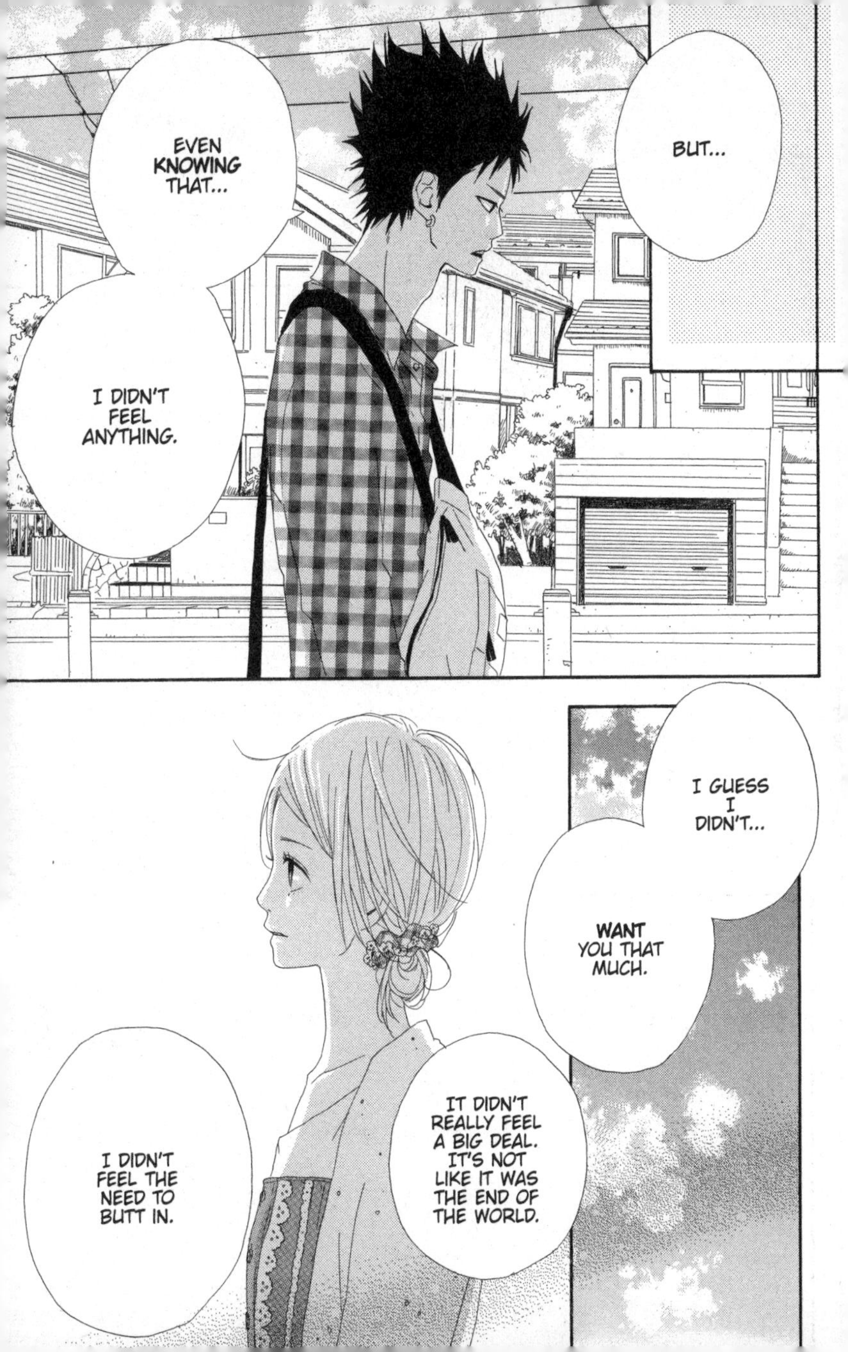
BUT...
EVEN KNOWING THAT...
I DIDN'T FEEL ANYTHING.
I GUESS I DIDN'T...
WANT YOU THAT MUCH.
IT DIDN'T REALLY FEEL A BIG DEAL. IT'S NOT LIKE IT WAS THE END OF THE WORLD.
I DIDN'T FEEL THE NEED TO BUTT IN.

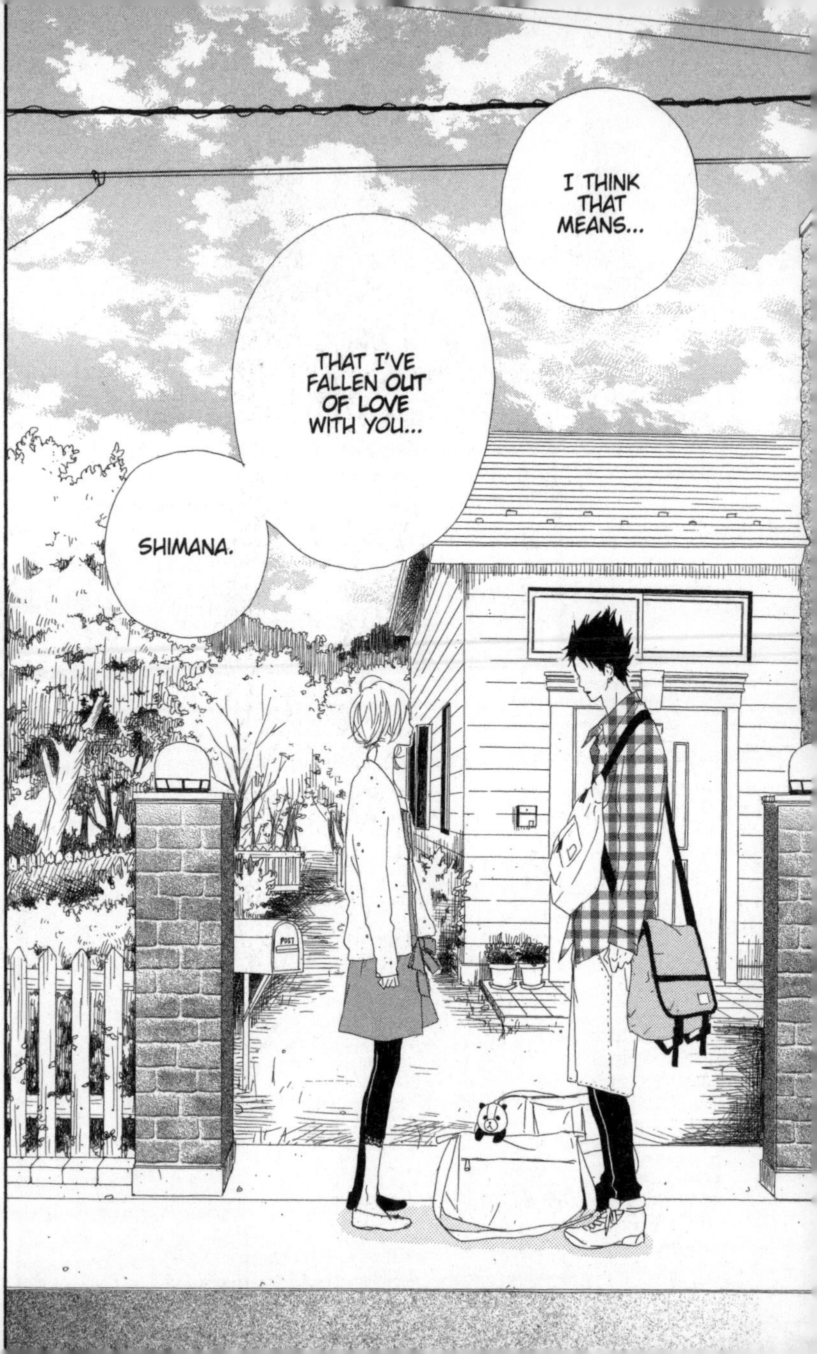
I THINK THAT MEANS...
THAT I'VE FALLEN OUT OF LOVE WITH YOU...
SHIMANA.

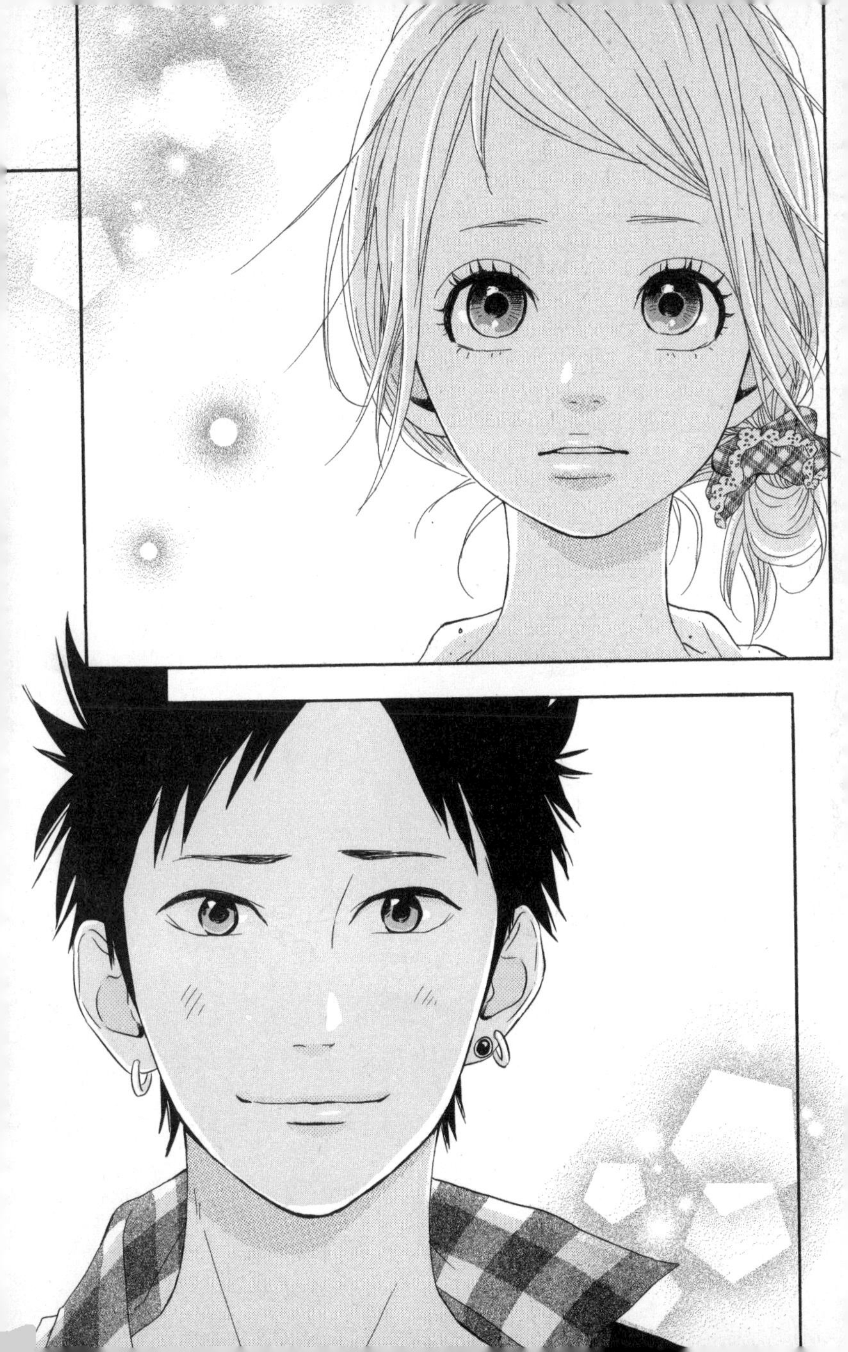

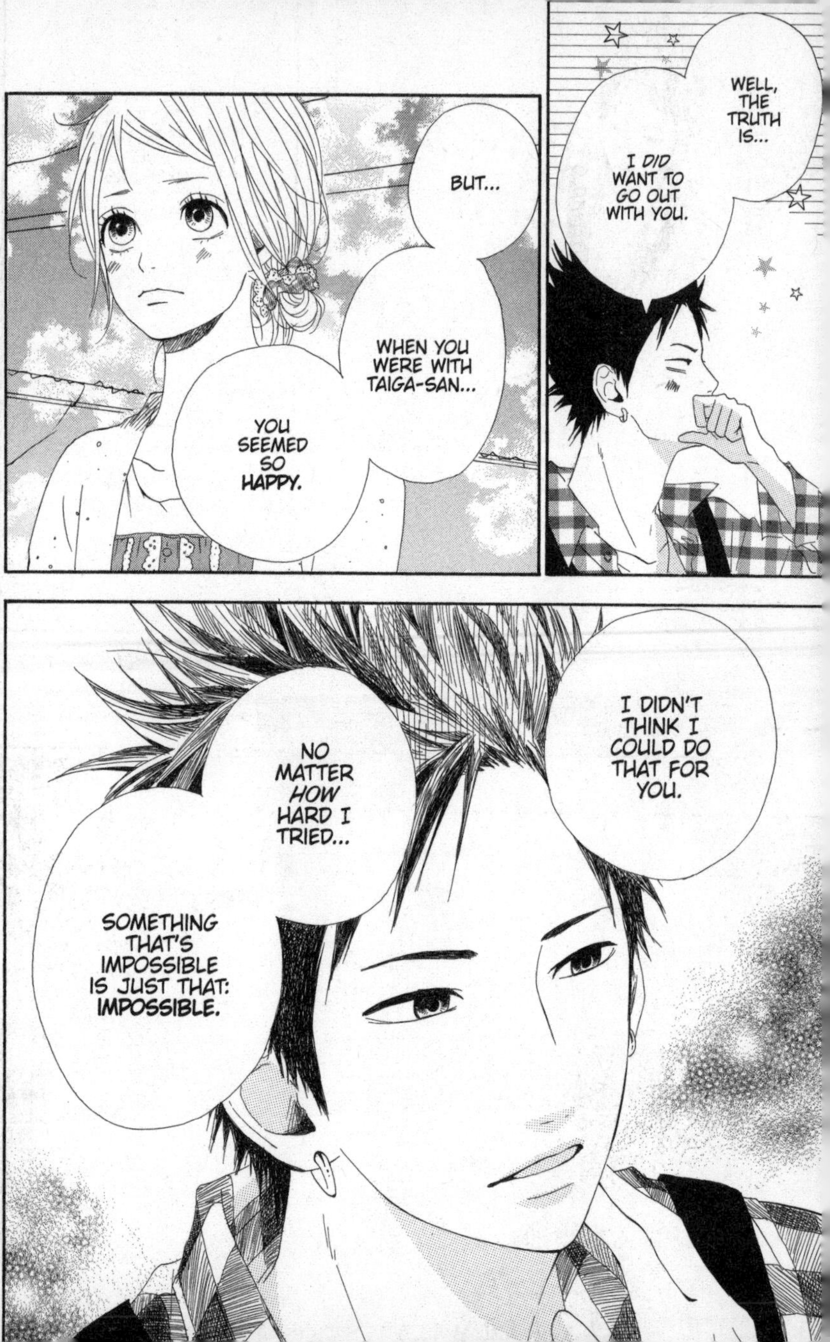
WELL, THE TRUTH IS...
I *DID* WANT TO GO OUT WITH YOU.
BUT...
WHEN YOU WERE WITH TAIGA-SAN...
YOU SEEMED SO HAPPY.
I DIDN'T THINK I COULD DO THAT FOR YOU.
NO MATTER *HOW* HARD I TRIED...
SOMETHING THAT'S IMPOSSIBLE IS JUST THAT: IMPOSSIBLE.

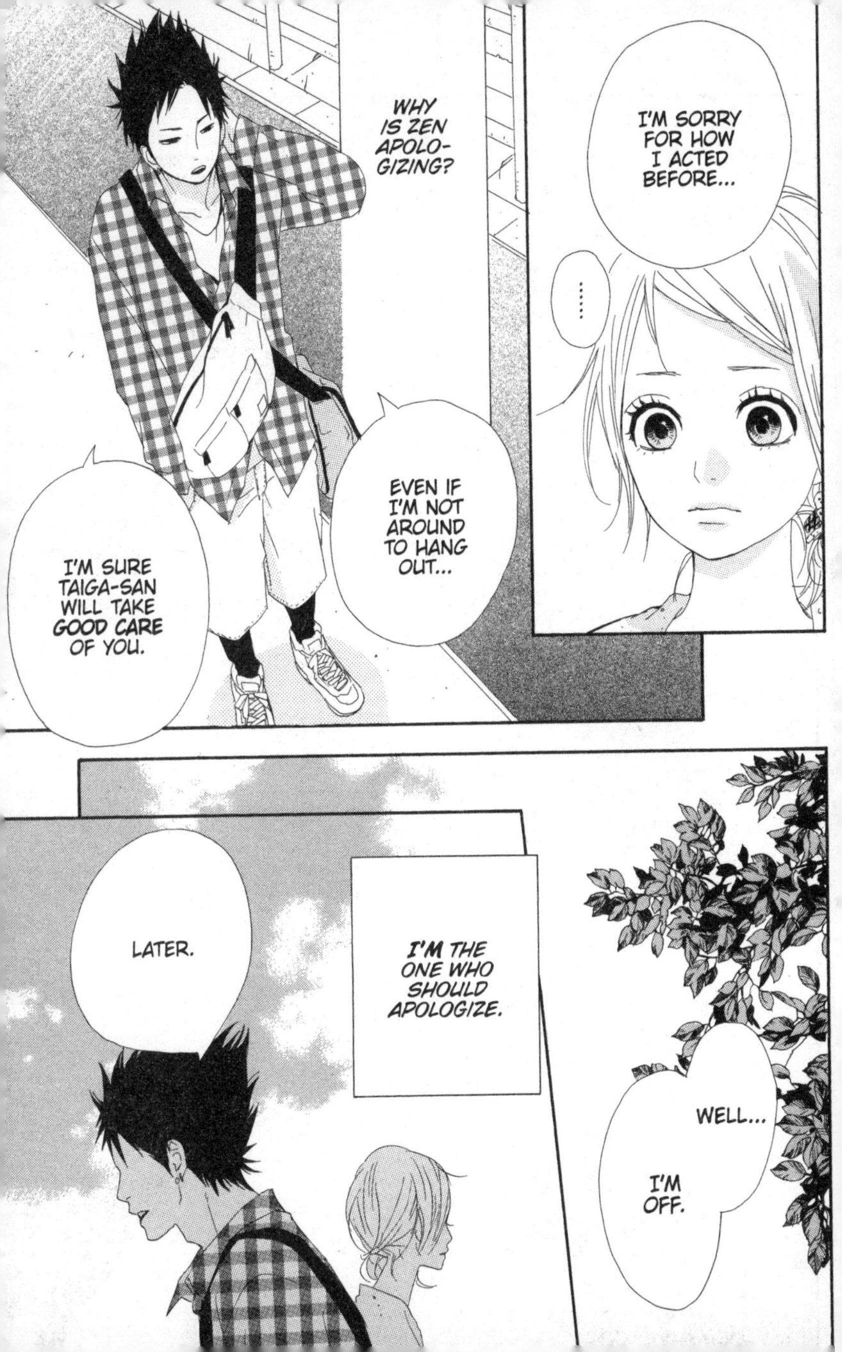
I'M SORRY FOR HOW I ACTED BEFORE...
......
WHY IS ZEN APOLOGIZING?
EVEN IF I'M NOT AROUND TO HANG OUT...
I'M SURE TAIGA-SAN WILL TAKE GOOD CARE OF YOU.
WELL...
I'M OFF.
I'M THE ONE WHO SHOULD APOLOGIZE.
LATER.

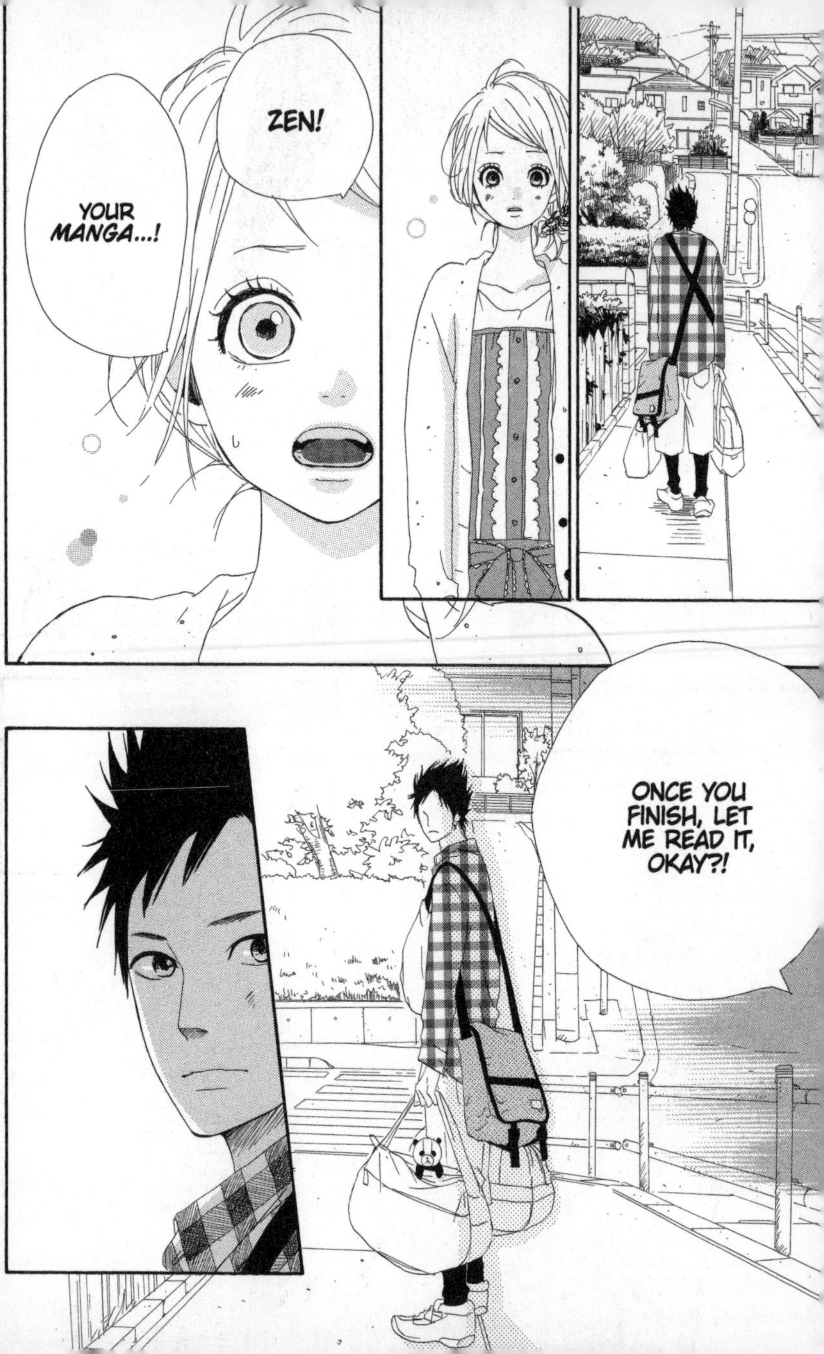
ZEN!
YOUR MANGA...!
ONCE YOU FINISH, LET ME READ IT, OKAY?!

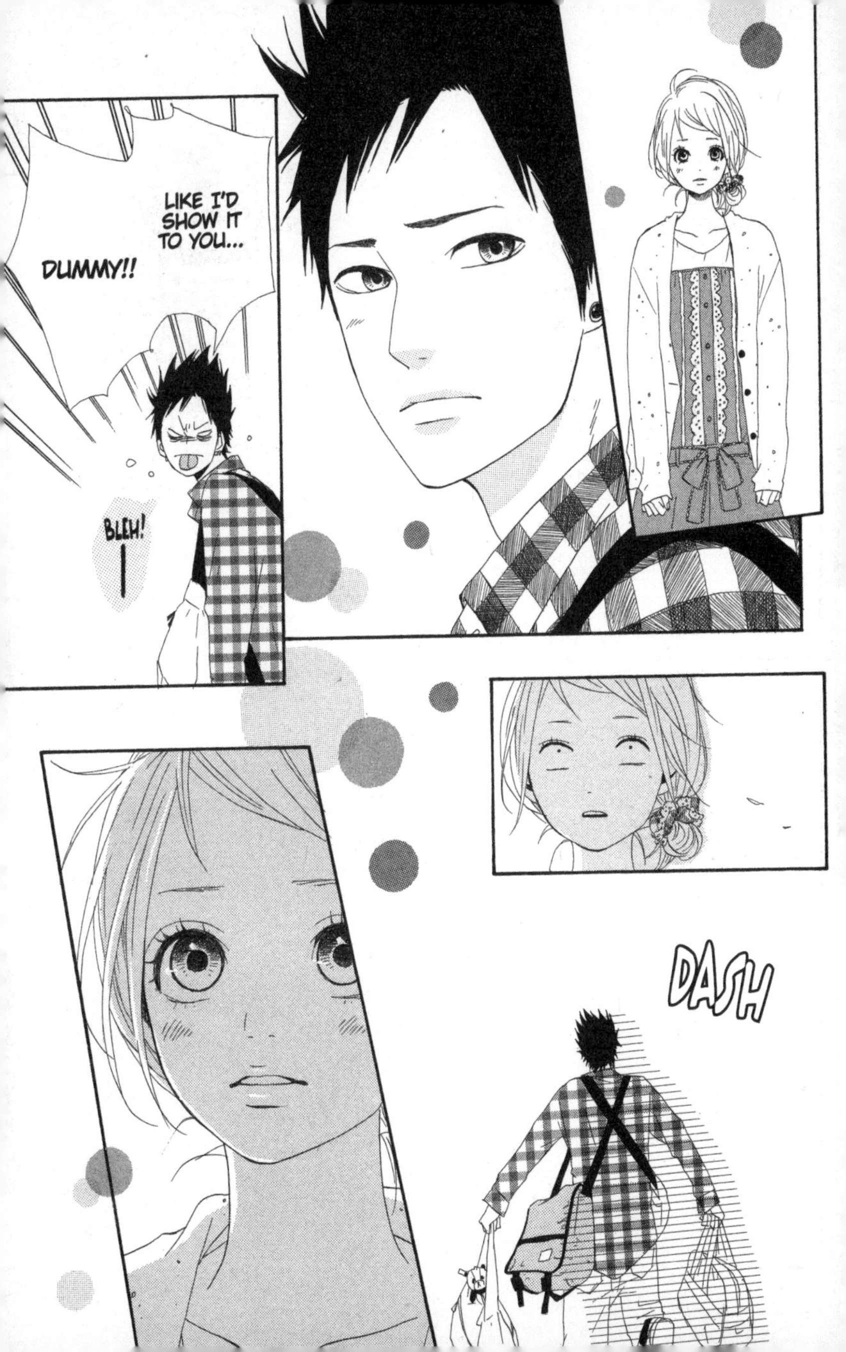
LIKE I'D SHOW IT TO YOU...
DUMMY!!
BLEH!
DASH

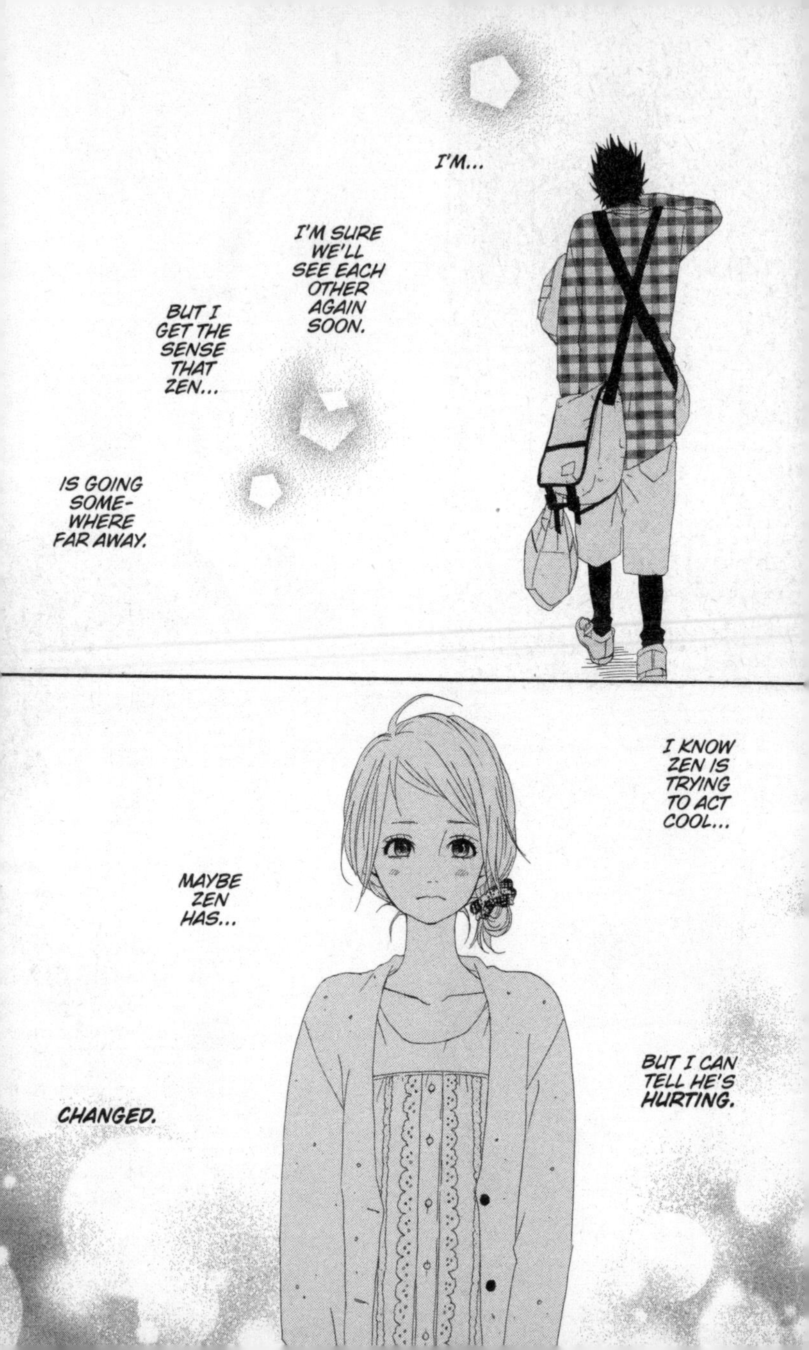
I'M...
I'M SURE WE'LL SEE EACH OTHER AGAIN SOON.
BUT I GET THE SENSE THAT ZEN...
IS GOING SOME-WHERE FAR AWAY.
I KNOW ZEN IS TRYING TO ACT COOL...
BUT I CAN TELL HE'S HURTING.
MAYBE ZEN HAS...
CHANGED.

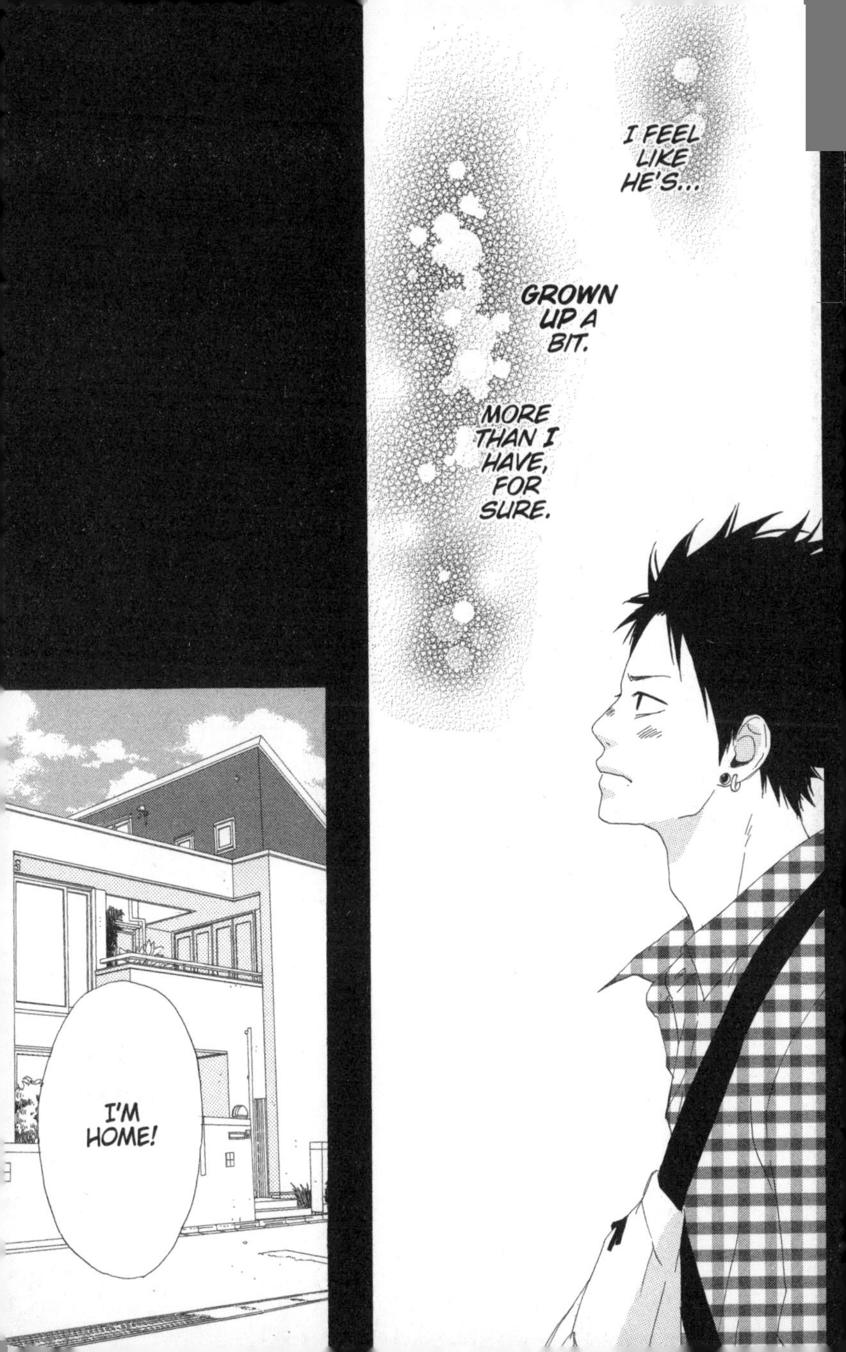
I FEEL LIKE HE'S...
GROWN UP A BIT.
MORE THAN I HAVE, FOR SURE.
I'M HOME!

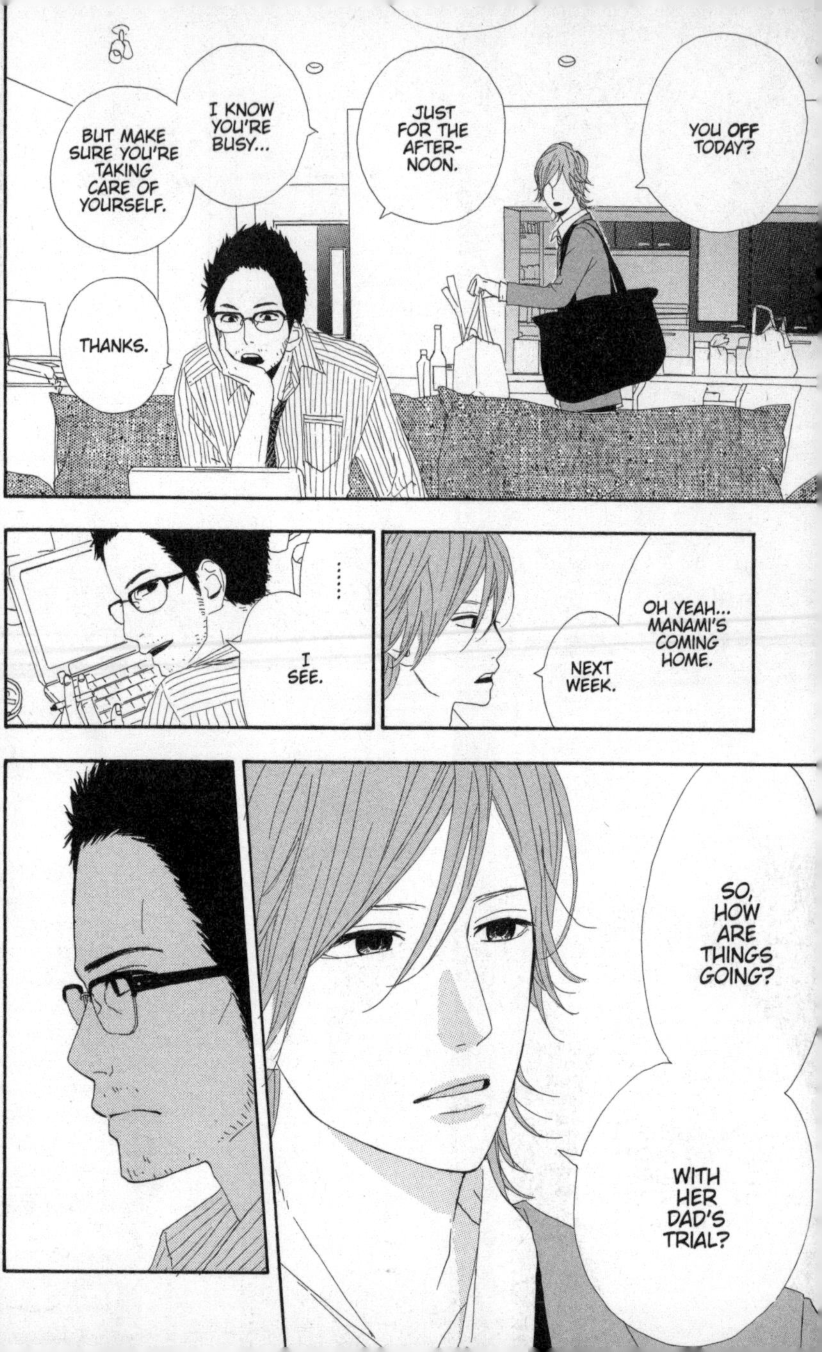
YOU OFF TODAY?
JUST FOR THE AFTER-NOON.
I KNOW YOU'RE BUSY...
BUT MAKE SURE YOU'RE TAKING CARE OF YOURSELF.
THANKS.
OH YEAH... MANAMI'S COMING HOME.
NEXT WEEK.
......
I SEE.
SO, HOW ARE THINGS GOING?
WITH HER DAD'S TRIAL?

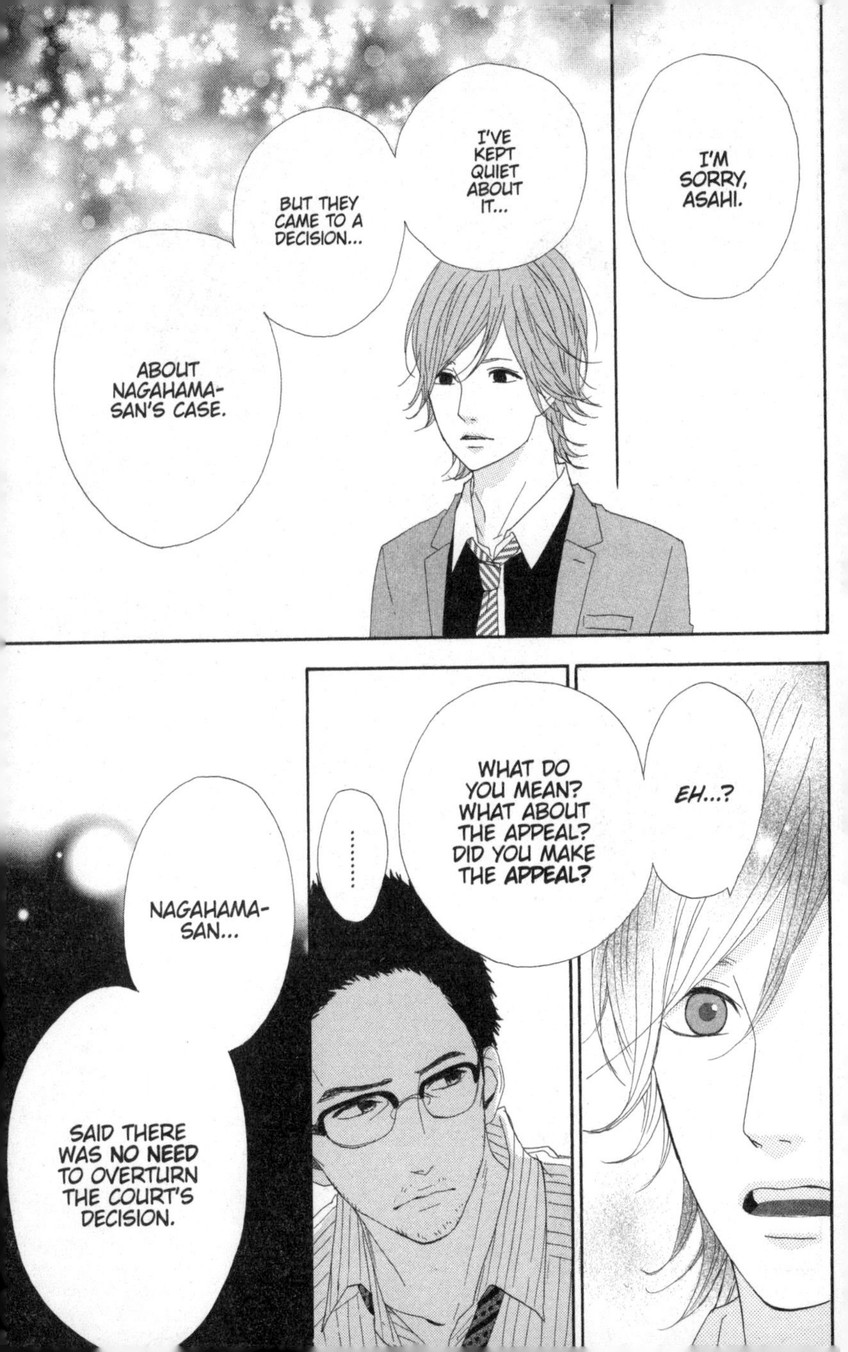

I'M SORRY, ASAHI.
I'VE KEPT QUIET ABOUT IT...
BUT THEY CAME TO A DECISION...
ABOUT NAGAHAMA-SAN'S CASE.
EH...?
WHAT DO YOU MEAN? WHAT ABOUT THE APPEAL? DID YOU MAKE THE APPEAL?
....
NAGAHAMA-SAN...
SAID THERE WAS NO NEED TO OVERTURN THE COURT'S DECISION.

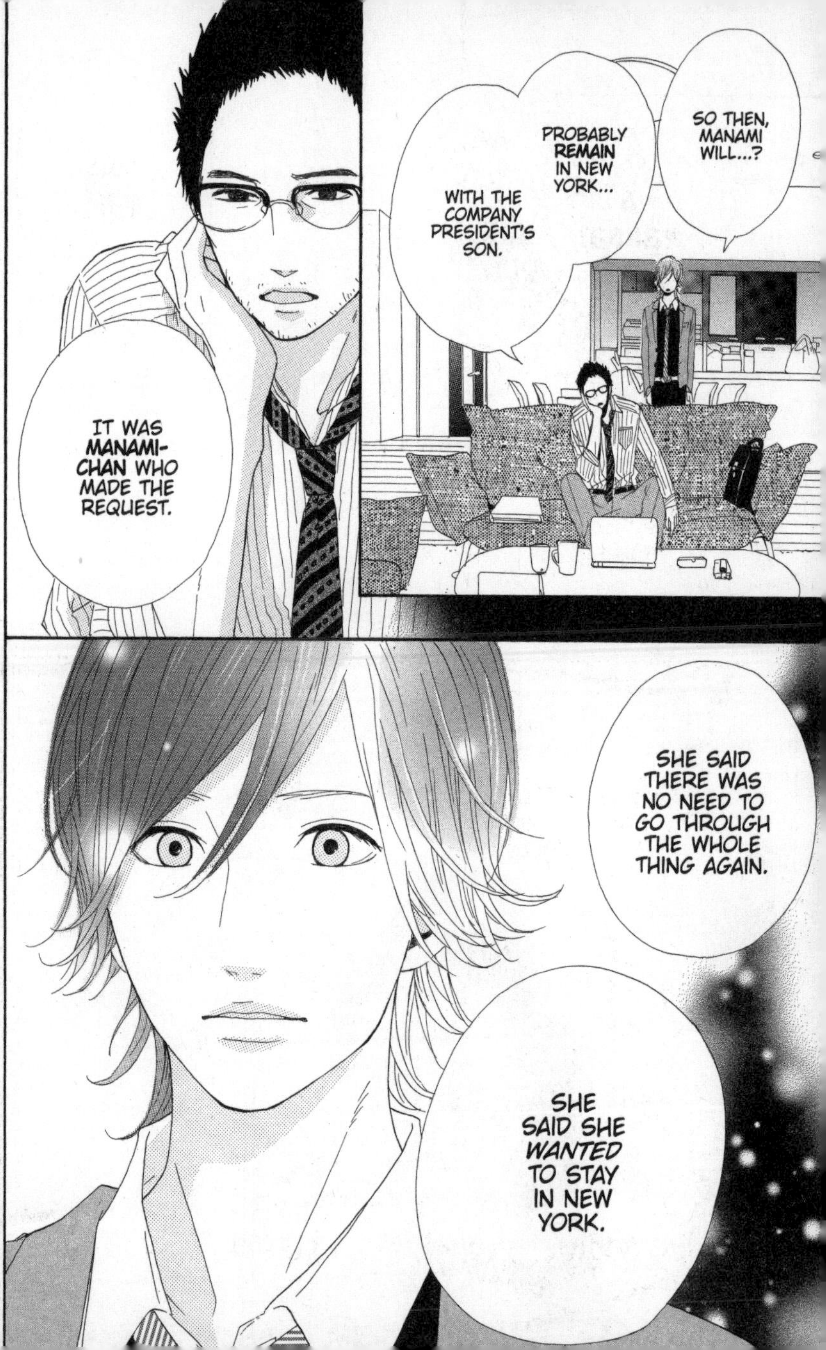
SO THEN, MANAMI WILL...?
PROBABLY REMAIN IN NEW YORK...
WITH THE COMPANY PRESIDENT'S SON.
IT WAS MANAMI-CHAN WHO MADE THE REQUEST.
SHE SAID THERE WAS NO NEED TO GO THROUGH THE WHOLE THING AGAIN.
SHE SAID SHE *WANTED* TO STAY IN NEW YORK.

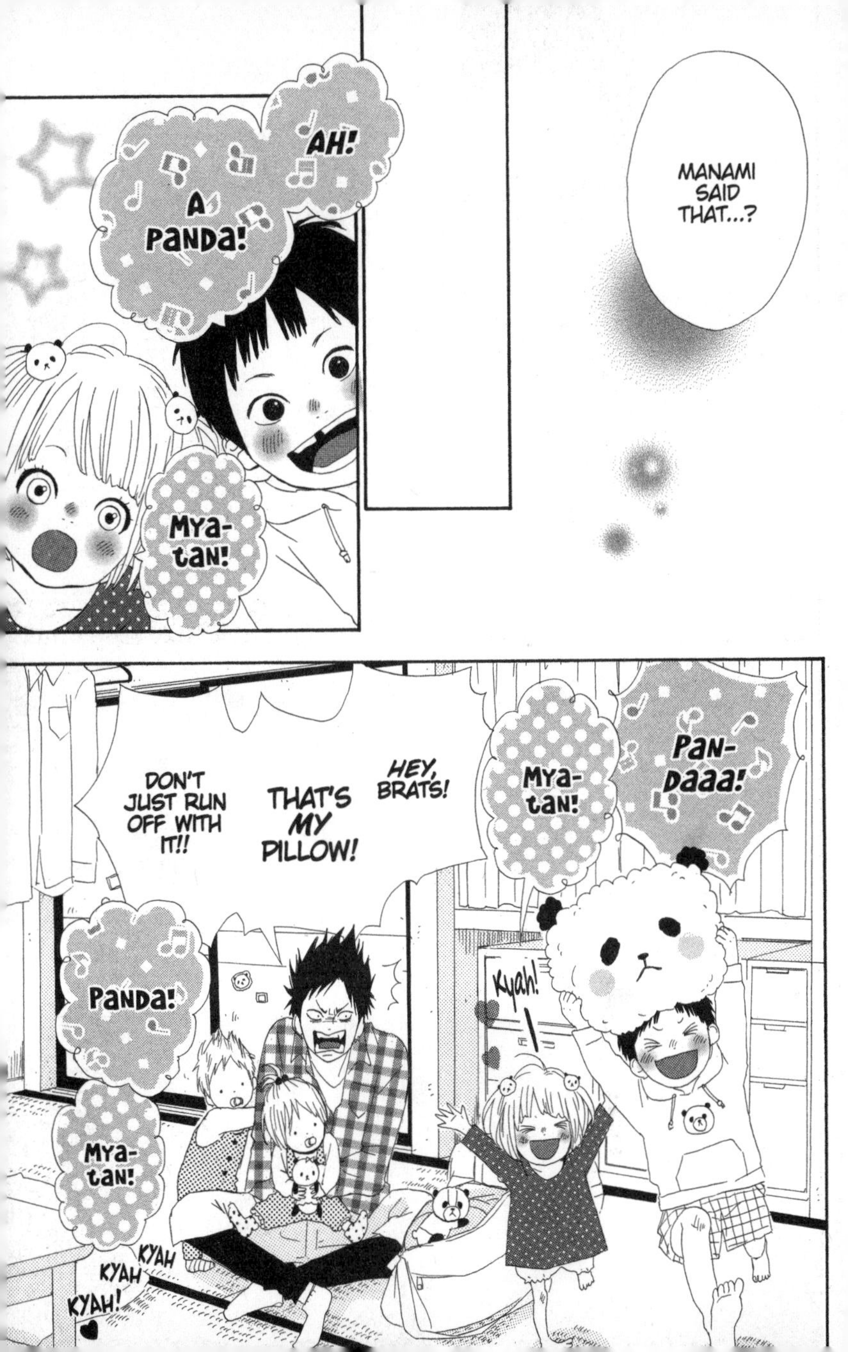
MANAMI SAID THAT...?
AH!
A PANDA!
MYA-TAN!
PAN-DAAA!
MYA-TAN!
HEY, BRATS!
THAT'S *MY* PILLOW!
DON'T JUST RUN OFF WITH IT!!
KYAH!
PANDA!
MYA-TAN!
KYAH
KYAH
KYAH!

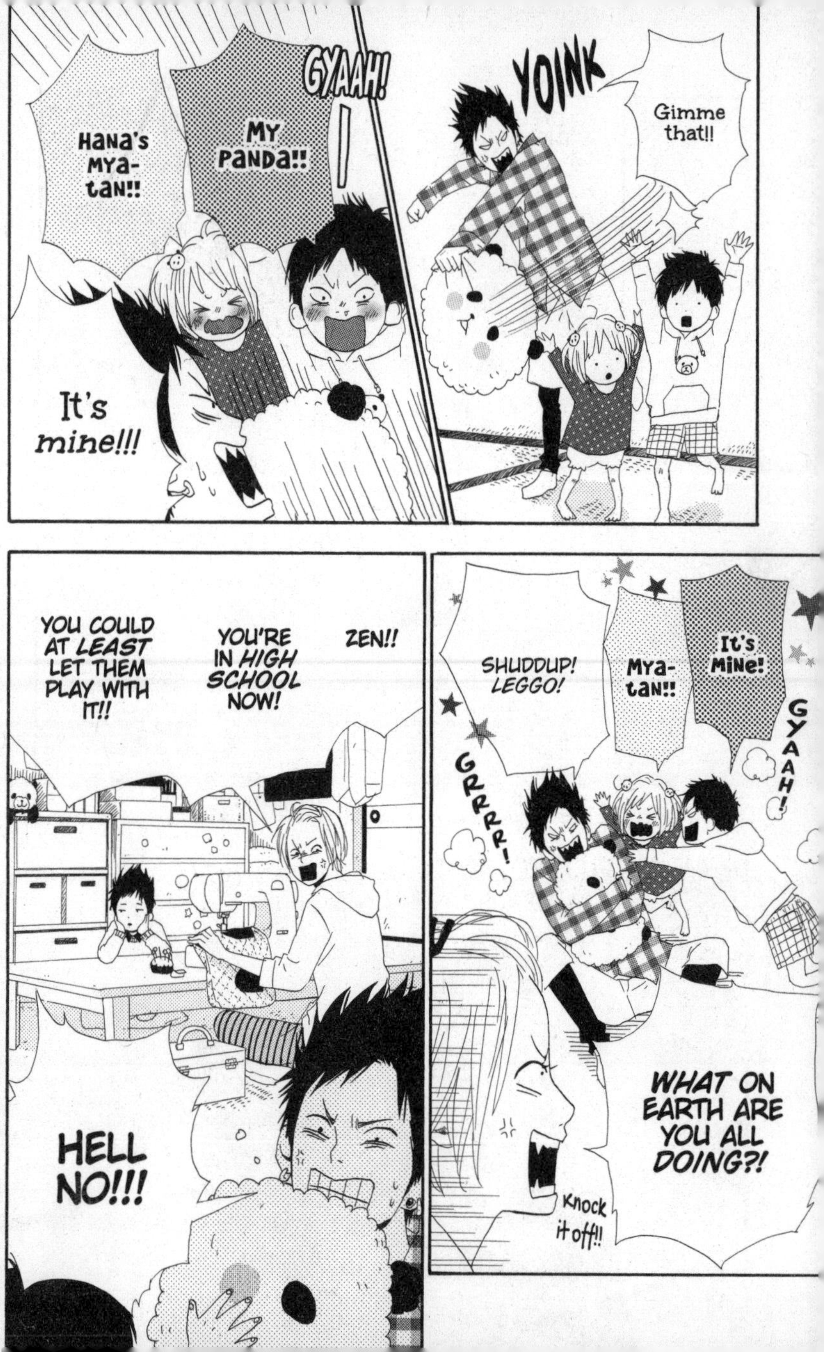
YOINK
Gimme that!!
GYAAH!
MY PANDA!!
Hana's Mya-tan!!
It's mine!!!
It's mine!
Mya-tan!!
SHUDDUP! LEGGO!
GYAAH!
GRRRR!
WHAT ON EARTH ARE YOU ALL DOING?!
Knock it off!!
ZEN!!
YOU'RE IN HIGH SCHOOL NOW!
YOU COULD AT LEAST LET THEM PLAY WITH IT!!
HELL NO!!!

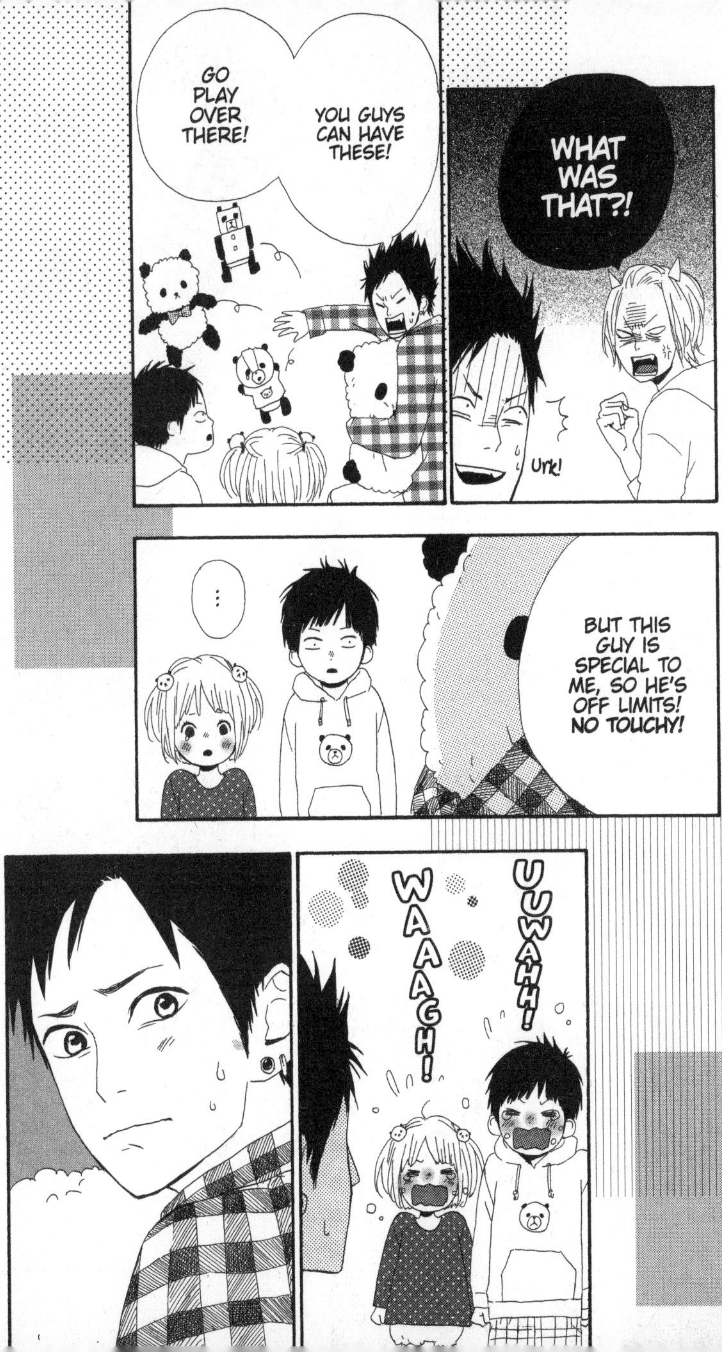
WHAT WAS THAT?!
Urk!
YOU GUYS CAN HAVE THESE!
GO PLAY OVER THERE!
BUT THIS GUY IS SPECIAL TO ME, SO HE'S OFF LIMITS! NO TOUCHY!
...
UUWAHH!
WAAAGH!

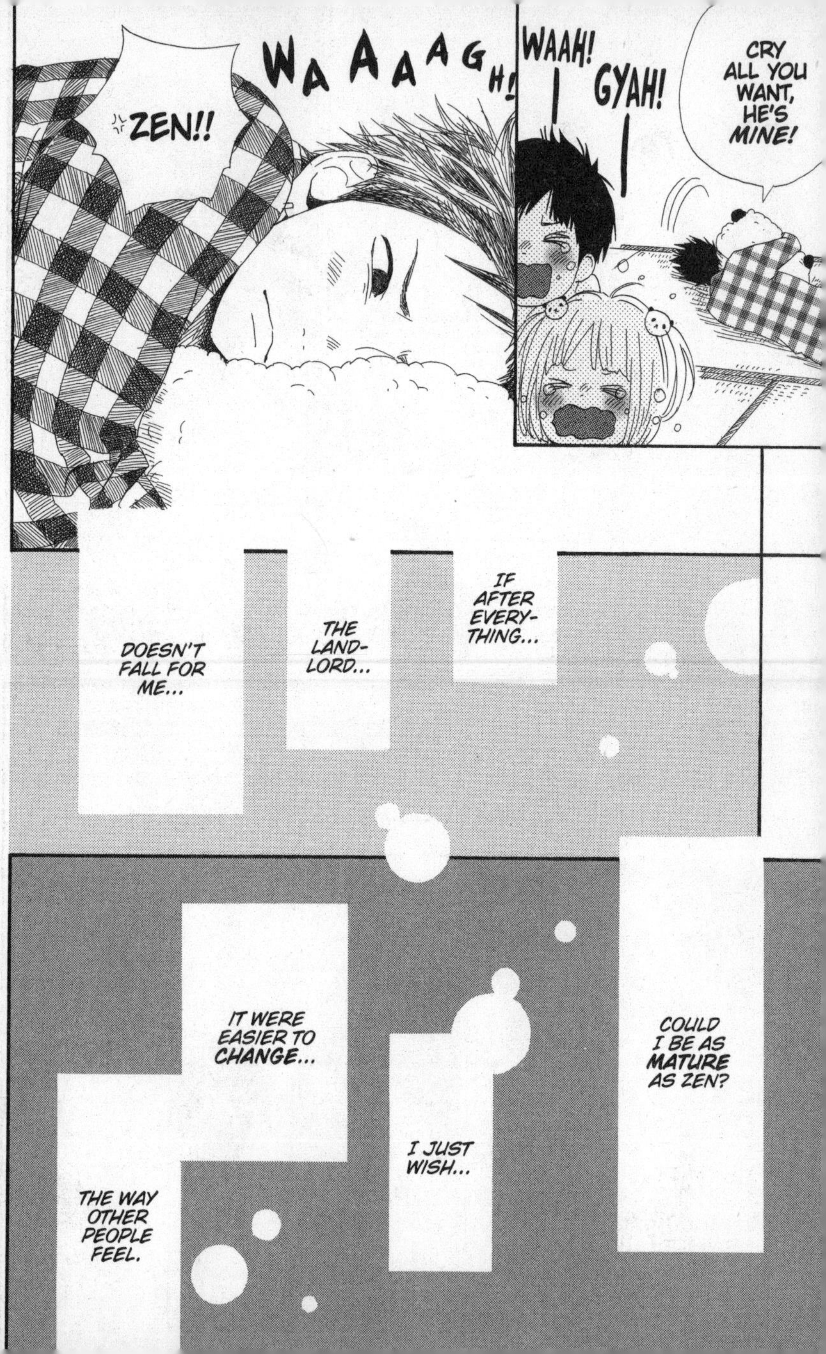
CRY ALL YOU WANT, HE'S MINE!
WAAH!
GYAH!
WAAAAGH!
ZEN!!
IF AFTER EVERYTHING...
THE LANDLORD...
DOESN'T FALL FOR ME...
COULD I BE AS MATURE AS ZEN?
I JUST WISH...
IT WERE EASIER TO CHANGE...
THE WAY OTHER PEOPLE FEEL.

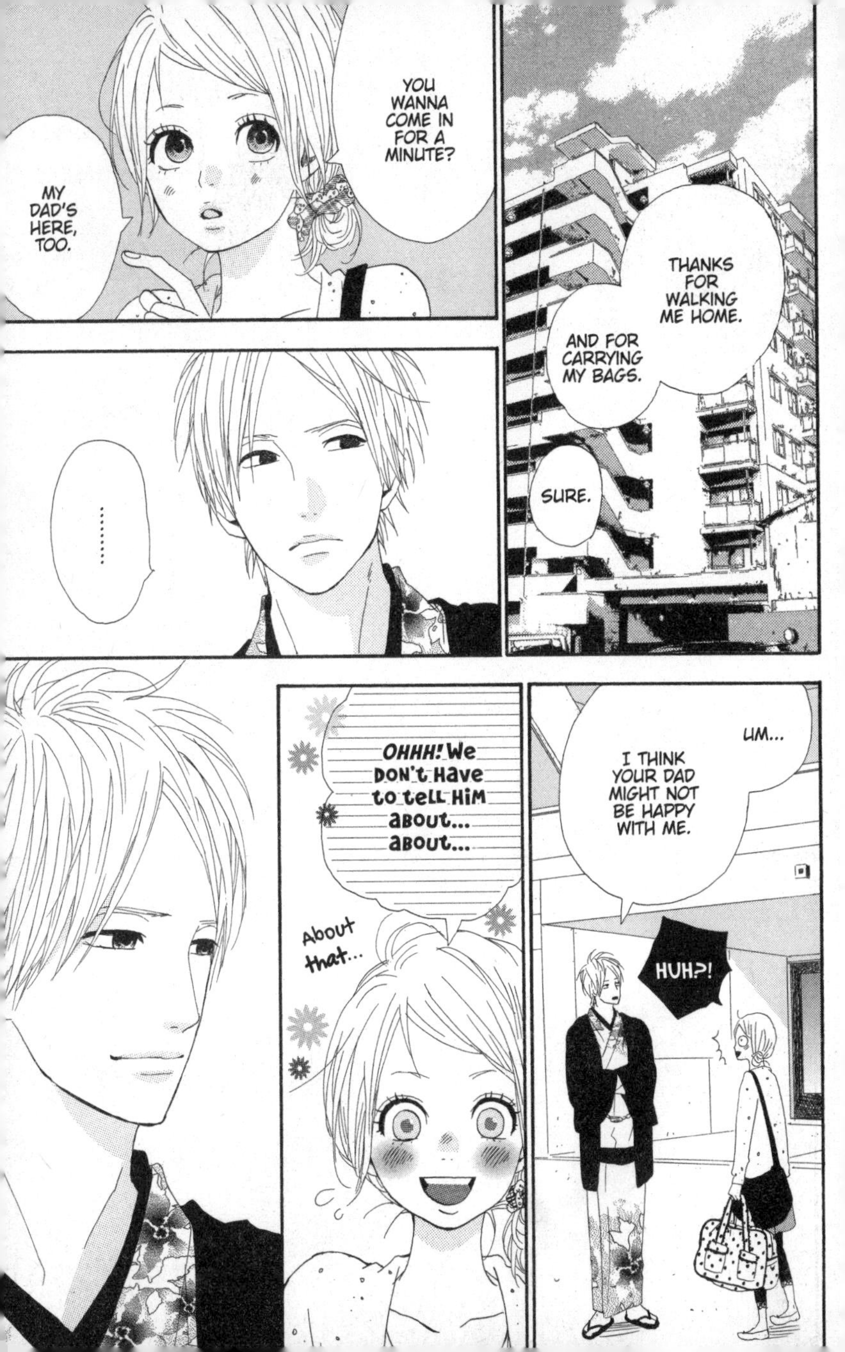
THANKS FOR WALKING ME HOME.
AND FOR CARRYING MY BAGS.
SURE.
YOU WANNA COME IN FOR A MINUTE?
MY DAD'S HERE, TOO.
......
UM...
I THINK YOUR DAD MIGHT NOT BE HAPPY WITH ME.
HUH?!
OHHH! We DON'T Have to tell HIM about... about...
About that...

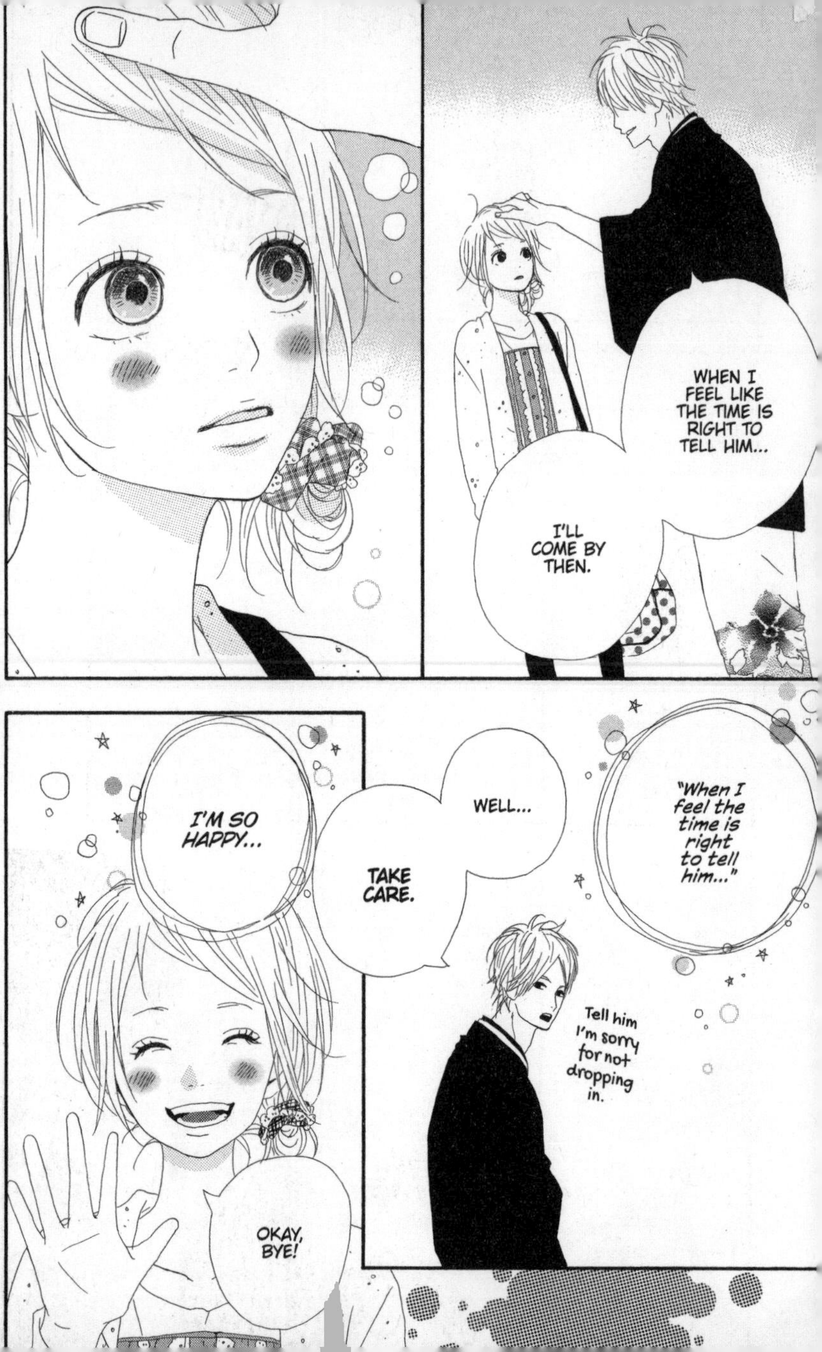
WHEN I FEEL LIKE THE TIME IS RIGHT TO TELL HIM...
I'LL COME BY THEN.
"When I feel the time is right to tell him..."
Tell him I'm sorry for not dropping in.
WELL...
TAKE CARE.
I'M SO HAPPY...
OKAY, BYE!

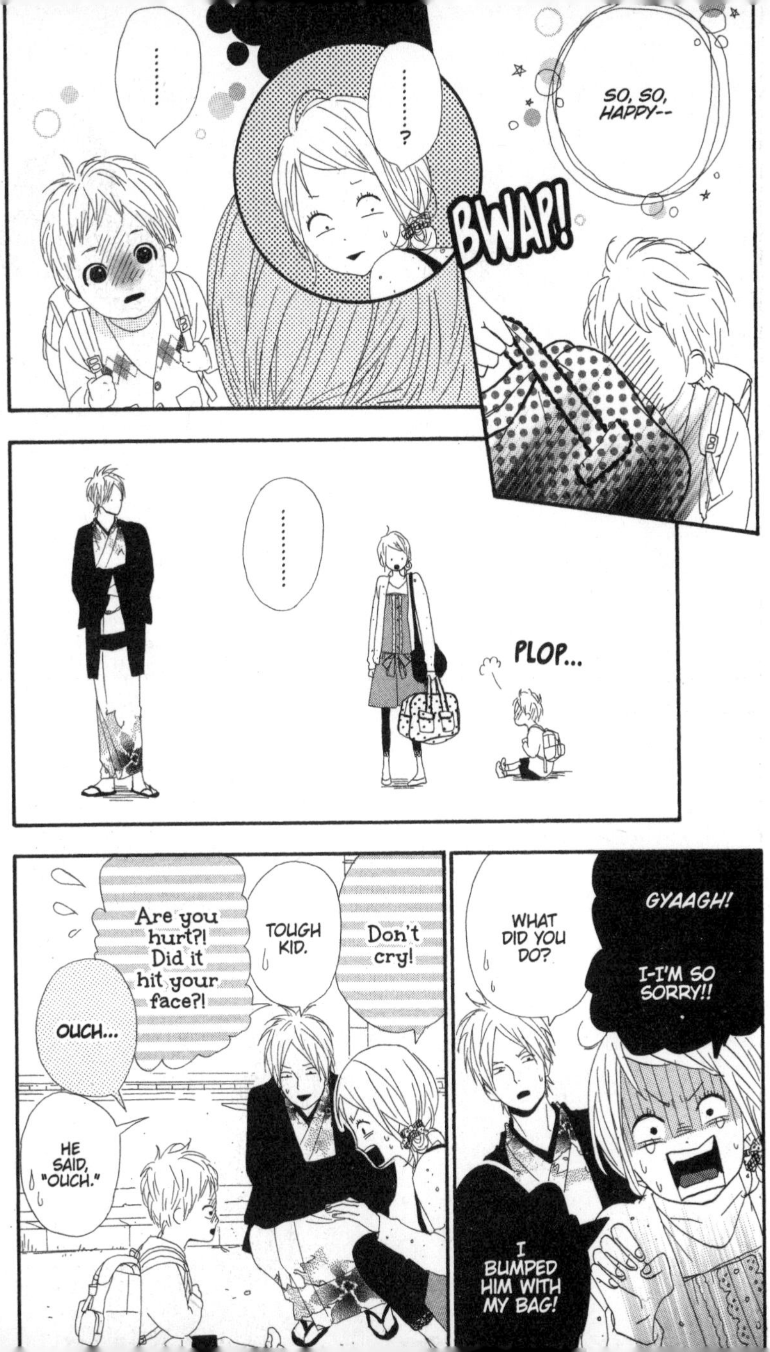
SO, SO, HAPPY--
BWAP!
......?
......
......
PLOP...
GYAAGH!
I-I'M SO SORRY!!
WHAT DID YOU DO?
I BUMPED HIM WITH MY BAG!
Don't cry!
TOUGH KID.
Are you hurt?! Did it hit your face?!
OUCH...
HE SAID, "OUCH."

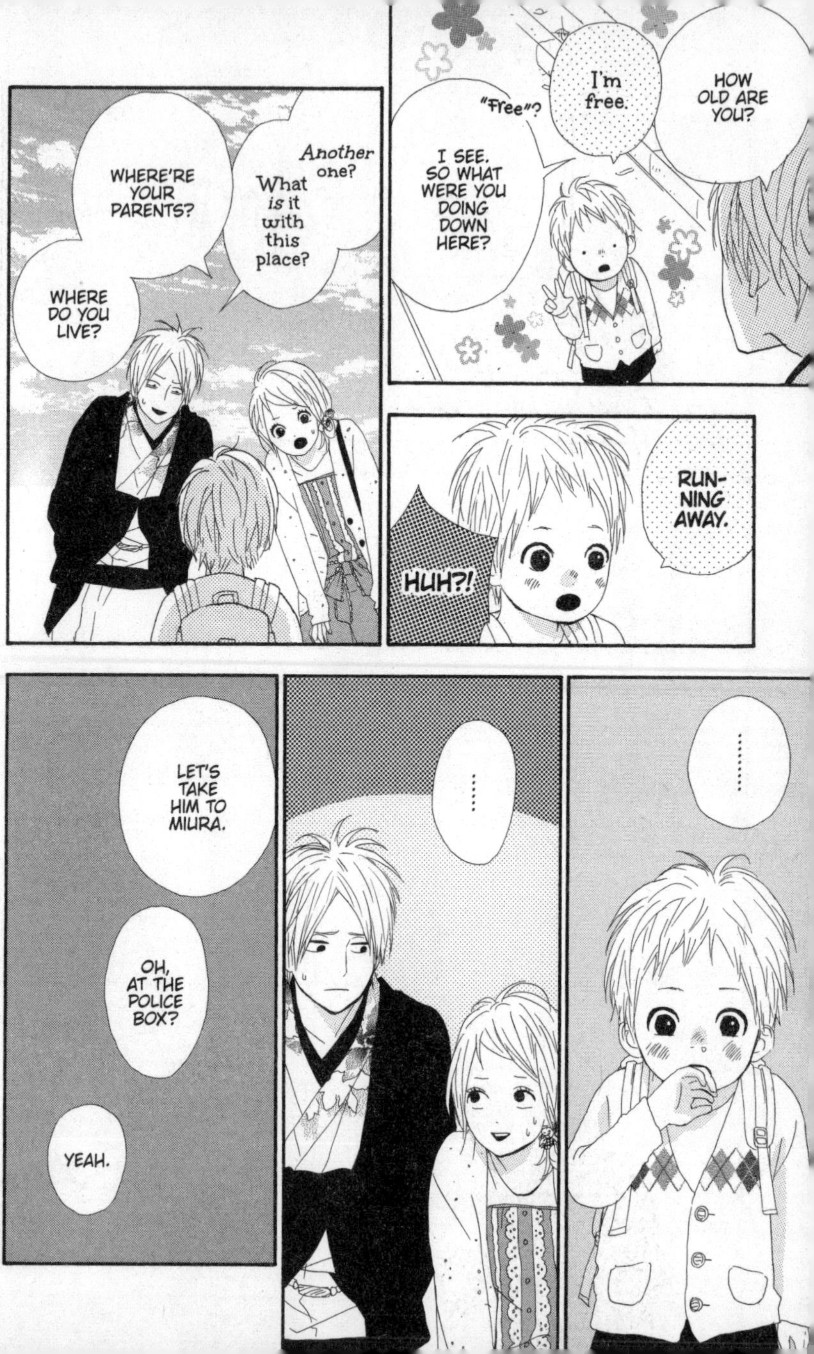
HOW OLD ARE YOU?
I'm free.
"Free"?
I SEE. SO WHAT WERE YOU DOING DOWN HERE?
RUN-NING AWAY.
HUH?!
Another one? What *is* it with this place?
WHERE'RE YOUR PARENTS?
WHERE DO YOU LIVE?
......
......
LET'S TAKE HIM TO MIURA.
OH, AT THE POLICE BOX?
YEAH.

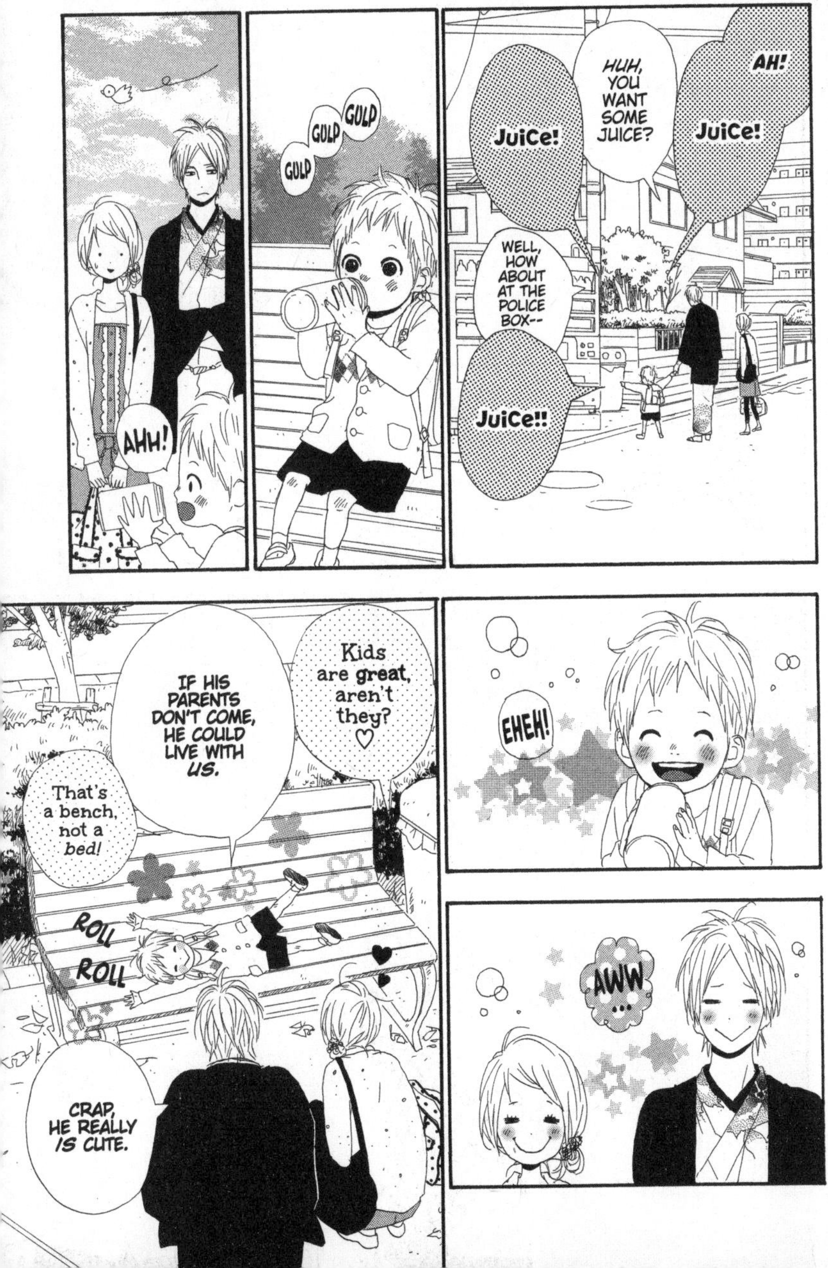
AH!
JuiCe!
HUH, YOU WANT SOME JUICE?
JuiCe!
WELL, HOW ABOUT AT THE POLICE BOX--
JuiCe!!
GULP
GULP
GULP
AHH!
EHEH!
AWW
Kids are great, aren't they? ♡
IF HIS PARENTS DON'T COME, HE COULD LIVE WITH US.
That's a bench, not a bed!
ROLL
ROLL
CRAP, HE REALLY IS CUTE.

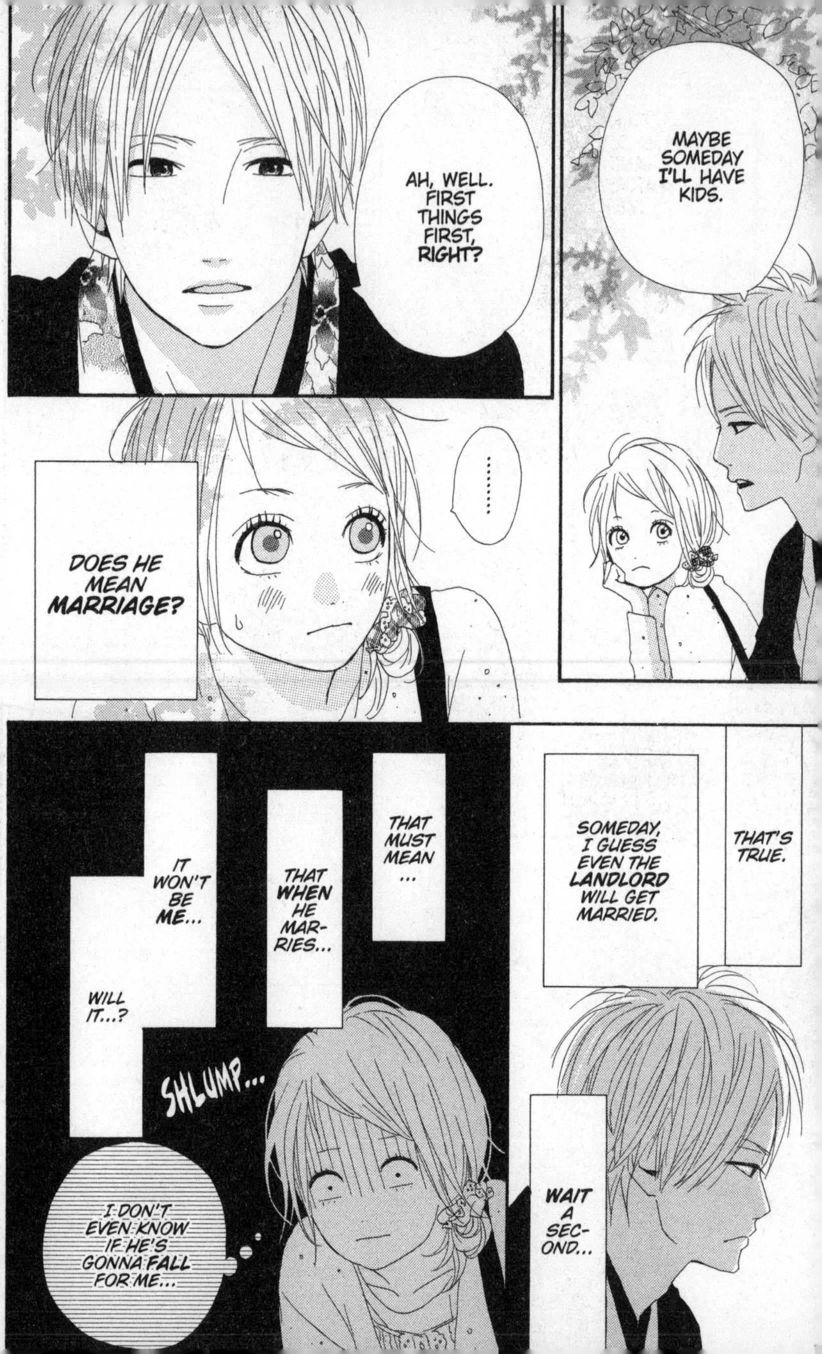
MAYBE SOMEDAY I'LL HAVE KIDS.
AH, WELL. FIRST THINGS FIRST, RIGHT?
......
DOES HE MEAN MARRIAGE?
THAT'S TRUE.
SOMEDAY, I GUESS EVEN THE LANDLORD WILL GET MARRIED.
WAIT A SEC-OND...
THAT MUST MEAN...
THAT WHEN HE MAR-RIES...
IT WON'T BE ME...
WILL IT...?
SHLUMP...
I DON'T EVEN KNOW IF HE'S GONNA FALL FOR ME...

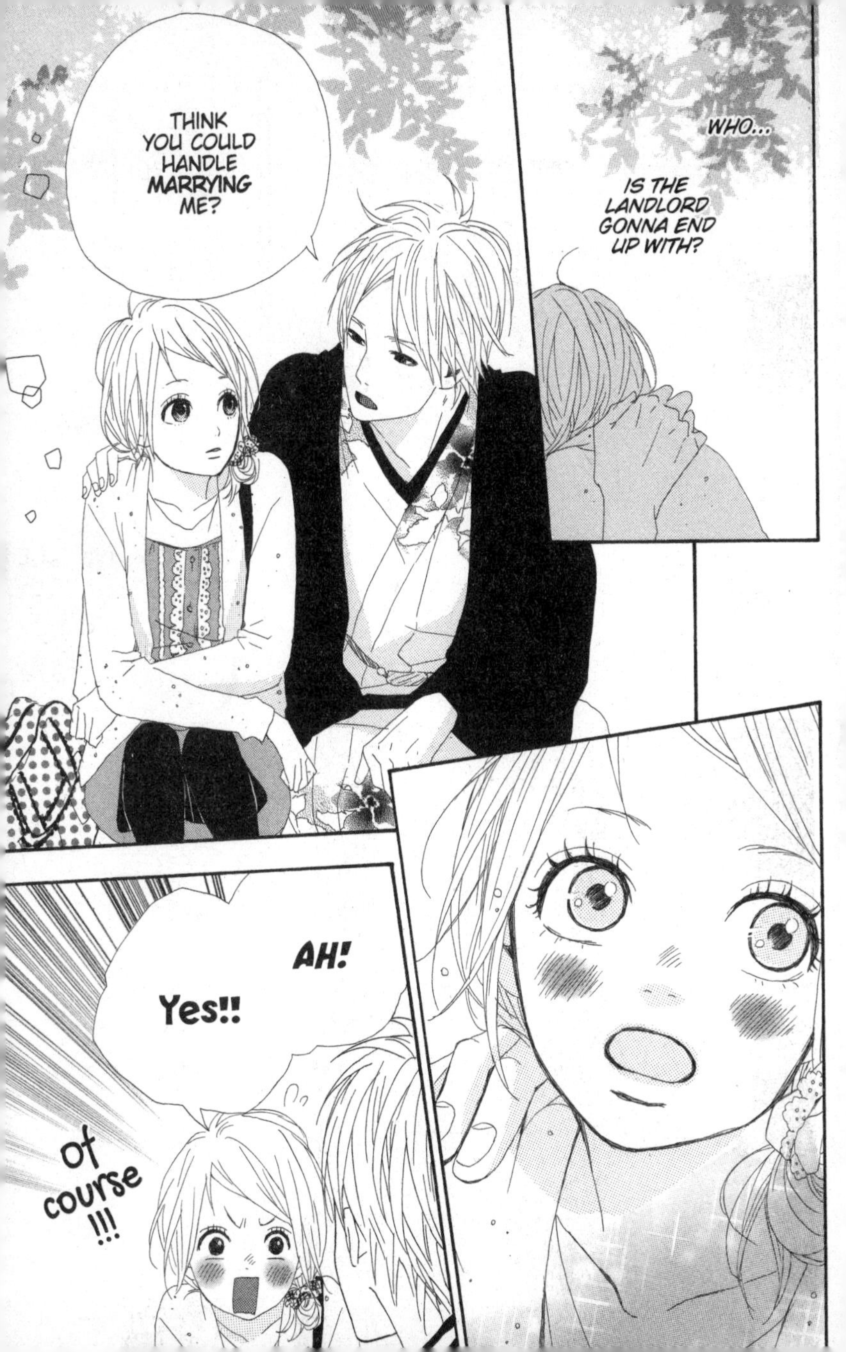
WHO...
IS THE LANDLORD GONNA END UP WITH?
THINK YOU COULD HANDLE MARRYING ME?
AH!
Yes!!
Of course!!!

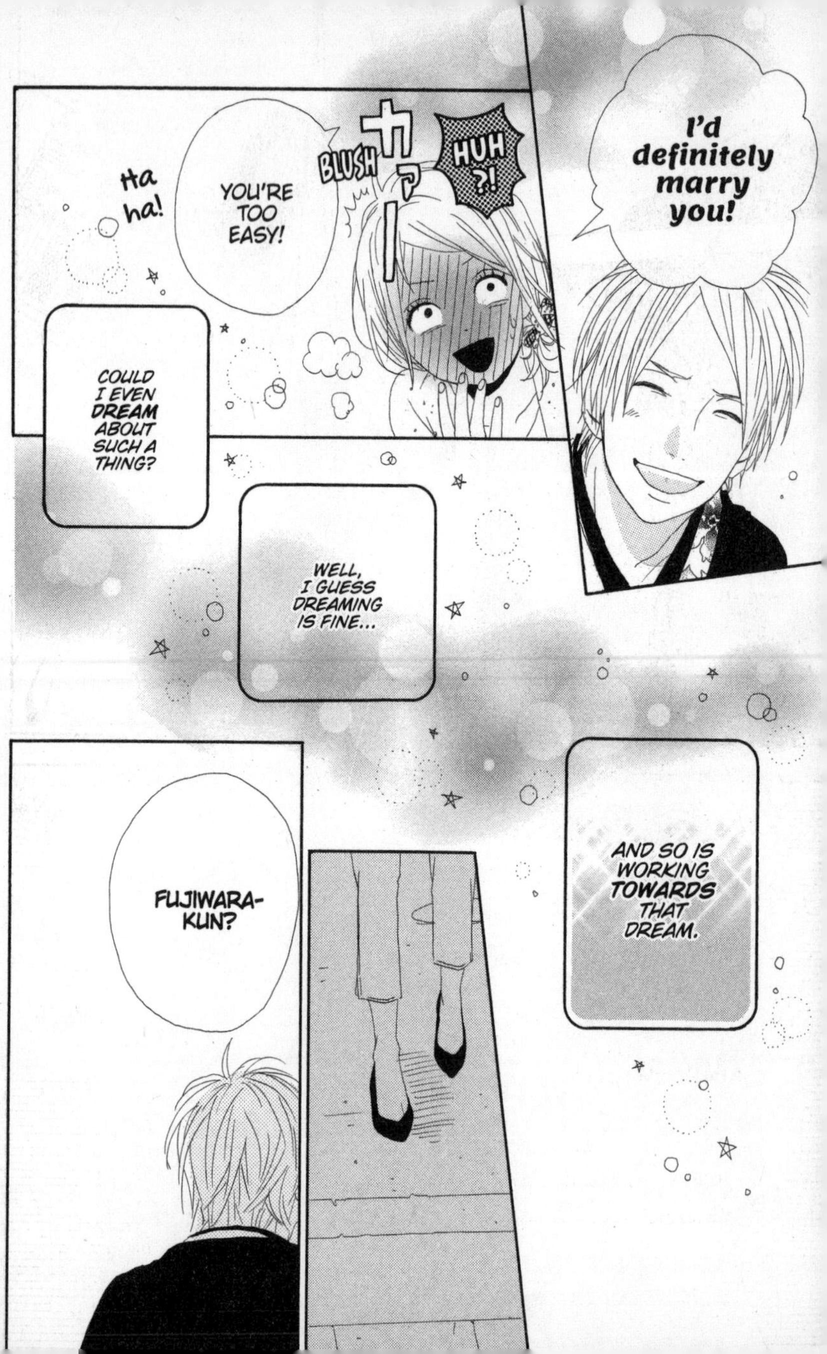

I'd definitely marry you!
HUH ?!
カァー
BLUSH
YOU'RE TOO EASY!
Ha ha!
COULD I EVEN DREAM ABOUT SUCH A THING?
WELL, I GUESS DREAMING IS FINE...
AND SO IS WORKING TOWARDS THAT DREAM.
FUJIWARA-KUN?

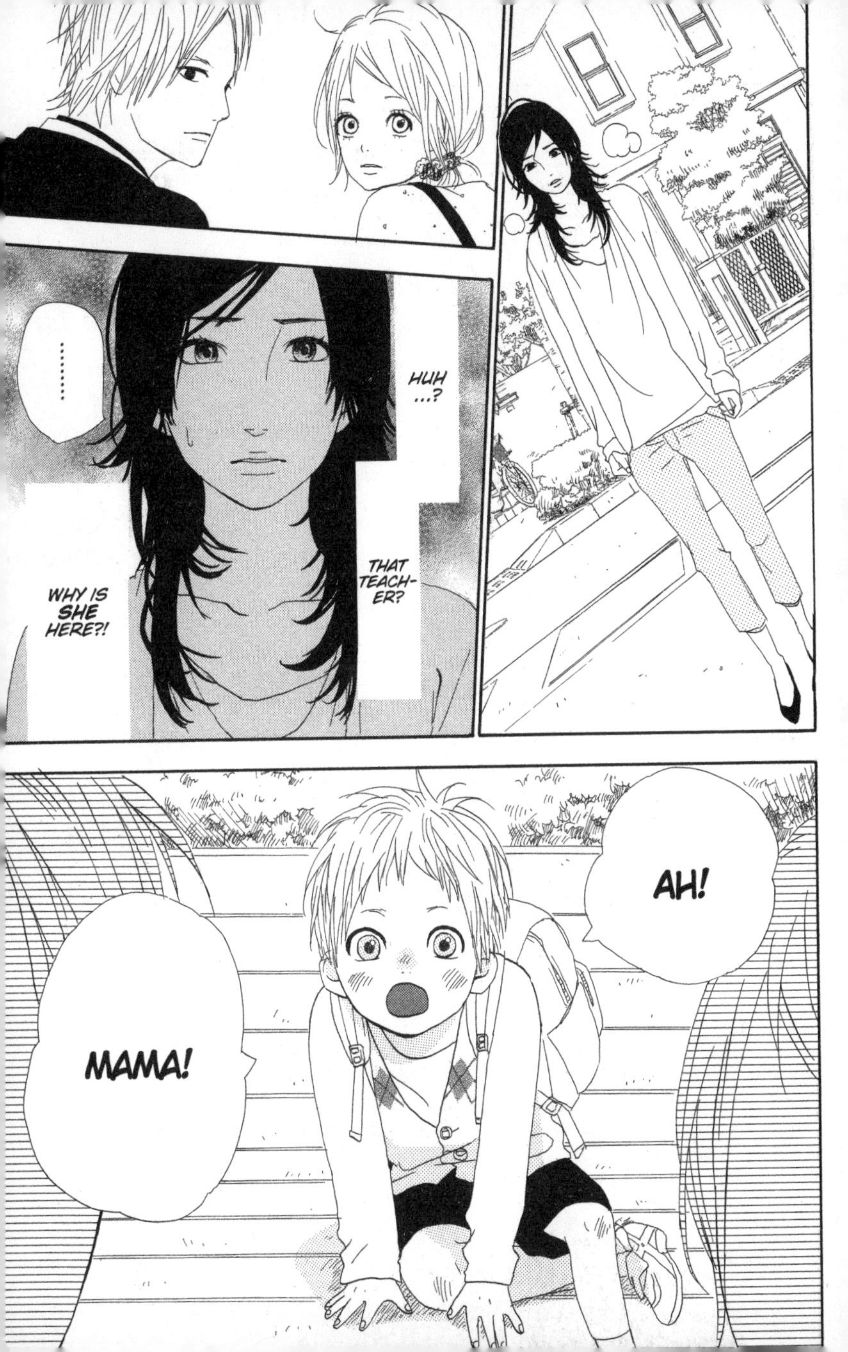
HUH ...?
THAT TEACHER?
......
WHY IS SHE HERE?!
AH!
MAMA!

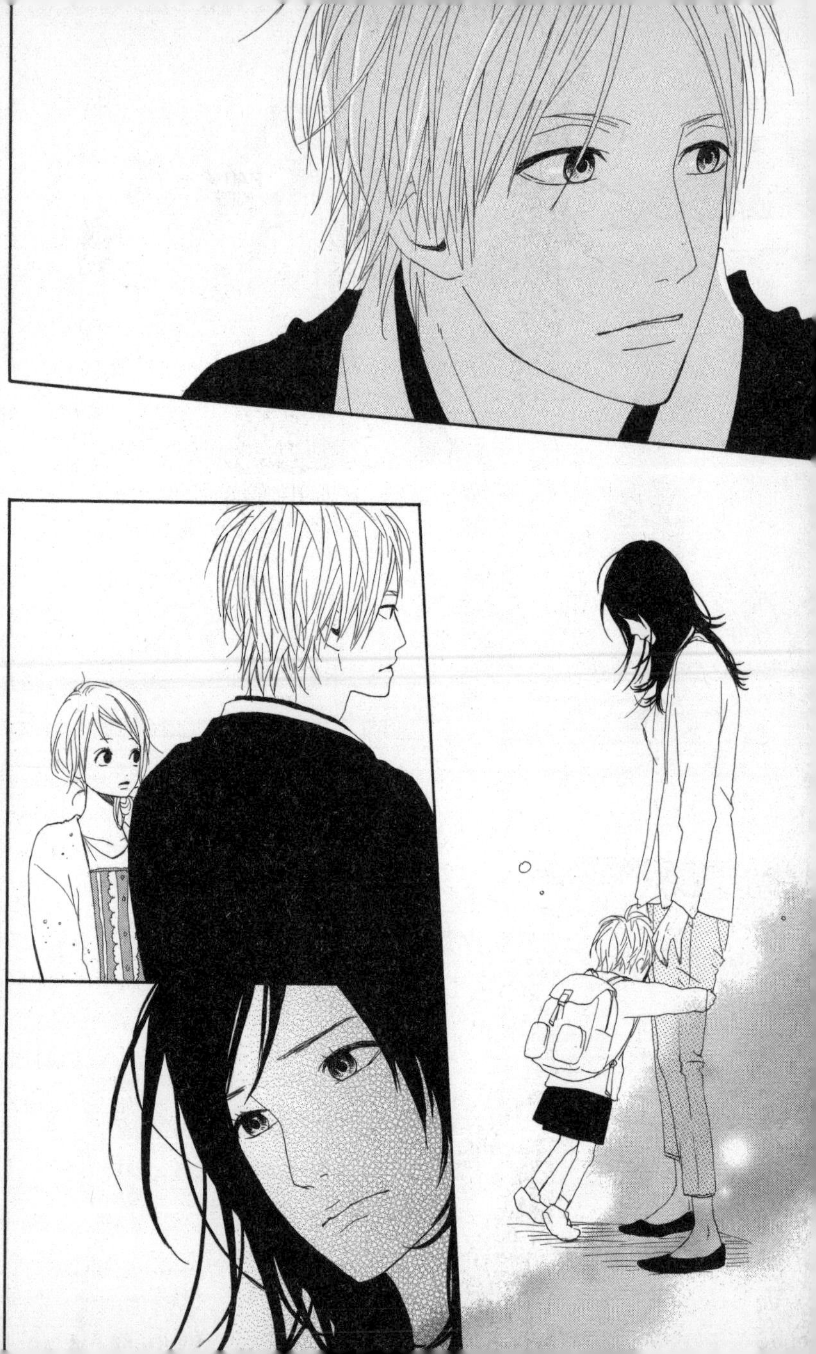

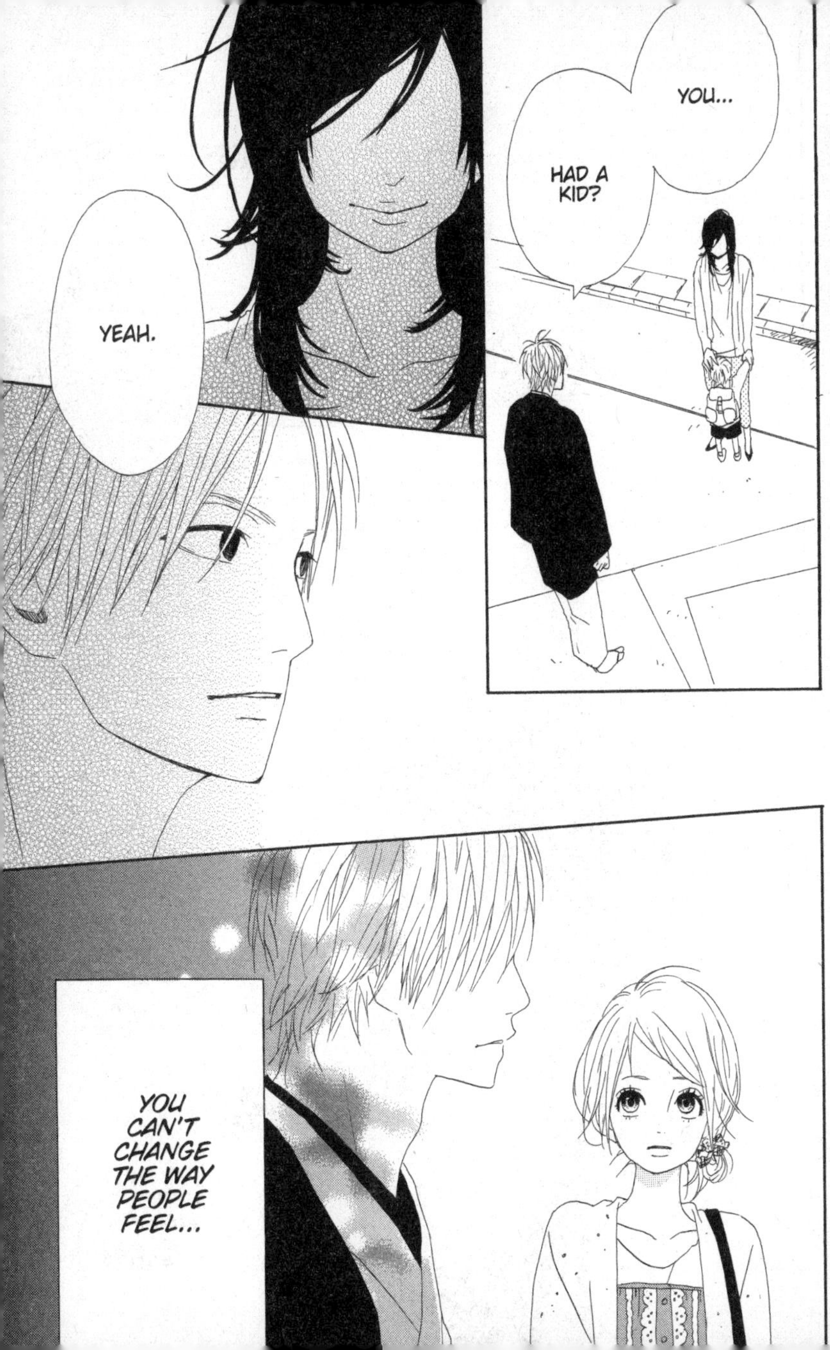
YOU...
HAD A KID?
YEAH.
YOU CAN'T CHANGE THE WAY PEOPLE FEEL...

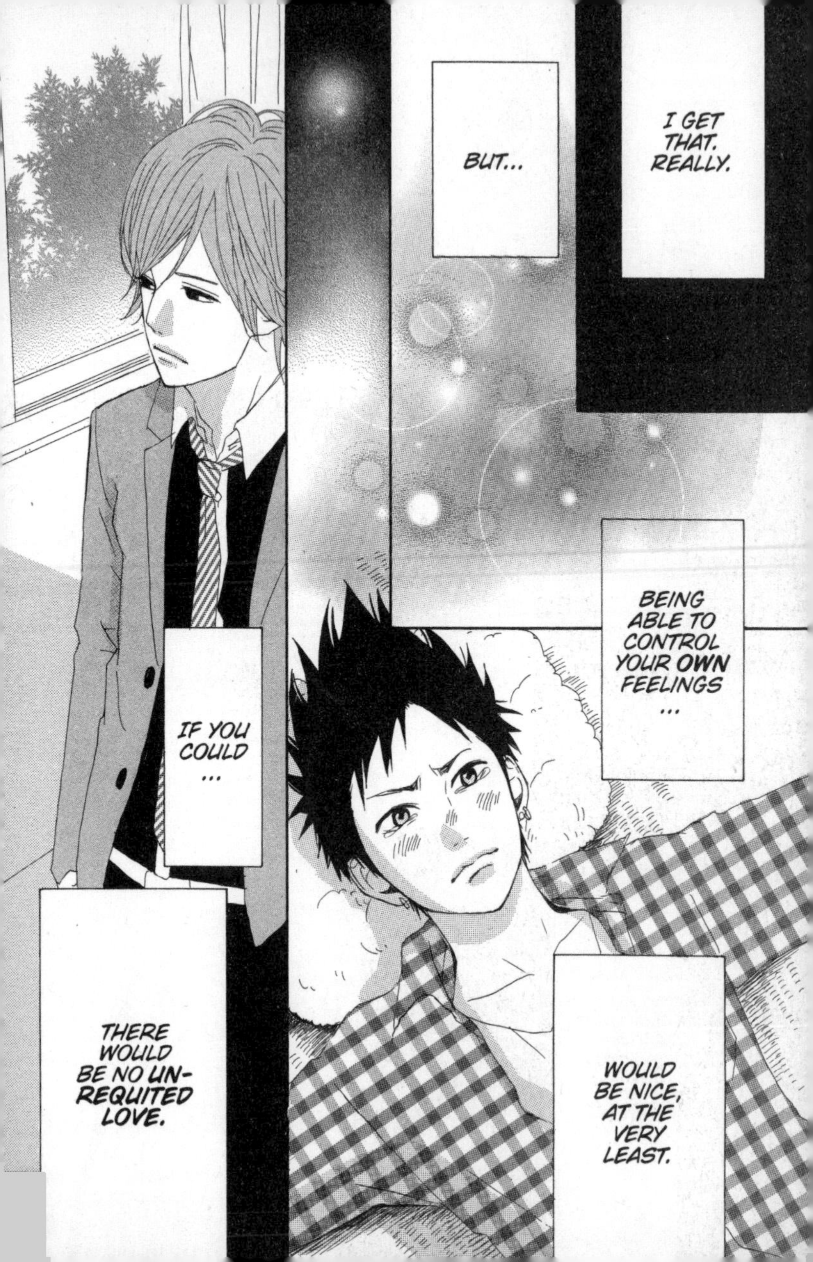
I GET THAT. REALLY.
BUT...
BEING ABLE TO CONTROL YOUR OWN FEELINGS...
WOULD BE NICE, AT THE VERY LEAST.
IF YOU COULD...
THERE WOULD BE NO UN-REQUITED LOVE.

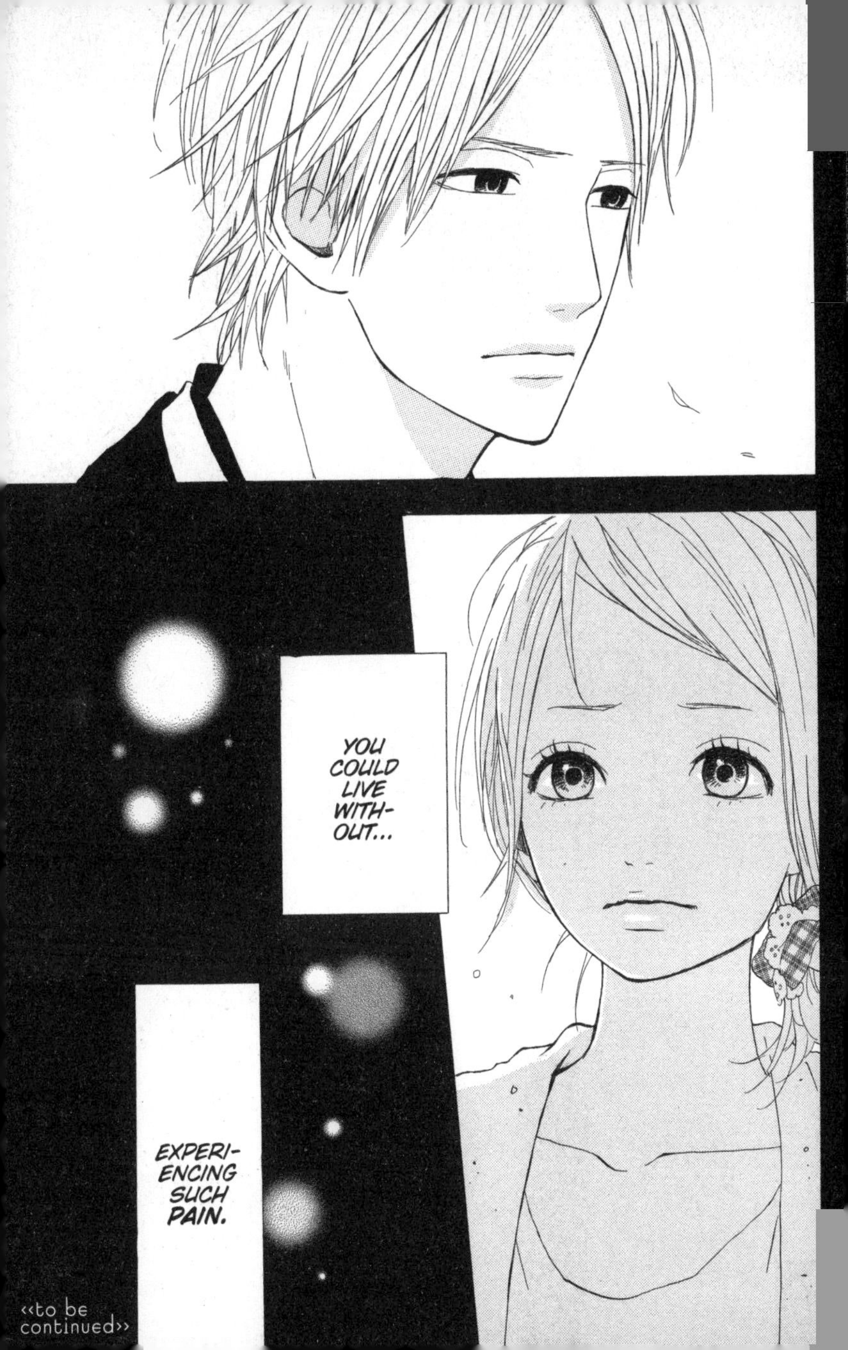
YOU COULD LIVE WITH-OUT...
EXPERI-ENCING SUCH PAIN.
<<to be continued>>

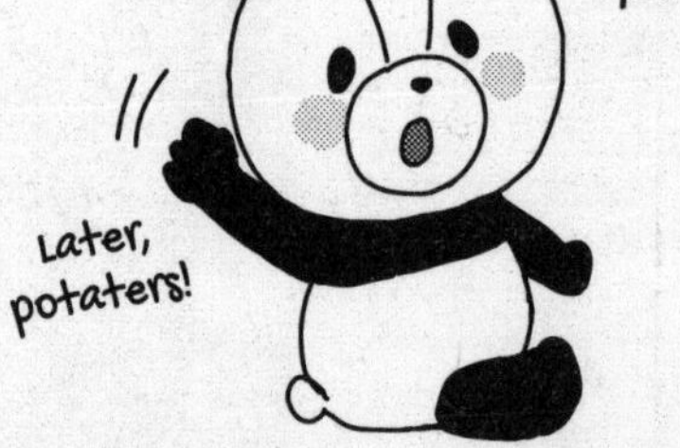
Bye bye!
Later, potaters!

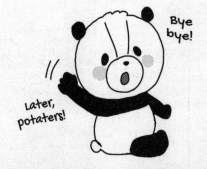

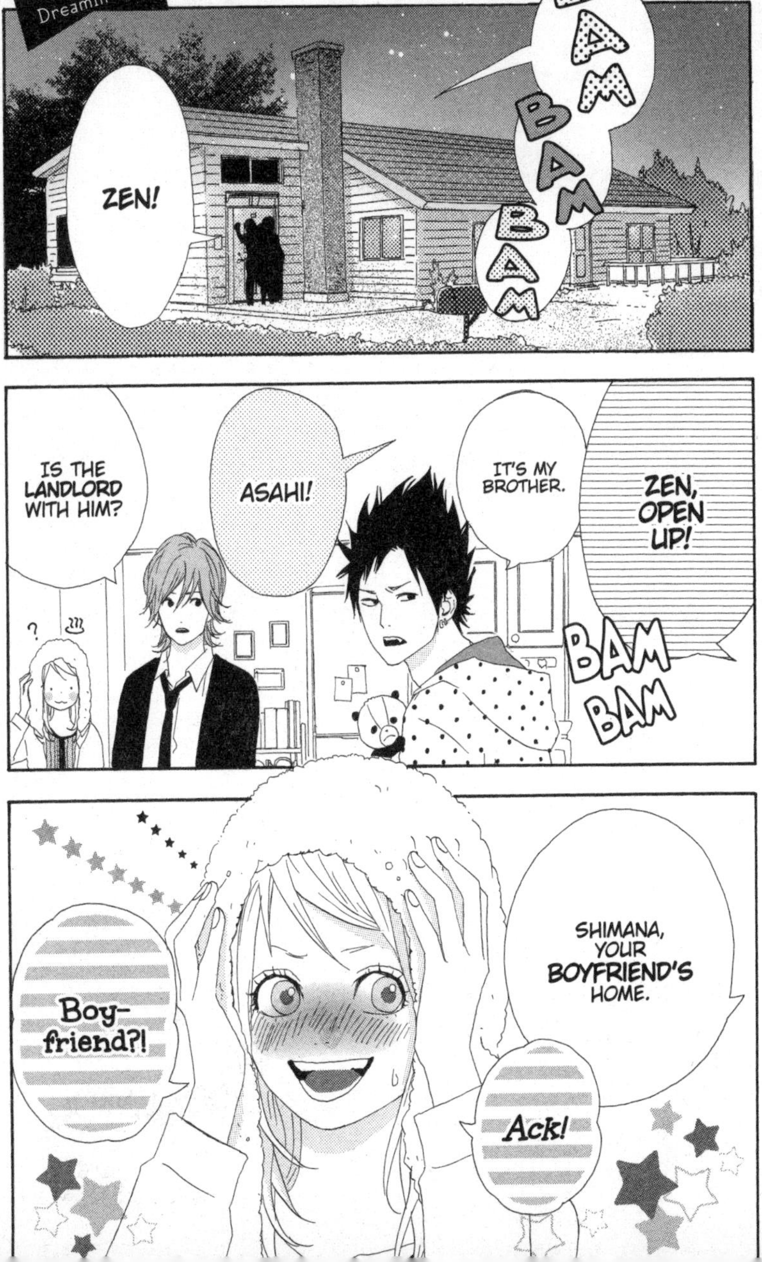
BAM BAM BAM
ZEN!
ZEN, OPEN UP!
BAM BAM
IT'S MY BROTHER.
ASAHI!
IS THE LANDLORD WITH HIM?
?
SHIMANA, YOUR BOYFRIEND'S HOME.
Ack!
Boy-friend?!

[Side Story]
Dreamin' Sun
20.5th DOOR
THAT'S RIGHT...
HE'S MY "BOY-FRIEND" AS OF TODAY.
THERE ARE SO MANY THINGS...
THAT I WANT TO TALK TO HIM ABOUT.

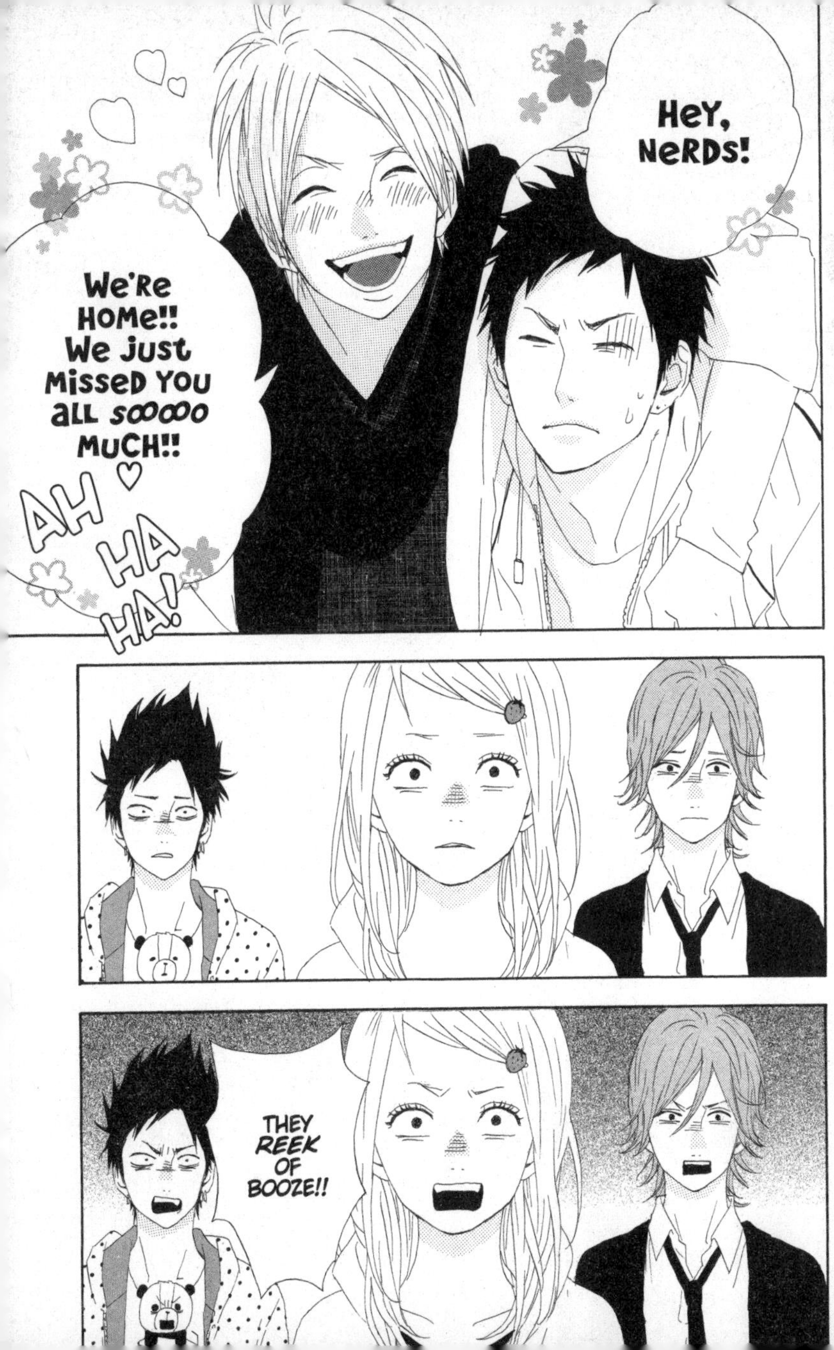
Hey, Nerds!
We're Home!! We just Missed You all sooooo MUCH!! ♡
AH HA HA HA!
THEY REEK OF BOOZE!!

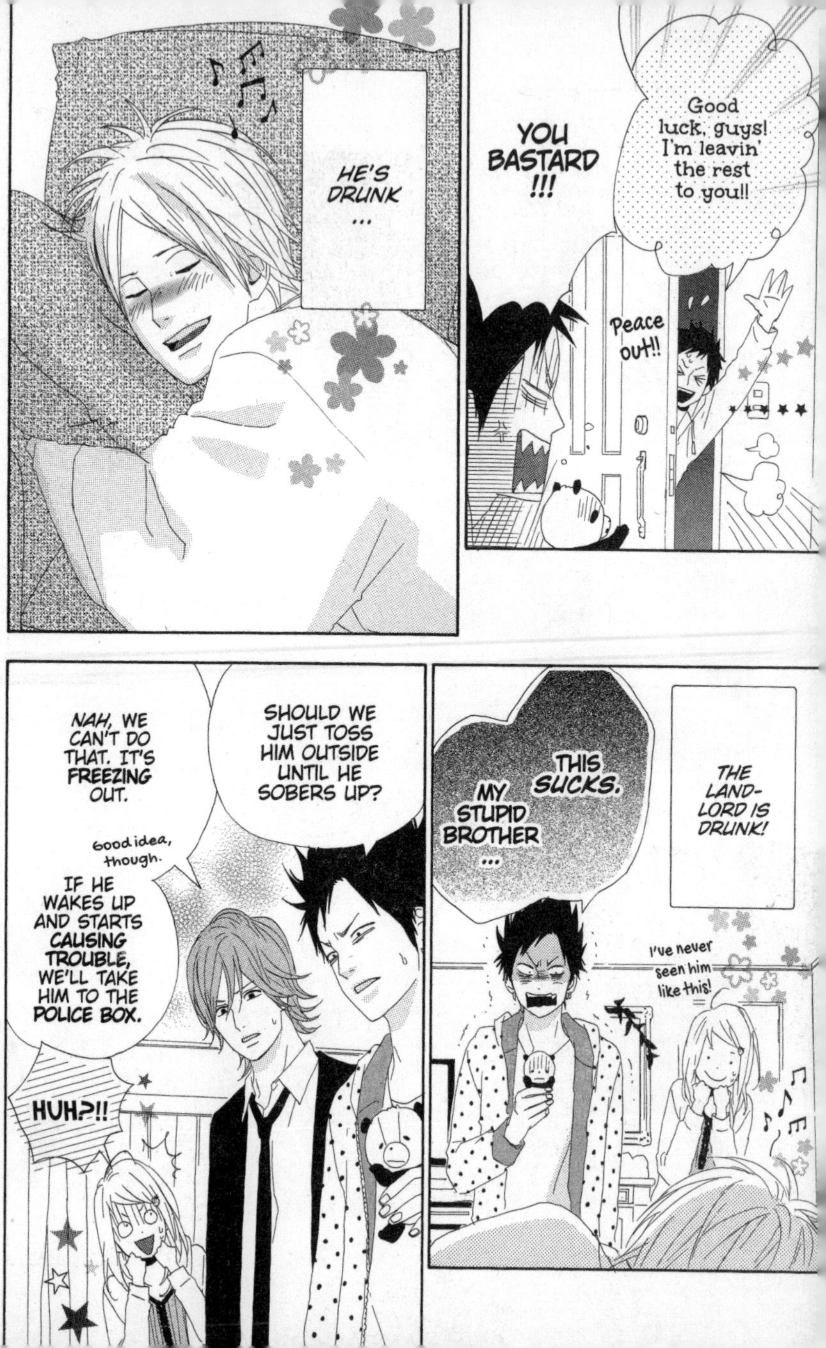
Good luck, guys! I'm leavin' the rest to you!!
YOU BASTARD !!!
Peace out!!
HE'S DRUNK ...
THE LANDLORD IS DRUNK!
THIS SUCKS.
MY STUPID BROTHER ...
I've never seen him like this!
SHOULD WE JUST TOSS HIM OUTSIDE UNTIL HE SOBERS UP?
NAH, WE CAN'T DO THAT. IT'S FREEZING OUT.
Good idea, though.
IF HE WAKES UP AND STARTS CAUSING TROUBLE, WE'LL TAKE HIM TO THE POLICE BOX.
HUH?!!

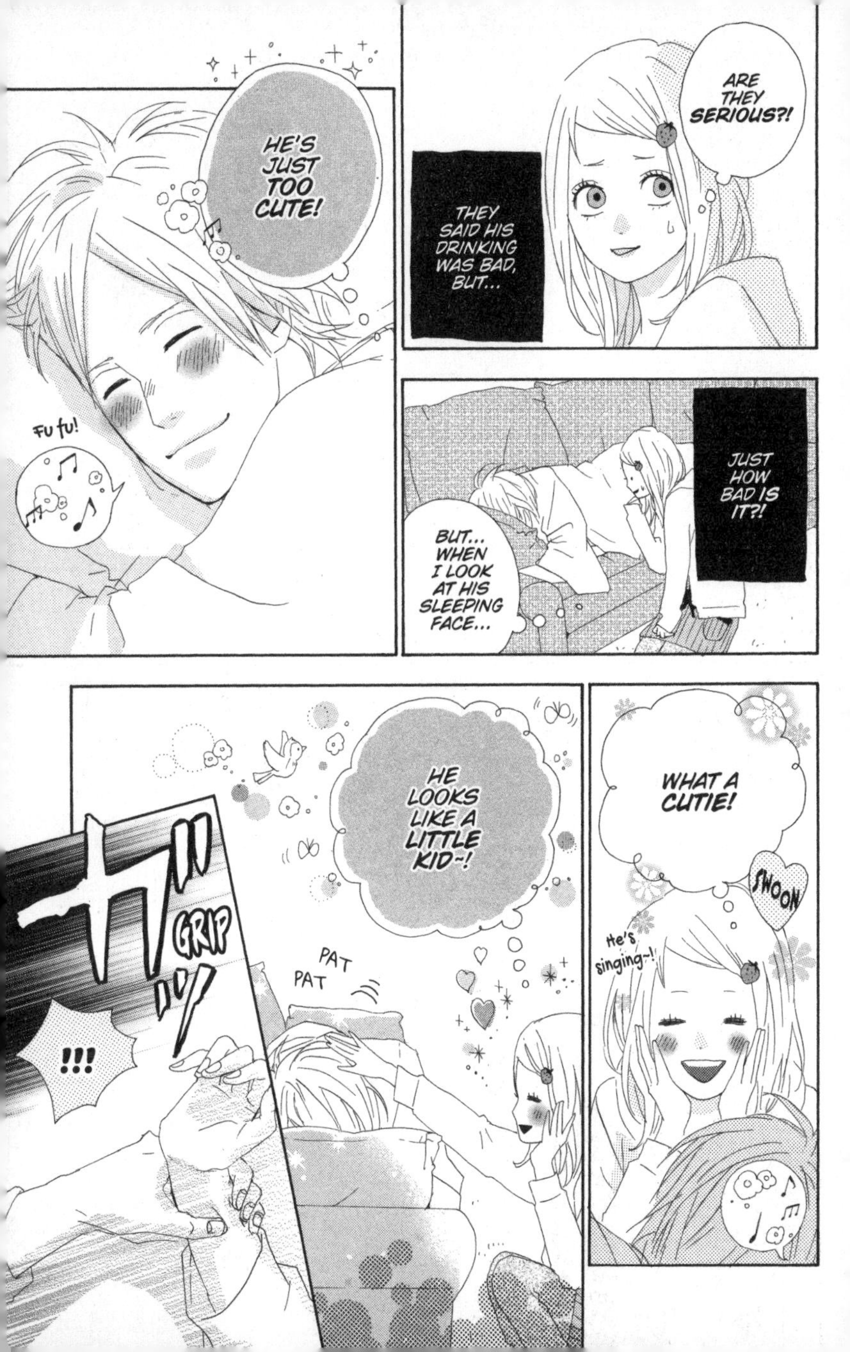

ARE THEY SERIOUS?!
THEY SAID HIS DRINKING WAS BAD, BUT...
JUST HOW BAD IS IT?!
BUT... WHEN I LOOK AT HIS SLEEPING FACE...
HE'S JUST TOO CUTE!
Fu fu!
WHAT A CUTIE!
SWOON
He's singing~!
HE LOOKS LIKE A LITTLE KID~!
PAT PAT
GRIP
!!!

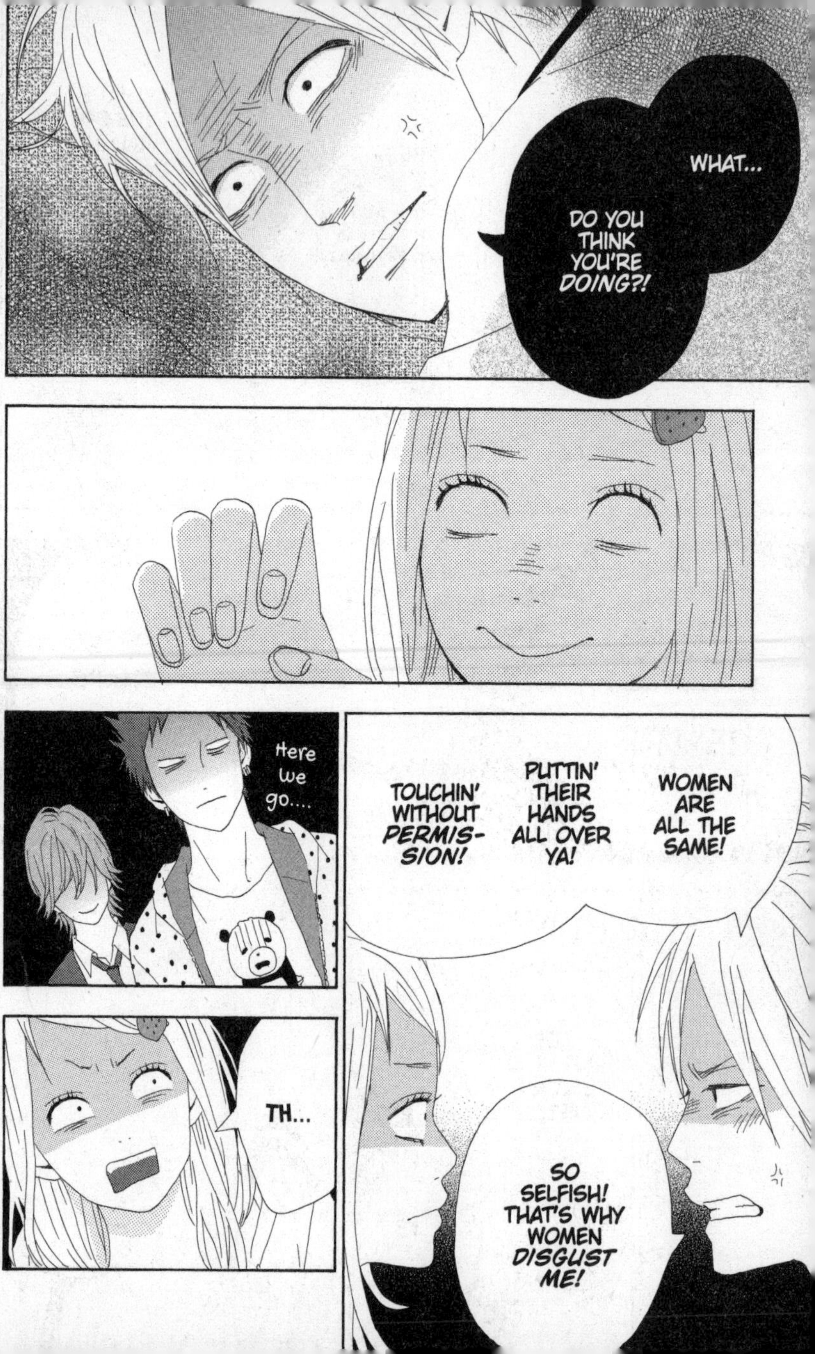
WHAT... DO YOU THINK YOU'RE DOING?!
WOMEN ARE ALL THE SAME!
PUTTIN' THEIR HANDS ALL OVER YA!
TOUCHIN' WITHOUT PERMIS-SION!
SO SELFISH! THAT'S WHY WOMEN DISGUST ME!
Here we go....
TH...

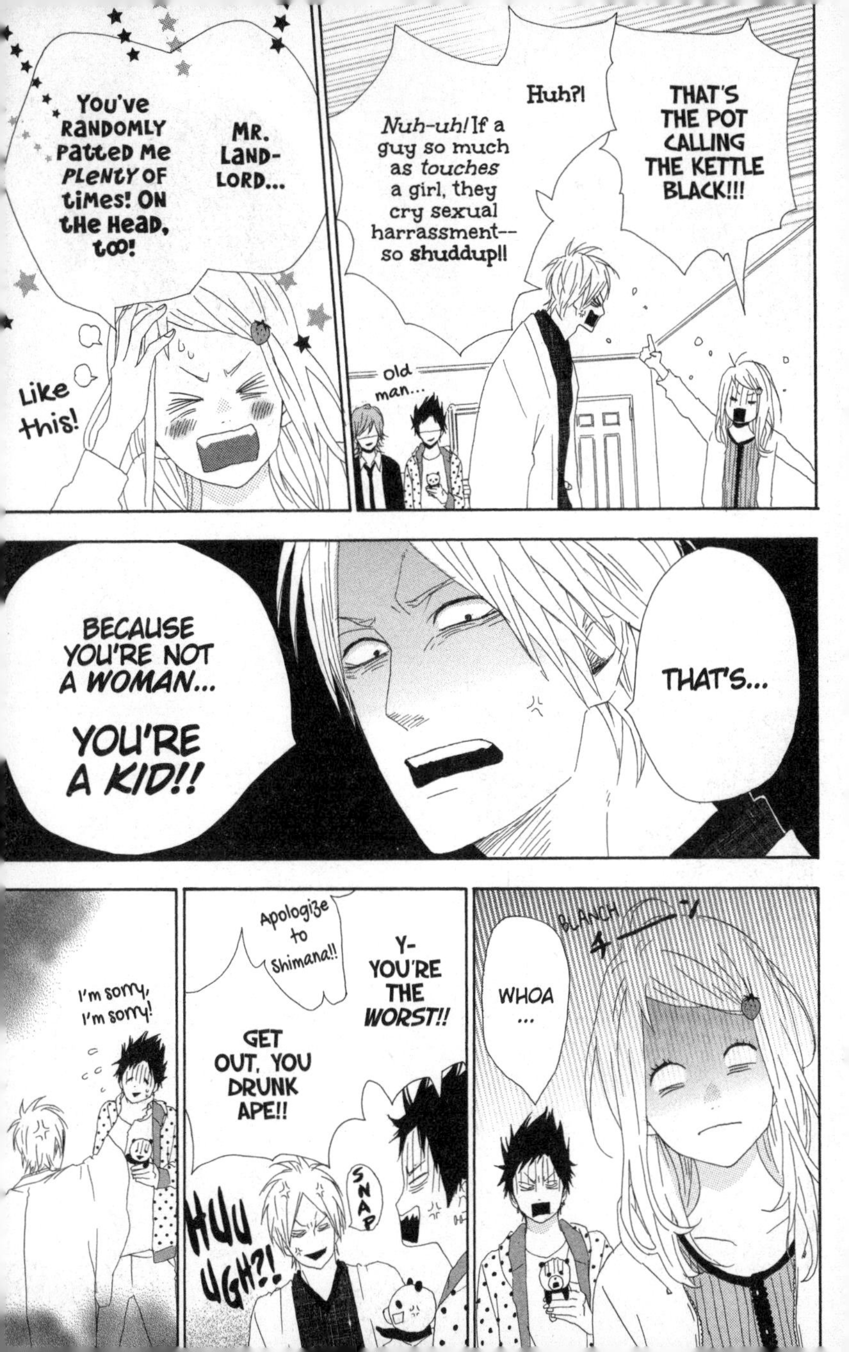

THAT'S THE POT CALLING THE KETTLE BLACK!!!
Huh?!
Nuh-uh! If a guy so much as touches a girl, they cry sexual harrassment-- so shuddup!!
old man...
MR. LANDLORD...
You've RANDOMLY patted me PLENTY OF times! ON the head, too!
Like this!
THAT'S...
BECAUSE YOU'RE NOT A WOMAN... YOU'RE A KID!!
BLANCH
WHOA ...
Y- YOU'RE THE WORST!!
Apologize to Shimana!!
GET OUT, YOU DRUNK APE!!
SNAP
HUUUGH?!
I'm sorry, I'm sorry!

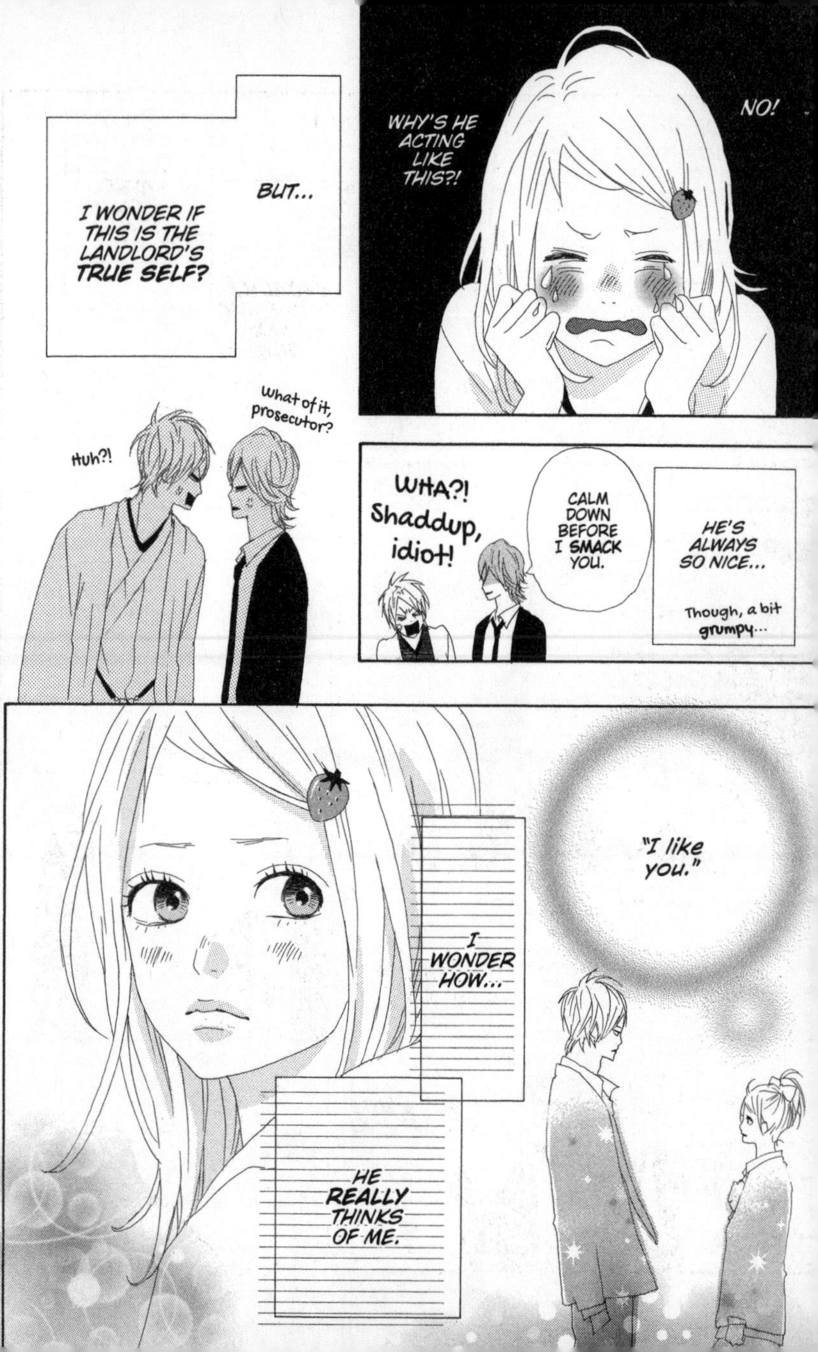
NO!
WHY'S HE ACTING LIKE THIS?!
BUT...
I WONDER IF THIS IS THE LANDLORD'S TRUE SELF?
HE'S ALWAYS SO NICE...
Though, a bit grumpy...
CALM DOWN BEFORE I SMACK YOU.
WHA?! Shaddup, idiot!
What of it, prosecutor?
Huh?!
"I like you."
I WONDER HOW...
HE REALLY THINKS OF ME.

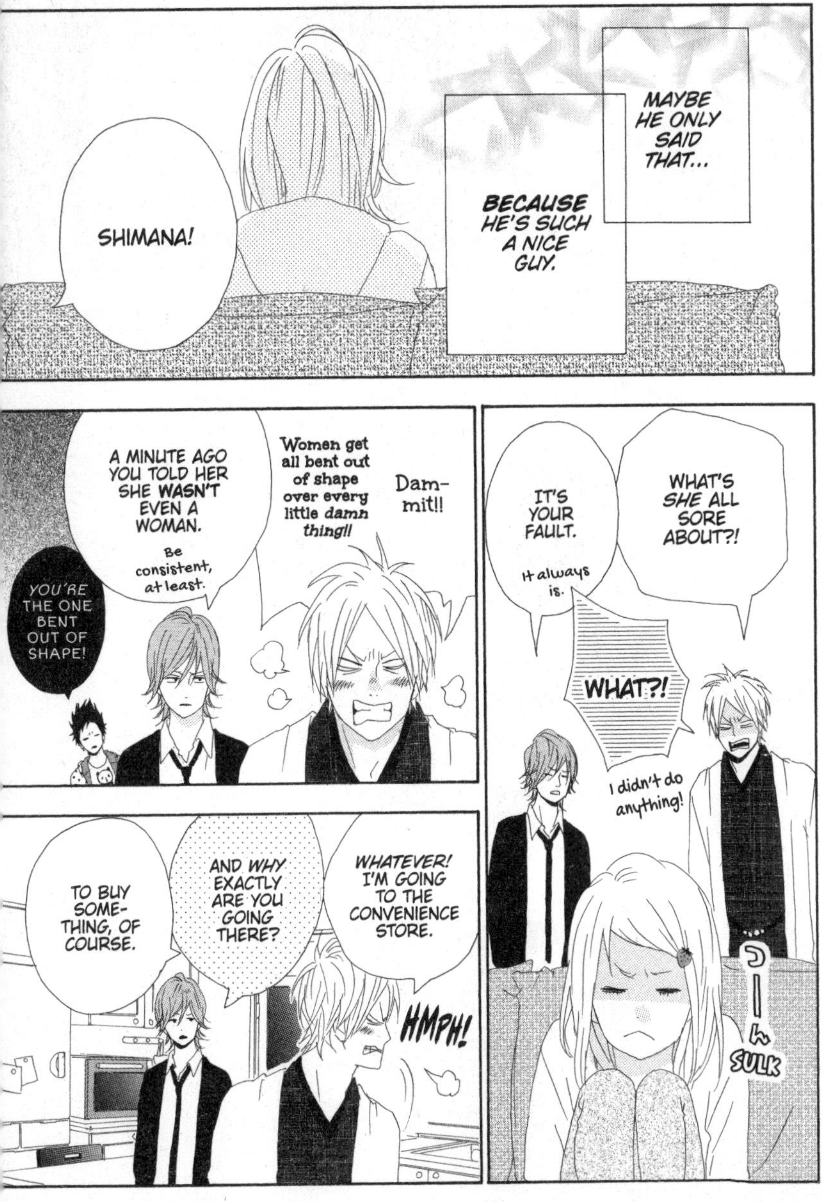
MAYBE HE ONLY SAID THAT...
BECAUSE HE'S SUCH A NICE GUY.
SHIMANA!
WHAT'S SHE ALL SORE ABOUT?!
IT'S YOUR FAULT.
It always is.
WHAT?!
I didn't do anything!
コーん
SULK
Dam-mit!!
Women get all bent out of shape over every little damn thing!!
A MINUTE AGO YOU TOLD HER SHE WASN'T EVEN A WOMAN.
Be consistent, at least.
YOU'RE THE ONE BENT OUT OF SHAPE!
WHATEVER! I'M GOING TO THE CONVENIENCE STORE.
HMPH!
AND WHY EXACTLY ARE YOU GOING THERE?
TO BUY SOME-THING, OF COURSE.

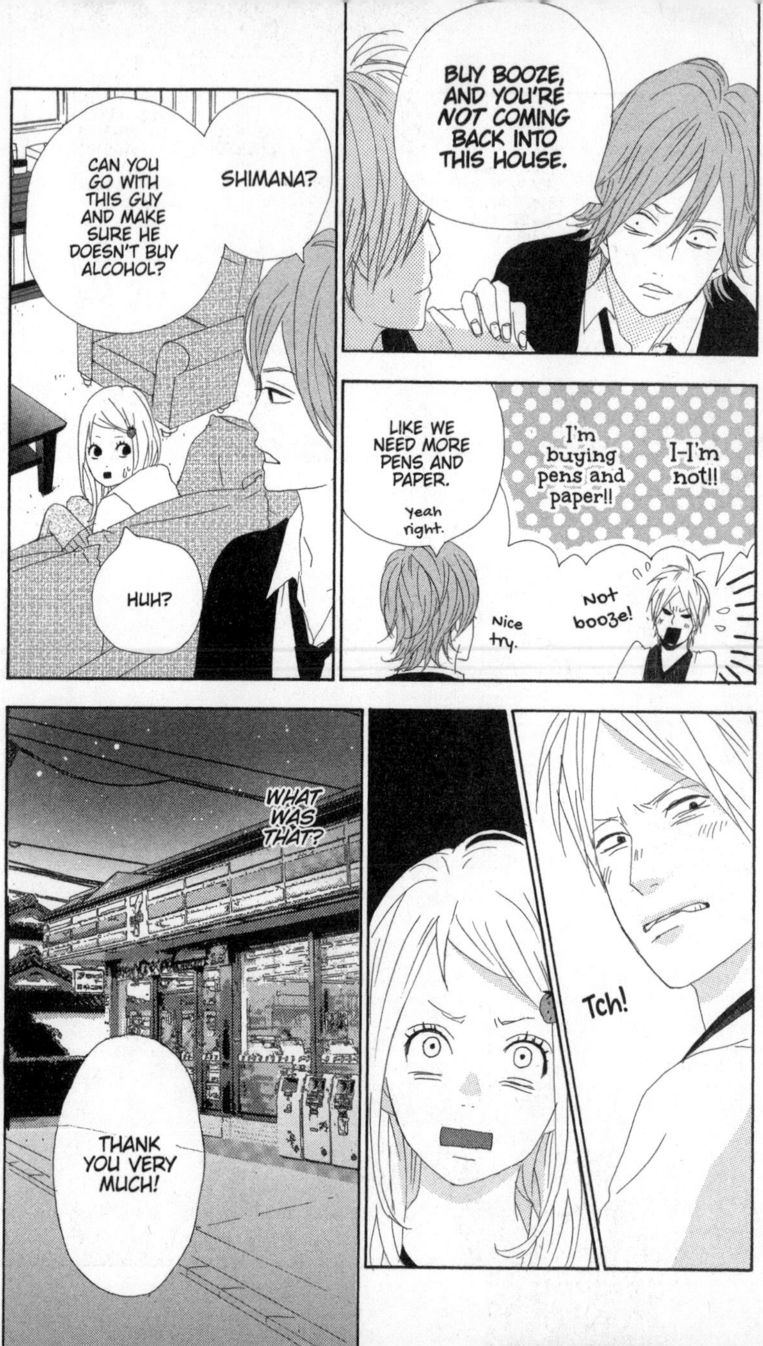
BUY BOOZE, AND YOU'RE *NOT* COMING BACK INTO THIS HOUSE.
I-I'm not!!
I'm buying pens and paper!!
Not booze!
LIKE WE NEED MORE PENS AND PAPER.
Yeah right.
Nice try.
SHIMANA?
CAN YOU GO WITH THIS GUY AND MAKE SURE HE DOESN'T BUY ALCOHOL?
HUH?
Tch!
WHAT WAS THAT?
THANK YOU VERY MUCH!

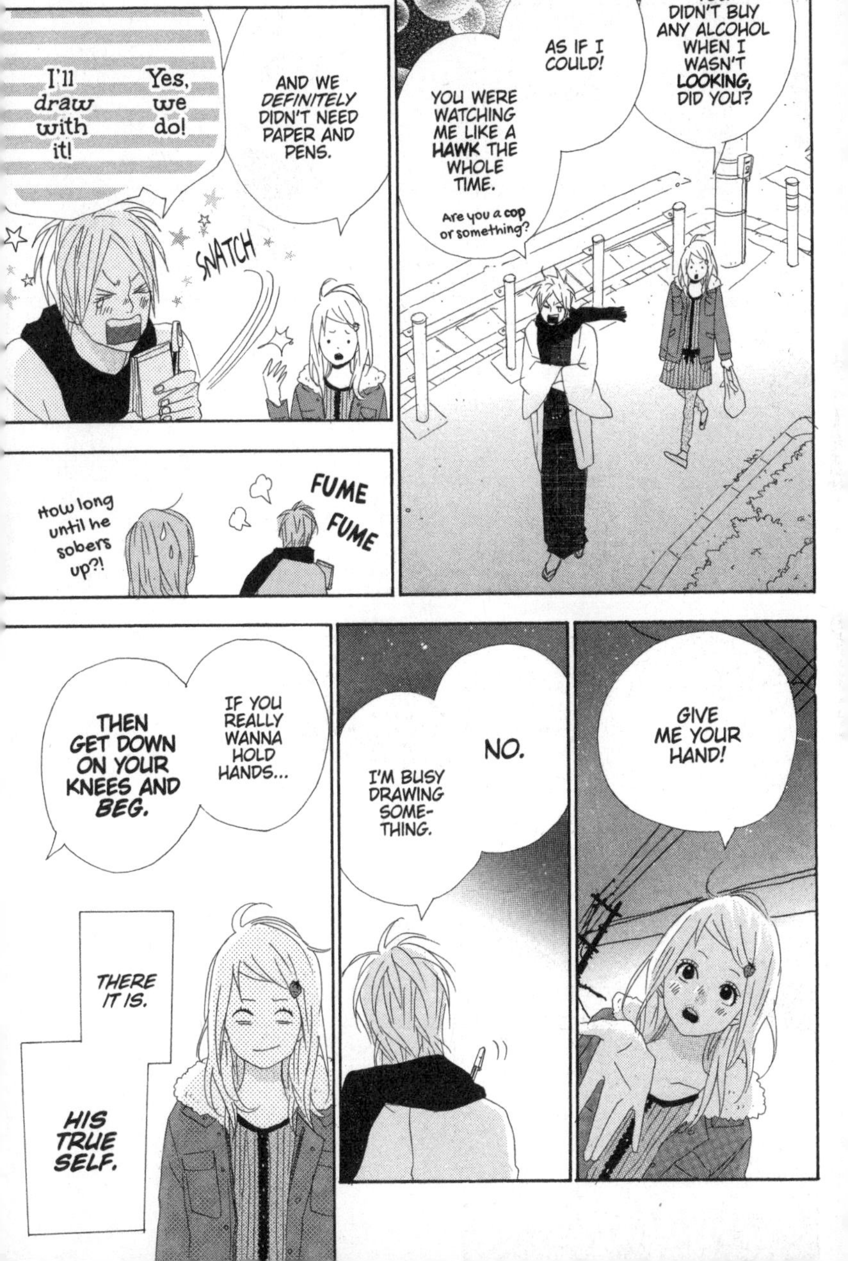
YOU DIDN'T BUY ANY ALCOHOL WHEN I WASN'T LOOKING, DID YOU?
AS IF I COULD!
YOU WERE WATCHING ME LIKE A HAWK THE WHOLE TIME.
Are you a cop or something?
AND WE DEFINITELY DIDN'T NEED PAPER AND PENS.
Yes, we do!
I'll draw with it!
SNATCH
FUME FUME
How long until he sobers up?!
GIVE ME YOUR HAND!
NO.
I'M BUSY DRAWING SOME-THING.
IF YOU REALLY WANNA HOLD HANDS...
THEN GET DOWN ON YOUR KNEES AND BEG.
THERE IT IS.
HIS TRUE SELF.

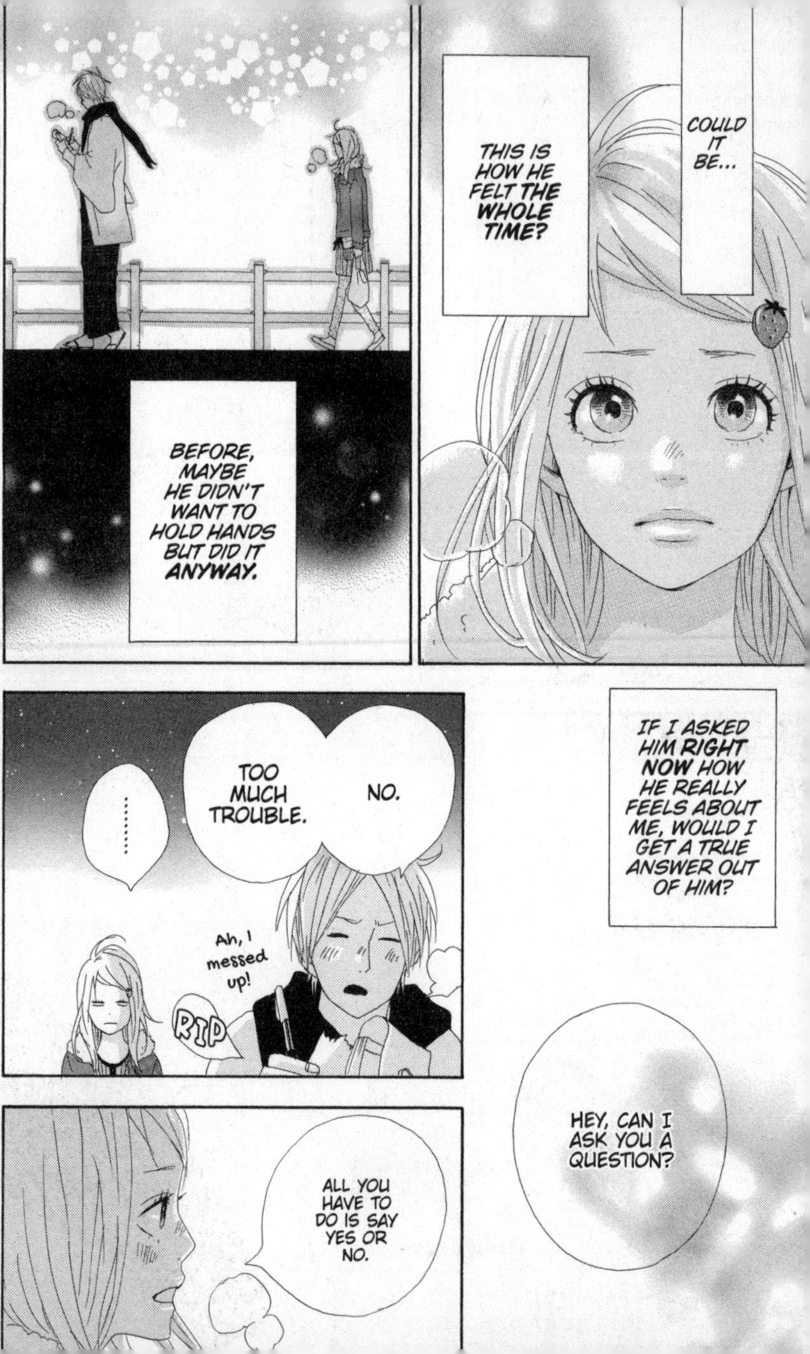
COULD IT BE...
THIS IS HOW HE FELT THE WHOLE TIME?
BEFORE, MAYBE HE DIDN'T WANT TO HOLD HANDS BUT DID IT ANYWAY.
IF I ASKED HIM RIGHT NOW HOW HE REALLY FEELS ABOUT ME, WOULD I GET A TRUE ANSWER OUT OF HIM?
NO.
TOO MUCH TROUBLE.
......
Ah, I messed up!
RIP
HEY, CAN I ASK YOU A QUESTION?
ALL YOU HAVE TO DO IS SAY YES OR NO.

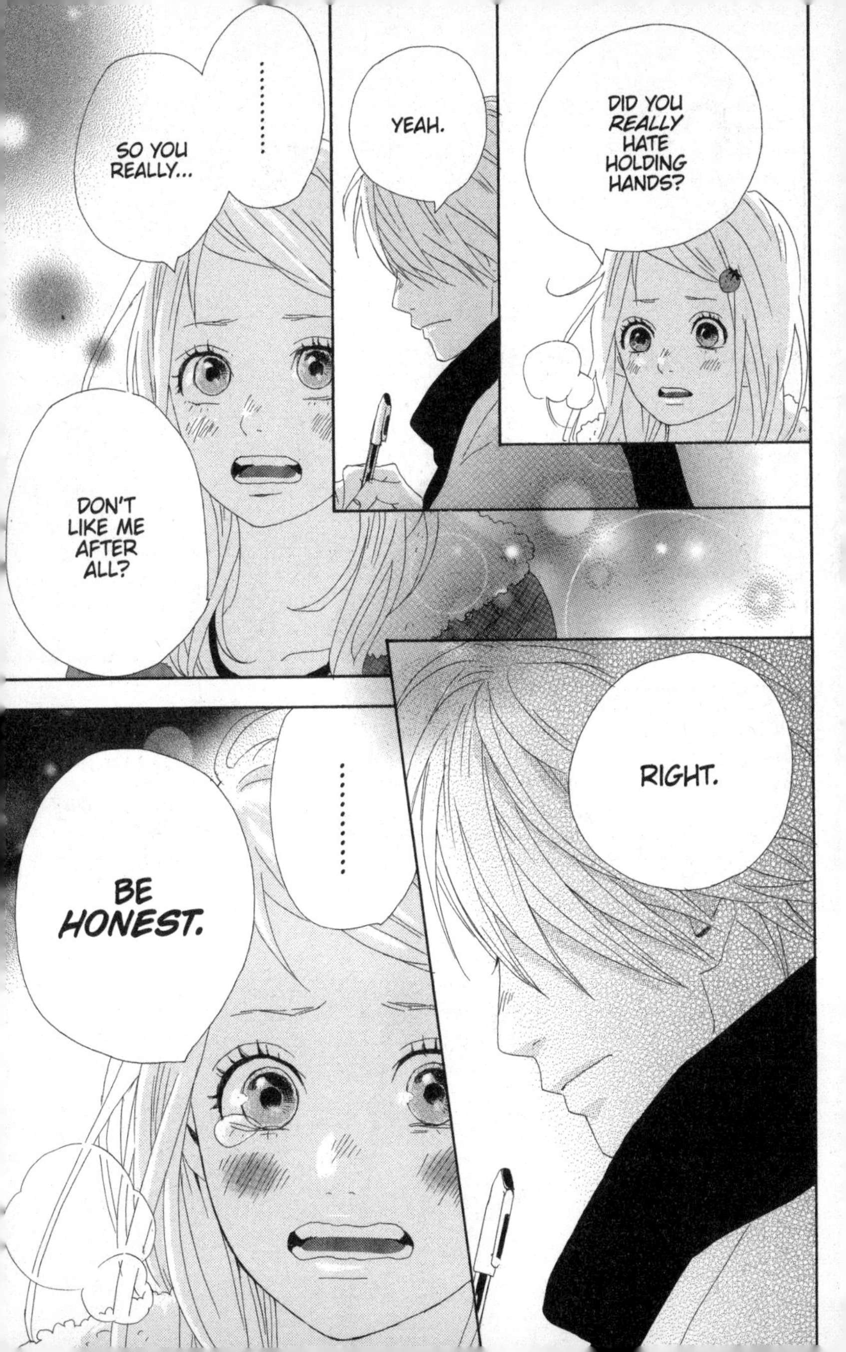
DID YOU *REALLY* HATE HOLDING HANDS?
YEAH.
......
SO YOU REALLY...
DON'T LIKE ME AFTER ALL?
RIGHT.
......
BE *HONEST.*

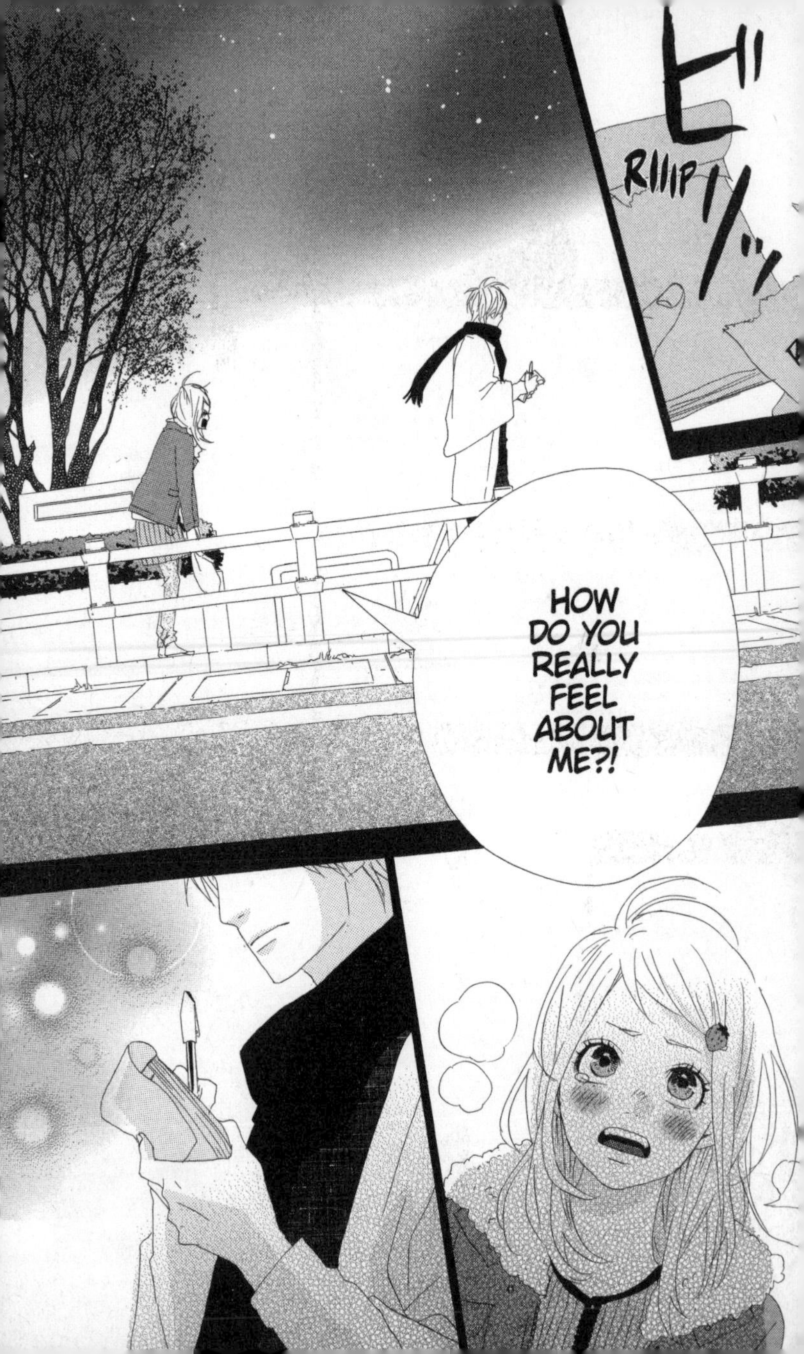
ビリッ
RIIIP
HOW DO YOU REALLY FEEL ABOUT ME?!

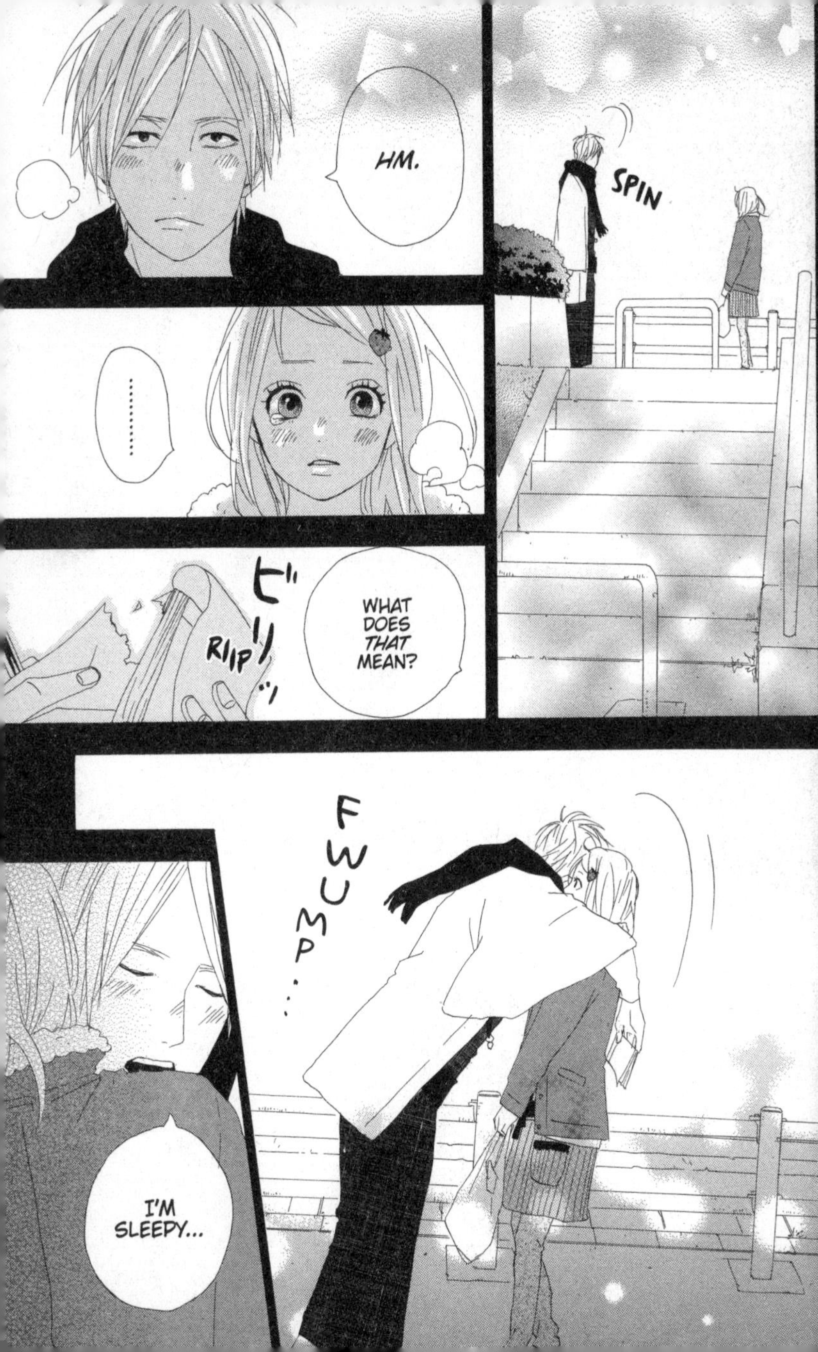
SPIN
HM.
......
ビリッ
RIIP
WHAT DOES THAT MEAN?
FWUMP...
I'M SLEEPY...

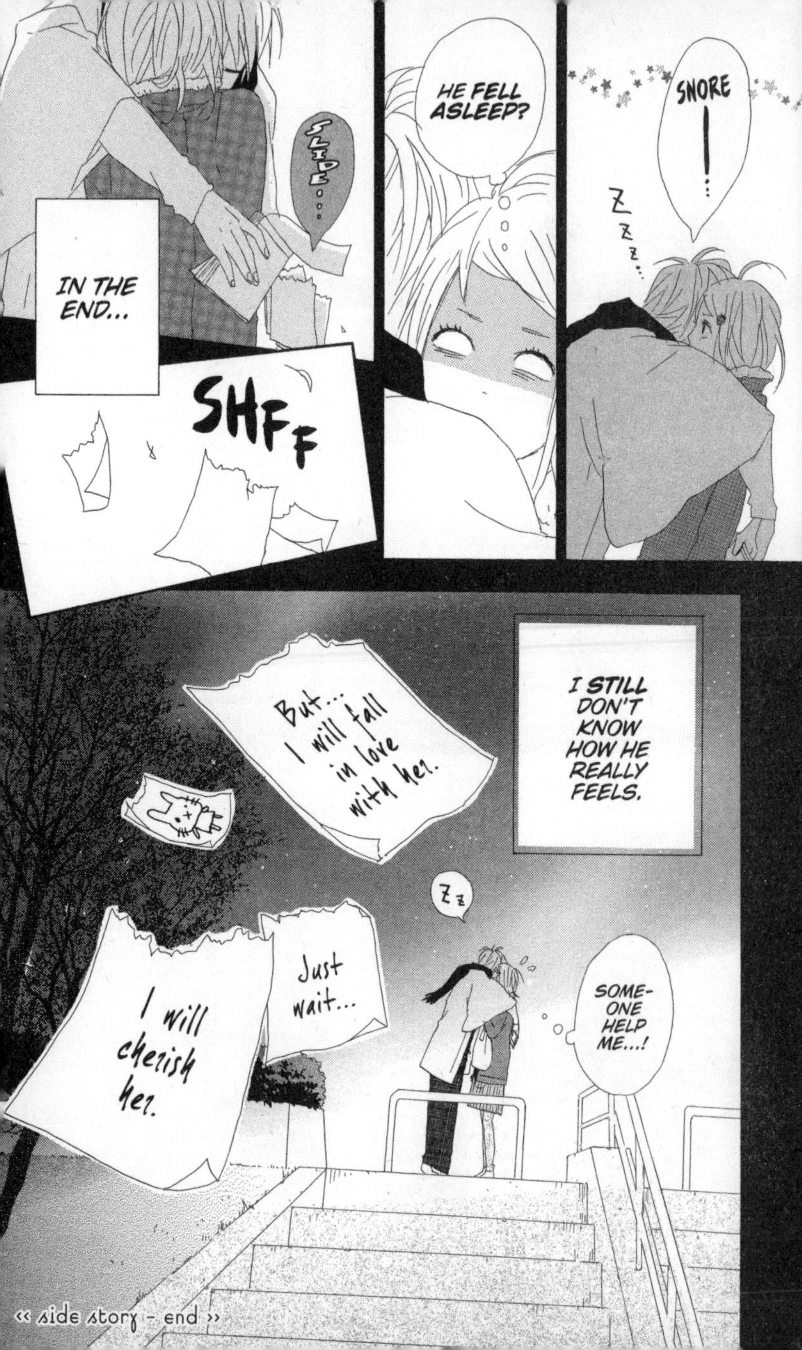
SNORE
!...
Z z z...
HE FELL ASLEEP?
SLIDE...
IN THE END...
SHFF
I STILL DON'T KNOW HOW HE REALLY FEELS.
But... I will fall in love with her.
Z z
SOME-ONE HELP ME...!
Just wait...
I will cherish her.
« side story - end »

THE FIND POKO GAME

Poko is hidden
throughout the
manga! Find him!

HINT: There aren't
any in the side story.

This time,
there are 4 POKOS.

BONUS MANGA

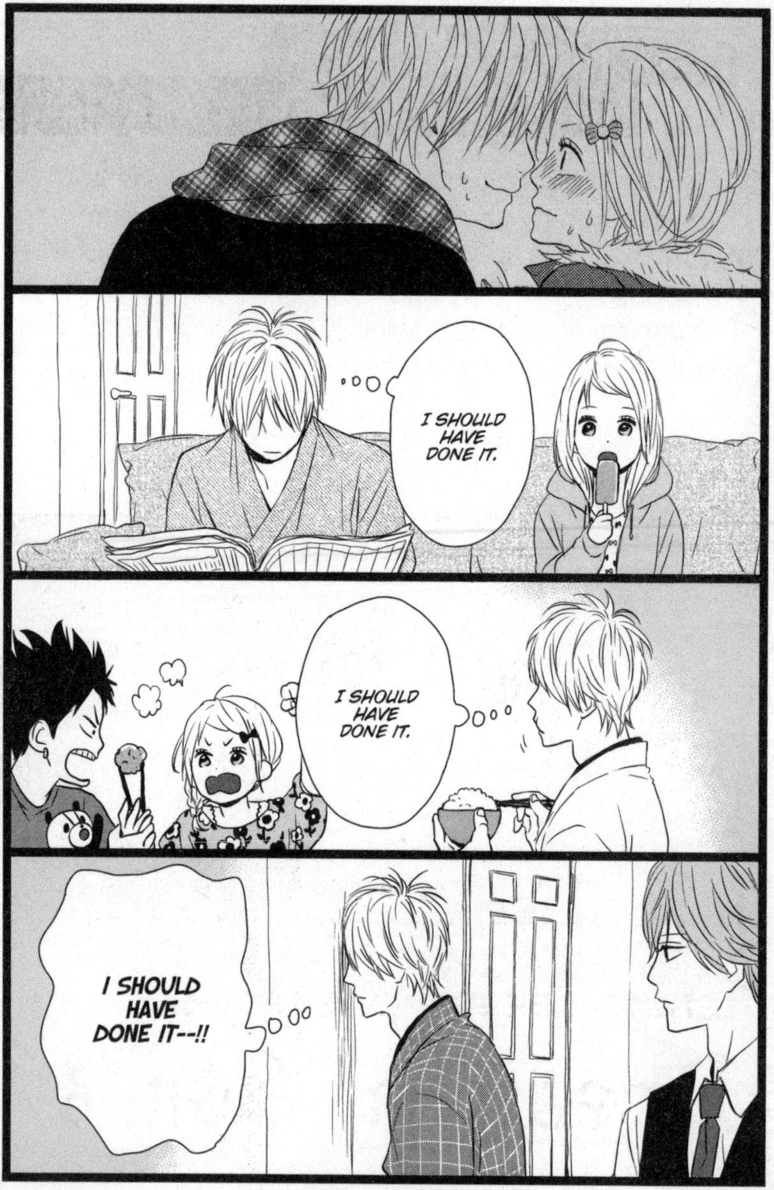
I SHOULD HAVE DONE IT.
I SHOULD HAVE DONE IT.
I SHOULD HAVE DONE IT--!!

THE END

Next Volume Preview

"At the most crucial moment, I couldn't say what was truly important."

When the landlord reconnects with his old flame, Shimana's anxiety about her relationship with him skyrockets. To avoid seeing him, Shimana goes to stay with her family as the spring semester begins. Will Shimana ever be able to face the landlord?! And what about the group camping trip?!

Includes *Dreamin' Sun* chapters 24~28

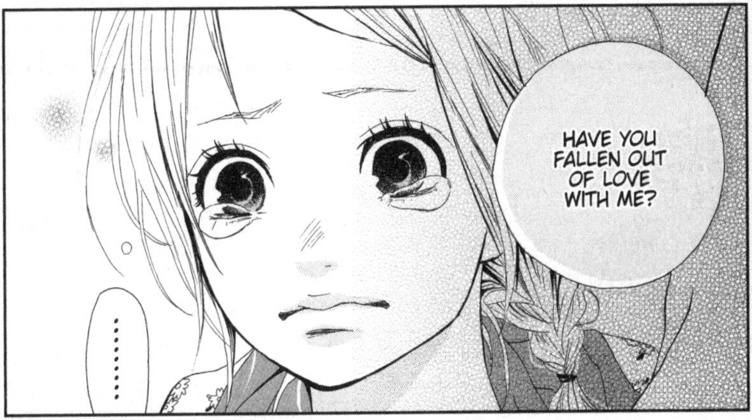
HAVE YOU FALLEN OUT OF LOVE WITH ME?
....

Ichigo Takano presents

Dreamin' Sun 6

Coming Soon!

SEVEN SEAS ENTERTAINMENT PRESENTS

Dreamin' Sun

story and art by **ICHIGO TAKANO** **VOLUME 5**

TRANSLATION
Amber Tamosaitis

ADAPTATION
Shannon Fay

LETTERING AND RETOUCH
Lys Blakeslee

COVER DESIGN
Nicky Lim

PROOFREADER
Danielle King
Holly Kolodziejczak

ASSISTANT EDITOR
Jenn Grunigen

PRODUCTION ASSISTANT
CK Russell

PRODUCTION MANAGER
Lissa Pattillo

EDITOR-IN-CHIEF
Adam Arnold

PUBLISHER
Jason DeAngelis

DREAMIN' SUN VOLUME 5

First published in Japan in 2015 by Futabasha Publishers Ltd., Tokyo.
English version published by Seven Seas Entertainment, LLC.
under license from Futabasha Publishers Ltd.

ISBN: 978-1-626926-71-4

Printed in Canada

First Printing: January 2018

10 9 8 7 6 5 4 3 2 1

FOLLOW US ONLINE: ***www.gomanga.com***

READING DIRECTIONS

This book reads from ***right to left***, Japanese style. If this is your first time reading manga, you start reading from the top right panel on each page and take it from there. If you get lost, just follow the numbered diagram here. It may seem backwards at first, but you'll get the hang of it! Have fun!!

1
2
3
4
5
6
7
8
9

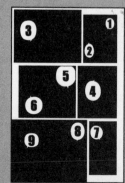